Interactive Group Counseling and Therapy

William B. Kline
Idaho State University

Merrill
Prentice Hall

Upper Saddle River, New Jersey
Columbus, Ohio

Library of Congress Cataloging-in-Publication Data

Kline, William B.
  Interactive group counseling and therapy / William B. Kline.
    p. cm.
  Includes bibliographical references and index.
  ISBN 0-13-012100-2
  1. Group counseling. 2. Group psychotherapy. I. Title.

BF637.C6 K54 2003
158′35—dc21   2001059176

Vice President and Publisher: Jeffery W. Johnston
Executive Editor: Kevin M. Davis
Associate Editor: Christina Kalisch Tawney
Editorial Assistant: Autumn Crisp
Production Editor: Mary Harlan
Production Coordination: Emily Hatteberg, Carlisle Publishers Services
Design Coordinator: Diane C. Lorenzo
Cover Design: Thomas Borah
Cover Image: SuperStock; © 2002 Artists Rights Society (ARS), New York/ADAGP, Paris, Wassily Kandinsky,
  "Sketch for Composition II" (detail)
Text Design and Illustrations: Carlisle Publishers Services
Production Manager: Laura Messerly
Director of Marketing: Ann Castel Davis
Marketing Manager: Amy June
Marketing Coordinator: Tyra Cooper

This book was set in Garamond by Carlisle Communications, Ltd. It was printed and bound by R. R.
Donnelley & Sons Company. The cover was printed by Phoenix Color Corp.

Pearson Education Ltd.
Pearson Education Australia Pty. Limited
Pearson Education Singapore Pte. Ltd.
Pearson Education North Asia Ltd.
Pearson Education Canada, Ltd.
Pearson Educación de Mexico, S.A. de C.V.
Pearson Education—Japan
Pearson Education Malaysia Pte. Ltd.
Pearson Education, *Upper Saddle River, New Jersey*

10 9 8 7 6 5 4 3 2 1
ISBN: 0-13-012100-2

Preface

This text presents principles, theories, and procedures to help readers develop their understanding of group interaction and begin their practice of group counseling and therapy. It will also expand experienced leaders' understanding of group work and offer new ideas that might invigorate their practice. To meet these goals, experienced group workers will be challenged to "try on" new perspectives and procedures, and students new to group work will be challenged to view group work as a distinct and uniquely powerful mode for counseling and therapy. Such students will find that the perspectives and procedures offered in this text are different from what they have learned in their training in individual counseling and therapy.

The perspectives on group work that have guided the preparation of this text vary from the perspectives present in most group counseling and therapy texts. First, the principles, theory, and procedures presented here heavily emphasize group process. This emphasis assertively stresses that the quality of group members' interactions is the most critical determinant of member change. This point of view has significant implications for the roles of group leaders.

Second, although group leaders play a critical part in the therapeutic success of group members, their roles are more indirect than those typically described in most texts. This means that leaders emphasize creating and maintaining a therapeutic environment, teaching members effective communication skills and tools for interpersonal learning, and structuring interaction so that members can learn from one another. This approach is far more indirect than leaders performing the role of an individual therapist in the group setting. The interaction of members provides the medium for therapy, not the individual therapeutic technique of the group leader.

Third, this text operates from a systemic perspective, which means that counseling and therapy groups are seen as social systems. Proponents of a systems perspective believe that the environmental context of the group, the composition of the group's membership, the goals of the group, the internal and external communications boundaries of the group, and members' problems are contextually intertwined. This perspective means, among many other factors, that social, multicultural, and diversity issues present in the environment in which the group takes place are invariably present in every group. This perspective also means that group members' interactions inevitably reflect the relationship issues all members share and experience outside the group.

Finally, this text emphasizes how group dynamics principles and group theory should be used to define leaders' actions. This text maintains that leader interventions made without theoretically based conceptualizations of group interaction are severely limited. Having theoretically based conceptualizations of group interaction offers leaders information about which intervention to use, when to use an intervention, and why an intervention they have used may not be effective. Surprisingly, this emphasis is relatively uncommon.

ORGANIZATION

This text includes two sections. The first section provides information designed to help leaders understand group interaction. The second section describes the essential tasks leaders perform in planning, conducting, and concluding groups.

The first section presents essential group dynamics principles, classic research-based models of group development, and theories especially suited for group work. A chapter and a chapter conclusion synthesize group development models and group counseling and therapy theories so that readers have concise statements of the common denominators of group development and group counseling and therapy.

The second section presents a description of the leader's role; basic leadership skills and interventions; strategies for developing membership skills; ongoing leadership tasks; intervention strategies; suggestions for planning, preparing, operating, and terminating groups; and a final chapter designed to encourage readers to reflect on the process of becoming effective group leaders. Although this text was intended to be comprehensive, it was impossible to include every topic group leaders should consider because of length limitations.

ACKNOWLEDGMENTS

This text is the product of my professional relationships. I thank my instructors, NTL trainers, NTL Human Interaction Laboratory group coleaders, counseling and therapy group members, students, and my colleagues for their role in shaping my thinking about group work. I'd also like to thank the reviewers of this book: Fred Bemak, George Mason University; James M. Benshoff, University of North Carolina, Greensboro; Adrian Blow, St. Louis University; Breda Bova, University of New Mexico; Duane Brown, University of North Carolina, Chapel Hill; James S. Delo, West Virginia University; Janice Delucia-Waack, State University of New York at Buffalo; Hardin K.

Coleman, University of Wisconsin, Madison; Kevin A. Fall, Loyola University, New Orleans; Brenda Freeman, Northwest Nazarene University; Chuck Gregg, University of Utah; Roger D. Herring, University of Arkansas, Little Rock; Mark M. Leach, University of Southern Mississippi; Sandy Magnuson, University of Northern Colorado; Chris McCarthy, University of Texas, Austin; Diane McDermott, University of Kansas; Bernard Nisenholz, California State University, Northridge; John G. Pappas, Eastern Michigan University; Woodrow M. Parker, University of Florida; Paul Power, University of Maryland, College Park; and Simeon Schlossberg, Western Maryland College.

This text is also the product of my experiences as a student, group leader, group member, supervisor, and teacher. Being a doctoral student at the University of Michigan set my mind free to question the status quo, challenge myself to keep striving, explore new ideas and perspectives, and dream about making a meaningful contribution to my profession. I hope I have lived up to the values and aspirations I developed there. Experiences as a group leader and member and as a teacher and supervisor have helped me test and deepen my thinking. Because my experiences in groups have continuously and powerfully reinforced the meaningfulness of group work, I thank my group leaders, fellow group members, members of the groups I have led, group leader supervisees, and students. The experiences they have offered me are priceless.

A number of very dear people provided the encouragement I needed to complete this text. I thank Jerry Donigian for being there. His thinking, guidance, and friendship helped me to believe in the value of my ideas and to complete this text. I thank Scott Hinkle and Ronnie Zuessman for being my friends and believing in me no matter the distance or circumstance. I thank Steve Feit for being Steve Feit (he knows how important that is to me.). I thank David Kleist for our brain-stretching conversations. I thank Arthur P. Lloyd and Jean H. Cecil for being my models of integrity and professional conviction. Jean and Arthur, although being miles apart and only acquaintances, have been my professional parents. I thank Ron Riggs, Kevin Davis, and Christina Tawney for helping me to become a better writer. I thank my students, particularly my doctoral students, for their questioning, trusting, risking, experimenting, and understanding.

I especially thank Elinor; there is no way I could have completed this text without her. She read, edited, challenged, questioned, and loved me throughout the entire project. I thank Sally for being patient, challenging me to be me, and not allowing my head to swell. I also thank Susie, Dave, and Huckleberry for their attention and willingness to be scratched. Finally, I thank Roz and George, coleaders of my first group. They never understood rock and roll but rocked nevertheless. I loved them dearly.

Finally, doing this project has taught me to go skiing as often as possible to celebrate living, go backpacking when life is overwhelming, and to fly fish when there is a need to find meaning.

Discover the Companion Website Accompanying This Book

THE PRENTICE HALL COMPANION WEBSITE: A VIRTUAL LEARNING ENVIRONMENT

Technology is a constantly growing and changing aspect of our field that is creating a need for content and resources. To address this emerging need, Prentice Hall has developed an online learning environment for students and professors alike—Companion Websites—to support our textbooks.

In creating a Companion Website, our goal is to build on and enhance what the textbook already offers. For this reason, the content for each user-friendly website is organized by topic and provides the professor and student with a variety of meaningful resources. Common features of a Companion Website include:

FOR THE PROFESSOR—

Every Companion Website integrates **Syllabus Manager**™, an online syllabus creation and management utility.

- **Syllabus Manager**™ provides you, the instructor, with an easy, step-by-step process to create and revise syllabi, with direct links into Companion Website and other online content without having to learn HTML.
- Students may log on to your syllabus during any study session. All they need to know is the web address for the Companion Website and the password you've assigned to your syllabus.
- After you have created a syllabus using **Syllabus Manager**™, students may enter the syllabus for their course section from any point in the Companion Website.

- Clicking on a date, the student is shown the list of activities for the assignment. The activities for each assignment are linked directly to actual content, saving time for students.
- Adding assignments consists of clicking on the desired due date, then filling in the details of the assignment—name of the assignment, instructions, and whether it is a one-time or repeating assignment.
- In addition, links to other activities can be created easily. If the activity is online, a URL can be entered in the space provided, and it will be linked automatically in the final syllabus.
- Your completed syllabus is hosted on our servers, allowing convenient updates from any computer on the Internet. Changes you make to your syllabus are immediately available to your students at their next logon.

FOR THE STUDENT—

- **Counseling Topics**—17 core counseling topics represent the diversity and scope of today's counseling field.
- **Annotated Bibliography**—includes seminal foundational works and key current works.
- **Web Destinations**—lists significant and up-to-date practitioner and client sites.
- **Professional Development**—provides helpful information regarding professional organizations and codes of ethics.
- **Electronic Bluebook**—send homework or essays directly to your instructor's email with this paperless form.
- **Message Board**—serves as a virtual bulletin board to post—or respond to—questions or comments to/from a national audience.
- **Chat**—real-time chat with anyone who is using the text anywhere in the country—ideal for discussion and study groups, class projects, etc.

To take advantage of these and other resources, please visit the *Interactive Group Counseling and Therapy* Companion Website at

www.prenhall.com/kline

Brief Contents

CHAPTER 1   The Social Context   1

SECTION I   **Understanding Group
             Interaction**   **13**

CHAPTER 2   The Interactive Group
             Environment   15

CHAPTER 3   Group Development
             Theory   33

CHAPTER 4   Interactive Group
             Development Theory   53

CHAPTER 5   Group Theory Introduction
             and Focal Conflict Theory   69

CHAPTER 6   General Systems Theory   85

CHAPTER 7   The Interpersonal Approach
             and Group Theory
             Summary   95

SECTION II   **Leading Groups**   **111**

CHAPTER 8   Organization and
             Operation   113

CHAPTER 9   Interactive Group
             Leadership   145

CHAPTER 10   Basic Skills and
             Interventions   175

CHAPTER 11   Developing Effective
             Group Membership Skills   209

CHAPTER 12   Ongoing Leadership Tasks   235

CHAPTER 13   Intervention Strategies   255

CHAPTER 14   Becoming a Group Leader   275

APPENDIX 1   ACA Code of Ethics and
             Standards of Practice   289

APPENDIX 2   Association for Specialists
             in Group Work Best
             Practice Guidelines   309

APPENDIX 3   Association for Specialists
             in Group Work
             Principles for Diversity-
             Competent Group Workers   313

Contents

CHAPTER 1

The Social Context   1

INTRODUCTION   1

SOCIAL CONNECTEDNESS, RELATIONSHIPS, AND MENTAL HEALTH   2

INTERPERSONAL RELATIONSHIPS   3

CHANGE   4
- *Interpersonal Learning and Group Interaction*   4
- *The Relevance of Change in Group Interaction to Real Life*   5

ESSENTIAL VALUES FOR GROUP WORK   5
- *Group Interaction as a Reflection of the Social/Cultural Context*   6
- *Social Issues and Social Responsibility*   6
- *The Critical Need for a Multicultural Perspective*   7
- *Multicultural Group Counseling and Therapy*   7

THE EFFICACY OF GROUP COUNSELING AND THERAPY   8
- *The Accounts of Joseph Pratt, Trigant Burrow, and Lewis Wender*   8
- *The Evolution of Group Work*   9
- *Research on the Efficacy of Group Counseling and Therapy*   11
- *The Current Need*   11

ORGANIZATION OF THIS TEXT   12

SECTION I   Understanding Group Interaction 13

CHAPTER 2

The Interactive Group Environment 15

INTRODUCTION   15

ESSENTIAL GROUP DYNAMICS   16
Norms   17
Roles   23

MEMBERSHIP ATTITUDES   30
Participation   30
Personal Responsibility   31
Risk Taking   31
Commitment to Others' Learning   32
Leader and Member Attitudes   32

CONCLUSION   32

CHAPTER 3

Group Development Theory 33

INTRODUCTION   33

MODELS   34

CLASSIC GROUP DEVELOPMENT THEORIES   34
Bion   35
Bennis and Shepard   37
Schutz   41
Tuckman   47

ESSENTIAL GROUP DEVELOPMENT CONCEPTS   50
Counseling and Therapy Groups Are Social Systems   50
Groups Address Core Interpersonal Issues   50
Anxiety Is Always Present   51
Conflict and Anger Are Inevitable, Indispensable, and Productive   51
*Members Have Varying Degrees of Success Resolving Core
    Interpersonal Issues*   52

CONCLUSION   52

CHAPTER 4

Interactive Group Development Theory 53

INTRODUCTION   53

CORE INTERPERSONAL CONCERNS   54
Involvement   54
Dependency   54

    Authority   55
    Individuation   55
    Intimacy   56
    Loss and Loneliness   56
  INTERACTIVE GROUP DEVELOPMENT THEORY   56
    Involvement   58
    Dependency   59
    Authority   60
    Individuation   62
    Intimacy   63
    Loss and Loneliness   65
  CONCLUSION   66

CHAPTER 5

Group Theory Introduction and Focal Conflict Theory   69

  INTRODUCTION   69
  FOCAL CONFLICT THEORY   71
    Group Process   71
    The Group Members' Therapeutic Experience   77
    The Therapeutic Process   81
  CONCLUSION   83

CHAPTER 6

General Systems Theory   85

  INTRODUCTION   85
  ESSENTIAL CONCEPTS   86
    Systems, Subsystems, and Suprasystems   86
    Isomorphy   86
    Homeostasis   86
    Boundaries   87
  BOUNDARY FUNCTIONING   87
    Impermeable Boundaries   88
    Diffuse Boundaries   88
    Effective Boundarying   89
    Autonomy   90
    Hierarchy   91
  THERAPEUTIC PROCESS   92
    Basic Assumptions   92
    Implications for Group Counseling and Therapy   92
    Process   93
  CONCLUSION   94

CHAPTER 7

The Interpersonal Approach and Group Theory Summary   95

INTRODUCTION   95

THEORETICAL FOUNDATIONS   96

ESSENTIAL CONCEPTS   98
Therapeutic Factors   98
Interpersonal Learning   98
Cohesiveness   100
Here and Now   100

THERAPEUTIC PROCESS   101
Necessary Conditions   101
Process of Therapy   101

ROLE OF THE LEADER   102
Creating a Facilitative Culture   102
Activating the Here and Now   103
Process and the Self-Reflective Loop   103
Conceptualization of Members' Concerns   104

CONCLUSION   104

ESSENTIAL THEMES IN GROUP COUNSELING AND THERAPY THEORY   105
Origin and Significance of Interpersonal Difficulties   105
Relatedness of Members' Concerns   106
Here and Now   107
Intervention Focus   107
The Therapeutic Group Environment   108
Interpersonal Objectives   108
Therapeutic Process   108

CONCLUSION   109

SECTION II   Leading Groups   111

CHAPTER 8

Organization and Operation   113

INTRODUCTION   113

PLANNING   114
Planning Decisions   114
Recruiting Group Members   117
Member Selection, Group Composition, and Member Preparation   119

ESSENTIAL OPERATING GUIDELINES   125
Prohibition of Physical or Psychological Harm   125
Confidentiality   125

Limits on Out-of-Group Socializing   126
Boundaries for Leaders' Relationships with Members   127

MANAGING OPEN GROUPS   128
Group Development Issues   128
Coping with Open Groups: Realistic Goals   128

COLEADERSHIP   129
Coleadership Benefits   129
Coleadership Issues   130
Coleader Relationships and Group Issues   131
Working Together in and out of Group   132
Postgroup Processing   132
Planning Time   132
Supervision   133
Dealing with Coleader Relationship Issues   135

LEADING SOLO   136
Support and Supervision   136

STARTING AND ENDING GROUP SESSIONS   137
Starting Sessions   137
Ending Sessions   138

TERMINATION   139
Premature Termination   139
Termination of a Group Member   141
The Process of Ending a Time-Limited Group   141
Termination Sessions   142

CONCLUSION   143

CHAPTER 9

Interactive Group Leadership   145

INTRODUCTION   145

TRUST AND GROUP BOUNDARIES   146

DEVELOPING EFFECTIVE INTERACTIVE SKILLS   147

LEADERSHIP ROLE   148
Factors Influencing the Leadership Role   148
Establishing Therapeutic Factors   150

INTERACTIVE THERAPEUTIC FACTORS   152

LEADERSHIP FUNCTIONS   153
Norm Setting   154
Boundary Management   155
Structuring   157
Instruction   158
Regard   160

Languaging   162
Administration   163

LEADERSHIP FUNCTIONS: LEADER BELIEFS AND MEMBER ATTITUDES   165

LEADERSHIP STYLE   166

The Authoritarian, Democratic, and Laissez-Faire Continuum   166
Active Versus Passive   169
Personal Involvement and Technical Skills   171
The Interactive Leadership Role   172

CONCLUSION   173

CHAPTER 10

Basic Skills and Interventions   175

INTRODUCTION   175

AFFECTIVE, COGNITIVE, AND BEHAVIORAL OBJECTIVES   177

Affective Objectives   177
Cognitive Objectives   178
Behavioral Objectives   179

INTERVENTION LEVELS   180

Individual-Level Skills and Interventions   180
Subgroup (or Interpersonal) Skills and Interventions   181
Group-as-a-System Skills and Interventions   181

INTERVENING: TIMING, BALANCE, AND INTENSITY   182

Timing   182
Balance   184
Intensity   185

BASIC SKILLS AND INTERVENTIONS   186

Listening Skills   186
Directives   187
Observation   188
The Basic Facilitation Sequence   189
Bridging   191
Confrontation   193
Challenges   197
Communication Clarification   199
Contracting   200
Boundary Setting   202
Requesting Input   204
Structuring   205

WHEN BASIC SKILLS AND INTERVENTIONS DO NOT WORK   206

CONCLUSION   207

CHAPTER 11

Developing Effective Group Membership Skills 209

INTRODUCTION 209

EFFECTIVE INTERPERSONAL COMMUNICATION 210

Guidelines for Effective Communication 211

Teaching Communication Skills 213

Communication Problems 216

Self-Disclosure 218

Feedback 221

Teaching Feedback Exchange 224

Teaching Members to Receive Feedback 226

Involving the Group in Feedback Exchange 227

EXPERIMENTATION 229

CONCLUSION 234

CHAPTER 12

Ongoing Leadership Tasks 235

INTRODUCTION 235

PROCESSING 237

Processing Skills 237

OPTIMIZING THE GROUP'S FACILITATIVE QUALITIES 241

Supporting Enabling Solutions 241

Identifying and Frustrating Restrictive Solutions 242

ESTABLISHING A SHARED PERCEPTION OF SAFETY 244

PROTECTING MEMBERS FROM HARM 246

Members Pressuring Other Members 247

Members in Isolation 248

Group Boundary Problems 249

ENSURING INDIVIDUAL MEMBERS' CHANCES OF SUCCESS 250

Monitoring Group Interaction for Focal Conflicts and Themes 253

CONCLUSION 254

CHAPTER 13

Intervention Strategies 255

INTRODUCTION 255

OBSTRUCTING NORMS 256

Implementing New Ground Rules 256

Observing Obstructing Norms 257

Observing and Directing Members to Discuss Obstructing Norms   258
Experimentation with New Norms   259
Confronting Obstructing Norms   261
Norms Interventions: Final Considerations   262
INTERPERSONAL AND RELATIONSHIP ISSUES   262
Interpersonal Boundary Interventions   263
Interpersonal Contracts   264
PROBLEMATIC MEMBER ROLES   265
Conceptualizing Problematic Roles   266
Intervening with Problematic Roles   267
Leader Precautions When Intervening with Problem Roles   270
CONFRONTING SOCIAL ISSUES   271
The Nature of Social Issues in the Group Context   271
Confronting Diversity Issues in the Group Context   272
CONCLUSION   273

CHAPTER 14

Becoming a Group Leader   275

INTRODUCTION   275
EMOTIONAL CHALLENGES   276
LEADERS' PERSONAL ISSUES   278
KNOWLEDGE   279
EXPERIENCE   280
PERSONAL DEVELOPMENT   282
PERSONAL LEADERSHIP STYLE   283
THE PERSONAL BOUNDARIES OF THE GROUP LEADER   283
Power, Authority, and Responsibility   284
Gender, Racial, Religious, and Cultural Issues   285
Being an Anarchist and Orchestrator   286
CONCLUSION   287

Appendix 1: ACA Code of Ethics and Standards of Practice   289

Appendix 2: Association for Specialists in Group Work
            Best Practice Guidelines   309

Appendix 3: Association for Specialists in Group Work
            Principles for Diversity-Competent Group Workers   313

References   319

Name Index   323

Subject Index   325

The Social Context

After reading this chapter, you should be able to:

✔ Discuss the importance of relationships in individuals' lives.

✔ Describe how changes occur in counseling and therapy groups and how these changes are relevant to individuals' lives.

✔ Name the core values of group counseling and therapy.

✔ Outline the origins of group counseling and therapy and how group work has evolved.

✔ Discuss the research on the effectiveness of group counseling and therapy.

✔ Discuss the current need for group counseling and therapy.

INTRODUCTION

We become group members the instant we are born, and we become members of many other groups as our lives unfold. These multiple memberships define the roles we play in our life stories and shape our relationships with others. We refer to ourselves in terms of the roles we play. I am a human being, a son, a husband, a father, a brother-in-law, an uncle, a friend, a group therapist, a researcher, a teacher, a supervisor, a storyteller, a skier, a backpacker, a fisherman, a frustrated golfer, and a writer. Because I am a human being, I am a part of many groups—a family, an extended family, friendship groups, a profession, and groups of persons who share similar passions and problems. We cannot escape group membership;

to be human is to be a member of many groups as well as a member of the largest group: humanity. We are connected to all those who live in the world with us, all who have preceded us, and all who will follow.

SOCIAL CONNECTEDNESS, RELATIONSHIPS, AND MENTAL HEALTH

Social connectedness is a sense of closeness and belongingness that develops in relationships that range from acquaintances to intimate relationships (Lee & Robbins, 2000). If we are effective in our interactions with others, we are likely to meet our social needs and develop a sense of social connectedness in our primary groups and the world. Effective interactions contribute to our sense of personal value and self-esteem. When we are not successful in our interactions, we become lonely and lose our sense of social connectedness and identity. Ineffective interactions also lead to a diminished view of our own personal worth and to lowered self-esteem.

The literature affirms that individuals' ability to effectively self-disclose in relationships plays a significant role in the effectiveness of their social functioning and sense of well-being (Davis & Franzoi, 1987). Self-disclosure leads to connectedness, which leads to a sense of well-being and mental health (Davis & Franzoi, 1987; Jourard, 1964). Without a sense of connectedness, individuals become lonely, lack a clearly defined sense of identity, and do not have the feeling of belonging in society in general.

Many theorists representing a wide range of perspectives (e.g., Bugenthal, 1965; Freud, 1922; Maslow, 1970; Rogers, 1961; Schutz, 1966) describe the essential role of relationships in meeting core human needs. Bugenthal discusses rootedness and relatedness as core existential needs and suggests that individuals are motivated to develop a sense that they are a part of humankind and involved in authentic relationships with others. Freud held that individuals have a basic psychological need for affiliation. Maslow believed that individuals need to experience a sense of belonging as well as a need for love and intimate relationships. Rogers held that individuals develop a sense of self-worth in the context of their relationships and strive to gain acceptance from others. Rogers also stressed that, as individuals age, their "need for positive regard from others increases. Such needs include being loved by others, being emotionally and/or physically touched, and being valued and cared for" (Sharf, 1996, p. 220). Finally, Schutz identified three essential interpersonal needs—inclusion, control, and affection—that can be satisfied only in relationship with others. All these theorists support the essential need of individuals to be in connected relationships where they feel valued and accepted.

Individuals must be able to self-disclose effectively to develop connections with others. However, being able to communicate one's internal experiences to others effectively is a complicated feat. Fears that have their origins in damaging relationships with peers or painful experiences in families of origin limit what individuals feel prepared to disclose. Limitations in what individuals feel prepared to disclose restrict their capacity for intimate involvement with others. For example, individuals who hear significant others comment that their ideas and emotions are stupid are unlikely to disclose thoughts and emotions that could make them vulnerable to crit-icism. Thus, to build authentic relationships, acquire a sense of social connected-ness, and develop a clear sense of personal identity, individuals must resolve interpersonal issues that influence how they communicate and respond to the com-munications of others. The resolution of interpersonal issues is a crucial prerequi-site for mental health.

INTERPERSONAL RELATIONSHIPS

Individuals learn how to view themselves and how to act in relationships with oth-ers because of experiences in their families of origin and later because of interac-tions with others in their family, social, and occupational groups. Theorists such as Sullivan (1953), Bowen (1966), and Kernberg (1976), despite their varied perspec-tives, contend that family-of-origin experiences shape the roles that individuals as-sume and the way in which individuals fulfill those roles. From the perspective of these theorists, experiences with significant others shape how individuals interact and influence their choices about forming relationships and interacting with others throughout their lives.

Relationship patterns formed in their families of origin define the behaviors and roles that individuals perform in all their relationships. This means that individuals' interactions, although looking somewhat different, are fundamentally consistent at home, at work, at school, or in any other social context. For example, an individual who suppresses the expression of her anger at home probably suppresses it at work and with her friends. An individual who believes he needs to please others to be ac-ceptable in his family is likely to work very hard to please his friends, his peers at work or school, and his employers or teachers.

Learning how to be in a relationship is a result of experiences individuals have in their families of origin. At times, the "rules" families have about how to be ap-propriate, acceptable, and noticed create self-perceptions and relationship behaviors that cause pain and limit how fulfilled individuals are able to be in their relation-ships. Family rules that forbid the expression of painful emotions severely limit how openly family members are able to share their feelings to gain support from other family members. Later in life, individuals who have grown up operating by these rules are not likely to know how to ask for or receive the support offered in more fulfilling relationships. Conversely, many families have rules that lead to self-perceptions and relationship behaviors that are fulfilling and allow individuals to de-velop and prosper. These families provide a nurturing environment in which it is safe to be vulnerable, share emotions, openly seek support, and experience acceptance.

Individuals who experience problems in their relationships are commonly dis-satisfied with their lives and are often less mentally healthy than individuals who do not experience relationship problems. When individuals who experience relation-ship problems become members of counseling or therapy groups, they have an op-portunity to identify their relationship problems and the self-perceptions that lead to unfulfilling relationships. Helping group members learn effective ways to make fulfilling interpersonal connections, change limiting self-perceptions, and acquire the interpersonal behaviors necessary to develop healthy relationships are the primary goals of group counseling and therapy.

CHANGE

From a group counseling and therapy perspective, two fundamental beliefs are useful guides for the work of group counselors and therapists. These beliefs pertain to how individuals develop relationship problems and how individuals can best change how they relate to others. The first belief is that individuals form and enact their personalities in relationship to others. In addition, because of their relationships, individuals develop a pattern of "acceptable" interpersonal behaviors that they believe are appropriate to use in their relationships. The second belief is that because individuals form self-perceptions and interpersonal behaviors in relation to others, they are more likely to change how they interact with others in relation to others.

Interpersonal Learning and Group Interaction

Literature as early as 1905 described the powerful impact that group members have on one another. This impact involves the power that group dynamics have to influence members and the interpersonal learning mechanisms (Yalom, 1995) that allow members to learn from their here-and-now interactions in groups. Bloch and Crouch (1985) analyzed the factors that research had identified as most crucial for achieving therapeutic goals in therapy groups. A common denominator in the factors Bloch and Crouch described was that interacting with each other was the most crucial factor in helping members achieve therapeutic success. That is, members profit the most from their interactions with each other, not from their interactions with the group counselor or therapist. The idea of members profiting from their interactions with other members is foreign to group counselors and therapists who have been trained in traditional, individually oriented approaches to counseling and psychotherapy. This idea is foreign because counselors and therapists, because of their training, perceive themselves as the primary agent of change in their work with clients.

From the perspective of this text, effective group leaders are those who can successfully create environments that promote effective member interaction. When members interact effectively, they experience the profound power of group interaction to influence their interpersonal behavior. When leaders recognize that their goal is to establish and maintain conditions that allow interpersonal learning, the way they lead groups often changes dramatically. Members who participate in groups that demonstrate necessary conditions and emphasize interpersonal learning become intensely engaged and acutely aware of their relationships with each other. This awareness can often lead to significant changes in how members relate to each other in groups and ultimately in members' relationships outside their groups.

The Relevance of Change in Group Interaction to Real Life

Ultimately, group members develop the realization that the way they interact with each other in group and the way they interact in relationships outside group are essentially identical. Because members participate in counseling and therapy groups to deal with their relationship problems, members' relationship issues are eventually enacted in the here and now of group interaction. On occasion, members will also see how their perceptions of others and their interactions in their group relationships are related to early experiences in their families of origin.

When members become aware of the behaviors and perceptions that create problems in the way they relate to others in group, change is possible. Group members who become aware of what they do to cause relationship problems are in a position to make choices about using different behaviors in their relationships. Changes that members make in group to improve their relationships with other group members can be applied to improving their relationships outside group.

Issues can arise, however, when members do not transfer what they learn in group to their out-of-group relationships. Leaders who are sensitive to this transfer of learning involve members in fine-tuning their behavior changes in group and making conscious decisions about when and how to use their new interpersonal behaviors in their relationships outside group. When considering the relevance of group interaction to "real life," new leaders and members must recognize that relationship behaviors in group correspond with relationship behaviors outside group. They also should recognize the need and value of a conscious decision-making process for transferring what is learned in group to out-of-group relationships so they have no doubt about the relevance of in-group changes to real-life situations.

ESSENTIAL VALUES FOR GROUP WORK

Helping people become more satisfied in their relationships with others is the core objective for group counseling and therapy. This objective can be translated, if necessary, into such terms as promoting mental health, increasing the effectiveness of interpersonal behaviors, improving boundary functioning, bettering social adjustment, changing limiting cognition, developing congruence, increasing self-acceptance, or ameliorating developmental issues. However counselors and therapists might express the objective for group counseling or therapy, the foundational value is that effective and fulfilling relationships are necessary for optimal functioning and mental health. This value has implications for the perspectives that leaders have about the role of groups in improving the quality of their social environment.

Leaders who understand that group interaction mirrors the interaction that occurs in the social environment outside the boundaries of their groups see the relevance of group work for improving the social environment. Among the things members should learn in groups are how to be sensitive to the needs of others, how to accept and live with differences, how to communicate to ensure more complete understanding, and how to deal productively with conflict. Thus, each member who leaves a group with these learnings can potentially contribute to the quality of the social environment. In addition, issues in the social/cultural context outside counseling and therapy groups have a powerful impact on individuals' relationships, both limiting and defining possibilities for personal development and life satisfactions. Leaders who are concerned about their members leading satisfying lives cannot ignore the social/cultural conditions that limit the possibilities of group members outside counseling and therapy groups.

Group Interaction as a Reflection of the Social/Cultural Context

The social issues present in the social/cultural context in which counseling and therapy groups are conducted invariably appear in group interaction. Most commonly, these issues emerge when members treat each other according to stereotypes. Blatant examples include a female member accusing a male member of not valuing the expression of emotions, a male member accusing a female member of not being able to make rational decisions, or a member suggesting that another member has limited capacities because of race. Other occasions in which stereotyping occur are less blatant but just as demeaning. For example, members may treat another member very carefully (e.g., making sure that another member understands what is going on or that another member does not have hurt feelings) or patronize that member because of their assumptions about how to get along with "that kind of person." In many cases, careful or patronizing treatment is a more subtle demonstration of stereotypes that limit what a member can learn and the relationships that a member is able to develop with other group members. In the case of stereotyping, it often seems that many members are unaware that their stereotypes limit the choices they make about their treatment of others. Many members are unaware that they inadvertently cause others pain. Perhaps most tragically, these members are totally unaware of how their stereotypes severely limit their opportunities for satisfying relationships and what they can learn from those whom they stereotype.

The most obvious and immediately damaging example of the emergence of social/cultural issues in counseling and therapy groups occurs when there is an open expression of bigotry or intolerance. These expressions are the clearest manifestation of social/cultural issues in the group context. Although the open expression of prejudice is appalling, it is only a more obvious expression of the same limiting beliefs expressed in more subtle examples of stereotyping. In all cases, members bring the biases they learn in their social environments into the counseling and therapy groups they attend. Considering counseling or therapy groups as "cultural" islands free of intolerance and bigotry is an enormous mistake.

Social Issues and Social Responsibility

Leaders who witness social issues appearing in their counseling and therapy groups are responsible for identifying and confronting these issues. Confronting social issues is a fundamental aspect of leaders' social responsibility. At a minimum, leaders who are sincere about helping members make productive changes in their lives are concerned about the social issues that cause members pain and limit their potential for growth.

Leaders must recognize that members live in environments where devastating social issues, such as religious and cultural bigotry, intolerance of differences, racism, ageism, or sexism, exist. These socially exhibited attitudes and beliefs significantly influence what persons can be and limit their opportunities to have social relationships that could contribute to their well-being. These realizations have three important implications for the work of group counselors and therapists. First, the leaders' responsibility to proactively identify and confront these issues during group interaction is critical. Second, leaders must help members learn not only how to confront and cope with the tyranny of social issues but also how to help others outside the group confront these issues. Finally, group counselors and therapists must find a meaningful way to confront social and cultural issues in their own lives.

The Critical Need for a Multicultural Perspective

Individuals from diverse cultures, races, religious practices, and worldviews populate the earth we live on. These diverse perspectives enrich us all because they offer alternative perspectives and variety; each of us becomes richer in our experiences when we embrace and respect diversity. Our relationships with diverse people demand that we reciprocate the gifts we receive. Treating others with respect and valuing the development of common understanding and acceptance completes a cycle of relationships that increases the possibility that social systems will come nearer to nurturing all individuals and their potential.

Multicultural Group Counseling and Therapy

In a sense, all group counseling and therapy is multicultural. Each group member represents diverse communities and the diverse qualities, histories, and circumstances of their families and experiences. Later discussion will describe various ways to compose groups and the advantages and disadvantages of composing groups of people who are alike or different in some way. At this point, prospective leaders should understand that diversity exists even in the most homogeneous groups. Leaders who assume diversity, even when members appear and act similarly, are most likely to develop an effective group environment.

Assuming diversity means that leaders presume that each member differs from others in meaningful ways. Leaders who assume diversity always strive to help members confront and answer the question, "How can we work together in a way that benefits us all?" Confronting this question means acknowledging members' differences and finding a common ground for members working together in the group. Confronting and acknowledging diversity means that members' differing perspectives can benefit all group members. For example, men and women can learn about their relationships from others' perspectives. Individuals who struggle with emotions and those who are comfortable with emotions can learn to empathize and tolerate others' way of expressing themselves. Spontaneous members and members who are more measured in their interactions can learn different ways to act in their relationships from each other. In each of these examples, members learn tolerance, experience alternative ways to interact, and broaden their perspectives about others.

THE EFFICACY OF GROUP COUNSELING AND THERAPY

The first description of group counseling and therapy appeared in an article by Joseph Pratt in 1905. This article described the powerful influence that group interaction had on group members. Pratt's ideas have evolved continuously since the publication of his accounts. At present, there continues to be overwhelming support for group counseling and therapy and an ever growing need for group interventions.

The Accounts of Joseph Pratt, Trigant Burrow, and Lewis Wender

Because of their accidental discoveries, practical demands, and curiosity about social interaction, the pioneers of group therapy learned about the power of group interaction to change individuals. Pratt (1907) was the first to write about the curative effects of group interaction. He used groups because of overwhelming practical demands and stumbled on the discovery that group interaction had a powerful influence on those who participated. Burrow (1928), curious how loneliness affected individuals, explored how relationships with others influenced psychiatric issues. Wender (1936) faced the practical issues of applying individually focused psychoanalytic therapeutic interventions to hospitalized psychiatric patients. He discovered that group interaction was productive because of some essential dynamics present in group interactions.

On July 1, 1905, Pratt began treating tuberculosis patients in groups because he was overwhelmed with a constant stream of new patients (MacKenzie, 1992; Pratt, 1907). Pratt's Emmanuel Church Tuberculosis Class was a group of 25 members who met weekly at Massachusetts General Hospital for socializing and education. Members of the classes represented many races and "sects." Pratt noted that the members, although different in many ways, shared the common bond of their disease. Invariably, those who attended the weekly meetings "were in good spirits." The outcome of Pratt's classes was the recovery of 75% of the tuberculosis patients, many of whom were given no hope for recovery.

On April 30, 1928, Burrow presented a paper at the Phipps Psychiatric Clinic at Johns Hopkins Hospital (MacKenzie, 1992). Burrow initiated his work with groups because of his interest in exploring the effects of isolation. He believed that many psychiatric problems were related to how individuals interacted with others in their communities. To study problems in community living, Burrow examined the here-and-now interactions of individuals in groups. He concluded that interventions designed to address "mental disorder and insanity, in industrial disorders and crime" (1928, p. 206), should focus extensively on how individuals relate to each other. He also reached the conclusion that interpersonal relationships play a critical role in the development and enactment of psychopathology.

Wender (1938) published a paper that described the practical realities of making efficient psychotherapeutic interventions with an inpatient population. Using a psychoanalytic frame of reference, Wender faced the issues of time, cost, patients' unsuitability for analytic procedures, and the difficulties he perceived in establishing productive transference relations. Wender determined that analytic procedures were unsuitable for his situation and that he needed to devise a therapeutic program that could overcome the limitations of analytic procedures. After extensively applying group therapeutic interventions in his setting, Wender identified several essential "dynamics" that operated in group psychotherapy: intellectualization, patient-to-patient transference, and catharsis in the family. Essentially, Wender was the first to articulate what are now referred to as group therapeutic factors.

The contributions of Pratt, Burrow, and Wender were the products of accidental discovery, curiosity, and practical demands. Pratt accidentally discovered the powerful effects of group interaction. Burrow forwarded concepts that describe the role of group interaction in the development and amelioration of psychopathology. Wender was the first to identify some of the critical group therapeutic factors. Each of these contributions plays an important role in current conceptualizations of the purposes and applications of group counseling and therapy.

The Evolution of Group Work

Although group work has been practiced for nearly a century, its practice dramatically expanded in the 1940s in response to the overwhelming needs of military personnel after World War II (Rutan, 1993; Scheidlinger, 1993). During the mid-1940s, group therapy grew dramatically in terms of theory and practice. "The group therapists of those days did the best they could through trial and error and by incorporating their dyadic psychotherapy skills in a group setting" (Rutan, 1993, p. xvii). Although the group therapists during this time were relatively unsophisticated, they recognized that something powerful was taking place in their groups (Rutan, 1993; Scheidlinger, 1993).

In the 1950s, therapists continued to recognize the power of their groups to heal members. Along with this recognition, numerous debates emerged. One of the first of these debates occurred between individually oriented therapists and group therapists and focused on the relative efficacy of individual and group therapy. Individual therapists argued that group therapy offered only superficial treatment (Rutan, 1993). This debate ended as groups persistently demonstrated their effectiveness and advantages over individual therapy. In particular, individual therapists, most of whom were analytically oriented, argued that group therapy diluted transference and that group therapy patients could thus make only superficial changes. This argument came to an end when group therapy consistently demonstrated that group interaction actually enhanced transference (Rutan, 1993). Subsequent debates occurred between group therapists over theory and the most effective group therapy techniques (Rutan, 1993; Scheidlinger, 1993). Despite these debates, by the end of the 1950s the literature recognized group therapy as a powerfully effective and versatile form of treatment.

In the 1960s and 1970s, major advances were made in the applications of psychoanalytic theory and object relations theory for group therapy (Scheidlinger, 1993). Also during this period, Whitaker and Lieberman (1964) presented a new theory that continues to make a significant contribution to the practice of group counseling and therapy. At the same time, various applications of group therapy developed and became highly popular. In particular, encounter groups and variants such as T groups and sensitivity training groups emerged as media for personal growth.

One of the foremost advocates of encounter groups was Carl Rogers, who stated, "For more than thirty-five years, individual counseling and psychotherapy were the main focus of my professional life. But nearly thirty-five years ago I also experienced the potency of the changes in attitudes and behavior which could be achieved in group. This has been an interest of mine ever since" (1970, p. v). Many authors echoed Rogers's enthusiasm during the 1970s, especially William Schutz (1973).

Unfortunately, many practitioners of encounter and related "growth" groups were insufficiently trained and were overenthusiastic, which often led to members having adverse experiences in their groups. These groups "challenged and embarrassed the professional group work field because many people began to equate those controversial and at times even harmful group enterprises with group therapy" (Scheidlinger, 1993, p. 5). In order to clarify the difference between the abuses of group work and competent practice, practitioners of group work recognized the need for increasing the professionalization of group work.

In response to the need for professionalization, the Association for Specialists in Group Work (ASGW) was founded in 1973. The ASGW joined the American Group Psychotherapy Association (AGPA), founded in 1942, in the advancement of professionalism in group work. Currently, both organizations have made substantial contributions to group work practice. *The International Journal of Group Psychotherapy*, published by AGPA, and the *Journal for Specialists in Group Work*, published by ASGW, make significant contributions to knowledge and practice. In 1994, AGPA, along with its standards for clinical membership and ethical practice, supported the initiation of certification for group therapists who meet stringent standards for training and experience. Currently, the Clinical Registry of Certified Group Psychotherapists manages the certification and recertification of group psychotherapists. ASGW has made substantial contributions to the professionalization of group workers in the fields of counseling and psychotherapy. It has also defined standards for training, practice, and multiculturalism in group work. In the field of psychology, the recognition of group work was slow to develop. In 1991, the American Psychological Association formed the Group Psychology and Group Psychotherapy division, which in 1996 began publication of the journal *Group Dynamics* (Gladding, 1999).

Since the 1970s, group therapy has seen continued growth and development. Dies (1993) points out that new group paradigms, such as time-limited therapy groups and self-help groups, have replaced the encounter movement of the 1970s. Scheidlinger (1993) describes the growth of the group therapy movement since the

1970s as "an unprecedented growth spurt" (p. 9). Evidence of the continued growth in group work includes the ever increasing presence of group research in psychotherapy and counseling literature and the rapidly increasing presence of group treatments in inpatient, outpatient, community, school, and "virtually all human service facilities" (Scheidlinger, 1993, p. 9). The substantial evidence of the effectiveness of group work interventions fuels the ongoing rapid expansion of group work.

Research on the Efficacy of Group Counseling and Therapy

Bernard and MacKenzie (1994), in describing the 15 years of psychotherapy research prior to 1994, note findings that approximately 85% of the individuals involved in psychotherapy do better than individuals in control groups. They go on to state that "the results are essentially the same whether the psychotherapy is delivered in an individual or group format" (p. viii). Yalom (1995) concurs that "the answer is very clear: there is considerable evidence that group therapy is at least as efficacious as individual therapy" (p. 218). Piper (1993) also makes this point: "Reviews of the outcome literature during the past decade have confirmed the general effectiveness of group therapy and its similar efficacy to that of individual therapy" (p. 674).

In 1993, Dies summarized 40 years of research in group psychotherapy. He noted several persistent trends in the findings. Among these trends, the literature communicates continued growth in the confidence that group treatments are effective. This confidence follows from meta-analytic studies of group research, surveys, comprehensive reviews of outcome studies, and studies that demonstrate the effectiveness of group interventions with specific client groups (e.g., depressed, bulimic, and sexually abused) (Dies, 1993). In general, authors (e.g., Bernard & MacKenzie, 1994; Dies, 1993; Piper, 1993; Scheidlinger, 1993; Yalom, 1995) agree that group treatment is effective and cost-efficient.

The Current Need

Group work has grown dramatically since the 1940s. This growth and the ever increasing professionalization of group counseling and therapy have progressed even more dramatically since the 1970s. Currently, group work has a solid grounding in research that supports its effectiveness. Group work is a primary treatment modality practiced in a wide array of settings. Now, as demands for cost-effective and efficient treatment become more intense, group work will continue its explosive growth. The environment demands it.

At present, the demands of managed health care and the need to provide cost-effective psychotherapy are mounting (Piper, 1993). These demands translate into pressure to provide brief and inexpensive treatment. Group treatment offers the most effective response to these demands. As Piper puts it, "If one were asked to select a form of verbal therapy that is maximally economical in terms of therapist time, short-term group therapy would be the obvious choice" (p. 676). Dies (1993) summarizes what the future might hold for group therapy if the current demand for cost-effective treatment continues: "It is conceivable that clinicians may face even greater challenges to explain why the treatment of choice for most patients is not group psychotherapy" (p. 476). In addition to economic demands, practitioners in human service settings and schools, in particular, face diminishing resources and increased demands for services. These environmental realities further forecast a continuously increasing need for group work. The future of group work is very bright.

ORGANIZATION OF THIS TEXT

This text contains two sections. The first section discusses theories and concepts that help group leaders conceptualize group interaction and develop group interventions. The second section provides practical information regarding the roles and functions of group leaders, basic leadership skills and interventions, ongoing leadership tasks, intervention strategies, and important considerations for forming and organizing groups. It concludes with a discussion of the process of becoming an effective group leader.

For experienced group leaders, I hope this text offers you new perspectives and ideas that might invigorate your practice. For students, fasten your seat belts—becoming a group leader is quite a ride!

SECTION

I

Understanding Group Interaction

The first section of this text presents concepts that help group leaders comprehend group interaction and begin to conceptualize group interventions. These concepts are organized into six chapters.

Chapter 2, "The Interactive Group Environment," presents group dynamics principles that are essential for group leaders. The chapter discusses norms and roles in terms of their importance, development, and implications for effectively functioning groups. These primary concepts are also discussed in terms of how they influence members' attitudes regarding group membership.

Chapter 3, "Group Development Theory," presents four theories of group development and a discussion of the essential themes in group development theory. The four theories were selected because of their contributions to the group counseling and therapy literature. Bion's theory of group development was one of the first theories to describe group development and was the first group development theory to illustrate the recurring nature of group members' concerns.

Bennis and Shepard's theory provides one of the most complete descriptions of group development phases. It also includes an important discussion regarding the significance of members' personalities and interpersonal issues on how groups develop over time.

Schutz's theory provides a perspective that was the culmination of the most comprehensive research in the area of group development. His theory contains perspectives on recurrent group issues, the role of interpersonal needs in group development, and the significance of members' personalities on group development and interaction.

Finally, Tuckman's theory of group development is presented for several important reasons. First, his initial and revised theory represents a complete overview of the findings of many group development articles. Second, his theory is probably

13

the most widely cited group development theory in the group counseling and therapy literature.

More recent group development research is extremely limited and does not contradict the findings of these classic and still state-of-the-art group development theories. Readers may encounter texts that present group development phases to organize their discussion. These organizational schemas are rarely based on research and are not intended to be formal theory.

Chapter 4, "Interactive Group Development Theory," systematically presents common themes in group development theory. This synthesis, presented as a theory, emphasizes an interactive perspective on group development. An extensive example of ongoing group interaction illustrates how these common themes impact group interaction and development.

Chapter 5, "Group Theory Introduction and Focal Conflict Theory," discusses criteria for selecting group counseling and therapy theory and introduces the theories that meet these conditions, concluding with a discussion of focal conflict theory. Although focal conflict theory is an elegant approach to comprehending group interaction, it appears very rarely in group counseling literature (e.g., Donigian & Malnati, 1997).

Chapter 6, "General Systems Theory," discusses the applications of general systems theory for group counseling and therapy. This discussion shows how basic systems concepts can be used to conceptualize group interaction and interventions. Not included here are more recent applications of general systems theory to group therapy that stress the synthesis of systems and analytic thinking to group therapy (e.g., Agazarian, 1997).

Chapter 7, "The Interpersonal Approach and Group Theory Summary," presents an overview of important interpersonal processes. This presentation stresses concepts related to interpersonal learning. The chapter concludes with a discussion of the common themes presented in these theories.

Each of the theories presented in Chapters 5 to 7 makes special contributions to the conceptualization of group interaction and to defining interventions that address counseling and therapy groups as social systems. Because these theories recognize groups as social systems, they offer perspectives that use the power of group interactions to help members change. Using such power is the essence of the interactive perspective.

2

The Interactive Group Environment

OBJECTIVES

After reading this chapter, you should be able to:

✔ Demonstrate an understanding of group dynamics concepts that are useful for interactive group counseling and therapy and for conceptualizing groups as social systems.

✔ Describe the relationship between group process and structure.

✔ Describe how group norms develop and what norms are consistent with effective and ineffective group functioning.

✔ Discuss how group member roles develop and the factors that influence their enactment.

✔ Discuss how member roles can facilitate or hinder effective group functioning.

✔ Indicate how norms and roles influence member attitudes and what member attitudes are consistent with productive group experiences.

INTRODUCTION

A crucial leadership goal is to develop a group environment that facilitates the development of essential member attitudes. To accomplish this goal, leaders need to understand some essential group dynamics properties that influence the effectiveness of the group environment. Once leaders have learned how to observe these properties, they can identify the restraining and facilitating forces in their groups and intervene to help members develop attitudes that support interpersonal learning.

ESSENTIAL GROUP DYNAMICS

Various disciplines interested in understanding group interaction have used the term *group dynamics* (Vander Kolk, 1985). Because these disciplines operate from diverse perspectives, there are many variations in the definition of group dynamics. This section defines group dynamics in a way that will help leaders observe and conceptualize group interaction. **Group dynamics** describes the purposes of group interaction (group process) and the interactive patterns (group structure) that emerge from these interactions.

A **group process** consists of interactions that "promote behavioral and attitudinal conformity with the group's emerging culture" (Wheelan, 1994, pp. 60–61). That is, group interaction involves members negotiating how to communicate, participate, and perceive group involvement. Group interactions include negotiations about how intimately members should interact, whether and how members should acknowledge and handle conflict, the acceptable level of honesty, what to expect from each member, and how to respond to each others' concerns. As leaders observe group interaction, the questions "What is the purpose of this interaction?" and "What are members negotiating?" will help them identify group process. Leaders can intervene to shape the development of the group environment after identifying group process negotiations. These interventions are discussed in the chapters of section 2.

The following discussion is a common example of negotiation in an early group meeting and depicts the group process of directly negotiating sharing emotions.

FRANCIS: "I'm not sure why having to share my feelings is so important. We shouldn't have to do it."

GEORGE: "I agree; it seems like we can talk about our problems, and that would be enough to help."

DAVE: "That's right, we should talk about what we're having problems with and not have to get into feelings!"

Group process also includes more subtle, indirect negotiations. Indirect negotiations occur as members observe the outcomes of others' interactions. These observed outcomes shape what members regard as safe or acceptable group behavior. Interactions that appear to have productive or nonthreatening outcomes are repeated, and those that have apparently negative outcomes are less likely to recur. Thus, indirect negotiations have the same effect on interaction as direct negotiation. For example, if sharing emotions seems productive, members are more likely to share emotions. If, on the other hand, sharing emotions seems damaging, members will attempt to avoid sharing emotions.

A more specific example of an indirect negotiation occurred in the third meeting of a group. During this meeting, Brian expressed his anger about Sally's participation. Rob, another group member, reacted. "Stop! Can't you see Sally is hurt?" The other group members looked on in stunned silence until Sally spoke. "Brian, your anger really hurt me. I didn't come here to be hurt like this!" In this example, a powerful indirect negotiation took place. All group members experienced anger as hurtful and as something to be avoided.

Direct and indirect negotiation processes frequently have the purpose of avoiding risky interaction. When they are successful, members are not likely to share honest reactions or to participate spontaneously. Consequently, leaders should be alert to members negotiating "rules" for interaction that limit what can be shared. Members use negotiations to add certainty and safety to interaction and to avoid the uncertainty of group membership. Unfortunately, these negotiations can block interchanges that can help members learn.

Group process negotiations inevitably establish stable patterns in group interaction. These patterns include consistencies in the attitudes that members develop about participation and how they interact with each other. These stable patterns are referred to as **group structure** (Forsyth, 1999). The most significant of these patterns are norms and roles. **Norms** describe consistent patterns in the behaviors of all group members. **Roles** describe unique behaviors consistently performed by individual group members.

Norms

When people talk about a group they belong to, they usually describe the behaviors they perform as a member. These behaviors identify the norms that operate in that group. Norms are the "unwritten code of behavioral rules . . . that guide the interaction of the group" (Yalom, 1995, p. 109). Because norms dictate how members interact, they determine a group's effectiveness.

Leaders should be aware that the behaviors necessary for productive group interaction become norms only when they become a pattern in group interaction. This means that the guidelines leaders suggest for effective interaction or the ways in which members agree to interact do not have an effect on what members actually do until they become norms. For example, a group leader may suggest that members restate feedback to ensure they understand the feedback. Following this suggestion, some members immediately accept feedback, and some restate it. At this point, restating feedback is not a norm and does not have a meaningful impact on group interaction. Later, when members restate feedback and correct others who do not, restating feedback has become a norm and has an effect on how feedback is exchanged.

Norms prescribe a range of productive or ineffective group interactions and indicate attitudes members share about participation. If a group's norms preclude meaningful interaction, this indicates that group members share attitudes that block important interaction. For example, in a group that changes subjects whenever conflict surfaces, members likely share the attitude that conflict is too dangerous to address. Leaders who identify norms that hinder group interaction can identify objectives for their interventions.

Because most norms develop through indirect negotiation, conversation about what members should or should not do is rare; thus, new norms often evolve before leaders are even aware of them. Fortunately, alert leaders can identify a norm when it is broken. A number of interactions indicate that a norm has been broken. Most often, when leaders observe members correcting each other's behavior (e.g., "Irwin, own that statement."), it indicates that a group norm has been broken. Other ways that group members will respond to a member breaking a norm include challenges (e.g., "Gerald, you can give better feedback than that."), criticisms (e.g., "That's so insensitive. You really don't care about getting along."), and angry reactions (e.g., "Shut up, you jerk! You don't belong here!").

By observing the strength of a group's reaction to the "norm violation," leaders can judge a norm's importance. The following situation demonstrates how members might react to the breaking of an important group norm.

SUE: "Ted, I can't believe you said that. That's not the way we're supposed to talk in here."

WANDA: "I'm really offended by that, too. I hope you never attack me like that."

TED: "Wow! I really feel like I've broken some kind of rule in here and you all want to punish me. I was only being honest!"

HARRY: "You'd think by now, Ted, you'd know how we're supposed to get along. I'm not sure I ever want you to talk with me like that."

JANE: "I'm not sure this group is for you. Have you thought about taking care of your problem somewhere else?"

A strong reaction to a norm violation indicates that members believe that the behaviors defined by the norm are important. By observing the norms that members require each other to obey, leaders can gain insight into members' apprehensions about participation. Once identified, these apprehensions should be explored. For example, when the norm "anger will not be expressed" is stringently enforced, members will vigorously correct, challenge, or criticize those who express anger or who attempt to discuss sharing anger. Leaders who observe a group enforcing rigid norms about expressing anger can assume that members have fears about expressing anger and should explore those fears.

When leaders observe members working hard to maintain a norm, they should also expect members to resist changing that norm. This is because members attempt to maintain norms that will protect them from the anxiety associated with being involved in experiences they perceive as risky. In general, the harder members fight to maintain a norm, the more difficult it will be to change that norm. Chapter 14 includes a discussion of intervention strategies designed to address norms that block group progress and to form productive norms.

The Formation of Norms.   Norms are the products of negotiations that involve members influencing one another. When members are uncomfortable with a certain behavior, their shared reactions establish the inappropriateness of that behavior. For example, a member may express anger toward another member. In response to this expression, some group members might show their discomfort, whereas others may discuss how "negative" feelings have been damaging in their personal relationships. Thus, without any specific mention of group rules, the development of a norm commences. The following interaction depicts this process.

ARTHUR: "Jim, I'm really angry with you! You can't say that!"

LUCY: "Arthur, you're so judgmental!"

JIM: "You really hurt my feelings. That kind of talk is not helpful for me!"

SUE: "You are just like my first husband. His anger was so destructive. It never did anyone any good."

LIZ: "Your anger has really got me upset. I don't think this is the place for that kind of emotion."

LUCY: "Yeah, I thought we were going to be here to help each other. I'm really upset."

These reactions begin to establish the norm that expressing anger is unacceptable. Conversely, when members admire a behavior, their reactions will establish the acceptability of that behavior. For example, after a member shares fears about confronting another member, the others share how impressed they are by this sharing. Consequently, the norm that expressing fears is appropriate begins to be established.

ARTHUR: [Tears in his eyes] "Rita, I really want to share how I feel about you. I can't; I'm so scared you'll hate me. I just want you to care about me."

LIZ: "I'm really moved by what you've said, Arthur. That took a lot of courage."

RITA: "Arthur, I never wanted to hurt you. I feel so close to you now."

ARTHUR: "This is the first time I ever experienced anything like this. I guess I was scared because I thought I was going to get hurt, but I wasn't. I'm so relieved."

SUE: "This is so incredible. I feel like I can talk about my fears, you know, what scares me, and that's okay."

These examples illustrate how indirect negotiation forms group norms. Norms form when members' negotiations result in a consistent pattern of group behavior. This process is most notable in a newly formed group, where norms are unclear and members are uncertain how to behave.

Sherif (1936) described the reciprocal influence process of norm development as a funnel pattern. When a new group begins, members use the behaviors they ordinarily use in social situations when they are unacquainted with what is expected. Over time, based on members' reactions to each other and the interventions of the leader, the variability of members' interactive behaviors decreases. After a while, members' behaviors begin to conform. At the point where "members align their behaviors until they match certain standards" (Forsyth, 1999, p. 121), norms have developed (see Figure 2.1).

The following scenario illustrates norm development during a group's first two sessions. During the early moments of the first session, members are engaged in a discussion about their families, their job situations, and the current weather conditions. Members interact spontaneously and shift from topic to topic; often several members talk at once and laugh nervously. The group leader intervenes by sharing some ideas about how the group can interact most effectively. The leader's suggestions include listening to each other and staying with a topic as long as it is productive. Some members use these suggestions, whereas others continue to interact as they had earlier. By the end of the session, after several leader interventions, members begin to be more attentive, talking one at a time and staying with a topic for longer periods.

Figure 2.1
Funnel Pattern of Norm Development

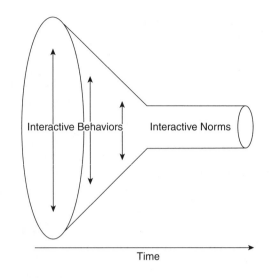

The second session begins with the same interaction patterns as the first meeting, but this does not last long. Without the leader saying anything, members stop their customary social interactions and focus on being in the group; a period of silence ensues. After a moment, a member talks, without interruption, about a relationship problem while others listen attentively. At the end of the member's sharing, other members take turns offering their ideas on how to solve the problem. Eventually, discussion drifts as others share experiences with relationship problems. Occasionally, a member interrupts, but others remind that member to wait until the current speaker has finished.

In this example, group behaviors became less variable. The group rapidly established the norm of one speaker at a time. Interaction began to conform to a standard of behavior, and the group committed to enforcing the standard. In addition, it appears that the group made progress in developing a "staying on the topic" norm. Although the member did not resolve the problem, the group stayed focused on relationship concerns.

By being aware of how norms are formed, leaders can encourage the inclusion of effective group behaviors and the exclusion of counterproductive behaviors. Clearly, the development of productive norms is most easily accomplished during the process of norm formation. To change a norm, the leader must identify the norm, obstruct its use, and replace it with a more productive norm (see chapter 13).

Obstructing Norms.   Obstructing norms support behaviors that are inconsistent with group objectives. These behaviors develop tension among members, create a risky environment, and encourage defensiveness. Obstructing norms include behaviors such as criticizing, denying feelings, talking about events external to the group, avoiding responsibility for personal reactions, assuming motivations behind others' behaviors, demanding conformity, and engaging in competitive interactions. They emerge during early phases of group interaction because members fear being hurt. For example, members might negotiate norms that support withholding emotions, changing topics when conflict emerges, or discussing events external to the group. Members' worst fears become realities when they cannot address their concerns without breaking a norm developed to protect themselves. Members who share feelings and concerns risk the criticism of others for breaking the group's norms.

Consequently, obstructing norms discourage openness, honesty, creativity, risk taking, and experimentation with new behaviors. A group that operates with obstructing norms is unlikely to provide members with productive experiences.

Example 1 demonstrates the presence of obstructing norms: "criticize those who do not conform to group norms" and "do not disclose negative feelings." In Example 2, members are using the norms "topic changing" and "avoid responsibility for personal opinions." Continuation of the norms in both examples paints a grim picture for the future of these groups. The first example involves a scenario where an obstructing norm is broken; the second demonstrates a group conforming to its obstructing norms.

Example 1

URSULA: "Linda, why can't you just get along and stop being so nasty! You're so defensive and hostile!"
LIZ: "Yeah, Linda, when you're angry like that, it doesn't work for me. You seem to have some real problems!"
JEFF: "If you were more agreeable, the group would be better for all of us."
LINDA: "I'm really upset that I'm angry and can't share it."
URSULA: "Listen, Linda, if you want to get along, you'll need to stay positive. Why can't you understand that?"

Example 2

JESSE: "You just can't imagine how I was treated in that store."
PHIL: "We are really getting somewhere in here. This is great."
SUE: "Phil, you know how important it is that we continue to progress the way we have."
JESSE: "Did you all see the news last night?"
PHIL: "I'm really tired of how they cover the same story over and over again."
LUCILLE: "It's supposed to be warm tomorrow."

Helping Norms.   Helping norms encourage members to use behaviors that help members meet their group counseling and therapy objectives. Generally, helping norms contribute to a facilitative group environment where members can self-disclose without fear of criticism, trust others to act in their best interest, and be confident that their concerns and feelings will be respected.

Behaviors indicative of helping norms include sharing and exploring emotions, working with a member's concern as long as it is productive, interacting in the here and now, being responsible for personal opinions and reactions, checking for understanding, accepting negative feelings, openly addressing conflict, and observing and discussing group process. These behaviors, along with the shared attitudes of respect and acceptance, result in a group environment that promotes the growth and change of members.

Groups often have trouble establishing group norms even though they reduce many of the anxieties associated with group membership. This is because helping norms are inconsistent with the way individuals customarily interact. To develop helping norms, leaders ask members to exchange customary social behaviors for more risky modes of interaction. For example, customary social interaction does not involve giving feedback, confronting, or sharing immediate feelings and reactions. Leaders should be aware that members need to be convinced that the behaviors associated with helping norms actually do work before they can become norms.

The following examples demonstrate the presence of helping norms. In Example 1, members are reacting to a member breaking a valued helping norm: "use responsible language." In Example 2, members are conforming to two helping norms: "paraphrase for understanding" and "stay in the here and now." These norms suggest that both groups are becoming productive learning environments.

Example 1

JOHN: "You just get so angry when you don't get your way."

JESSE: "Are you saying that's your reaction to me?"

JOHN: "I'm not going to talk to you about it."

RICHARD: "John, it seems to me that you are the angry one here, but you won't admit it!"

LINDA: "I'm experiencing you as really hard to get to know. I don't know how you feel or what you think. I feel shut out by you!"

RICHARD: "Why don't you just say how you feel for a change? I tried it, and it worked for me."

JOHN: "Okay, I get your point. I am angry. I'm angry that none of you seem to be getting to know me. I'm sorry, Jesse, what you said really hit home! It's what I've been struggling with in here and at home and work."

Example 2

DIANE: "I'm reacting to what you just said to me, Rick. Are you saying that I put you off because of the way I look at you and that you perceive me as angry?"

RICK: "I'm scared now. But, yes, I feel intimidated right now. I feel like you'll hurt me. Your brow is furrowed, your voice is raised, your fists are clenched, and you're staring at me."

JULIE: "Diane, I agree with Rick. I'm perceiving you as angry, and I'm feeling like I want to back away from you. I'm scared now, too. Most of it has to do with the way you're looking and the volume of your voice."

NANCY: "Diane, I'd find you easier to approach if you would relax your face
            and hands and talk in a softer voice."

DIANE: "So I'm putting all of you off, scaring you, because of the loudness of
            my voice and the expression on my face?"

ALL: "Yes!"

Summary.   Norms are a significant determinant of a group's therapeutic effectiveness. Most norms are established covertly through indirect negotiation. The norms
that emerge in a group reflect members' shared attitudes about participation. Members, especially during early group meetings, usually consider the norms necessary
for effective interaction very risky and will attempt to develop norms that provide
safety. Once group members experience the value of effective group interaction and
begin to associate interpersonal anxiety with potential learning opportunities, the behaviors associated with helping norms will be established.

Roles

Roles, like norms, are a group structural property. Whereas norms are the behaviors
expected of all group members, **roles** are the unique behaviors group members expect from an individual member. As groups form, they become social systems composed of member roles. Member roles develop so that the group can meet the needs
of its members; this means that each member will behave differently to perform necessary functions. This is important to remember, as members do not always appear
to be acting in a way that helps members meet their needs when in fact they are.

Role Development.   Groups become social systems very rapidly. Even as members form initial impressions of each other, they establish expectations for the roles
each other will fill. Wheelan (1994) discusses how members' roles develop during
the initial stages of a group:

> Role assignment . . . is not entirely the product of rational assessment of each mem-
> ber's skills and talents. Rather, it is based on first impressions, external status, and
> initial self-presentation as well as the group's needs at the moment. Members may
> or may not secure a role that will facilitate group goal achievement. On an individ-
> ual level, a member may find him- or herself in a role that is comfortable and allows
> for positive contribution to group effort. On the other hand, the member may find
> his or her assigned role inhibiting and unfamiliar. (p. 57)

Wheelan (1994) makes several other key points group leaders need to understand. First, roles form covertly. Members seldom discuss which member will fill a
particular role. Second, members are not initially aware that they are assuming a role
assigned to them by other group members. Finally, roles develop early in the life of
the group and are difficult to change.

When groups form, members are concerned about what they and others will be
doing in the group. Members will ponder role questions such as "What will others
want from me?," "What should I expect from others?," and "What am I supposed to
do?" Ultimately, the reactions of other members to their behaviors determine the

roles members assume—an indirect negotiation process. Although members seek and desire a role that meets their needs and is acceptable to them, they will enact roles on the basis of the expectations communicated by others in their interactions with them. Even members who enact roles that employ behaviors that receive a negative response in the group are responding to the expectations of other members. Wheelan (1994) states,

> The power of social roles to influence the behavior and attitudes of both the role occupant and others viewing the role should not be underestimated. Roles shape attitudes and behavior. Once a person assumes a role, the role creates a new mental perspective in the individual. (p. 56)

Direct negotiation of roles occurs only when members and leaders openly discuss the performance of a group function or when a leader intervenes to modify the role of a particular member. Examples of direct negotiation include members agreeing on who will be responsible for keeping the group on task or for making sure that members are seated and ready to start the group on time or the leader asking a particular member to monitor the expression of emotions in feedback exchange.

Role Types.   The roles that members assume have been classified and defined in terms of specific member behaviors (e.g., Benne & Sheats, 1948; MacKenzie, 1990). MacKenzie (1990) offers a role typology that views roles as a part of a group's social system. He believes that members must perform four complementary roles for a group to be therapeutically viable: sociable, structural, divergent, and cautionary roles. Any number of members can fill these roles, and the performance of each of these roles facilitates or inhibits group effectiveness.

Sociable roles (MacKenzie, 1990) are filled by members who share emotion, develop positive interpersonal relationships, involve others in interactions, and care about others. These roles are necessary if the group is to develop a safe and facilitative group climate. Members who fill sociable roles try to ensure that all members have positive relationships. However, extreme forms of sociable role behaviors block the expression of anger, confrontation, and discussion of member conflicts.

Structural roles (MacKenzie, 1990) are filled by members who attend to group organization so that the group can provide effective learning experiences. Structural role behaviors are concerned with meeting goals and achieving positive outcomes. Structural role behaviors, such as asking for guidelines or clarifying procedures, help members develop an understanding of group process and reduce the anxiety associated with the ambiguity of group interaction. Members who fill this role tend to be cognitive and push for structure. In their extreme, structural role behaviors block the expression of emotion and retard spontaneous interaction.

MacKenzie (1990) characterizes members who fill **divergent roles** as continuously challenging others and expressing points of view that differ from others. Members perceive those who fill divergent roles as hostile and critical. Because of the antagonistic attitudes displayed by these members, others face the challenge of having to clarify their own perspectives and learn how to accept divergent points of view. In addition, these members make the positive contribution of introducing the expression of anger into group interaction. Extreme forms of divergent role behaviors have a harmful effect on group interaction. When unsuccessfully managed, divergent members' behaviors cause groups to polarize around issues and experience unresolved hostile feelings.

Cautionary roles (MacKenzie, 1990) are demonstrated by members who withhold personal information. When cautionary members join groups, they are apprehensive and often withdraw from interaction. The reluctant involvement of cautionary members forces other members to examine their commitment to the group and willingness to self-disclose. Members who fill cautionary roles usually frustrate other members' efforts to involve them in group interaction. Cautionary members also force other group members to deal with their concerns about being unacceptable. In extreme cases, cautionary role behaviors increase other members' apprehensions about self-disclosing in the group. If interventions do not succeed, cautionary role behaviors threaten group cohesion.

MacKenzie believes that these four roles, each with positive and negative manifestations, are essential. It is important for leaders to remember that all roles, no matter how they are perceived, can be used for the benefit of group members. Only extreme role behaviors have a seriously negative impact on a group. A group social system that includes these roles has a structure that allows it to confront the essential interpersonal issues associated with these roles.

Role Performance.   The performance of any role ranges in its impact on group interaction. Members who perform roles that improve interpersonal communication and contribute to establishing helping norms are needed for a group to become an effective learning environment. Examples of **facilitative role performance** for each of MacKenzie's (1990) role types show how each role can make an important contribution to group effectiveness.

> Facilitative Sociable Role: "Art, you're the only one who hasn't shared your feelings with Steve. I hope you'll do it."
>
> Facilitative Structural Role: "Bill, you got a bunch of feedback. Do you understand what Holly said to you?"
>
> Facilitative Divergent Role: "Why do we always have to agree on everything? I don't agree, and I think my point of view is just as valid as yours!"
>
> Facilitative Cautionary Role: "Just because other people want me to share all my feelings doesn't mean I have to!"

Roles may also hinder group progress. **Hindering role performance** serves the agenda of individual members at the group's expense. The performance of these roles ordinarily includes ineffective behaviors developed to satisfy interpersonal needs in family-of-origin and social environments. Hindering role performance has the consequence of diverting other members from productive interactions. Examples of role performance for each of MacKenzie's (1990) role types show the enactment of roles that hinder group effectiveness.

> Hindering Sociable Role: "There seems to be a lot of negative feelings in here. We need to stop this and focus on the good things that are going on in the group."

Hindering Structural Role: "As the leader of the group, aren't you supposed to tell us what to do now? Some people have shared emotions, and that doesn't work! What exactly is the procedure?"

Hindering Divergent Role: "It's all your fault; you've just succeeded in getting us all upset. Where did you learn how to lead groups?"

Hindering Cautionary Role: Silence.

Some members play roles that help other group members meet their needs for safety and threaten group effectiveness. **Avoidant role performance** helps members avoid confronting their shared apprehensions. Individuals in sociable, structural, cautionary, and divergent roles can enact their roles as avoidant role performers. For example, when a member performs an avoidant divergent role, he or she is likely to be the only member who shares anger. This member performs a role that serves the purpose of helping others who have difficulty expressing anger avoid having to express it. The following dialogue demonstrates this process.

WALLY: "Ryan, I'm really angry! How dare you!"
HAYDEN: "Wally, I'm sure you're not really angry; it's just a misunderstanding. Anger doesn't help."
LAURA: "That's right, Wally. I'm sure if you would just listen to what Ryan is saying, you wouldn't be angry. Your anger is not useful."
RON: "Wally, I'm really uncomfortable with how you continue to be angry. It's like you're ready to throw a chair or something. You just don't know how to get along!"
LAURA: "If you would just try to understand what Ryan is saying, you wouldn't have to be angry. You always seem angry!"
BOB: "Wally, what's your problem? Can't you control yourself?"

This illustration shows how group members deal with their fears about anger by confronting an individual whose role involves expressing anger. Instead of talking about their fears, group members use an avoidant role performer as a means to escape dealing directly with their concerns. This process involves members criticizing the member in the avoidant role for unacceptable behavior instead of directly discussing their fears. If this process continues, it has the effect of establishing norms that preclude the enactment or discussion of the behaviors members' fear. When these norms are established, members avoid confronting the fears that lead to their becoming group members.

Filling any role as an avoidant role performer can be very difficult because no matter what a member does, he or she will continue to represent the fears that other members want to avoid. When members persist in labeling a member as a problem, that member's behaviors and the group's avoidance of a shared fear will continue. Leaders should be aware that a member who fills any role as an avoidant role performer is in danger of becoming a scapegoat. Later chapters discuss the process of scapegoating and leader interventions that address scapegoating.

Leaders can differentiate hindering and avoidant role performance by examining how a role affects the group. If members are dealing with interpersonal fears and a member diverts the group's attention to him or her, that member is performing a

Table 2.1
Facilitative, Hindering, and Avoiding Dimensions of MacKenzie's (1990) Group Roles

	Facilitative	Hindering	Avoiding
Sociable roles	Supports and encourages the expression of emotions and caring. Is sensitive to the feelings and needs of other members.	Attempts to suppress the expression of "negative" emotions and conflict. Stresses the importance of "being nice."	A member who persistently blocks interactions that include conflict and "negative" emotions.
Structural roles	Organizes and clarifies group processes in order to help the group meet its goals and function effectively.	Pushes to establish structure and firm procedures. Attempts to maintain cognitive interaction and suppress spontaneity.	A member who consistently attempts to preclude the expression of emotion and pushes for rigid structure.
Divergent roles	Challenges members to clarify perspectives and examine group interaction from different viewpoints. Introduces the expression of anger and confronting conflict.	Polarizes the group around conflicts by frequently challenging or "finding fault" with group processes and objectives.	A member who persistently attacks group processes and objectives, criticizes the perspectives of other members, and refuses to accept other points of view.
Cautionary roles	Helps members examine their commitment to the group and anxieties associated with acceptance and self-disclosure because of their reluctance and apprehensions about participation.	Withholds personal reactions and threatens group safety because of their hesitancy. Is ambivalent when others attempt to involve him or her.	A member who remains silent and presents rigid interpersonal boundaries despite repeated attempts by others to involve him or her in group interaction.

hindering role. If the group has a strong reaction to a member's behavior, avoids dealing with their own reactions to the issues that member presents, and criticizes that member for the behavior, that member is performing an avoidant role. By differentiating avoidant and hindering roles, leaders can intervene more effectively. Chapter 14 discusses leader interventions that address these role issues. Table 2.1 depicts how each of MacKenzie's (1990) roles can involve facilitative, hindering, or avoidant characteristics.

Role Problems.   When members do not perform the behaviors expected of their role, other members will respond. These responses involve exerting pressure on the member who is not behaving as expected to perform expected behaviors. The pressure to perform a role can cause members to struggle with participating in a personally congruent manner. The following are some common scenarios.

Martha is expected to offer spontaneous opinions. She has the latitude to offer opinions in a personally congruent way as long as she offers opinions—quickly. When she decides not to offer opinions because she wants to experiment with being more reflective, other group members pressure her to offer opinions. Some members ask her for her opinions, and others confront her, saying that they feel rejected by her because she is withholding her ideas.

When the group begins, John tries to act according to how he perceives himself—caring and emotionally sensitive. Ideally, others would support his acting this way, but this is not the case. Other members persistently try to influence him to angrily confront those members who break the group's norms.

The group has been meeting for several months. Recently, Scott has become progressively annoyed about other members' reactions to him. He shares his anger: "I thought we were supposed to be honest and care about each other! But every time I'm honest and show I care, I get criticized. Some of you seem to want me to go away."

During the group's third session, Sally makes an emotionally charged statement: "What the h— am I supposed to do! I can't figure it out. All I know is that whatever I do, it's not what I'm supposed to do!"

These scenarios are indicative of the pressures members experience finding and filling their roles. When these pressures are vague or conflicting, they create role problems. Forsyth (1999) describes these problems as **role stress**, of which he describes two basic categories: **role ambiguity**, which is the outcome of ambiguous role expectations, and **role conflict**, which is the product of conflicting expectations for a role or conflicts between the various roles a member may fill inside and outside the group.

Role Ambiguity.   Role ambiguity occurs when members are uncertain what they are supposed to do or doubt whether they are capable of doing what is expected of them (Forsyth, 1999). Role ambiguity is also related to Gladding's (1995) description of **role confusion**, which depicts members who do not understand what they are supposed to do. Role ambiguity and role confusion often occur in newly formed groups or when new members enter an ongoing group. These role issues are common in the early stages of group development.

Role Conflict.   Role conflict occurs when members experience incompatible role expectations (Forsyth, 1999). **Intrarole conflict** arises when members are expected to perform a role that involves seemingly incompatible behaviors. For example, a member who is expected to provide support and at the same time confront others experiences intrarole conflict. Intrarole conflicts also emerge when other members expect different behaviors from a particular member.

Interrole conflicts emerge when members struggle with roles that are inconsistent with their self-image and the roles they normally perform. Gladding (1995) uses the term **role incompatibility** to describe this aspect of role conflict. He states, "In role incompatibility a person is given a role within the group . . . that he or she neither wants nor is comfortable exercising" (p. 38). Members who are influenced to act in unfamiliar ways commonly experience interrole conflict. In some cases, members experiencing interrole conflicts are making productive changes in their inter-personal behaviors. For example, a member who fills the role of the listener in the group and never listens at home experiences interrole conflict. Occasionally, how-ever, interrole conflict involves members filling roles that do not include productive behaviors (e.g., interrupting those who express emotions). The group leader needs to decide when it is necessary to support or challenge the roles performed by mem-bers experiencing interrole conflicts.

Leaders who understand the significance of roles and role problems have a means to conceptualize the behavior patterns of each group member in the context of the group social system. Remember that members are always responding in some way to the expectations of other members. In addition, roles are parts of a group's social system, a product of negotiation. Clearly, leaders should consider these dy-namics when they intervene to help members change their roles.

Roles in Effectively Functioning Groups.   In general, members must enact a va-riety of roles in order to bring essential group issues to the surface. A group where all members are performing sociable roles (MacKenzie, 1990) will not be as effective as a group where members also enact structural, cautionary, and divergent roles (MacKenzie, 1990). Groups will stall when they do not have members who create in-teractive issues. This is because the interactions of apparently "difficult" members cause other members to address their own concerns.

In a productive group experience, members learn to develop the flexibility to enact a range of roles that will work effectively in a wide range of relationships. To do so, members need to develop comfort and competence with a range of relation-ship skills. Groups that encourage experimentation with new behaviors have norms that allow members to experiment with alternative roles.

Summary.   Each member's role is necessary for the continuation of the group's so-cial system. This does not mean that the group operates effectively. Rather, it means that the social system created through group members' negotiations persists. The im-plication is that the roles that form the structure of the group's social system can sup-port or block a group in accomplishing its purposes.

When members chastise a member for acting "inappropriately," the leader should carefully examine what is occurring. A member who does not perform ac-cording to role expectations threatens the continuation of the group's social system. On observing a group attempting to force a member into a role, leaders should ask themselves, "What purpose does this role serve for the group?" It is highly probable that a member's inappropriate behavior is consistent with a concern that the other members want to avoid.

Leaders should understand that a group that keeps a member in a particular role might hinder the progress of the member and the group. The leader must in-tervene if the expectations of members are keeping a member in a role that does not allow growth. At the same time, the leader should be cognizant that a group that keeps a member in a role sustains the status quo in the group social system. Defining this status quo is an important diagnostic step in understanding a group's functioning.

MEMBERSHIP ATTITUDES

The norms and roles members negotiate and attempt to sustain represent their attitudes about participation. These attitudes bring about opportunities for learning and changing and shape the social structure and effectiveness of group environments. Leaders should understand that a systemic relationship exists between effective participation attitudes and facilitative norms and roles. Norms and roles influence members' attitudes while, at the same time, members' attitudes influence group norms and roles they attempt to negotiate. A group will be effective when it develops norms and roles that support essential member attitudes and when members' attitudes support facilitative norms and roles.

Members value participation when they experience a group structure that supports interaction that leads to productive change. Once developed, attitudes that value participation lead members to become more actively involved and committed to group participation. Conversely, members who have not had productive experiences will display attitudes that question the value of participation. This skepticism is usually associated with norms and roles that do not support interactions that allow interpersonal learning. The longer a group structure persists that does not support interpersonal learning, the more likely it is that members will begin to regard the group as a waste of time and honest participation as excessively risky. To reverse this skepticism, members must experience what it is like to experience productive group interactions.

As leaders work to develop a social structure that creates an effective group environment, they should be cognizant of a number of essential member attitudes. Leaders who are able to help members develop these attitudes are more likely to develop an effective interactive group environment. These attitudes include members' beliefs about the potential outcomes of participation, personal responsibility for learning, the usefulness of risk taking, and commitment to learning from one another. It is also important that the attitudes leaders demonstrate are consistent with the attitudes they attempt to develop in members.

Participation

Participation that is based on a shared commitment to personal learning and the learning of others is a hallmark of an effective group environment. Participation attitudes describe members' beliefs about the potential benefits of participation. Members will believe in the benefits of participation when they observe or personally experience productive learning. Because of these observations and experiences, members develop participation attitudes that lead to greater investment in group participation. For instance, when members observe another member learning to communicate more effectively, the entire group observes productive learning. Consequently, members experience the group as an effective learning environment and understand the value of participation.

Members will be successful when they believe that participation will benefit them and they act on this attitude. The emerging attitude that participation is worthwhile eventually develops group norms and roles that support the importance of participation. In turn, norms and roles that support the importance of participation further develop attitudes that the group is meaningful and important for its members. On the other hand, when members question the value of participation, they create an environment that is less likely to develop norms and roles that support productive learning experiences. If most of a group's membership shares this attitude, the group is boring and unproductive.

Personal Responsibility

Members who act on the attitude that they are personally responsible for their own learning will have productive group experiences. During the initial stages of a group, however, members are unclear regarding how to learn. Members often expect the leader to provide specific instructions or the answers to their concerns. Initially, most members balk at the prospect of being personally responsible, wanting the leader to be in charge. These members may also have no idea what to do to be responsible for their learning.

Once members understand that learning depends on the choices they make about their participation, they comprehend what it means to be responsible for their own learning. Members who comprehend this actively self-disclose, participate in feedback exchange, and experiment with new behaviors. Members who persist in the fantasy that the leader knows what each member needs to learn are not likely to benefit from their experience in an interactive group.

Risk Taking

As group members develop attitudes that value participation and personal responsibility for learning, risk taking increases. Risk taking means that members choose to participate despite their anxiety. Members who take risks choose to disclose, offer feedback, or experiment with behaviors in ways that challenge what they believe they need to do to be safe or acceptable to others.

Members' uncertainty about the way others might respond and their needs for acceptance when taking a risk influence the amount of anxiety they experience. Members who are very uncertain about the outcome of the risk they take and believe that their participation could lead to rejection take a major risk. Conversely, persons who are more certain that the risk they take will have a positive outcome face a less threatening risk and less anxiety. The greater the uncertainty, the greater the anxiety.

Groups that have norms and roles that support risk taking as an essential aspect of participation become exciting environments for learning and change. Because members must first learn to tolerate the anxiety associated with taking risks, the belief that risk taking is desirable is not easily developed. As members confront their fears and learn that risk taking can lead to important learning, they reframe the anxiety associated with risk taking as excitement.

Commitment to Others' Learning

Members of groups that are especially productive share the attitude that being committed to the learning of others is extremely important. This shared commitment is the outcome of observing and experiencing interpersonal learning. When members learn productively from each other and understand that they rely on each other for learning, they develop norms and roles that support collaborative learning.

Leader and Member Attitudes

The development of essential member attitudes is necessary if a group is to be an effective learning environment. Achieving these attitudes is unlikely when leaders' attitudes are inconsistent with the attitudes they attempt to develop. Leaders who act congruently on the beliefs that participation leads to learning, that personal responsibility for learning is essential, that risk taking leads to growth, and that collaborative learning is critical will communicate attitudes that lead to the development of a powerful learning environment. Leaders who have not experienced the impact of this form of interpersonal learning or who doubt members can learn from each other will not communicate these attitudes effectively.

CONCLUSION

The effective interactive group environment is one where members interact openly and honestly. For this to happen, a group must have a social structure that encourages interpersonal learning. Groups that have norms and roles that encourage members to accept personal responsibility, believe in active participation, commit to collaborative learning, and value risk taking are powerful learning environments.

3

Group Development Theory

OBJECTIVES

After reading this chapter, you should be able to:

✔ Discuss the usefulness of group development theory for group leaders.

✔ Describe various group development theory models and the essential components of a practical group development theory.

✔ Explain four classic group development theories.

✔ Discuss how group member characteristics influence group development and the issues that emerge during group interaction.

✔ Outline essential themes in group development theories.

INTRODUCTION

Group development theory helps leaders anticipate events that occur regularly during a group's life span. Group development theories describe "patterns of growth and change that occur in groups throughout their life cycle, from formation to dissolution" (Forsyth, 1990, p. 76). Similarly, group development theory presents phases of interpersonal activity organized around the resolution of specific interpersonal concerns.

Group counselors and therapists need to understand group development theory for several important reasons. First, all groups encounter similar phases of development, each of which addresses a significant interpersonal issue. Because group development theory suggests a sequence in which interpersonal issues arise, leaders can plan initial and concluding sessions, anticipate the emergence of interpersonal issues, and understand surfacing issues as naturally occurring phenomena. Second, group development theory provides a framework that organizes and contextualizes the observation of process and structure. This framework describes how interpersonal concerns influence the nature of interaction and evolving group structure. Finally, group development theory offers leaders a means to understand and predict dominant group issues and patterns of group interaction on the basis of the interpersonal styles of group members.

MODELS

Group development theories have been formulated from a variety of theoretical and research perspectives. These theories have been structured using different developmental models that are important to understand because they provide a system for evaluating and applying group development theory. Gibbard, Hartman, and Mann (1974) categorized these models and described their strengths and limitations.

The **linear-progressive model** links group development with movement toward a goal. This model sees groups moving from an initial stage of tentative interaction, to the resolution of interactive problems, and finally to a stage of productivity. It ignores the presence of recurring group issues and group termination.

The **life-cycle model** addresses the omission of the final stage of group development by describing the experiences members have as they adjust to group termination. However, this is also a linear model that suggests that once group problems are resolved, they never recur.

The **recurring-cycle model** describes cycles of recurring themes in group interaction. These themes represent critical issues that emerge and reemerge during group interaction. According to Gibbard et al. (1974), the recurring-cycle model focuses on how group members attempt to manage anxiety in order to maintain equilibrium, deal with interpersonal boundaries, and resolve their individual concerns.

Although the recurring-cycle model addresses the limitations of the linear models, it is not the only model to consider. Probably the best group development theory is a synthesis of these models but not one that oversimplifies the complexity of group development (Gibbard et al., 1974).

From an interactive perspective, a useful group development theory must meet certain criteria. It must account for issues that occur as groups begin and conclude and that recycle as groups progress. At the same time, a useful group development theory must address how the interactive styles of group members influence the emergence of initial, concluding, and recycling issues.

CLASSIC GROUP DEVELOPMENT THEORIES

This chapter, in order to illustrate group development theories and their essential themes, presents four classic group development theories. The theories of Bion

(1961), Bennis and Shepard (1956), Schutz (1966), Tuckman (1965), and Tuckman and Jensen (1977) are presented because they are the most widely cited and researched models of group development. More recent presentations of group development theories, for the most part, include similar components and the same developmental stages (Forsyth, 1999). Other recent presentations of group development, in addition to showing similar stages, are stage models that are used to organize the presentation of group counseling texts (Corey & Corey, 1997; Gladding, 1999). These models are also based on classic group development theory and are not intended to be construed as formal group development theories.

The classic theories presented in this chapter emerged from diverse origins. Bion's (1966) theory emerged from his clinical experience in Great Britain, Bennis and Shepard's (1956) was developed from research on unstructured groups of American college students, Schutz's (1966) initially emerged from research on work groups in the U.S. Navy, and Tuckman's (1965) and Tuckman and Jensen's (1977) was the product of meta-analyses of existing group therapy literature. Despite their diverse origins, a number of consistent themes emerge that are important to understand.

Bion

Bion (1961) viewed group interaction as members' attempts to deal with the anxiety created by recurring interpersonal issues. Although these issues are dealt with as they occur, groups can reach only a temporary resolution. These essential interpersonal issues inevitably resurface. Bion's theory was the initial recurrent-cycle model of group development.

Rioch (1975) credits Bion with initiating a paradigm shift from thinking about group interaction as an indication of individual members' concerns to thinking about group interaction as a demonstration of the concerns of a social system. Bion extended this premise to maintain that the concerns members experience in groups mirror the problems they experience in society. Bion's work constituted a major theoretical shift by originating the group-as-a-whole perspective (MacKenzie, 1990) and emphasizing a here-and-now focus (Yalom, 1975).

Bion's fundamental premise was that every group behaves "as if" there are two groups present: the **work group** and the **basic assumption group**. Thus, a group will act as if it is a work group at times and at other times as if it is a basic assumption group.

The Work Group.   The work group functions on a rational level to accomplish its objectives. Rioch (1975) characterized the work group as follows:

> The work group takes cognizance of its purpose and can define its task. The structure of the group is there to further the attainment of the task. . . . The members of the work group cooperate as separate and discrete individuals. Each member of the group belongs to it because it is his will and his choice to see that the purpose of the group is fulfilled. He is therefore at one with the task of the group and his own interest is identified with its interest. The work group constantly tests its conclusions in a scientific spirit. It seeks for knowledge, learns from experience, and constantly questions how it may best achieve its goal. (p. 23)

Groups that act as if they are a work group are rare, although many groups, for limited periods, occasionally act this way (Rioch, 1975). Most of Bion's theory describes why groups do not act as if they are work groups.

Basic Assumption Groups.   The term *basic assumption* refers to the irrational assumptions that serve as the basis for group members' interactions; that is, members act as if their assumptions about the conditions that exist in the group are true. These assumptions are not often shared verbally. However, by observing consistency in member behavior, leaders can identify the assumption that the group is acting on. Bion believed that group members experience three primary emotional states: dependency, fight/flight, and pairing. These emotional states categorize the basic assumptions.

The **dependency assumption group** members act as if they must have someone protect and reassure them. Members often assign leaders the ability to understand what they need without having to share their concerns and expect leaders to supply solutions. These members "deskill" themselves by acting as if they are unable to deal with their own concerns. These members are often passive and expect leaders to make their groups anxiety free. Because leaders cannot possibly meet these expectations, members become angry and disappointed. Eventually, members become angry that they have depended on the leader to take care of them.

The **fight/flight assumption group** members "cluster together as if threatened by a dangerous force. The language of the group centers around the themes of threat and the need to defend itself or escape. . . . Such groups may experience rapid alternations between themes of fear and themes of revenge" (MacKenzie, 1990, p. 9). When members act on fight/flight assumptions, leaders come under direct attack because members believe they have not adequately taken care of them. Sometimes members' attacks are indirect. Such attacks take the form of being late or absent, storytelling, having "social" conversations, or trying to sidestep the purposes of the group (Rioch, 1975).

The group focuses on pairs of members during the **pairing assumption group**. This focus takes several forms. First, the group can focus on improving the relationship of a pair of members. This attention indicates that if this member pair could get along better, it would have some critically important effect on the group. Second, pairs develop intimate relationships that occasionally take on a sexual overtone. Third, the group develops a hopeful atmosphere, and positive feelings shared in dyads permeate interaction.

Bion's work served as the transition from conceptualizing interaction in terms of individual dynamics to thinking about the group as a social system. His thinking also initiated a transition from practicing individual treatment techniques in a group setting to using interventions that focus on the entire group. Although Bion's work tends to be somewhat obscure, his perspectives are helpful for understanding the dynamics of the group as a whole and issues that recur in groups.

It is important to remember that the concerns that characterize the basic assumptions will recur regardless of leaders' effectiveness and the intentions of the group members. Bion's most important idea is that consistency in members' interactions is related to shared, erroneous, and usually unspoken assumptions about group interaction.

Bennis and Shepard

Bennis and Shepard's (1956) theory describes the effects of subgroups and personalities on group interaction and development. This theory uses a linear-progressive model. It suggests that once issues are handled, they are forever resolved. It does not account for members' experiences as the group approaches termination.

Bennis and Shepard contended that communication is the most essential concern of all groups. Without effective communication, a group cannot adequately address its conflicts, members are unlikely to benefit from participation, and members cannot overcome the issues that prevent effective group functioning. Bennis and Shepard describe two essential areas of interpersonal concern that are obstacles to effective communication: dependency and interdependence. They describe **dependence** and **interdependence** as the two major phases of group development during which individual members' styles of coping with relationships emerge (Golembiewski & Blumberg, 1970).

Dependency describes members' attitudes toward authority, beliefs about the use and distribution of power, and how responsibility should be assigned. Interactions indicating the presence of dependency issues include discussions about norms and ground rules, why the group should or should not be structured, members' responsibilities, conflict over the leader's role, and direct challenges to leaders. During interaction about dependency concerns, members can be withdrawn, aggressive, or submissive. Group development is demonstrated when members move from being concerned about authority to addressing concerns related to intimacy.

Interdependence addresses members' attitudes and feelings toward relationships. Intimacy, or how emotionally and psychologically open members are to one another, forms the basis of interdependence issues. Interaction that depicts interdependence concerns focuses on members' relationships.

Members' personal styles of interaction and the extent to which they have resolved personal issues with authority and intimacy play a significant role in group development. Bennis and Shepard describe three personality types that emerge during dependence and interdependence.

The personalities emerging during the dependence phase are **dependent**, **counterdependent**, and **independent**. Dependents seek out authority relations. Leaders who provide structure and clear rules comfort them. In effect, dependents want leaders to take care of them. Counterdependents, on the other hand, resent authority. They challenge leaders because they do not trust authority. Outspoken counterdependents often challenge the group's usefulness and have conflicts with assertive dependents. Independents have successfully resolved authority issues. These members are flexible in their authority relations, being submissive or rebellious as circumstances dictate. They tend to be objective in their relationships with the leaders.

During the interdependence phase of group development, **overpersonal**, **counterpersonal**, and **independent** personalities emerge. Overpersonals will not rest until they have achieved a high level of intimacy with others. Counterpersonals, conversely, are not interested in intimate relationships and try to avoid them. Independents have successfully resolved intimacy issues and do not compulsively seek out or avoid close relationships with other members.

Table 3.1
Bennis and Shepard's Dominant Personalities (Phases and Subphases)

Phase	Subphase	Dominant personalities
	Dependence-flight	Dependents
Dependence	Counterdependence-flight	Dependents and counterdependents
	Resolution-catharsis	Independents
	Enchantment-flight	Overpersonals
Interdependence	Disenchantment-flight	Overpersonals and counterpersonals
	Consensual validation	Independents

These personalities have a profound influence on group development because their shared issues become themes in group interaction. Groups composed of an outspoken majority of one personality type will develop very slowly and may stall in a phase of development. For example, a group composed of individuals who have not successfully dealt with their authority concerns (counterdependents) is not likely to progress beyond authority issues. Conversely, in a group with a balanced distribution of member personalities, the group is much more likely to have interactions that can move it forward (see Table 3.1).

Phase I: Dependence. During the initial phase of development, members encounter issues with people in authority. Members begin group by having successfully resolved authority issues, distrusting authority, or needing the security offered by an authority who offers specific instructions on how to behave. The interplay of these personalities is the basis of interaction occurring during this phase.

Subphase 1: Dependence-flight. During this subphase, members struggle with the anxiety involved in a new and uncertain experience. Interactions tend to be social exchanges where members attempt to find similarities or common experiences. Usually, members look to the leaders to offer them instructions on how to interact and for specific information about the goals they should have for the group. When leaders are unable to provide answers that reduce members' anxiety, the members have a dilemma. They face the ambiguity of not knowing exactly what they need to do and of having leaders who are either incapable or unwilling to tell them what to do. Dependent members try harder to get directions from the leaders. At the same time, counterdependents look for excuses to stage a rebellion, and independents observe, waiting to see what transpires. This subphase ends as members exhaust ways to acquire direction and approval from the leaders. Members become increasingly uncomfortable with their anxiety.

Subphase 2: Counterdependence-fight. Because group leaders have failed to reduce anxiety and dependents' attempts to get direction have not succeeded, counterdependents become more outspoken. Consequently, two subgroups emerge, and the anger that was avoided during the dependence-flight subphase surfaces as dependents and counterdependents battle for control. Dependents attempt to find a way to structure the group and reduce anxiety, whereas counterdependents oppose any attempt to structure the group. This battle is accompanied by disenchantment with the leaders. Members of both sides see the leaders as ineffective or incompetent because they have not met the members' needs. Input from leaders is ignored or discounted as the conflict over control of the group continues. During this time, independents present compromise solutions to group issues and urge finding a middle ground. These attempts are fruitless, and the conflict continues.

Subphase 3: Resolution-catharsis.   Conflict reaches its peak, but interaction begins to change. This subphase begins when independents who are less affected by dependency concerns begin to be heard. Independents, who have been unsuccessful in introducing compromise solutions, now become successful mediators. Independents are heard because dependents and counterdependents realize they cannot resolve their disputes and because the conflict has become excessively uncomfortable.

The independents' mediation initiates a transition in group interaction that allows members to look at the group's potential usefulness. When group members make this transition, they address norms, members' responsibilities, and the importance of group membership. The outcome of conflict over group control is the emergence of group cohesion. Members become aware that they are not helpless or isolated, that they are able to solve problems, and that they can successfully communicate their apprehensions.

Phase II: Interdependence.   As the interdependence phase begins, members have endured conflict and resolved issues. Members now share a commitment to the group. Members enjoy "the end" of conflict and the positive feelings experienced in the group. Interaction stresses maintaining these feelings, and members begin to face their concerns about intimate relationships.

Members are in various stages of resolution over the emerging intimacy concerns. Overpersonal members feel a desperate need to establish and maintain intimacy, counterpersonals fear intimacy and wish to avoid it, and independents are comfortable with varying levels of interpersonal intimacy. During this phase, the interactions of these personalities shape group development.

Subphase 4: Enchantment-flight.   This subphase begins with members enjoying the relaxed atmosphere that has emerged after a difficult period of group conflict. Many members share the attitude that everyone must be happy. This shared attitude produces norms that insist that conflict be avoided at any cost and that decisions be unanimous. Bennis and Shepard (1956) characterize the beginning of this subphase as "sweetness and light" (p. 429). As this phase continues, however, "the myth of mutual acceptance and universal harmony must be recognized for what it is" (p. 429).

Eventually, the pressure to conform to the group's norms begins to meet resistance. Members subgroup into two camps: one that urges the maintenance of harmony and the other that rebels against the demands of forced agreement. Counterpersonals challenge the "fake attempt to resolve interpersonal problems by denying their reality" (Bennis & Shepard, 1956, p. 430). As this subphase closes, conflict over norms that demand harmony builds.

Subphase 5: Disenchantment-fight.   At the beginning of this subphase, two subgroups represent opposing views on how intimate interaction should be. Overpersonals urge complete openness and present "a demand for unconditional love" (Bennis & Shepard, 1956, p. 430). Counterpersonals oppose intimacy and argue for more closed interpersonal boundaries.

The members of these opposing subgroups share a common apprehension about maintaining self-esteem. Counterpersonals believe they can maintain self-esteem by avoiding intimacy, and overpersonals believe that by establishing very intimate relationships, they can gain acceptance and maintain self-esteem. As members interact during this subphase, a theme emerges: "If others really knew me, they would reject me" (Bennis & Shepard, 1956, p. 431). Overpersonals believe that by requiring intimacy, they will be safe: "If we know each other completely, we couldn't possibly hurt each other." Counterpersonals believe that by avoiding intimacy, they will be safe: "If I don't let you know me, you can't reject me."

As intimacy issues are confronted, anxiety increases. In response, members use defensive behaviors to avoid facing their fears of intimacy. These defenses include absenteeism, intellectualization, questioning the value of the group, and boredom. At the conclusion of this subphase, overpersonals and counterpersonals are involved in sustained conflict over the acceptable level of intimacy in the group.

Subphase 6: Consensual validation.   This subphase often begins when members become aware that the conclusion of the group is approaching. Independents believe that the resolution of conflict is necessary, express confidence in the value of the group, and begin to look earnestly at their roles. The actions of the independents encourage members to confront their fears by disclosing emotions and personal reactions. The disclosing members discover that others, because of their disclosures, do not reject them as they had anticipated. Members speak about the assumptions they have made about themselves and others and how these assumptions influence their perceptions and understanding of their behaviors and those of others.

During this subphase, numerous values surface that are consistent with highly effective group functioning:

1. Members accept each other and do not attach a value to others' characteristics.
2. Conflict over emotional issues ceases, yet conflict over tangible group issues (e.g., logistical problems, norms, and so on) is tolerated.
3. Although consensus is important, agreement is not forced. Instead, hearing divergent views is valued and encouraged.
4. Members discuss group process and personal involvement in the group without alarm.
5. Communication explores thinking, emotions, and behaviors. Because of their composition, not many groups accomplish this level of effectiveness.

The contributions of Bennis and Shepard's theory are in the areas of group composition, crucial interpersonal concerns, and communication. The personalities described by Bennis and Shepard offer group leaders guidelines for group composition decisions during pregroup screening. The personality characteristics of potential members in the areas of dependency and interdependence allow leaders to anticipate the communications problems a group will encounter as it deals with developmental concerns. Bennis and Shepard suggest that groups are neither good nor bad but that some groups are more effectively composed than others. When a group is poorly composed, the leader can do little to help it achieve optimal functioning.

Bennis and Shepard do not account for how members experience group termination or for recycling group issues. Despite these limitations, this theory offers leaders valuable information.

Schutz

Schutz's (1966) theory of group development and interpersonal behaviors were based on extensive empirical research. The cornerstone of his theory is his conceptualizations of interpersonal needs. These concepts describe patterns of interpersonal behaviors and essential relationship variables. Although Schutz has since modified his theory, his initial conceptualizations are extremely relevant to understanding group development.

Schutz emphasized that interpersonal behaviors are directed toward meeting interpersonal needs. These needs "may be satisfied only through the attainment of a satisfactory relation with other people" (1966, p. 15). These needs were **inclusion**, **control**, and **affection**. Schutz contended that "inclusion, control, and affection constitute a sufficient set of areas of interpersonal behavior for the prediction and explanation of interpersonal phenomena" (1966, p. 13).

Persons have deficient, excessive, or ideal levels of need fulfillment as adults because they had varied degrees of success in learning how to meet these needs as children. Persons who have deficient, excessive, or ideal level fulfillment in one need can demonstrate a different level of need fulfillment in the other areas. For example, people can have an ideal level of affection needs, a deficient level of control needs, and an excessive level of inclusion needs.

Inclusion: Needs and Personalities.   Inclusion involves establishing and maintaining satisfactory relationships. A satisfactory relationship involves experiencing a mutual interest between self and others and believing in the worth and significance of the self within the relationship. Inclusion needs are related to being attended to, acknowledged, and recognized. The interpersonal behaviors directed toward satisfying this need include participation, interaction, and involvement. Inclusion needs also define a desire to have an identity that separates an individual from others and to be recognized. Schutz characterizes the interpersonal behaviors of inclusion as seeking "prominence rather than dominance." Each individual, depending on his or her experience as a child, has varying inclusion needs and associated fears. Individuals who have deficient inclusion needs are **undersocials**, those who have excessive inclusion needs are **oversocial**, and those who have ideal inclusion needs are **socials**.

Undersocials tend to be withdrawn and avoid participation. They attempt to maintain distance from others and guard their privacy. Schutz contended that undersocials experience the inclusion needs of wanting to be attended to and of being regarded as significant. However, because they fear rejection, not being paid attention to, or being seen as insignificant, they choose to not be involved with others. They avoid interactions that could help them meet their needs in order to prevent their fears from becoming a reality. Schutz depicted the underpersonals' attitude as "No one is interested in me, so I'm not going to risk being ignored. I'll stay away from people and get along by myself" (1966, p. 26).

Oversocials experience the same fears and needs as undersocials. Instead of avoiding interaction, however, oversocials relentlessly seek it out. Oversocials confront their fears of being ignored by doing everything in their power to gain others' attention. Schutz characterizes the attitude of oversocials as "Although no one is interested in me, I'll make people pay attention to me in any way I can" (1966, p. 26). Oversocials seek opportunities to prove their worth by being involved with others. These efforts include intensive and occasionally exhibitionistic group participation.

Socials do not experience the fears of oversocials and undersocials. Socials perceive themselves as significant persons with unique identities who are worthy of attention. Consequently, interactions with others do not cause socials to experience significant anxiety. Socials feel comfortable being involved with others or spending time alone. Their group participation varies because they are comfortable participating frequently or infrequently. Socials experience the freedom of having a wide range of choices in interpersonal behaviors because their self-worth does not depend on how others respond to them.

Control: Needs and Personalities.   Control needs surface in interactions that involve influencing or being influenced by others (Schutz, 1966). Control describes individuals' needs for authority and power in relationships. Control refers to the need to influence others, whereas inclusion reflects the need to be involved with others. Control depicts needs for "dominance," whereas inclusion describes needs for "prominence" (Schutz, 1966). Individuals satisfy inclusion needs by being noticed and involved, and they satisfy control needs by winning. Schutz believed that control issues are most effectively resolved when individuals share a mutual respect for others' competence.

The extent of individuals' control needs reflects the intensity of their fears. The fears relevant to control needs have to do with being regarded as incompetent, irresponsible, stupid, or unreliable. The more concerned individuals are about others perceiving them as such, the more control issues will surface in their relationships. Schutz classified individuals with deficient control needs as **abdicrats**, those with excessive control needs as **autocrats**, and those with ideal control needs as **democrats**.

Abdicrats avoid situations that require them to act responsibly or participate in decision making with others. Schutz described abdicrats as being submissive, gravitating toward being subordinates, wanting to be relieved of obligations, and regarding themselves as untrustworthy. Abdicrats fear that others will not help them when they need help, cannot competently manage their responsibilities, and believe that others are aware of this. Because of these beliefs, abdicrats avoid circumstances that could demonstrate their incompetence. Abdicrats are passive-aggressive in interper-

sonal interactions because they are too fearful to confront or disagree with decisions
made by others.

Autocrats also fear that they are not capable of responsible adult behaviors and
that others know this. Autocrats, however, use behaviors designed to take charge
and establish themselves as the most powerful persons in their relationships. Autocrats deal with their fears by seeking out every possible opportunity to prove their
competence. Autocrats make decisions for others because they do not trust others
to make decisions that are in their best interest. Schutz describes autocrats' attitude
as "No one thinks I can make decisions for myself, but I'll show them. I'm going to
make all the decisions for everyone always" (1966, p. 29).

Democrats have resolved power and authority issues in their relationships. Consequently, democrats believe that they are capable, responsible, and trustworthy.
Democrats are not concerned about others perceiving them as helpless, stupid, or
incapable. Democrats believe in their own competence and trust themselves. They
perceive that others respect and trust them and believe that they are capable of making effective decisions.

Affection: Needs and Personalities.   Affection needs involve developing satisfactory intimate interpersonal relationships that include liking, affection, and love.
These needs can be met only in intimate interactions that express fondness and attraction and that lead to close relationships. Schutz contrasted affection needs with
inclusion and control needs by using polarities to describe how these needs surface
in relationships. Inclusion needs have to do with "in or out," control needs with "top
or bottom," and affection needs with "near or far."

To develop close emotional relationships, individuals must confront their inner-
most fears about revealing themselves to others: "If I reveal my private thoughts to
another person, will that person find me acceptable, or will I be rejected?" To meet
affection needs, individuals confront their apprehensions about others, perceiving
them as deserving affection: "Will this person care enough about me to return my
affection?"

The extent to which individuals fulfill affection needs and perform affection behaviors depends on their fears. Those who expect rejection will experience intense
fears when they attempt to meet affection needs. Conversely, individuals who believe that they are lovable and do not fear rejection will not be apprehensive about
meeting affection needs. Schutz classifies individuals with deficient affection needs
as **underpersonals**, those with excessive affection needs as **overpersonals**, and those
with ideal affection needs as **personals**.

Underpersonals believe that they are unlovable and unlikable and that they do
not deserve the affection of others. Consequently, underpersonals avoid close emotional connections and stay emotionally distant. Because they perceive themselves
as unlovable and unlikable, they do not trust others' expressions of positive feelings
toward them. Schutz described the underpersonal attitude as "I find the affection
area very painful since I have been rejected; therefore I shall avoid close personal
relations in the future" (1966, p. 30).

Underpersonals maintain distance by avoiding opportunities for close relationships and actively attempting to keep people away. These behaviors include being

overtly antagonistic and having superficial relationships with many people so that they will not have to get uncomfortably close to any one person. Underpersonals fear that allowing people to know them intimately would be devastating because others would only discover what makes them so unlovable. Schutz states, "As opposed to the inclusion anxiety that the self is of no value, worthless, and empty, and the control anxiety that the self is stupid and irresponsible, the affection anxiety is that the self is nasty and bad" (1966, p. 31).

Overpersonals work tirelessly to develop intimate relationships to confront the interpersonal fears of being unlovable, unlikable, and rejected. Their goal is to develop relationships that have a very personal quality. They want to be very close to as many people as possible. Schutz characterized the overpersonal attitude as "My first experiences with affection were painful, but perhaps if I try again they will turn out to be better" (1966, p. 31).

The incessant efforts of overpersonals to be liked and loved include blatant attempts to secure others' approval and making overly personal self-disclosures. Other overpersonal behaviors include manipulating others to sustain close, enmeshed relationships. As Schutz puts it, overpersonals "devour friends and subtly punish any attempts by [others] to establish other friendships" (1966, p. 31). Overpersonals are clinging and jealous.

Personals are comfortable in intimate relationships and in those that require emotional distance. They are not concerned with rejection, and they feel free to be emotionally and psychologically intimate whenever it feels right. Personals perceive themselves as lovable and as able to give and receive affection and are not excessively concerned with being liked. When others do not want to be involved in a personal relationship, it is not because they are unlovable. Rather, failed relationships are the consequence of incompatibility. Personals are self-accepting and can give and receive affection freely because they are not emotionally needy.

Schutz's Theory of Group Development.   Schutz's group development theory is formulated on the premise that individuals are motivated to meet inclusion, control, and affection needs in the group context. To meet these needs, group members use necessary interpersonal behaviors. When members attempt to meet a particular need, the behaviors they use characterize group interaction and define the group's stage of development. Thus, when group members are attempting to meet inclusion needs, their inclusion behaviors characterize group interaction, and the group is in the inclusion phase.

Group development follows a predictable course, dictated by the interpersonal needs of group members. Schutz's **principle of group integration** described the initial progression of development. This principle stated that group members' initial interpersonal behaviors are inclusion behaviors meant to meet basic inclusion needs. Then, as group members meet inclusion needs, they begin to use control behaviors to meet control needs. Once members meet control needs, affection behaviors emerge in order to meet affection needs. Schutz proposed that interaction related to meeting inclusion, control, and affection needs recycles repeatedly over the life span of a group.

Figure 3.1
Group Integration and Resolution

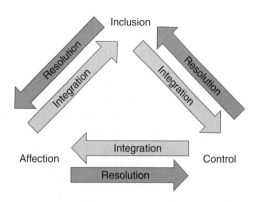

As groups conclude, the process of group integration is reversed. Schutz's **principle of group resolution** describes how groups confront termination: "Prior to a group's anticipated termination [group development] follow[s] the opposite sequence in that the predominate area of interpersonal behavior is first affection, then control, and finally inclusion" (1966, p. 168). As members of a group in the affection phase become aware of the group's ending, they again confront control and inclusion needs; that is, members will struggle with deciding how to finish being a group and then with what it means to no longer be involved with each other (see Figure 3.1).

Inclusion Phase.   During initial meetings, individuals are concerned about becoming group members. To address this concern, members make decisions about the extent of their involvement. These decisions range from choosing to be highly engaged to leaving. In the process of making involvement decisions, members confront their personal concerns about their identity and importance.

Group interaction during this phase concerns boundary issues (Schutz, 1973). That is, members decide whether they want to belong to the group and whether belonging to the group is safe. To reach this decision, members try to determine whether leaders are committed to their welfare and whether other members will pay attention to them and regard them as unique individuals.

Inclusion interaction is tentative and includes discussion of safe social topics. Although these discussions are irrelevant to the purposes of the group, they help members get to know each other and are unavoidable. Schutz (1973) states, "Groups not permitted this type of testing will search for some other method of obtaining the same information" (p. 52). Although all members experience some degree of inclusion concerns, oversocial and undersocial members will be especially concerned with inclusion issues.

Control Phase.   Once members are comfortable with inclusion concerns and begin to think of themselves as a group, control issues surface. When members confront control issues, they face concerns related to their ability to influence others and to assume responsibility. Autocrats and abdicrats, in particular, confront issues that involve their fears about competence.

Once the group enters the control phase, interaction becomes more confrontational. Interaction involves conflict over issues that include how feedback should be exchanged, whether anger is appropriate, how the group should be structured, rules for attendance and interaction, the leaders' roles, responsibility for learning, and so on. Interaction with leaders involves similar issues. Abdicrats want the leaders to have all the power and responsibility for how the group proceeds, whereas autocrats want the leaders to have none. Interaction has the purpose of sorting out how much influence, power, and responsibility members will have in the group. The control phase involves each member's attempt to find a comfortable way to participate in interactions regarding power, responsibility, and influence (Schutz, 1966).

Affection Phase.   After members become comfortable with control issues, they face intimacy issues. Members decide how close or distant they will be with each other, especially with one other member. Overpersonals and underpersonals are especially concerned about how lovable others perceive them to be.

Group interaction becomes progressively more emotional during the affection phase. Affection behaviors involve expressing positive feelings. This phase can also contain expressions of anger and jealousy. Members also direct affection behaviors toward leaders to determine whether the leaders like or approve of them. The prevalence of emotional expressions between pairs of members is the key to identifying this phase. Affection interactions have the objective of establishing a comfortable level of expressing and receiving emotional intimacy (see Table 3.2).

Schutz does not suggest a linear progression of developmental stages. Rather, group development characterizes members' greatest concern at any given moment. Inclusion, control, and affection issues always exist. This suggests that as members conclude considering the concerns of one phase and enter the next phase, they can reenter a previous phase. For example, members of a group have decided that membership in the group is desirable and look forward to being together. However, as

Table 3.2
Schutz's Stages, Concerns, and Personality Continua

Stage	Concern	Personality Continuum
Inclusion	In or out	Undersocial Social Oversocial
Control	Top or bottom	Abdicrat Democrat Autocrat
Affection	Near or far	Underpersonal Personal Overpersonal

they deal with control issues, interaction becomes heated, and members become frightened by the intensity of emotion in the group. In response, members reconsider inclusion in a group where intense emotions are expressed. The recurrence of inclusion, control, and affection concerns is confusing if group leaders expect a linear progression of developmental phases.

Group development is also heavily influenced by the interpersonal orientations of members and how assertively they try to meet their needs. A group composed of assertive autocrats, for example, will be overly concerned with control issues. Therefore, control issues will reappear over and over again, and the group will not enter the affection phase.

Group development is influenced by a group's duration. Groups meeting for extended periods are more likely to cycle and recycle through group development phases. Groups meeting for limited periods may not progress through the phases. Thus, a group composed of undersocials meeting for a brief time may never leave the inclusion phase.

Schutz's theory can assist leaders in a number of ways. First, group composition decisions can be made with an awareness of how potential members' personalities and interpersonal behaviors will influence group effectiveness. Second, knowing the combination of members' personalities allows leaders to anticipate how the group will confront developmental issues. Third, when members' interactions are conceptualized in terms of interpersonal needs, leaders have insight into issues that influence interpersonal behaviors in the group. Schutz's theory sensitizes leaders to the early needs of group members regarding inclusion, the factors that contribute to control issues that may result in leadership challenges, how affection concerns play out during the course of the group, and how termination issues will appear as the group nears conclusion.

Tuckman

Tuckman's (1965) group development model derived from his meta-analysis of group development research. His model defined group development concepts and the dominant themes in group development studies. Tuckman's work resulted in a linear-progressive group development model. Later, Tuckman and Jensen (1977) converted Tuckman's initial formulation to a life-cycle model by adding a termination stage.

Tuckman concluded that group members engage in activities designed to accomplish the purposes for which the group was convened. These activities are **task behaviors**. To accomplish a group's purposes, members interact. As a result of this interaction, patterns of interpersonal relationships emerge and change as the group progresses. Tuckman used the term **group structure** to define these relationship patterns.

Tuckman's initial model had four developmental stages: forming, storming, norming, and performing. Later, adjourning was added as a fifth stage (Tuckman & Jensen, 1977). Tuckman believed that these stages "hold up under widely varied conditions of group composition, duration of group life, and specific group task" (1965, p. 397).

Forming.   The first stage of group development witnesses members involved in testing and dependency as they acclimate to a new group. During this stage, members participate hesitantly, attempting to discover acceptable behaviors and what their relationships with other members and leaders will be like.

Structure (testing and dependency).   Initially, members attempt to establish relationships with the leaders and other members in a new and unfamiliar situation. This process involves testing out interpersonal boundaries. As this stage unfolds, members learn what behaviors are appropriate by judging the reactions of leaders and other members to their behaviors. This testing-out process is accompanied by dependency. Members often want the leaders or "some powerful group member" (Tuckman, 1965, p. 386) to offer direction and support in order to lower anxiety.

Task Behaviors (orientation to the task).   As group interactions begin, members try to achieve certainty about what they will be expected to do as group members and how these behaviors will accomplish the goals of the group. They also struggle to discover what information they will be required to share. During this stage, the members are seeking an understanding of the rules for group interaction.

Storming.   During the second stage, members engage in conflict with the leaders and one another. This conflict involves members challenging each other and the leaders, withdrawing from interaction, questioning the usefulness of the group's structure and task activities, and occasionally attacking the leaders directly. Members resist the demands of group involvement and want to maintain their individuality.

Structure (intragroup conflict).   Interactions are characterized by competition and defensiveness. Members become polarized around issues related to the anxiety involved in developing closer relationships with each other. Tuckman observed, "There are characteristic key issues that . . . boil down to the conflict over progression into the 'unknown' of interpersonal relations or regression to the security of earlier dependence" (1965, p. 386).

Task Behaviors (emotional response to task demands).   During this stage, members resist performing the behaviors required to accomplish group objectives. Members challenge the need to disclose personal information, the usefulness of group interactions, and the techniques and procedures used by the leaders. These challenges reflect members' concerns about the discrepancy between their customary interpersonal behaviors and the demands of the group's task activities. Members have emotional reactions to group demands that require making changes in their interpersonal behaviors. Commonly, leaders are the target of members' challenges resulting from these emotional reactions. Interactions at this point have the goal of avoiding involvement and exposure.

Norming.   As the third stage begins, members accept the usefulness of the group's structure and task activities. Members increasingly accept each other despite personality differences and regard group membership as important. Members commit to the group and to maintaining the interpersonal harmony that marks the initiation of this stage.

Structure (development of group cohesion and functional role relatedness). During this stage, the group becomes cohesive because it has become increasingly important to its members. At this point, members view minor disagreements as a threat to the harmony that has followed a period of conflict. Norms that suppress conflict and encourage conformity and agreement emerge and are vigorously enforced.

closer

Task Behaviors (discussing one's self and other group members). The overall theme of interaction in this stage is "probing and revealing by group members at a highly intimate level" (Tuckman, 1965, p. 390). Other related themes emerging during this stage are "confiding . . . discussing personal problems in depth . . . exploring the dynamics at work within the individual . . . and exploring the dynamics at work within the group" (Tuckman, 1965, p. 390). Members become increasingly intimate yet careful not to confront each other.

Performing.   The fourth stage sees the group reaching its greatest effectiveness. Members' task behaviors are highly productive in terms of reaching group goals. Roles that members assume promote therapeutic progress and "constructive action" in the group.

Structure (functional role relatedness).   This stage marks the time when members typically gain self-understanding and insight. Group goals are achieved, and members' roles achieve greater flexibility. The group has become a therapeutic environment, members are invested in the work of the group, and they are not resistant to the therapeutic process.

Task Behaviors (emergence of insight).   Members achieve understanding of their personal and interpersonal issues during the fourth stage. Members develop insight into personal concerns, achieve understanding of their interactions, and initiate therapeutic change. Members willingly exchange feedback, self-disclose, confront one another, take risks, and participate in therapeutic interactions.

Adjourning.   In the adjourning stage, members experience separation and the termination of the group as a significant event. At the conclusion of counseling and therapy groups, members usually have developed close emotional connections. When termination nears, members have significant emotional reactions to the end of the group and experience it as a significant loss.

Tuckman's paradigm, with the addition of the adjourning stage, described themes in group development research prior to 1977. Tuckman's model has two crucial limitations. First, it does not account for recurring issues. Second, it does not include a description of the effects of the interpersonal styles of group members on group development.

ESSENTIAL GROUP DEVELOPMENT CONCEPTS

The group development theories presented in this chapter evolved from the study of various groups in a variety of settings over a time span of nearly 30 years. Interestingly, despite this diversity, these theories share concepts and developmental themes.

Group development theories offer some important foundational concepts that help leaders comprehend group interaction. These concepts include the following: Counseling and therapy groups are social systems; groups address variations of core interpersonal issues; anxiety related to core interpersonal issues is always present; conflict is inevitable, indispensable, and productive; and members join groups having had varying degrees of success in dealing with core interpersonal issues.

Counseling and Therapy Groups Are Social Systems

Relationship patterns develop as members interact (Tuckman, 1965). Over time, these relationship patterns define a group as a distinct social system, a critical part of which is the group's normative structure. This structure expresses members' tolerance for the anxiety produced by shared interpersonal concerns (Bennis & Shepard, 1956; Bion, 1961; Schutz, 1966). This means that leaders can judge the strength and nature of members' apprehensions by observing how intensely members negotiate norms and apply their sanctions. For example, when members are very intense in negotiating norms that prohibit the expression of "negative emotions," leaders can conclude that members are especially concerned about safety or very fearful of the expression of anger.

A group's emerging social structure also establishes interpersonal boundaries that define the behaviors required for membership. These negotiated boundaries define how openly members should interact and the issues they should discuss. Consequently, interpersonal boundaries reflect members' decisions about becoming included in the group. Thus, when members avoid discussing emotions, a leader can conclude that members are reluctant to be fully involved in the group.

An especially significant social systems concept is that the issues members encounter in groups are not separate from the issues members experience outside groups (Bennis & Shepard, 1956; Bion, 1961; Schutz, 1966). They are isomorphic. Isomorphy means that the interpersonal dynamics and behaviors of members in group are identical to those that members demonstrate outside group. Isomorphy also means that the concerns each member experiences are shared, to some extent, by other members. Thus, when one member struggles with intimacy, other members also struggle, and all members (even the leader) indirectly confront their intimacy concerns outside the group. More broadly, isomorphy means that counseling and therapy groups confront the same issues confronted in larger social systems and in society in general (Bion, 1961).

Groups Address Core Interpersonal Issues

Group development theory (Bennis & Shepard, 1956; Bion, 1961; Schutz, 1966; Tuckman, 1965) describes how members struggle to deal with core interpersonal issues: involvement, dependency, authority, individuation, intimacy, and loss and loneliness. Variations of these core interpersonal issues emerge and recycle as long as groups remain intact (Bion, 1961; Schutz, 1966).

Two common factors influence the emergence of core interpersonal issues: how effectively members have resolved these core issues before coming to group and apprehensions related to intimacy. In groups composed of individuals who have unsuccessfully resolved a particular core issue, members will have an intense reaction when the issue emerges. Usually, the issue emerges, only to be avoided. When members avoid a core issue, it surfaces over and over again with no indication that progress is being made. Conversely, in groups where most individuals have had some success in dealing with a core issue, the issue will reemerge, but it will be addressed successfully, and the group progresses (Bennis & Shepard, 1956; Schutz, 1966).

When group interaction becomes more intimate, variations of issues that have been successfully addressed during earlier, less intimate interaction resurface. For example, when involvement is addressed during initial group meetings, members might readily accept what is required to be a group member. Later, when sharing increasingly personal information becomes a part of group interaction, members will reconsider involvement (Bion, 1961; Schutz, 1966).

Anxiety Is Always Present

Anxiety is a persistent element of group interaction. Bion (1961) stressed that group interaction seeks to maintain a homeostasis that keeps anxiety at a level members can tolerate. Even when members successfully confront a concern that creates anxiety, apprehensions remain. These apprehensions are related to the fears that subsequent interaction may demand greater intimacy or that other, more risky issues may surface. Anxiety related to core interpersonal issues is commonly related to fears associated with intimacy: rejection, abandonment, incompetence, and significance (Schutz, 1966).

Conflict and Anger Are Inevitable, Indispensable, and Productive

Conflict is associated with members' attempts and inescapable failure to avoid anxiety. Direct and indirect expressions of anger aimed at group leaders include members reacting to leaders' failing to provide freedom from anxiety or a group structure that provides total safety (Bennis & Shepard, 1956; Bion, 1961; Schutz, 1966; Tuckman, 1965). At the same time, members conflict and become angry with each other when they disagree over how to best avoid anxiety (Bennis & Shepard, 1956; Schutz, 1966).

Conflict and anger are indispensable if groups are to become highly productive. Conflict is productive because it exposes members' interpersonal concerns. For example, when members conflict over the expectations of group membership, leaders can direct members to explore their inclusion needs. This intervention directs members to confront the concerns they are experiencing in the here and now. Leaders who understand that the potential for change exists whenever conflict emerges are more likely to look for opportunities to identify conflict.

Members Have Varying Degrees of Success Resolving Core Interpersonal Issues

Individuals who enter counseling and therapy groups have had varying degrees of success resolving core interpersonal issues (Bennis & Shepard, 1956; Schutz, 1966). Very few new members likely have achieved the resolution depicted by Schutz's (1966) socials, democrats, and personals or Bennis and Shepard's (1956) independents. It is more likely that members have developed personality patterns that reflect varying degrees of success in meeting interpersonal needs and confronting core issues in their relationships. This means that when core interpersonal issues emerge, members will react with various degrees of intensity. These reactions will have a definite impact on group functioning.

Counseling and therapy groups function effectively when members develop insight and a deeper understanding of their interactions with others (Tuckman, 1965). These outcomes are likely to occur when members communicate effectively (Bennis & Shepard, 1956). Unfortunately, groups encounter barriers to effective communication that are closely related to members' shared core interpersonal concerns. A group composed of individuals who share the same interpersonal issue has a prearranged dominant issue and is likely to stall when that issue emerges (Bennis & Shepard, 1956; Schutz, 1966). If a group is to function effectively, it requires the presence of individuals who have, to some degree, resolved the interpersonal issue being addressed (Bennis & Shepard, 1956).

CONCLUSION

Group development can be described in a number of different ways. Despite their different descriptions, group development theories display common themes. Understanding these theories and their common themes is important because it allows leaders to anticipate and conceptualize surfacing concerns and group events. In addition, by understanding how the interactions of individual members influence group development, leaders can make informed decisions about group composition and anticipate more specific developmental issues. Decisions about group composition and more information on dealing with the impact of individual members on the group social system are addressed in later chapters.

4

Interactive Group Development Theory

OBJECTIVES

After reading this chapter, you should be able to:

✔ Describe the core interpersonal issues that surface during group interaction.

✔ Discuss a group development theory and an illustrative narrative that emphasizes interpersonal issues and the circumstances that lead to the recycling of these issues.

✔ Explain how the recycling of interpersonal issues influences group development and members' interactions.

✔ Discuss how variations in members' personalities and unresolved interpersonal issues influence group development.

✔ Describe how a model that recognizes the influences of member personalities, describes recycling issues, and employs a life-cycle model depicts group development.

INTRODUCTION

The previous chapter described classic group development theories and the essential concepts they share. This chapter presents a theory of group development that emphasizes the core interpersonal issues presented in those classic theories. This theory recognizes that the essential concepts of classic group development theories (i.e., counseling and therapy groups are social systems; anxiety related to core interpersonal issues is always present; conflict is inevitable, indispensable, and productive; and members join groups having had varying degrees of success in dealing with core interpersonal issues) exist as group development realities.

CORE INTERPERSONAL CONCERNS

A theme in classic group development theory describes how groups address core interpersonal issues. These issues, discussed in the following sections, are involvement, dependency, authority, individuation, intimacy, and loss and loneliness. Groups address these issues in the context of group interaction that becomes increasingly intimate. The issue a group confronts at any particular time during its interaction denotes its stage of development.

Involvement

When groups begin, members confront the same concerns they experience whenever they become initially involved in any relationship. In the group setting, however, these concerns are magnified because members are asked to interact in a way that is more self-revealing than customary interaction. Accordingly, members confront fears about being rejected and ignored (Schutz, 1966) and react emotionally (Tuckman, 1965). From the start, members are faced with anxiety.

Most members try to establish certainty to lower their anxiety (Schutz, 1966; Tuckman, 1965). Members test each other initially to judge what their relationships will be like (Tuckman, 1965). In so doing, members are attempting to ensure that other members will acknowledge their presence, uniqueness, and importance and to hear whether they share mutual interests (Schutz, 1966). Members also test the leaders to ensure that they care about them. Ultimately, members examine what is required to participate and face the decision to engage or disengage.

Members who decide to be involved in the group begin to engage each other more honestly, whereas those who remain uncertain assume a more disengaged stance. Although members must make a range of decisions about their involvement in the group, all share a common experience: anxiety. Anxiety about participation demands increasingly personal interaction and operates in the background throughout the life of most counseling and therapy groups.

Dependency

Once members become uncomfortably anxious, they act as if they need leaders to take care of them and protect them (Bennis & Shepard, 1956; Bion, 1961; Schutz, 1966; Tuckman, 1965). Members want guarantees that the group will not be too scary so that they can avoid excessive anxiety. However, if the group is to have any real impact on its members, anxiety cannot be avoided. The efforts of leaders who believe they can create an anxiety-free environment will be futile.

Authority

Members react angrily when they learn that leaders cannot or are not willing to remove anxiety from their interactions (Bion, 1961). Members blame leaders for their anxiety, challenge leaders' competence, question the need for self-disclosure, and debate the structure and usefulness of the group (Bennis & Shepard, 1956; Bion, 1961; Schutz, 1966; Tuckman, 1965). Members may express their anger directly in verbal attacks or indirectly by ignoring or refusing to respond to leaders' interventions, being late, refusing to act according to the group's ground rules, and so on (Bennis & Shepard, 1956; Bion, 1961; Schutz, 1966; Tuckman, 1965).

During this stage, conflict over control of the group emerges between members who distrust authority and those who cling to the belief that leaders can rescue them from anxiety (Bennis & Shepard, 1956; Bion, 1961; Schutz, 1966). Depending on the group's composition, this conflict can become heated, and anger surfaces between members. Even though members' opposing points of view might be far apart, all members struggle with the question of how to interact in a way that guarantees safety from anger and anxiety (Bennis & Shepard, 1956; Bion, 1961; Schutz, 1966; Tuckman, 1965). Attempts to find a useful solution to the problem of anxiety inevitably fail.

As anxiety and anger continue to build, members air their apprehensions about group interaction, responsibility for learning, and the leader's role. Eventually, members become aware that airing their apprehensions, although creating anxiety, helps them confront important issues. Group cohesion emerges when members see that they are able to solve problems and survive intense expressions of emotion (Bennis & Shepard, 1956; Schutz, 1966; Tuckman, 1965). At this point, a palpable sense of relief occurs in the group.

Authority issues can recur whenever interaction becomes excessively threatening. This happens because members have turned to their leaders for a rescue rather than confronting their fears (Schutz, 1966).

Individuation

This stage begins as members experience the relief of having reached a conclusion to their conflict. Members enjoy the harmony and unquestioned endorsement of the group's importance that follow the intense conflict (Bennis & Shepard, 1956; Schutz, 1966; Tuckman, 1965). So that these feelings of well-being can be sustained, norms emerge that forbid the expression of "negative" emotions. These norms also demand that members ignore conflict and maintain the status quo (Bennis & Shepard, 1956; Schutz, 1966; Tuckman, 1965). After a time, members become disgusted with the phoniness and contrived nature of group interaction (Bennis & Shepard, 1956; Schutz, 1966). Anger builds, and a new battle begins.

Members conflict over norms that maintain contrived harmony. Those who value diverse points of view and want to confront interpersonal issues are eventually the most persuasive. Ultimately, members come to value the expression of individual perspectives and sincere emotions. They develop increased tolerance for conflict and see it as productive. As a result, the valuing of differences becomes a norm.

This stage closes when members express themselves and accept others as unique individuals. The pressure to conform has transformed into valuing individuality and encouraging members to express a full range of perceptions and feelings. As long as the group atmosphere is one of acceptance, anxiety about intimacy will build.

Intimacy

When group acceptance norms support individuation, members openly express their emotions, values, beliefs, and perceptions. As a result, questions about intimacy come into intense focus. Members share their fears about vulnerability to rejection, their own acceptability, maintaining self-esteem, and how deserving they are of affection (Bennis & Shepard, 1956; Bion, 1961; Schutz, 1966; Tuckman, 1977). Conflict at the onset of this stage concerns how intimately members should interact (Bennis & Shepard, 1956; Schutz, 1966; Tuckman, 1965).

Members confront the issues they experience in their intimate relationships during this stage (Bennis & Shepard, 1956; Bion, 1961; Schutz, 1966). Whereas previous stages have allowed members to address interpersonal concerns, the work of members during this stage can be the most intense and productive (Tuckman, 1965).

As this stage progresses, members are increasingly open and develop intimate relationships (Bennis & Shepard, 1956; Bion, 1961; Schutz, 1966). Intimacy and the open expression of emotions, perceptions, and ideas permeate this stage. For many members, this is the most personally open and connected they have ever been. As termination nears, members confront what it means to lose these relationships.

Loss and Loneliness

At the termination of a group, members have learned how to overcome isolation by openly sharing their emotions and perceptions. They have interacted meaningfully and have developed close emotional relationships (Schutz, 1966; Tuckman & Jensen, 1977). These experiences make termination an emotionally and symbolically significant event (Schutz, 1966; Tuckman & Jensen, 1977). Members confront the prospective loss of significant relationships and the loneliness of being disconnected from those who have had a profound effect on their lives. At termination, members leave with an understanding of how to confront loss and loneliness in their lives.

INTERACTIVE GROUP DEVELOPMENT THEORY

A useful model of group development describes the core interpersonal issues that emerge and recycle during the life of a group. It explains interaction among members by identifying the influences of members' personalities, and it describes stages in terms of their interactive dynamics and the events and emotional climate that accompany transitions to preceding or ensuing stages. Finally, this model describes the experiences that members face as their group reaches termination. The following model builds on the concepts and themes that appear in classic group development theory and attempts to meet the demands of a useful group development model.

Figure 4.1
Interactive Group Development Model

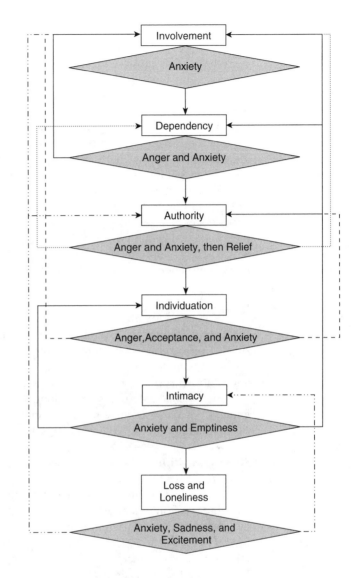

Figure 4.1 illustrates a model that employs the themes that appear in group development theory. The rectangles represent various stages of development, whereas the diamonds describe the dominant emotions of group members. These emotions and the energy they generate serve as **stage transitions**. That is, intense emotions shared by group members often serve as the end of one stage and the initiation of the next.

The lines and arrows below the diamonds describe how group development would progress were a group flawlessly composed (see the section titled "Members Have Varying Degrees of Success in Resolving Core Interpersonal Issues" in the previous chapter). Lines that connect the stages describe common paths of recycling concerns, while the arrows show the direction of these recycling issues. For example, when members struggle with intimacy concerns, they may look to the leader to take care of them (i.e., intimacy recycling to dependency) or may reconsider their involvement in the group (i.e., intimacy recycling to involvement). Although the issues members encounter at the Intimacy and the Loss and Loneliness stages are the most common initiators of recycling, any stage, except Involvement, can result in recycling to a previous stage.

The following narrative describes the interactive content occurring during the various stages and the events that lead to the transitions that occur between stages. This narrative is presented along with an ongoing group dialogue that illustrates typical group interaction and the effects of members' personalities. Recall that members' personalities reflect varied levels of resolution in the areas of inclusion, control and authority, and intimacy and affection. For simplicity, the narrative describes experiences that are likely to occur in a closed, time-limited group. As you read the interactive content of each stage, stage transitions, and dialogue, reflect on how and when recycling might occur and on how other group compositions could affect development.

Involvement

Interactive Content.   Members face the prospect of establishing new relationships. However, because members are there to discuss sensitive material and leaders direct them to interact in a more personal way, members become anxious. Initial interaction is superficial as members attempt to get to know each other and cope with their anxiety. Members are making several decisions at this point: "Will I be safe in here?," "What does it take to be a member?," and "How involved do I want to be?" As members decide to get involved, self-disclosures become more revealing.

Stage Transition.   As members begin revealing more personal information related to the purposes of the group, anxiety increases. Along with initial concerns about acceptance, members are now approaching the discussion of material that has the potential to result in embarrassment, ridicule, and rejection. This stage concludes when members experience what they perceive as excessively uncomfortable anxiety.

Dialogue.   Seven members are present in a group convened for its second meeting. The leader, Terry, greets the members and briefly reminds them of a few ground rules. She then asks the members to share what being in the group is like for them. Wanda, Susie, Dave, Phyllis, Chester, Maggie, and George take turns offering comments. Terry asks the members to describe their reactions to what they have heard others say.

WANDA:	"I'm not sure what you're asking us to do. What are we supposed to say? I want to belong to a group where I know other people care about me. It's kind of scary to say stuff before you know what they want to hear."
TERRY:	"You all listened carefully to what others had to say. I'd like to hear you share your impressions with each other—you

know, the emotions you experienced, the connections you may have made with others. Maybe you found that you have some things in common, or maybe you had a negative reaction to something you heard."

PHYLLIS: "You are not really telling me what I need to do. I think Wanda is right; I don't want everyone to think I'm a real jerk by telling them something they don't want or need to hear. I want to be part of a group where others like me."

DAVE: "Phyllis, I'm like you. I need more specific instructions before I make a fool of myself."

SUSIE: "I'm having a reaction to what you folks are saying. Sure, I'd like to be friends with everybody, but if I just say what you want to hear, you wouldn't learn anything. I want to hear what your real reactions are to me."

GEORGE: "Me too. Let's be real in here."

MAGGIE: "Hold the phone you two! This is making me real nervous. I don't know if I'm ready to hear everything people think about me. I don't want to get hurt."

WANDA AND PHYLLIS: [In unison] "Right!"

TERRY: "Chester, you haven't said anything. What's going on?"

CHESTER: "I'm kind of agreeing with Wanda, Phyllis, Dave, and Maggie. I don't want to get hurt. I came here to feel better about myself, not get slammed. Anyway, I've already said too much."

Dependency

Interactive Content.   This phase begins as members' anxiety about participation reaches a peak. Anxiety about self-disclosure and safety is extremely uncomfortable for most members. Members turn to the leader, asking for a guarantee that they will not be hurt, a "silver bullet" that removes their anxiety. Some members want the leader to offer specific guidelines for how they should interact. Others are less active, watching and occasionally commenting. An observer would characterize members' nonverbal communication as anxious and their interactions as cautious.

Stage Transition.   After repeated attempts to get the leader to remove anxiety, members realize that the leader is not able or willing to provide them with the comfort they desire. This stage concludes as members continue to experience intense anxiety about participation. At this point, they also become angry with the leader for abandoning them and being incompetent.

Dialogue.   Tonight is the group's fifth meeting. Wanda, Phyllis, Dave, Maggie, and Chester are becoming increasingly agitated. They appear anxious, shifting in their chairs and looking intently at the footwear worn by other members. Meanwhile, Susie and George seem excited to begin.

SUSIE:	"This has been great for me, being able to share what's going on with me. I don't do that enough."
PHYLLIS:	[Sarcastically] "I'm glad you've been having such a wonderful time."
GEORGE:	"Whew, Phyllis, what's your problem?"
PHYLLIS:	"George, I'd like to get into this with you, but this is not the time. I'm at loose ends. I need more information about how this group thing is supposed to work."
WANDA:	"Terry, can't you have us do an exercise or something?"
DAVE:	"I really don't want to get involved in pointing fingers, but I need to say something. Terry, it really seems that you could do something to make this easier."
CHESTER:	"I'm with Dave, I'm going to hold back until I know what to expect. I've been hurt enough."
MAGGIE:	"I think this group is getting out of hand."
TERRY:	"I can see that all of you are at least a little scared and some of you are very scared. I'm also getting the impression that I'm the one whose responsible for how uncomfortable you are. I wonder what would happen if you started to talk about what's scaring you?"
PHYLLIS:	"What! Are you tripping or something?"
DAVE:	"Whatever, this is bull——!"

Authority

Interactive Content.   Members typically begin this stage by holding the leader responsible for their anxiety. Some members are angry because they see themselves as being abandoned by the leader. Other members interpret their anxiety as the result of the leader's incompetence. Some members continue to believe that the leader can make the group anxiety free, whereas others directly and indirectly express their anger toward the leader.

Eventually, members conflict with each other over how best to remove anxiety from interaction. As a result, members engage in heated conflict with each other. This conflict has many variations, depending on how members have dealt with authority issues and their tolerance for anxiety. This conflict draws out members' concerns about participation.

Stage Transition.   The intensity of the anger and anxiety in the group is almost unbearable. As members become increasingly angry and frustrated about their failed attempts to avoid anxiety, they begin to understand how sharing their fears and interpersonal concerns can help them. This stage concludes as members experience profound relief that their conflict has been "resolved."

Dialogue.   About halfway through the sixth meeting, Phyllis and Dave voice their anger. Wanda and Chester express their concern that Terry is holding back a strategy that would make interaction easier. Phyllis and Dave argue with Wanda and

Chester about how members should interact. Susie, George, and Maggie watch and eventually join in the conflict.

PHYLLIS: "Terry, I don't think you know what you're doing. We can't trust you to run this group in a way that will work for us!"

TERRY: "Phyllis, I know you're angry with me and that being in this group is frightening for you. I'm not really sure what's scaring you . . ."

PHYLLIS: [Interrupting] "Stop! Stop doing that! You're the one that's scary!"

DAVE: "Terry, I hope you never push me like that. It only hurts and doesn't do any good."

CHESTER: "Terry, I'm sure that with all your experience, you could make this all go so much more easily. Please tell me what I need to do to make this safe."

WANDA: "I kind of agree with Chester here. I want to get along with everyone. But you keep talking about us being scared or afraid of something or other, when you could do something."

TERRY: "Sounds like some of you think I'm holding back on the magic and others think I have no clue. All this seems to be about whose responsible for all these uncomfortable feelings."

PHYLLIS: "I think we should decide that we're going to get along and decide for ourselves what we should talk about."

Thirty minutes of conflict over how the group should operate goes nowhere. Members are becoming increasingly agitated.

DAVE: "I think we should share what we see as each others' strengths. That would help us all feel better."

PHYLLIS: "Dave, nobody asked for your opinion. We need to decide on topics that deal with our concerns and assign a person to present on a topic each week, and then we can discuss it."

DAVE: "Phyllis, who made you the queen of the universe?"

PHYLLIS: "Go to h——, Dave! Your ideas are stupid. I know what I'm doing."

CHESTER: "Wow, you two! Cool off. I'm not comfortable with these negative emotions."

DAVE: [Ignoring Chester] "Yeah, right. You can't deal with not being in control of everything."

PHYLLIS: "Don't you dare say that about me! That hurts!"

DAVE: "How do you think I feel? I've always been scared about making an a—— of myself."

WANDA: "Chester, you're right on target. These are the kinds of feelings that scare me. They just hurt, and nothing gets any better."

SUSIE: "Do you guys see what's going on?"

GEORGE: "Yeah, you're fighting over how to make it safe in here, and it's bringing up what you're afraid of."

MAGGIE: "Terry, what happened?"

TERRY: "Maggie, it looks like when people begin to share what's scary for them, something happens to their fears. Let's talk about what's happening."

Individuation

Interactive Content.   Members enjoy the respite after a period of ongoing conflict. They now regard the group as important and meaningful in their lives. Norms emerge that demand the expression of positive feelings and the avoidance of conflict. Some members eventually tire of the phoniness of these norms and angrily challenge other members who enforce the "harmony at all costs" norms. The outcome of this conflict is norms that support the expression of divergent points of view, addressing conflict, sharing the full range of emotions, and prizing the diversity of the membership. As these new norms take effect, members become more accepting of each other, and self-disclosure becomes increasingly intimate.

Stage Transition.   Acceptance builds, and members feel freer to disclose more personal reactions and emotions. This stage concludes as members become increasingly anxious about the level of intimacy building in the group.

Dialogue.   After the preceding conflict, the group is relieved. All the members, regardless of how upset they have been, seem to be enjoying the fact that the group has survived intense conflict and expressions of anger. Interaction has been led by Wanda and Phyllis, who seem to enjoy sharing positive feelings and the absence of conflict in the group.

WANDA: "I am so pleased we finally understand that staying positive and not getting into ridiculous arguments is what we need. You know, I wish my family would understand this. Stay positive and your troubles go away."

PHYLLIS: "I never would have guessed that this group could have become so helpful. I'm glad we all agree with what Wanda has been saying. There's no reason to get so upset when staying positive is so productive."

SUSIE: "You know, I kind of agree with you two. I like that we're being so positive and not at each others' throats. But I'm not so sure this is real. I don't know if I can agree with the idea of always staying positive."

MAGGIE: "Susie! Don't go spoiling what we have worked so hard to achieve. I think this is one of those times you need to go along with things. This is so wonderful!"

PHYLLIS: "That's right, Susie, things are going so well. I know what a positive person you are at heart. You can fit in here, can't you?"

SUSIE: "Oh, come on! I'm just saying what's on my . . ."

WANDA: [Interrupting] "There! That's it. You know, Susie, I have some feedback for you. When you say what's on your mind, I get the impression that you're trying to turn our discussions into some kind of whining contest. I feel really positive about you anyway."

TERRY: "Some folks are shifting around in their seats after your feedback Wanda. Susie, would you share what you heard Wanda say and your reactions to her feedback."

SUSIE:	"Wanda, I'm stunned. No, no I'm not stunned. I'm really ticked off! You said that when I talk about what's on my mind, you think I'm whining but that you like me anyway?"
WANDA:	"Yeah, Susie, that's pretty much it. You shouldn't be ticked off because I can see you becoming such a positive person."
SUSIE:	"Yeah, whatever. This is feeling a little weird to me. I'm wondering if anyone else agrees with Wanda's feedback?"
DAVE:	"Susie, you're right, this is getting really weird. I'm not believing what you said Wanda. Susie, it seems to me that you're just trying to be honest. Wanda, what you said to Susie really annoys me, too!"
PHYLLIS:	"Wait a minute, Dave! We don't need to start with this kind of talk. The group is great the way it is!"
GEORGE:	"I'm not so sure, Phyllis. What do you want us to do—pretend everything smells like roses when there's a skunk in the room?"

Over a period of 30 minutes, the interaction becomes intense, one faction of members arguing to "stay positive" and another arguing for the need for honesty, whether "positive" or "negative."

CHESTER:	"I've been reluctant to say anything until now, but I'd like to know that I can be honest with you all, even though it's really scary for me. I sure don't want to pretend I go along with what you're saying when I don't. That's always been my problem, and it's got me nowhere."
DAVE:	"Chester, I couldn't say it better! You know, Chester, I feel like I'm beginning to get to know you. I'm like you, I get into trouble when I pretend. You know, 'Go along to get along.' It works for a while, then it starts to stink!"
SUSIE:	"Wanda, Phyllis, and you Maggie, I know how scary anger is for you three. I don't want to hurt you or frighten you. I just want you to understand that we don't all have to be alike to get along."
PHYLLIS:	"Susie, I hate to admit it, but I am scared of what happens when people get angry. I'm beginning to see that I'm not having much success controlling how you feel about me. That scares me, too."
SUSIE:	"I had no idea. Phyllis, I just thought you hated me!"
PHYLLIS:	"No, Susie, I've wanted you to care about me from the start, but I don't know how to get close to someone who's as honest as you. Funny, that goes for most of you. But now I'm wondering if I really know anyone. Wanda, Maggie, I'm thinking I don't really know who you are, I was just comfortable with you."

Intimacy

Interactive Content.   Conflict between members emerges over the acceptable level of intimacy. Interaction addresses fears related to rejection, acceptability, vulnerability, and exposure. These intense interactions include the open expression and experiencing of emotions and the development of insight into members' relationship concerns. Members directly confront issues that contribute to loneliness and isolation and make intense connections with each other. These connections foster emotionally and psychologically open relationships. It is in this context that termination enters members' awareness.

Stage Transition.   As this stage concludes, many members may have experienced the most meaningful and open relationships in their lives. Termination means the loss of these relationships. Members' sadness is associated with the impending emptiness of losing meaningful relationships, and their anxiety is associated with fears that they may once again be lonely.

Dialogue.   Interaction is emotionally intense as members explore their relationship concerns in the group and understand how these issues influence their family and social relationships. As the group concludes, members become aware of termination.

MAGGIE: [Looking at Phyllis] "I've been thinking everyday about what you said to me a few weeks ago, that you don't really know who I am and that you're just comfortable around me. I was home the other day and was not liking how my kids and husband were not really paying attention to me, and I realized that no one does. Oh, I get along with everybody, but I don't have a real relationship with anybody. [Starting to cry] I'm so lonely and scared."

WANDA: [Tears in her eyes] "Maggie, I've been having the same reaction. I'm like this 'let's everybody be happy and nice person.' But who I am is anybody's guess. I hold back because I'm scared. I don't even know who Wanda is any more."

A few minutes of silence.

TERRY: "As I look at your faces, I see what look's like some intense reactions to what's going on between Wanda and Maggie. Some of you are having reactions, but you aren't saying anything."

CHESTER: "Yeah, I'm having two reactions. One is, I can't believe how real Wanda and Maggie are. I'm amazed and so happy for them! The second reaction is to the feelings I'm having. It's like you two have the exact same hole inside that I have."

PHYLLIS: "I want to know what you two think and how you feel about me. I want to be real with you, and I want you to be real with me."

TERRY: "Dave, tears are running down your face."

DAVE: "I'm feeling so lonely. I feel like I have a chance right now to do something about it, but I'm really scared."

TERRY: "Do it anyway."

DAVE: [Voice shaking] "Phyllis, I feel such a deep connection with you. I share your fears, and I want you to know that I really care about you. I wish I could take your pain away. I really hope you can let me know what's going on inside you."

PHYLLIS: [Face flushing] "Dave, I'm so scared of men. I've been hurt so many times, by my father, by my ex-husband, and by any man I've tried to

DAVE: get close to. I feel like 'damaged goods'! I don't want any more pain like that."

DAVE: "Phyllis, I don't want to hurt you. I care about you. What do I need to do for you to believe me? What have I done to scare you?"

Dave and Phyllis continue for several minutes.

TERRY: "Phyllis, you seem very open with Dave. Yet I'm not seeing you reacting like you're getting hurt. Instead, you seem to be getting more vulnerable with Dave."

PHYLLIS: "I'm beginning to feel like I can trust Dave. I don't think he'll just use me and leave me. I can tell by the way he listens and the expression on his face. He's not like the others."

TERRY: "Let's talk about what's happening here. How are the rest of you experiencing what's happening here?"

For the next 45 minutes, members process their experiences and apply these experiences to their lives.

TERRY: "We have about 15 minutes to wrap up. Who wants to comment?"

SUSIE: "This has been so powerful for me tonight. I feel so grateful to have been here. I am really scared, though. I remember what Terry said a few weeks ago about the group ending. We only have three more weeks. I don't know what I'll do when this group ends."

The others nod quietly.

Loss and Loneliness

Interactive Content.   This stage begins as members experience the prospect of losing meaningful relationships. The leader reminds members that they have learned how to develop meaningful relationships. If they have not already done so, members discuss how to apply what they have learned in the group to their outside relationships. Eventually, the group concludes.

Stage Transition.   The group concludes as members experience loss. At the same time, members experience the excitement of awareness, understand how to confront their needs and fears effectively, and have the relationship skills and understanding necessary to develop fulfilling relationships. Members have learned how to connect and meet their emotional needs in their relationships because they have done so in the group. They have encountered their fears and survived.

Dialogue.   At the start of the last meeting, before a structured closing experience, Terry asks members to describe their experiences during the group and how they are applying what they have learned in their lives. Members are often tearful in describing their experiences, and some suggest ways that members can stay in contact after the group ends. Some members share their reluctance to end the group, whereas others seem ready to do so.

SUSIE: "I'll start. I wasn't sure at first if I was going to learn anything in here. Then, boom, it all hit me. I had to deal with how my expectations of other people get in the way of my relationships. I have always wanted to be real, and I have never cut any slack for anyone who wasn't. I'm not so type A about that anymore. I feel like I'm more patient and I want to get to know people more than I did before, you know, before I make some kind of stupid snap judgment. I like me and other people much more than I did before. I'm excited about getting on with my life!"

WANDA: "Susie, you scared the living s—— out of me at first. I finally figured out why. It was because you were doing what I was so afraid of doing, being real. I have to say, I know this will blow your mind, that I've come to admire you and am trying to be more open myself. I've figured out why I stay hidden, and I've decided that I can't afford to let it get in the way of being close to others. I got that out of this group. I want a real relationship more than I want to be safe. We're starting family therapy in two weeks!"

CHESTER: "I have lived my life being afraid of being hurt by other people. Looking back on what it was like for me as a kid helped me make sense of that. But what didn't make sense is that I acted like that was how everyone everywhere would treat me, even though I'm not little Chester anymore, wanting to please so I wouldn't get screamed at. After a while in here, I realized I had a choice, I could choose to not do that anymore. I could actually act differently. It has been really hard being more honest, really scary at first. Now, after really working hard to be that way in here, it's working. I see some real benefits at work and with my friends. I don't know how to thank you guys."

MAGGIE: "My family does not take me for granted anymore. I won't let them. I found that not holding back gets me what I thought holding back would get me. I feel much closer to my husband, even though I really blew him away at first. I don't know if he had ever really heard any of my opinions before."

GEORGE: "You all have come to mean so much to me. I have made lots of progress, but I don't want to just say good-bye and leave. Does anyone besides me want to stay in touch after group ends?"

The remaining members make similar disclosures until Terry introduces the closing experience.

CONCLUSION

Interactive group development theory describes core interpersonal issues that members encounter during their group experiences. These issues emerge as members confront opening their interpersonal boundaries. The emergence of these issues is not necessarily linear. Groups will return repeatedly to issues confronted earlier in the group to deal with the anxiety generated by increased intimacy. Increased intimacy can almost always be equated with increased vulnerability. This means that members encounter increasingly intense fears of rejection and alienation as group interaction progresses.

Group counseling and therapy theory describes how boundary issues originate and emerge during group interaction. Being conversant with group development and group therapy theory helps leaders achieve their potential as effective group counselors and therapists.

CHAPTER 5

Group Theory Introduction and Focal Conflict Theory

OBJECTIVES

After reading this chapter, you should be able to:

✔ Describe the characteristics of theories that are most appropriate for group counseling and therapy.

✔ Discuss the limitations of theory designed for individual work for group applications.

✔ Describe focal conflict theory's conceptualization of group process.

✔ Explain how focal conflict theory conceptualizes group members' therapeutic experiences.

✔ Explain how focal conflict theory conceptualizes the work of the group therapist.

✔ Outline focal conflict theory's implications for practice.

INTRODUCTION

Group therapy and group development theories differ in several ways. Group development theory describes when and how issues common to group members surface, how these issues temporarily resolve, and how these issues recycle. Group therapy theory, on the other hand, depicts the dynamics of members' interactions, how leaders use these interactions therapeutically, the conditions necessary for change, how members change, and the roles of group leaders. Group leaders can use group development theory to anticipate group events and how individual personalities will influence group interaction. Leaders can use this theory to more deeply understand interaction and how to use it for the benefit of group members.

A theory that is appropriate for group counseling and therapy offers leaders a number of critically important benefits (Hansen, Warner, & Smith, 1980; Lonergan, 1994). First, an appropriate theory offers concepts that reduce the complexity of group interaction. These concepts offer leaders a framework they can use to structure their observations of group interaction. Second, a useful theory presents a model of effective interaction and suggests procedures to facilitate that interaction. These elements help leaders define possible interventions and their objectives. Third, because a pertinent theory structures observation, conceptualizes interaction, defines objectives, and suggests interventions, leaders become more confident in their ability. Finally, and possibly most important, group leaders who use a theory in which they believe are more convincing to group members. When leaders are confident and believe in their theory, members become more actively involved in group processes (Lonergan, 1994).

To be appropriate for group counseling or therapy, theories must meet at least two basic requirements. Appropriate theories must make group interaction understandable and clearly describe how group interaction is used to benefit group members. Nevertheless, the literature, especially in the field of group counseling, presents theories that do not meet these requirements. This literature extends the use of individual counseling theories to the group setting (see, e.g., Cappuzzi & Gross, 1992; Corey, 2000; Gladding, 1999).

Theories that are designed to understand individuals do not meet the demands of group work. Hansen et al. (1980) called attention to this issue over 20 years ago: "Various theories of counseling have viewed the group situation as an extension of individual counseling" (p. 14). Donigian and Malnati (1997) addressed the history and implications of this issue:

> Historically, most group therapy models developed out of individual psychotherapy. This means that, essentially, therapists conducted individual therapy within a group setting. Hence, the crucial elements for change were limited to the dynamics of the interaction between therapist and client. (p. 1)

Conyne, Wilson, and Ward (1997) addressed the implications of this issue for training group leaders:

> A chronic difficulty in the training of group counselors has been the lack of a comprehensive theory of group counseling which is grounded in the special environment of the group. Because of this lack, group counseling has relied on attempts by various authors to apply the theories of individual counseling and psychotherapy to the group context. (p. 97)

The consensus of these authors is that theories designed for individual counseling are not appropriate for group applications. The most glaring deficiencies in individually focused theories are that they do not conceptualize group interaction and how group interaction can be used to benefit members.

Donigian and Hulse-Killacky (1999) argued that individually focused theories fail to address essential systemic aspects of the group milieu. They identified four specific limitations: (a) Individual therapy theories do not offer a framework for comprehending the information generated by interaction, (b) they do not address the impact of group-as-a-whole dynamics on members, (c) they do not offer an adequate explanation of group process, and (d) they do not describe how group process can be used to help members change. Simply stated, applications of individual therapy theory to group settings are inadequate. Conyne et al. (1997) agree: "We eagerly await the development of a theory of group counseling that is interpersonally based and articulates the systemic dynamics of persons in groups" (p. 98).

This text presents three theories grounded in learning and change in an interpersonal context: focal conflict theory, systems theory, and the interpersonal approach. Focal conflict theory explains the shared concerns of members and how interaction reflects these concerns. Systems theory provides critical concepts for viewing groups as social systems and a useful structure for observing group interaction. The interpersonal approach discusses important interpersonal learning processes, suggests essential leadership procedures and perspectives, and conceptualizes members' interactions. Each of these theories is grounded in research and the experiences of their authors as group therapists.

FOCAL CONFLICT THEORY

Focal conflict theory conceptualizes the interpersonal concerns of group members and how these concerns surface in here-and-now group interaction. Whereas systems theory originated from the study of biological systems (von Bertalanffy, 1968) and the interpersonal approach applies concepts developed for individual psychiatry (Sullivan, 1953), focal conflict theory originated from the specific study of groups. Focal conflict theory (Whitaker & Lieberman, 1964) is grounded in its authors' experiences as group leaders and in their research, which included the systematic observations of a broad range of group members and group formats.

Whitaker and Lieberman (1964) presented focal conflict theory as a series of propositions about group therapeutic processes. They organized these propositions into three categories: group process, members' therapeutic experiences, and therapist contributions. Group process propositions include the basic focal conflict model, how the forces of equilibrium and change operate in therapy groups, how themes emerge in members' interaction, how group culture develops, and how group interaction recurrently addresses vital group issues. The propositions that describe group members' therapeutic experiences include descriptions of members' perceptions and behaviors as well as how members change or maintain habitual interactive patterns. Later chapters will discuss therapist contributions in depth.

Group Process

The Group Focal Conflict.   Focal conflict theory (Whitaker & Lieberman, 1964) proposes that themes in members' verbal and nonverbal behaviors reflect shared concerns. The shared covert wishes of members are termed **disturbing motives**, which are what members wish they could do in the group. For example, group members may want to make their feelings known to others to obtain support. However, the desire to disclose feelings means that members must confront their shared fears about the consequences of revealing these feelings, possibly the fear of rejection. These fears are called **reactive motives**. The conflict that results from opposing disturbing and reactive motives is the **group focal conflict**, which invariably causes members to experience anxiety.

Solutions.   Members' interaction commonly has the goal of responding to a group focal conflict. When members agree to a way to respond to a focal conflict, they have developed a **solution**. For example, in a group where the focal conflict involves the disturbing motive of expressing emotions and the reactive motive of fearing rejection, the group might use a solution such as talking about safe topics (see Figure 5.1).

To be successful, solutions require the agreement of the entire group and must either lower the intensity of the members' anxiety or satisfy the disturbing motive by allowing its expression. The solution of talking about safe topics will become successful only when all members agree to talk about safe topics, actually discuss safe topics, and are no longer uncomfortably anxious.

Group focal conflicts have two types of solutions: a **restrictive solution** and an **enabling solution**. Restrictive solutions manage the intensity of the group's anxiety by avoiding the discussion or experience of the disturbing and reactive motives. By avoiding these wishes and fears, members achieve a temporary reduction in their anxiety (see Figure 5.2).

Enabling solutions, however, satisfy disturbing motives and confront the fears associated with reactive motives. Because they confront fears, enabling solutions temporarily increase members' anxiety. If an enabling solution is successful, anxiety eventually decreases because members confront a shared fear and satisfy the disturbing motive. For example, members who disclose emotions and share fears of rejection ultimately reduce their fear of rejection by talking about it. When the fear of rejection diminishes and members continue to disclose feelings, the group will

Figure 5.1
The Group Focal Conflict

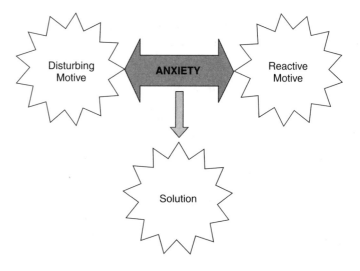

Figure 5.2
Group Focal Conflict Solutions

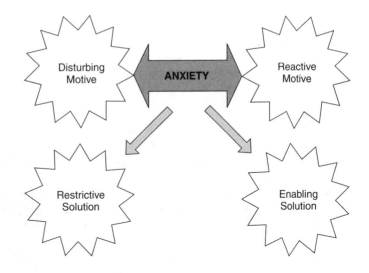

demonstrate a sense of accomplishment, become more cohesive, and move on to its next focal conflict. Table 5.1 provides some examples of focal conflicts and solutions. Figure 5.3 shows how a focal conflict can be diagrammed.

Solutional Conflict.   Although members do agree about solutions to focal conflicts, they can also disagree about them. When members express opposing solutions, they become involved in a **solutional conflict**. When a solutional conflict occurs, some members may strongly advocate continuing to "talk about safe topics" as a way to avoid anxiety. At the same time, others may believe a better solution is available and, for example, advocate challenging the usefulness of group interaction.

Solutional conflicts have two common variations. One version involves two separate restrictive solutions to avoid anxiety. Here, members might openly disagree about whether to talk about safe topics or question how involvement in the group can be helpful. Another version occurs when members experience varying degrees of anxiety. Members who are not anxious about the focal conflict might advocate an enabling solution, such as "Let's talk about our feelings." Others, who are more anxious about the focal conflict, could insist on the restrictive solution, "We need to talk about safe topics" (see Figure 5.4).

Members' attempts to deal with the anxiety created by a focal conflict continue until the group has successfully used an enabling solution. Restrictive solutions temporarily reduce anxiety but never attend to the fears of the reactive motive or satisfy the disturbing motive. Consequently, focal conflicts related to particular disturbing and reactive motives constantly recur throughout the life of the group.

Equilibrium.   Focal conflicts are products of group interaction. As members interact, they are exposed to a range of disturbing and reactive motives. Focal conflicts emerge, anxiety surfaces, and solutions are developed. Once members develop a successful enabling or restrictive solution, a new focal conflict emerges. For example, a group that has dealt with a focal conflict created by a "share your

Table 5.1
Examples of Focal Conflicts

Disturbing motive	Reactive motive	Restrictive solutions	Enabling solutions
Members want to share their emotions.	Fear of rejection and criticism.	Talk about cognitive topics.	Talk about feelings and the fears associated with sharing them.
Members want to openly share what aggravates them about other members.	Fear of being criticized for their own "shortcomings."	Ignore "aggravating members" and focus on deciding what it takes to get along in group.	Share reactions and fears of what it would be like to be criticized in group.
Members want to discuss issues of interpersonal attraction.	Fear of rejection and looking foolish.	Attempt to avoid the issue by talking about relationships outside group.	Discuss fears about vulnerability and what attracts members to each other.
Members want to resolve conflict.	Fear of others' anger and looking incompetent.	Pretend there is no conflict.	Discuss reservations about being seen as incompetent and areas of conflict.
Members want to disagree.	Fear of being criticized and looking foolish.	Change topics whenever disagreements surface.	Talk about fears of being criticized and desire to disagree.

Figure 5.3
Group Focal Conflict Example

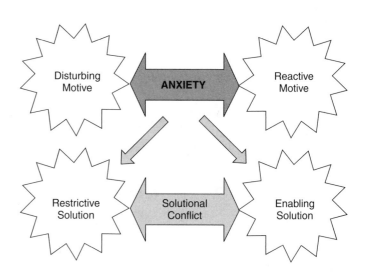

fears" disturbing motive and a "you'll be ridiculed" reactive motive by successfully employing a "discuss fears" enabling solution will experience a new focal conflict. The new focal conflict emerges because another disturbing motive, such as "share your perceptions of others," will follow. When this happens, the group begins a new search for another solution.

Figure 5.4
Solutional Conflict

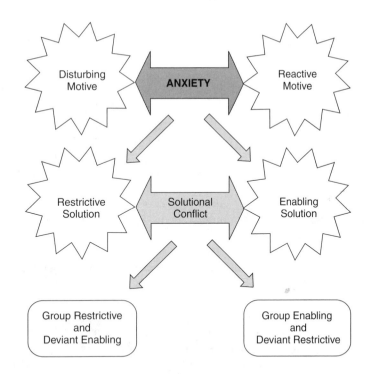

The process of finding solutions to focal conflicts is ongoing. The goal of members' interactions is to maintain an acceptable level of anxiety in the group by establishing **equilibrium**. Equilibrium occurs when a balance between the disturbing and the reactive motives is established with a solution.

Groups that avoid issues that generate an unacceptable level of anxiety are able to maintain equilibrium. When equilibrium is maintained, groups stall, at which point interactive issues continuously recycle and are repetitively avoided. Consequently, members learn very little.

Group Composition and Solutions.   Solutions to focal conflicts determine how a group progresses, and the individual characteristics of group members greatly influence those solutions. In large part, the success of solutions depends on the extent to which members share emotional reactions to emerging disturbing motives.

Solutions form readily when members have similar reactions to disturbing motives. An enabling solution that propels the group forward is probable when members can tolerate the anxiety generated by a disturbing motive. Conversely, when members cannot tolerate the anxiety created by a disturbing motive, a restrictive solution develops quickly. Quickly developed restrictive solutions lead to the persistent recurrence of focal conflicts and an overall reduction in the group's effectiveness. When members differ in their reactions to focal conflicts, solutions form slowly because negotiating a successful solution requires more extensive interaction.

Themes in Group Interaction.   Disturbing motives that persistently reemerge in groups have a definite influence on group functioning. Reemerging disturbing motives, or "a series of focal conflicts in which the disturbing motives are closely related" (Whitaker & Lieberman, 1964, p. 63), constitute a group's **theme**. That is, group themes surface when members have a common desire to avoid the anxiety associated with a particular disturbing motive. A group's theme can be identified when members use various restrictive solutions to respond to a reemerging issue. These restrictive solutions, however, only contribute to the reappearance of thematic disturbing motives.

For example, over the span of five sessions, members of a recently formed group have discussed how they could meet their counseling goals. Whenever members begin to discuss the usefulness of "being honest," one of the members presents a topic that diverts the conversation for most of the session. These topics have included "Let's get to know each other first," "Focusing on each other's strengths is the most important thing we can do," "Criticism is not useful," and "We should take turns talking about our concerns outside the group because that's why we're here." These topics are examples of a series of restrictive solutions designed to avoid the disturbing motive of "being honest." Because "being honest" has repeatedly reemerged, it has become this group's theme.

When members are adept at developing successful restrictive solutions, the number of group themes multiplies because they are not successfully resolved with an enabling solution. To counteract this process, leaders need to identify and frustrate these solutions by directing the group to discuss their disturbing motives and reactive fears. Although members respond uneasily to these interventions, interaction eventually becomes more productive.

Themes are also present in groups that develop successful enabling solutions. In contrast to groups that continuously develop restrictive solutions, these groups demonstrate increasing intensity and intimacy that slows when interaction becomes too intense and an acceptable level of anxiety is not maintained (i.e., equilibrium). At this point, members confront focal conflicts regarding the depth of intimacy.

Group Culture.   A group's culture is similar to its normative structure. It defines how members can interact, is the outcome of group interaction, and has a lasting influence on members' interactive behaviors (Whitaker & Lieberman, 1964). **Culture** is the composite of all the prescriptions for group behavior established by the group's solutions to its various focal conflicts. The solutions that determine a group's culture "define the character of the therapeutic enterprise, the relationships among patients and between patients and therapists, the boundaries on the expression of affect, acceptable content, and acceptable modes on interaction" (Whitaker & Lieberman, 1964, pp. 97, 98). For example, a group that persists in using restrictive solutions such as "don't share feelings" and "only compliments are acceptable" has developed a culture that limits how much members can learn from each other.

Group culture resists change because members cling to solutions that have proven to reduce anxiety. It does change, however, when established solutions no longer eliminate anxiety. This occurs when members or leaders focus the group's attention on its reactive fears. As a result, members' anxiety escalates and the group's solution no longer offers protection, at which point the group begins negotiations designed to develop new solutions. For example, a leader has frustrated the group's restrictive solution of "don't share your feelings" by consistently asking members to share their feelings. This increases their anxiety to an uncomfortable level, and they begin to negotiate a new restrictive solution. This negotiation is marked by discussion of topics like "How should we solve problems?," "How can we best support each other?," "Feelings are not important," and "Being forced to share feelings is inappropriate."

When groups interact to create new solutions, leaders can influence members to develop enabling solutions. This is accomplished by directly addressing the focal conflict. Ideally, a group's culture will be governed by a majority of enabling solutions.

The Group Members' Therapeutic Experience

Habitual Personal Solutions.   Members enter groups with **habitual personal solutions**. They develop these solutions in their families of origin to manage interpersonal concerns and anxiety (Whitaker & Lieberman, 1964). Ordinarily, people become group members because their habitual solutions no longer protect them from anxiety as they face developmental crises.

> For example, Michael joined a group with the habitual solution of "never share your feelings." Michael came to the group because he struggled with unsatisfying relationships, not being aware of his habitual solution and how it affected his life.

When starting a group, members are reluctant to abandon habitual solutions because these solutions have worked in the past. As group continues, the futility of members' continued attempts to use their habitual solutions becomes more obvious. Members become aware of their habitual solutions and how ineffective these solutions are. They acknowledge that these solutions no longer work. Consequently, members face the anxious prospect of abandoning a solution that has provided them safety in the past for a solution that may or may not work.

Resonance and Viability.   In addition to acknowledging that their habitual solutions no longer work, members encounter focal conflicts that are consistent with their habitual solutions. This consistency is referred to as **resonance** (Whitaker, 1989). When members' habitual solutions resonate with the focal conflict, their anxiety escalates dramatically, and they attempt to defend themselves to make the group **viable** (Whitaker & Lieberman, 1964).

> For example, Michael had a very difficult time sharing any information that would let others know that he cared about them and wanted to be their friend. Typically, when he wanted to develop a relationship, Michael would wait for others to share their feelings about their friendship but would never share what he felt. As Michael's group progressed, members confronted a focal conflict that concerned expressing emotions. During this discussion, Michael became very anxious. He argued that members should never have to share what they felt. Whenever another member would suggest that sharing emotions was important, Michael had a strong reaction,

offering sometimes-angry statements that appeared to be designed to shut down the conversation.

In this example, Michael's habitual solution of never sharing his feelings was challenged, and his anxiety escalated. As the group considered enabling solutions to the focal conflict, Michael did all he could to make the group viable by advocating his habitual restrictive solution and attempting to shut off conversation that supported alternative enabling solutions.

Viability occurs when a member is able to avoid a threatening interaction with habitual personal solutions. To maintain the group as a viable environment, members attempt to influence others to use their own habitual solutions. These attempts, however, are usually unsuccessful or short lived because group solutions to focal conflicts are constantly evolving and require ongoing negotiation.

> In Michael's case, his success was short lived. The other members decided to share feelings. This made being a member very difficult for Michael, and he became extremely anxious. Still, he argued for not sharing emotions.

Members who attempt to influence other members to use personally viable solutions and are not successful often settle for compromise solutions. Although the group environment continues to be threatening, such solutions are desirable because they make interaction less overwhelming.

> Michael, recognizing that the group would not go along with his solution of not talking about feelings, argued that members should participate in whatever way was comfortable for them. The other members could not be convinced to change their "sharing feelings is essential" solution.

If an acceptable compromise solution is not established, members will often withdraw from interaction to protect themselves. Ultimately, all members encounter situations for which they have no personal solutions, their solutions will not work, or the group solution does not reduce their anxiety.

> Michael was unable to convince others to back off their sharing emotion solution. As a result, he became progressively more anxious and closed off to interaction. Other members' attempts to involve him on a feeling level were unsuccessful.

The motivation to make the group viable increases whenever group solutions do not reduce a member's anxiety. Anxiety escalates whenever the group solution prescribes interpersonal behaviors that are particularly frightening for members. Members feel especially threatened when they become aware that the group solution makes it impossible to avoid anxiety. Whitaker and Lieberman (1964) point out that the member's perception of threat is specifically related to a personal solution that is not working. When members' habitual solutions no longer protect them, members become increasingly vulnerable. As the perception of vulnerability increases, members experience increasingly uncomfortable anxiety. The energy members invest in attempting to influence group solutions is proportional to the intensity of their perception of threat.

Compromise Solutions and Members' Influence on Solution Negotiation.
Solutions to focal conflicts are negotiated and involve compromise. These negotiations are usually conflictual, as members argue for their own habitual solutions. Because this process demands considerable energy, the group is relieved when a
compromise solution is determined; consequently, the group commits to implementing the solution. At this point, a member's chances of influencing the group to
change its solution are minimal.

When the group experiences a situation that threatens its equilibrium, a member's attempt to influence the group can be successful. Being able to influence the
group successfully is not related to a member's personality. A member's success depends on how much anxiety is generated by the current group conflict and the timing of the member's contribution. When a group is experiencing intense anxiety and
has not identified alternative solutions, members can more easily influence the
group to adopt their habitual solutions if their solutions offer immediate relief from
anxiety.

> Michael could have convinced the others to use his solution if they were
> very anxious about sharing emotions and were unable to come up with a
> solution that immediately lowered their anxiety. In Michael's case, how-
> ever, these conditions did not exist, and he was unsuccessful.

Members' Anxiety.   The anxiety experienced by an individual member depends
on the member's perceptions of group events, the extent to which his or her interpersonal fears resonate with the current disturbing motive and reactive fears, and
how inconsistent his or her habitual solutions are with the group's solutions.

> In Michael's group, other members were not uncomfortably anxious about
> sharing emotions. Michael, on the other hand, feared what would happen
> if he shared his feelings. The group's solution was very inconsistent with
> Michael's habitual solution, and his interpersonal fears were highly reso-
> nant with the group's reactive motive. Michael began to perceive the
> group as a hostile environment and the other members as persons who
> had the power to harm him. Michael became extremely anxious.

Deviant Members and Group Focal Conflict.   Each member's perceptions of
other group members shift. Shifting perceptions are influenced by the extent to
which other members contribute to making the group viable at any particular point
in time. Members perceive others more favorably when they support solutions and
less favorably when they do not. When a member is perceived as blocking the success of a group's solution, that member is perceived negatively by the other members. This member is known as the **deviant member**.

> Michael's perception of other group members changed, just as their per-
> ceptions of him changed. When conversation was superficial, all members
> shared positive impressions of each other. As members approached their
> solution of sharing feelings, they began to see Michael as a person who
> was attempting to hinder their progress.

The term *deviant* describes members who do not behave according to group-developed solutions (Stock, Whitman, & Lieberman, 1958). Members become deviants when they enact an enabling solution in the context of a restrictive group solution or a restrictive solution in the context of an enabling group solution.

Michael became a deviant member because he enacted a restrictive habitual personal solution in the context of the group's enabling solution (see Figure 5.5).

Because deviants' interactions call attention to disturbing motives and reactive fears, hard-earned group solutions are unsuccessful, and anxiety becomes uncomfortable. The group reacts emotionally and attempts to persuade the deviant to agree with the group solution (e.g., "Michael, you really need to start sharing your feelings. We have a real problem with you withdrawing and not sharing your feelings!"). The group may also, in response to a deviant's continued noncompliance, attempt to reinterpret the deviant's behavior so that it does not threaten the solution (e.g., "Michael really doesn't understand what he's feeling, so it's OK that he withdraws.") or modify their solution to accommodate the deviant's disagreement (e.g., "When Michael withdraws, we can ignore him.").

The quality of deviants' group experiences is threatened when they frustrate the group solution by not conforming to it. This frustration leads others to actively pres-

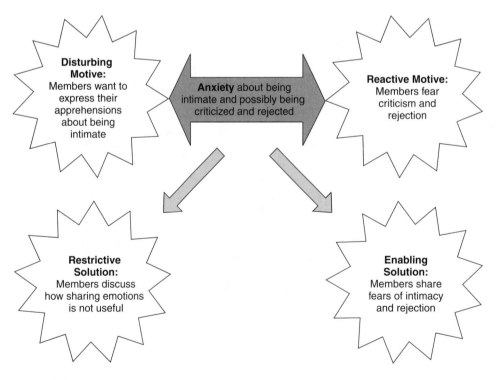

Figure 5.5
"Deviants" and the Group Focal Conflict

sure deviants to agree with their solution. Typically, groups are intolerant of members who do not conform to an agreed-on solution and will criticize the deviant for the anxiety experienced in the group.

> As members continued sharing their feelings, they became progressively uncomfortable with Michael's withdrawal from interaction. Members made numerous statements like "Michael, if it weren't for you, we could actually accomplish something in this group. Maybe you shouldn't be here."

Scapegoat.   The crucial issue associated with deviant members is their potential for being scapegoated. When a member is condemned for group difficulties, that member becomes a **scapegoat**. The leader should protect the deviant member from becoming a scapegoat by supporting solutions that deal with the deviant in a manner that has therapeutic benefit for the deviant and the group.

> Michael's group leader intervened when she recognized that he was becoming a scapegoat. She first directed members to address what it would be like for them to be pressured to do something that scared them. She focused on what it was like for them to believe that others did not honor their fears and apprehensions. Then she initiated a conversation with Michael that focused on relating his fears with what the group had just discussed, what it was like to have others not respect his fears. Ultimately, by continuously connecting Michael with others who shared similar reactions, the leader encouraged Michael to share his fears about sharing feelings with others.

The Therapeutic Process

The focal conflict approach has the objective of helping members develop more effective interpersonal solutions and self-perceptions that are more complimentary. These objectives are based on the assumption that persons entering groups use restrictive habitual personal solutions that limit their interpersonal effectiveness. For individuals to profit from their experiences as members, they must be involved in interactions that elicit change.

To elicit change, leaders intervene whenever needed to establish a level of anxiety that energizes members' interactions. Sometimes this means elevating the anxiety of a group that is avoiding its issues by directing members to discuss reactive fears and disturbing motives. This also means, when anxiety threatens to shut down interaction, that leaders may introduce or allow the group to use a restrictive solution. Change is also initiated when leaders identify and frustrate restrictive solutions that block the expression of disturbing motives and reactive fears. Finally, and possibly most important, leaders establish the group as an environment that provides enough safety for members to take risks and self-disclose. These objectives can be reached using a variety of interventions that will be described in later chapters.

Necessary Conditions for Change.   If members are to change, they must experience several essential conditions. First, members must encounter group focal conflicts that resonate with their concerns. Second, in order to learn more effective interpersonal solutions, members must participate in interactions where their habitual restrictive solutions *do not* allow them to avoid anxiety or meet interpersonal needs. Finally, members must have opportunities to learn about and use effective alternative solutions. Members are successful when they develop more effective interpersonal solutions, greater tolerance for anxiety, and flexibility in their interactions.

Therapeutic Environment.   Members are likely to develop effective interpersonal solutions when their group's culture is dominated by enabling solutions and they feel safe. Safety in the context of enabling solutions allows members to abandon habitual personal solutions without debilitating fear and develop a greater tolerance for anxiety. When a group is safe, members are also more likely to experiment with interpersonal solutions and abandon limiting habitual solutions. In a culture dominated by restrictive solutions, members are unlikely to share sufficient personal information or experience enough anxiety to compel them to abandon their habitual solutions.

In a group culture dominated by enabling solutions, members obtain information that leads to increased self-understanding and more effective personal solutions. This information emerges from members' presentations of solutions to satisfy the group's disturbing motives. For example, in a group where members are developing a solution for a focal conflict related to interpersonal boundaries, members might hear alternatives to their habitual solutions, such as share emotional reactions, ask for what you want, disagree, and so on. This learning process is especially productive when the group's focal conflict resonates with a member's concerns and the member has an opportunity to learn about and experiment with alternative solutions. In addition, as members receive feedback, become aware of their reactions to focal conflicts, and observe the reactions of others, they obtain information that can increase self-understanding.

The usefulness of the information members obtain through group interaction is limited in a group dominated by restrictive solutions, the negotiation of which involves conversation regarding how to escape anxiety. This conversation suppresses enabling solutions that can lead to more effective relationships. Because solutions developed in a group dominated by restrictive solutions are focused on avoidance, the information members obtain about alternative solutions is suspect.

Unsuccessful Group Experiences.   Focal conflict theory contends that members will be unsuccessful for several reasons. First, failure occurs when members are able to continue using ineffective habitual personal solutions. This allows members to avoid intense emotions that lead to abandoning ineffective solutions and experimentation with more effective solutions. Second, members who are able to successfully protect themselves by withdrawing from interaction also will be unsuccessful. Withdrawal allows members to avoid interaction that renders their solutions ineffective. Finally, members who are able to avoid anxiety by substituting their ineffective habitual solutions with new restrictive solutions will not be successful. This unfortunate substitution is common in groups dominated by restrictive solutions.

Consistently withdrawn or silent members are least likely to benefit from group interaction. By simply observing the emotions, personal concerns, and enabling solutions that emerge in the group, silent members achieve limited awareness and insight. Because silent members do not interact, they do not receive direct feedback, are unlikely to overcome fears, and cannot experiment with different solutions.

CONCLUSION

Focal conflict theory is a powerful tool for group leaders. It provides leaders with a conceptual framework for understanding the outcomes of group interaction and thus helps them comprehend group dynamics and formulate interventions. In addition, this theory provides a clear description of how to use group interaction to benefit members. Finally, focal conflict theory can help leaders develop an effective group environment and intervene when a group's culture limits what members can gain. Specific discussion of how leaders use focal conflict theory to conceptualize interventions is contained in the next section of this text.

6

General Systems Theory

OBJECTIVES

After reading this chapter, you should be able to:

✔ Discuss general systems theory concepts relevant to interactive groups.

✔ Describe how general systems theory can be used as a framework for understanding group interaction.

✔ Explain how leaders use their understanding of boundary functioning to understand and modify group interaction.

✔ Describe the assumptions and therapeutic process that derive from general systems theory.

✔ Discuss the implications for practice presented by general systems theory.

INTRODUCTION

In 1971, the American Group Psychotherapy Association charged a committee led by Helen Durkin to investigate the applications of general systems theory for group therapy (H. Durkin, 1981). This committee developed models for group therapy that departed from the prevailing theories and conceptualizations of the leader's role. This chapter describes applications of general systems theory for group counseling and therapy along with some of the ideas presented by Durkin and her associates. In addition, the work of family therapy theorists provides a more in-depth discussion of a number of concepts.

General systems theory and focal conflict theory are similar in several ways. Both share the assumption that members share common concerns. In addition, both describe how members interact to determine acceptable communication content (e.g., emotions or honest reactions are acceptable or unacceptable). General systems theory is more global in its conceptualization of interaction than focal conflict theory, as general systems theory focuses primarily on communication and not on members' conflicts or anxiety.

ESSENTIAL CONCEPTS

Systems, Subsystems, and Suprasystems

General systems theory describes how the constituent parts of a group interact. The group system is a collection of individuals who stand in dynamic relationship with each other. These dynamic relationships involve members interacting with and having a mutual influence on each other. The interaction of members develops a pattern and thus becomes a system. "Systems are the product of the interaction of their parts" (H. Durkin, 1981, p. 8). Within the group system, each member's interaction performs a function that maintains the group as a system.

Systems are not isolated; rather, they are parts of larger systems and are composed of smaller systems, or subsystems. **Subsystems** are subgroups of two or more members who share common characteristics. Individual members also constitute individual subsystems. **Individual subsystems** characterize "information about the individual that is known to others. It represents the individual's sense of self" (MacKenzie, 1990, p. 37). Counseling and therapy groups also exist within the context of larger systems. These larger **suprasystems** include the setting in which the group is convened (e.g., the agency, hospital, school, and so on) and even larger systems (e.g., the immediate community, city, county, and so on).

Isomorphy

Although systems are different, they all share common characteristics, or isomorphies. In a group setting, understanding the concerns of a member sheds light on the related concerns of all other members. Conversely, conceptualizing the concerns that characterize group interaction allows leaders to understand the concerns of each member. Thus, a member who describes difficulty with intimacy somewhat describes the intimacy concerns of other members. From the perspective of the group as a system, a group that avoids intimacy has members who have intimacy concerns.

More broadly, isomorphy implies that counseling and therapy groups reflect the social conditions of their suprasystems. Thus, all groups demonstrate the issues prevalent in their social contexts. This isomorphy has an important implication for group leadership in that leaders must confront issues of racism, sexism, ageism, and culture that invariably emerge in group interaction.

Homeostasis

All groups attempt to maintain homeostasis through interaction that regulates behavior. For example, members' interactions often involve establishing norms that prevent excessive anxiety. The resulting norms include **negative feedback loops** that limit behaviors that produce anxiety and **positive feedback loops** that encourage behaviors that manage anxiety. Whenever group norms have changed, as in the process of group development, the group will attempt to regain homeostasis. The homeostatic process involves "times of change followed by times of consolidation to accommodate the change" (MacKenzie, 1990, p. 37). Homeostasis explains why groups avoid issues after periods of intense, emotionally charged interaction and why they tend to avoid implementing norms that increase intimacy.

Boundaries

In attempting to understand how families function, family therapy theorists have utilized the concept of boundaries. Boundary concepts are especially relevant for understanding counseling and therapy groups. All subsystems and individual subsystems within groups have boundaries that differentiate them from other subsystems. Groups as systems have external boundaries that separate them from other systems. External boundaries define behaviors that are acceptable in a group, define the group's purpose, and differentiate the group from other groups.

Boundaries "define the amount and kind of contact allowable between members" (Becvar & Becvar, 1996, p. 191). Because boundaries define how much contact members can have, they also define the information members can share. These **interpersonal communication boundaries** thus regulate interaction. Groups that have ill-defined boundaries are not likely to have committed members. The lack of commitment occurs in these groups because members are uncertain about their relationships and what they should share. Groups that have rigidly defined boundaries are likely to become stale and boring because members are not likely to share or receive beneficial information about their relationships.

Subsystems or subgroups have boundaries that separate their members from others. Subgroup members usually share a common perspective, have a common function in the group, or have some common characteristic that defines subgroup membership. Occasionally, subgroups form in response to a particular group issue because of a shared point of view and disband once the issue is no longer relevant. As long as subgroups exist, they have a divisive effect on the group because subgroup boundaries exclude other members. For this reason, subgroups require energetic leader intervention.

In effective counseling or therapy groups, members have psychological boundaries that differentiate them from each other. Boundaries in effective groups allow members to interact meaningfully. When members reciprocally express opinions, emotions, and perceptions, they learn from, influence, and connect with each other and establish their uniqueness.

BOUNDARY FUNCTIONING

The development of members depends on how effectively they open and close their boundaries to define themselves and receive and share information. The process of members opening and closing their boundaries is called **boundarying** (J. Durkin, 1981). Boundarying implies that individual members have the necessary resources to open their boundaries to receive information and close them to consolidate their learning or protect themselves. Boundary functioning depends on the choices members make to open or close their boundaries.

Ineffective boundarying poses problems for members, subgroups, and the group as a system. These problems are related to boundary permeability, or "how easily [boundaries] permit information to flow to and from the environment" (Goldenberg & Goldenberg, 1991, p. 46). Permeability problems occur when boundaries do not allow information input or output or do not limit information to be input or output.

Impermeable Boundaries

When members do not consider the input of others or do not share personal information, they have impermeable boundaries. Members with such boundaries become disengaged from the social contexts in which they live and appear unaffected by others' concerns (Barker, 1992). Because these members are disengaged, they are autonomous. This autonomy, however, comes at the cost of not having the capacity to ask for or receive support or to establish emotional connections with others (Minuchin, 1974; Nichols & Schwartz, 1995). Consequently, these individuals do not appear sensitive to others' needs for support (Becvar & Becvar, 1996). These members are not likely to develop meaningful relationships with other members because of their reluctance to share emotion or be psychologically intimate. Disengaged members do not benefit from feedback and have the tendency to perseverate over particular issues.

> Jim is unemotional in his interactions with others and does not share enough personal information to allow others to know him. Occasionally, other members have a strong reaction to Jim and offer him feedback. Jim, however, ignores this feedback or states that he is not interested in hearing it. Whenever Jim struggles, he does not verbalize his concerns and clearly does not know how to ask for help. During a session, Jim repeatedly complained about not having many friends. He was then offered the following feedback: "Jim, when I ask you how you feel about me, you don't share your feelings and don't even say what you think about me. When you do that, I feel shut out and sad, and I assume you don't want to have a relationship with me." After this feedback, Jim stated, "I heard what you said, but I don't know why I don't have many friends."

Diffuse Boundaries

Members who are overly dependent on others have highly permeable or **diffuse boundaries** (Nichols & Schwartz, 1995). Members with diffuse boundaries develop enmeshed relationships with other members. These relationships are displayed by members who respond immediately to the emotional reactions of others (Minuchin, 1974) as if they cannot tell whether the expressed emotions belong to them or to other members (Becvar & Becvar, 1996). Members with diffuse boundaries are reluctant to state their opinions and avoid confrontation. They are vulnerable, overly concerned about the feelings of others, and tend to be very compliant. In effect, they do not seem able to close their boundaries to define themselves or to protect themselves from criticism or unhealthy influence.

Members with diffuse boundaries are depicted by Bowen's concept of fusion (Kerr, 1981). Members who are emotionally fused with others are extremely susceptible to being influenced by the emotions of other members and behave as if their well-being is dependent on others experiencing "positive" emotions. Emotionally fused members tirelessly pursue others' approval. In addition, fused members believe and act as if people cause others' emotions, are reluctant to take responsibility for their own emotions, and blame others for the emotions they experience.

> Over the last several weeks it has become apparent that Karen is investing most of her energy in trying to keep others happy. She seemed vulnerable and overly reactive to others' emotions and often came to tears over trivial comments. Other members often commented that she was "taking it too seriously." When confronted by another member for being "wishy-washy," Karen responded, "I'm sorry. Please tell me I haven't offended you. I know I shouldn't do that; tell me what you want me to do."

Effective Boundarying

Effective boundarying occurs when members intentionally open and close their boundaries when beneficial. Minuchin (1974) would characterize these members as having clear boundaries. These members are capable of balancing nurturing with receiving nurturing, giving support with receiving support, and belonging with autonomy (Becvar & Becvar, 1996). They open their boundaries to receive feedback, self-disclose, and experiment with new behaviors. They also open their boundaries to connect with others without becoming enmeshed. When it is time to reflect on what they have experienced and consolidate their learning, these members close their boundaries. Members who use their boundaries effectively can close them to protect themselves when necessary or open them to engage with others.

> Susie had received feedback from four other group members over a 25-minute period. She responded by verifying that she understood the feedback accurately and "checked out" the feedback with other members. Susie took some of the feedback to heart, tried on new behaviors, and openly shared emotions and perceptions related to the feedback. When she believed that she needed to reflect on the feedback she had received and had experienced enough intense emotion, she stated, "I need to stop now and reflect on what just happened."

Just as the permeability of individual boundaries affects interpersonal functioning, the permeability of system and subsystem boundaries affects group functioning. Groups operating with clear boundaries demonstrate fluid communication. These groups effectively negotiate and renegotiate boundaries so that members can learn and change. Change is less threatening when a group has effective boundarying. Members feel free to experiment with new behaviors and express opinions, emotions, and perceptions.

Groups with impermeable boundaries often have a disengaged membership. Members avoid contact with each other by withholding their emotions, opinions, and perceptions. The overall tone in these groups is cognitive and somewhat disinterested. Members in these groups are unlikely to profit from interaction, test out new behaviors, or develop satisfactory relationships with other group members. These groups can be highly cohesive, but this comes at the cost of being disengaged from the environment and potentially productive input.

Members of groups with highly diffuse boundaries are extremely sensitive to others' reactions. These members are intensely involved with each other and provide a smothering blanket of support. Maintaining comfort and the status quo are highly valued. These members also are overly concerned about others' "negative" emotional reactions and attempt to stifle the expression of these emotions. Members of these groups depend on leaders for direction and often seek leaders' approval. They have little success developing relationships with each other because they are unlikely to risk revealing themselves to others. The learning potential in groups with diffuse boundaries is minimal because members are unlikely to share honest reactions or risk experimentation with new behaviors. These groups are also so open to external input that they often become unproductive, focusing on external concerns as opposed to their own development (see Figure 6.1).

Autonomy

An important goal for group members is autonomy. Autonomy means that members have the capacity to act intentionally in their boundarying. Leaders thus have an objective of helping members make choices to open and close their interpersonal boundaries in a way that is self- and relationship enhancing.

Boundarying, as an autonomous system, opens up the possibility for personal development and allows members the freedom to change within the limitations of larger systems (J. Durkin, 1981). Individuals, however, have the freedom to be autonomous in terms of their personal boundaries, what they share, and what they choose to experience. The function of autonomy is **wholing**. "Wholing means achieving function through self-organization. Functioning in living structure involves maintaining and developing oneself in the face of environmental forces which work passively or actively against such adaptation" (J. Durkin, 1981, p. 37).

Autonomous members decide independently when to participate or not participate and how deeply involved they will be in any interaction. These members can self-disclose to develop intimate relationships and set appropriate limits on how intimate they become with others. The boundaries of autonomous members allow them to become involved but not enmeshed.

However, autonomy can lead to isolation if individuals close their boundaries excessively. Although members should strive for autonomous functioning, they need to learn to keep their boundaries open enough to form relationships. Autonomy

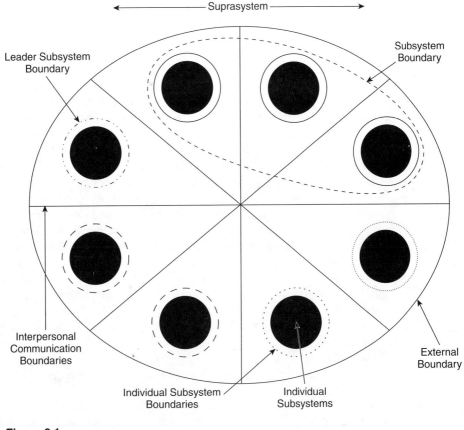

Figure 6.1
Systems Diagram

should be coupled with sufficient permeability to allow members to be open to feedback and be sensitive to others' experiences. Openness to others' experiences, knowing how and when to offer support or share emotions, is essential for members' growth and relationship development.

Hierarchy

Systems exist within suprasystems, and subsystems exist within systems. The activities of a system are organized by the system in which they exist (MacKenzie, 1990), and so the group organizes the behavior of group members. Therefore, in order to understand the behaviors of a member, the leader should consider how the members' behaviors fit how the group is functioning. For example, a person receiving feedback and experimenting with making requests for support may not make sense unless this person's behaviors are viewed in the context of a counseling or therapy group.

THERAPEUTIC PROCESS

Basic Assumptions

Helen Durkin (1981), in explaining the application of general systems theory to group therapy, described groups and their members as living systems. Effective living systems can open their boundaries to acquire energy and information and use this energy to change. By changing, these systems have the capacity to adapt to environmental circumstances to allow growth and development. In closing their boundaries, these systems are capable of maintaining a desired inner state and filtering out environmental events that can threaten this inner state. Closing boundaries also allows systems to preserve their identity and not become fused with other systems. In this context, relationships involve the reciprocal opening and closing of boundaries—opening for input and connection and closing for identity and integrity.

Living systems open and close their boundaries most effectively when they operate autonomously. "The goal of therapy, to help the group members restore or enhance their own autonomy, is concretized into the more practical goal of helping group members more effectively open and close their own boundaries" (H. Durkin, 1981, p. 6). By focusing on boundaries, leaders can simplify their work. "Focusing on system boundaries gives the therapist a single uniform approach to all levels which permit him, at times, to cut through the diversity of content to the underlying structure" (H. Durkin, 1981, pp. 11–12). In essence, the desired outcome for group counseling and therapy is members who can open their boundaries to receive and utilize necessary input and close their boundaries when needed to maintain identity and integrity.

Seeing the group, its members, and its leaders as living systems simplifies the understanding of interaction and development of interventions. Because groups operate as hierarchies, interaction observed at one level shows how a system functions at the next lower level. This also means that interventions directed at one level of the group system affect the subsystems of that level. Thus, when leaders intervene to improve group communication, leaders can assume that group subsystems and individual subsystems will be affected.

Isomorphism is a highly significant concept in general systems theory for group counseling and therapy. Because all levels of the group system share characteristics, leaders can learn about the issues of each member by identifying the issues encountered by the group as a system. The assumption of isomorphy also allows leaders to identify group issues by understanding the concerns of individual members.

Implications for Group Counseling and Therapy

The use of general systems theory in group counseling and therapy is all about boundarying. Leaders have the essential tasks of assessing boundary functioning and intervening to alter boundaries that limit members' capacity for adaptation and growth. The concept of autonomy serves as the criterion for assessing members' boundaries and as the objective for leaders' interventions. Once boundaries are assessed, interventions attempt to modify excessively closed or open boundaries at all levels of the group system. Additional concepts, such as isomorphism and hierarchy, are useful aids to comprehending boundary functioning, understanding the issues present at all system levels, and developing and implementing interventions.

Change involves modifying the inner structure of members' internal systems. "In order to change the inner structure of a system, its boundaries must be penetrated" (Gray, 1981, p. 204). Thus, the essential objective of group counseling and therapy is to help members develop the ability "to restructure themselves by regulating the permeability of their intra- and interpersonal boundaries" (H. Durkin, 1981, p. 19).

Process

The application of general systems theory to group counseling and psychotherapy involves a therapeutic process that focuses on the boundarying occurring at multiple levels of the group system. The primary role of leaders is to identify ineffective boundary structures and intervene to alter them (H. Durkin, 1981; MacKenzie, 1990). More specifically, leaders have the objective of optimizing the group's external boundaries, interpersonal communication boundaries, subsystem boundaries, and individual boundaries. Autonomy is the goal.

To assess boundary functioning, leaders select one level of the system to observe, be it individuals, subsystems, or the group as a system. When interaction indicates diffuse or impermeable boundaries, leaders can intervene. These interventions have the goal of helping members develop autonomous boundary functioning.

When boundary functioning indicates diffuse boundaries, interventions focus on helping to "firm up" boundaries. Leaders should help members with diffuse boundaries become more independent in their actions and thinking. These members can benefit from numerous interventions, including experimenting with sharing independent opinions, stating what they want as opposed to asking, and experimenting with anger and disagreeing.

When a group has diffuse external boundaries, it spends excessive time conversing about outside events and effort in smothering communication that could increase anxiety. Diffuse external boundaries are commonly seen in groups where members have "safety first" or less permeable interpersonal boundaries. These boundaries often occur in groups that incorporate new members on too regular a basis. Leaders of these groups are clearly challenged in their work to develop sufficiently closed boundaries and trust. Their only resort is to emphasize interventions that keep interaction focused on the here and now, to develop norms that contrast with outside systems (e.g., open sharing of emotions), and to use language that stresses the group as separate from external systems.

When boundary functioning indicates impermeable boundaries, interventions focus on opening boundaries. Impermeable boundaries require opening to allow the exchange of necessary information. One way individuals can be helped to open their boundaries is by leaders encouraging them to share emotions (MacKenzie, 1990). Other procedures such as feedback exchange that encourage effective communication and experimentation with new behaviors can also be effective.

Groups that have impermeable external boundaries can have the advantages of cohesiveness, trust, and intense here-and-now interaction. However, a group with impermeable boundaries that remains intact for long periods can become stale without occasional new members and suffers from being detached from the environment. Leaders can use the boundary-opening intervention of asking members to connect their in-group experiences with similar experiences outside the group. This intervention must be timed well and used carefully so as not to create norms that open the group's external boundary excessively (e.g., talk about outside material).

Groups are effective when boundaries allow communication to flow freely. In these groups, members exchange feedback and experiment with new behaviors that lead to change. Ineffective groups suffer from external boundaries that are too diffuse and internal communication boundaries that are impermeable. Such groups demonstrate an atmosphere of defensiveness that involves constant introduction of topics that have little impact on members to maintain safety and homeostasis. Ineffective groups rarely have meaningful feedback exchange or members who experiment with interpersonal behaviors.

CONCLUSION

General systems theory is a useful framework for understanding group interaction. The theory's principles define the characteristics of a productive group environment and help leaders conceptualize interventions. The concepts of isomorphy and hierarchy are especially helpful for understanding the shared aspects of members' concerns and the potential effects of interventions. Leaders who stress a systems approach have the primary role of boundary regulator. Leaders who focus on boundarying and who have autonomy as their primary goal can be very effective.

General systems theory greatly simplifies group interaction, so it is a useful framework for understanding the complexities of members' interactions. By itself, however, it lacks sufficient depth to explain the dynamics of group interactions or to provide a detailed description of the leader's role. Authors who utilize general systems theory, such as Donigian and Malnati (1997) and Agazarian (1997), add their own conceptualizations of the leader's role and borrow from other theoretical perspectives to deepen the understanding of members' interactive dynamics. Systems theory concepts will be incorporated in the discussion of leader interventions in the second section of this text.

The Interpersonal Approach and Group Theory Summary

OBJECTIVES

After reading this chapter, you should be able to:

✔ Discuss the theoretical foundations of the interpersonal approach.

✔ Explain the essential concepts of the interpersonal approach.

✔ Discuss the interpersonal perspective on the group therapeutic process.

✔ Describe the role of a leader who emphasizes the interpersonal approach.

✔ Outline the seven themes group counseling and therapy theories share and how these themes can be used in group practice.

INTRODUCTION

The interpersonal approach to group counseling and therapy emphasizes members learning from each other in a setting that accentuates here-and-now interaction, feedback exchange, the correction of interpersonal perceptual distortions, immediate emotional experiencing, the utilization of essential therapeutic factors, and cognitive processing. It views members' interaction in the group as the basis for interpersonal learning, the objectives of which are awareness, insight, and change in relationships both in and out of the group setting (Leszcz, 1992). The interpersonal approach to group therapy was made prominent by the work of Yalom (1970).

Focal conflict theory, general systems theory, and the interpersonal approach are similar in that they claim that members' group interactions mirror their interactions outside group. The interpersonal approach differs from focal conflict theory and general systems theory in that it does not emphasize the group as a social system. Thus, it does not stress group-as-a-whole interventions as an imperative aspect of the leader's role. In addition, the interpersonal approach stresses an interpersonal learning process, which the leader must facilitate. Finally, the interpersonal approach is heavily influenced by the work of Sullivan (1953), which was not specifically intended to be a group approach to therapy.

THEORETICAL FOUNDATIONS

The interpersonal approach to group therapy sees group interaction as the mechanism for change (Leszcz, 1992). This perspective is the product of Yalom's conceptualization of interpersonal learning as a therapeutic process. Yalom's ideas were based most extensively on the work of Harry Stack Sullivan.

Sullivan (1955) contended that self-esteem depended on individuals' perceptions of how significant others evaluate their behaviors. During childhood, "the developing personality embraces those parts of the self that are valued by his or her significant others" (Leszcz, 1992, p. 38). By behaving in a way that significant others approve, individuals are able to maintain their interpersonal attachments and build their self-esteem. Conversely, behaviors that do not gain the approval of significant others cause interpersonal anxiety because individuals perceive that such behaviors threaten their attachments with significant others. Because significant others disapprove, individuals' perceptions of their self-worth diminish. The behaviors that create interpersonal anxiety or threaten disapproval are "disavow[ed] through the process of selective inattention" (Leszcz, 1992, p. 38).

Because significant others disapprove, individuals disown personal experiences and avoid using interpersonal behaviors that communicate these experiences. Conversely, individuals learn to value interpersonal behaviors and their accompanying internal experiences when they gain the approval of significant others. Thus, individuals create their own personalities on the basis of how they perceive the evaluations of significant others by eliminating or maintaining interpersonal behaviors. The resulting composite, although formed at an early age, persists and influences relationships throughout an individual's life (Hall & Lindzey, 1978).

> When Steve was 5 years old, his parents scolded him on numerous occasions for feeling and acting sad and angry. When Steve experienced these scoldings, he perceived he was doing something inappropriate and that being sad and angry was unacceptable. Eventually, so Steve could maintain his parents' approval and his own self-worth, he stopped attending to these unacceptable feelings. Consequently, Steve came to believe that he had to conceal his feelings to maintain attachment with his parents and be worthwhile. Recently, when Steve, now 28 years old, joined a group, he described a number of failed relationships. He discussed feeling unable to

meet his needs for emotional support. He also stated that his partners complained they never knew when he was upset and felt shut out by him. When other members encouraged him to talk about his sadness, Steve denied feeling sad.

Yalom (1995) also stresses Sullivan's idea that individuals are disposed toward perceiving others in a way that distorts what actually occurs in their relationships. These distortions are associated with individuals' perceptions and possible misinterpretations of significant others' approval and disapproval. Sullivan coined the term *parataxic distortion* to describe this perceptual process. "A parataxic distortion occurs in an interpersonal situation when one person relates to another not on the basis of the realistic attributes of the other" (Yalom, 1995, p. 19). Rather, individuals react to others unrealistically because of their perceptions and internal reactions (Yalom & Vinogradov, 1993). These distortions define acceptable and unacceptable interpersonal behaviors and lead to impaired relationships.

Leaders will commonly observe a variety of parataxic distortions emerging in group interaction. The following example occurred during the early meetings of an adolescent group.

RENEE: "Brian, you just can't act that way. I won't like you if you do."
LEADER: "Renee, I'd like you to try a different way to..."
RENEE: "Shut up! You are so critical of me and everything I do. You think I can't do anything right! You go to h——!"

In this example, Renee's reaction was due to a parataxic distortion, which is indicated when a member's emotional reaction is far more intense than a situation warrants. Here, Renee's angry reaction was inconsistent with the content of previous and current interaction. Although this example involved the leader, parataxic distortions occur between members as well.

Parataxic distortions are correctable through the process of **consensual validation** (Sullivan, 1953; Yalom, 1995). Consensual validation is a process in which individuals learn how to value themselves, their internal experiences, and their behaviors differently, depending on others' responses and perceived evaluations. In this way, group members who encounter others' reactions that are contrary to their own perceptions can correct their interpersonal distortions. For example, if a member who is ashamed of having shared his feelings hears that other members deeply appreciate this sharing, it can change his belief that others will reject him because he is worthless when he shares feelings. This corrected interpersonal distortion helps this member value his emotions and become more emotionally open in his relationships.

Yalom (1995) regards interpersonal relationships as a critically important human need. "People need people—for initial and continued survival, for socialization, for the pursuit of satisfaction. No one—not the dying, not the outcast, not the mighty—transcends the need for human contact" (p. 21). Sullivan and Yalom view mental health in terms of healthy relationships. Therefore, the goal of group counseling and therapy is to help group members learn how to achieve healthy and satisfying relationships.

ESSENTIAL CONCEPTS

The interpersonal approach focuses on members' interactions "as the nucleus of change, growth, and improvement" (Leszcz, 1992, p. 37). This focus is grounded in the assumption that developing and sustaining relationships is a highly significant human need and that individuals' definitions of self-worth are a function of their relationships.

Therapeutic Factors

Yalom (1995) describes 11 factors that contribute to the process of change in a therapy group. These factors are "the essential things that make people get better" (Lonergan, 1994, p. 207) and are oversimplifications of the complex interactive phenomena that contribute to helping therapy group members (Yalom, 1995). These factors are valuable for their utility as leadership objectives.

Two of these factors are interpersonal learning and cohesiveness. Yalom (1995) treats these separately to emphasize their importance. Seven other factors—installation of hope, universality, imparting information, altruism, the corrective recapitulation of the primary family experience, developing socializing techniques, and imitative behavior—are also important contributors to change. Yalom (1995) sees the final two factors—existential factors and catharsis—best understood in the context of the other factors. Chapter 10 addresses therapeutic factors in much greater detail.

Interpersonal Learning

Interpersonal learning is a comprehensive term that encompasses the processes of consensual validation, corrective emotional experience, the group as a social microcosm, and transference and insight. Whereas other therapeutic factors contribute to change, interpersonal learning is the most essential mechanism of change (Yalom & Vinogradov, 1993). Interpersonal group therapy uses interpersonal learning to alter interpersonal distortions, provide insight, and help members master the interpersonal behaviors necessary to experience more satisfying relationships (Yalom & Vinogradov, 1993).

Interpersonal learning involves members gaining an understanding of how others perceive and react to their interpersonal behaviors. When members share their perceptions and reactions, others receive information that can correct interpersonal distortions. In addition, this information provides members with input about alternative interpersonal behaviors that can improve their relationships. As members become more adept at self-observation and effective interpersonal behaviors, they transfer their learning to relationships outside the group.

 Consensual Validation.   The most significant factor in interpersonal learning is the process of consensual validation, the most essential component of which is interpersonal feedback. Leaders encourage consensual validation on the premise that individuals can alter their interpersonal distortions when they compare their self-evaluations to others' evaluations (Yalom & Vinogradov, 1993). Thus, when members find that others see certain interpersonal behaviors positively, they can begin to regard those behaviors positively even though they previously have seen them as unacceptable. Consensual validation also affects behaviors that others see as unacceptable and that the member has seen as acceptable.

> John believed that sharing emotions was a sign of weakness and thus unacceptable. After an intense interaction with another group member, John heard that others believed he was being evasive and dishonest because he had not shared the emotions he was obviously experiencing. John received feedback that challenged his interpersonal distortion that sharing emotions was unacceptable. John also learned that others experienced his acting as if he had no emotions negatively. Thus, John received information that challenged his assumptions about acceptable and unacceptable interpersonal behaviors. This input offered John consensual validation that changed his interpersonal distortion that sharing emotions was unacceptable.

Consensual validation is achieved through feedback exchange. Feedback allows members to learn how others perceive their interpersonal behaviors. Effectively shared and processed feedback offers members information that increases their understanding of how their behaviors contribute to the emotional and cognitive reactions of others and challenges interpersonal distortions. This information enables members to self-evaluate on the basis of what actually happens in their relationships and not on their distorted perceptions of others' evaluations.

Corrective Emotional Experience.   Corrective emotional experiences involve members' experiencing intense emotion, reality testing, and cognitive processing that corrects interpersonal distortions. Two important conditions need to exist in groups for corrective emotional experiences to occur: safety and honest feedback exchange (Yalom, 1995). Corrective emotional experiencing includes consensual validation and emphasizes emotion or intense self-disclosure.

Corrective emotional experiencing involves the expression of intense emotion (positive or negative) or the sharing of a revealing and involving self-disclosure, sustained interaction that allows full expression of the emotion or disclosure, consensual validation that corrects an interpersonal distortion, and an improvement in members' ability to interact intimately with other members (Yalom, 1995). Often, it involves members anticipating a disastrous reaction to their display of emotion or disclosure and experiencing a response from others that is contrary to this anticipation.

> Beth believed that expressing her anger when she felt ignored would result in rejection and never gaining the acceptance of others. During the latter part of a session, she had felt that others had been ignoring and trivializing her input. She exploded with intense anger before she could stop herself. The other members attended to her and did not attempt to shut

down her anger. Beth, with the encouragement of the leader and other members, was able to share not only her anger but also her fears of disapproval and rejection. Instead of being rejected or criticized, she found that others appreciated her expressions. Others let her know that it was important for them to know whenever she felt ignored or angry. On the basis of this experience, Beth learned to share her anger more openly and confronted her fears of abandonment and rejection.

Social Microcosm.   Over time, members' relationships in counseling and therapy groups increasingly resemble members' relationships outside their groups (Yalom & Vinogradov, 1993). Yalom and Vinogradov (1993) point out that the interpersonal concerns that have led members to the group eventually are demonstrated in the context of the group's interaction. In other words, members' relationship difficulties and interpersonal distortions become evident as members interact. Members' group experiences also take on characteristics of members' families of origin. Ultimately, members use the same interpersonal behaviors they have developed in their families of origin.

The interpersonal issues that bring members to groups become apparent in the members' here-and-now interactions. These interactions are thus relevant to understanding and improving members' relationships. By observing members' interactions, leaders get information about members' interpersonal dynamics. This information shapes interventions that address relationship difficulties in the group and improves relationships outside the group.

Cohesiveness

Cohesion in group therapy is analogous to the therapeutic relationship in individual counseling and therapy (Yalom, 1995). Yalom (1995) defines cohesiveness as "the attraction that members have for their group and for the other members" (p. 67). A cohesive group has more consistent attendance, higher levels of member participation, more intense self-disclosure, more satisfying relationships between members, increased tolerance for hostility, and overall more effective outcomes than less cohesive groups. Members of cohesive groups are accepting and supportive of each other and open to being influenced by other members (Yalom, 1995).

Cohesiveness must exist if the other therapeutic factors are to operate (Yalom, 1995). When a group is cohesive, members accept each other and value each others' opinions and thus disclose more and risk more. Consequently, cohesiveness leads to positive outcomes. The development of a cohesive group environment depends on how effectively leaders have developed a safe therapeutic group culture.

Here and Now

An extremely important task for leaders is developing a group culture that emphasizes the here and now. When a group is engaged in the here and now, interaction focuses on what is occurring in the present between members in the group, not on past or outside events. This emphasis is critical for two reasons. First, interactions occurring in the group at any particular moment contain the interpersonal distortions that have brought members to the group. Second, interactions in the here and now are more likely to be affect laden and immediate. Such interactions have a greater impact and are more challenging to interpersonal distortions (Yalom & Vinogradov, 1993). Yalom (1995) puts the importance of the here and now into perspective: "to the degree that the therapy group focuses on the here-and-now, it increases in power and effectiveness" (p. 27).

Two conditions must be present if the here and now is to have a therapeutic impact. First, members must be in spontaneous, open, and authentic contact with each other. Second, members must reflect back on their experiencing of one another to make their experiencing therapeutically useful. This is a **self-reflective loop** that involves cognitive processing of experience and offers members opportunities to develop insight (Yalom, 1995). Yalom strongly cautions leaders not to see emotional experiencing in the here and now alone as adequate for therapeutic progress. "There [is] clear evidence that a *cognitive component* [is] essential; some type of cognitive map [is] needed . . . that [frames] the experience and [makes] sense of the emotions evoke[ed] in the group" (p. 29).

THERAPEUTIC PROCESS

The interpersonal approach uses necessary therapeutic conditions and a therapeutic process that stresses interpersonal learning. The goal is to optimize members' interpersonal functioning. To meet this goal, members' concerns are conceptualized as interpersonal difficulties stemming from interpersonal distortions. Next, by focusing on here-and-now interactions, leaders help members identify and correct the interpersonal distortions that hinder their interpersonal functioning.

Necessary Conditions

Yalom stresses the primacy of cohesiveness and interpersonal learning for the success of group members. These two therapeutic factors allow other therapeutic factors to emerge and operate. Whether cohesiveness and interpersonal learning are present depends on how effectively leaders have developed a facilitative group culture. For a group culture to develop and use necessary therapeutic factors, two conditions must exist: "(1) the members must experience the group as sufficiently safe and supportive so that . . . tensions may be openly expressed; (2) there must be sufficient engagement and honest feedback to permit effective reality testing" (Yalom, 1995, p. 25).

Process of Therapy

The therapeutic process is a process of interpersonal learning that includes consensual validation, corrective emotional experience, the group as a social microcosm, the activation of the here and now, and processing that uses the self-reflective loop. Members who are involved in this process learn to function more effectively in their relationships in group. This learning then transfers to relationships outside the group.

In brief, this process flows in the following way:

1. Members interact openly and honestly in the here and now.
2. Members' interpersonal distortions emerge in their here-and-now interactions.
3. Members become aware of these distortions because of interpersonal feedback and self-observation.
4. Interpersonal distortions are corrected through consensual validation and corrective emotional experiencing.
5. Members gain insight into how others perceive them, their motivations, and the etiology of their interpersonal distortions and behaviors.
6. Members take responsibility for using and changing ineffective interpersonal behaviors.
7. Members learn about and use behaviors that are consistent with more effective interpersonal functioning.
8. These behaviors are then used in interpersonal situations outside the group.

Yalom (1995) stresses that members' success depends on both emotional experiencing and developing a cognitive structure to define, gain insight, and change interpersonal distortions.

ROLE OF THE LEADER

The basic objective for leaders using the interpersonal approach is to mobilize the interpersonal learning process. Once in operation, interpersonal learning builds group cohesion and activates other therapeutic factors. To accomplish this, objective leaders perform roles that establish a safe and facilitative group culture and perform essential functions.

Creating a Facilitative Culture

"Leaders of interpersonal groups must initially work to create a safe, supportive, and therapeutic environment" (Yalom & Vinogradov, 1993, p. 190). Accomplishing this objective requires several important steps. First, leaders carefully compose their groups with members who meet five criteria. Potential members must be able to examine their interpersonal behaviors, motivated to change, open to giving and receiving feedback, willing to experiment with new interpersonal behaviors, and committed to regular attendance (Yalom & Vinogradov, 1993).

Second, leaders establish the group as a therapeutic social system that supports members' growth and change. This system is developed with the guiding principle that members helping members is the most effective and desirable outcome; that is, "the group is the agent of change" (Yalom, 1995, p. 109). Accomplishing this objective involves developing a normative structure much like the facilitative group environment discussed in chapter 2.

The norms that Yalom (1995) recommends include self-monitoring, self-disclosure, procedural, importance, agents of help, and support. Self-monitoring group norms help members become responsible for group functioning and include members making comments about interaction, pointing out conflict, encouraging each other to stay in the here and now, and monitoring each other's feedback. Self-disclosure norms facilitate members' disclosing here-and-now reactions and other information relevant to interaction. Examples are norms that do not force disclosures, that allow members to make choices about what to disclose, and that do not criticize self-disclosure. Procedural norms promote free-flowing and spontaneous interaction. Yalom (1995) warns that overly structured procedural norms prevent spontaneous interaction and make groups boring. Norms related to the importance of the group to its members are articulated in how members utilize the group for help. When such norms are in place, members participate, with the belief that interaction is helpful. Norms that communicate that members are the agents of help are in place when members turn to each other for input and feedback as opposed to looking to leaders for help. Examples are norms that allow members to ask each other for help, that encourage each others' risk taking, or that give feedback when others need it. Support norms establish safety and security in the group. Norms that communicate support include those that accept each others' feelings nonjudgmentally, that never criticize the person but that share reactions to behaviors, that stay with a member as long as work is productive, that guard against feedback overload, and that encourage risk taking.

Activating the Here and Now

Yalom and Vinogradov (1993) stress that one of the leader's primary responsibilities is teaching members about here-and-now interactions. During the early stages of a group, leaders have to continually instruct members to share immediate emotions, discuss what is happening in the present, share immediate reactions to each others' behaviors, and give immediate feedback. Donigian and Hulse-Killacky (1999) state that in order to activate the here and now, leaders need to help members focus on their interactions and reflect on group events. The important part of activating the here and now is attention to process (Donigian & Hulse-Killacky, 1999).

Process and the Self-Reflective Loop

The concept of process is a benchmark of the interpersonal approach. Process describes "the nature of the relationship between interacting individuals" (Yalom, 1995, p. 130). Process characterizes how interaction actually occurs (e.g., volume or rate of speech or nonverbal behaviors) and the purpose of the interaction. Yalom (1995) considers process the how and why of interaction. Thus, leaders who pay attention to process observe interaction, wonder about the motivations or purposes behind interaction, and consider what interaction says about the relationships of the interacting members.

Process describes not only a discrete interaction but also a series or sequence of interactions. These interactions may involve several members or the entire group. Examples of process include interactions designed to reduce anxiety, negotiate norms, or make decisions. In terms of dyadic interaction, process could involve developing a relationship, criticizing, supporting, and challenging. The interpersonal approach stresses the importance of leaders making statements identifying process. Yalom (1995) argues that process "is indispensable and a common denominator to all effective interactive groups" (p. 137). Becoming aware of process allows members to learn from their interactions and develop a different understanding of themselves (Yalom & Vinogradov, 1993). Process observations that help members reflect on their interactions are instrumental to this learning.

Leaders using the interpersonal approach perform several tasks to utilize process for interpersonal learning. The first task is activating a here-and-now focus. This is achieved by directing members to interact about what is transpiring in the group at the moment and directing members away from discussing events that occur outside the group (Yalom, 1995). Once here-and-now interaction takes place, the next task is "process illumination" (Yalom, 1995). This means that leaders make statements that describe the how and why of interaction. Examples of process statements include "The group seems to want to avoid talking about Mary's issue"; "John, it looks like you're trying to convince Shelley to like you"; or "Some of you want to confront the issue of how much emotion to share in here, while others would rather not talk about it."

Yalom characterizes the sequence of here-and-now experiencing and then reflecting on that experience as the self-reflective loop. Interacting in the here and now openly and with emotional honesty and then reflecting back on this experiencing is an essential aspect of interpersonal learning. The self-reflective loop allows members to conceptualize their experience and gain insight. Insight leads to understanding about relationships and interpersonal behaviors.

Conceptualization of Members' Concerns

The effectiveness of the interpersonal approach relies on leaders being able to conceptualize members' concerns as interpersonal difficulties (Yalom, 1995). Thus, the issue that caused a member to join a group is not as significant as how that member relates to others. Members' concerns and treatment goals are expressed in terms of altering interpersonal distortions, improving members' ability to relate effectively, and achieving healthy relationships. For example, members who enter groups because of "depression" could be seen as individuals who have restricted relationships. Possible goals of these members could include increased involvement with others, improved relationship skills, and spontaneity. The perspective that the life satisfaction and difficulties of individuals manifest themselves in interpersonal relationships is the foundation of the interpersonal approach.

CONCLUSION

The major strength of the interpersonal approach is its conceptualization of interpersonal learning. Interpersonal learning and its related concepts are rooted in a model of interpersonal relationships. This model accounts for how members develop and can change ineffective interpersonal functioning. Additional strengths of the interpersonal approach include its conceptualization of therapeutic factors that lead to the therapeutic progress of group members.

The interpersonal approach acknowledges that groups operate as therapeutic social systems and describes procedures for developing an effective therapeutic culture. Although Yalom (1995) recognizes that groups operate as therapeutic social systems, he describes but does not emphasize conceptualizing the group as a social system or interventions that address the group as a system.

ESSENTIAL THEMES IN GROUP COUNSELING AND THERAPY THEORY

The theories presented in this and the two preceding chapters reduce the complexity of group interaction, present models of effective interaction, and suggest interventions necessary to help members meet counseling and therapy goals. Leaders who use these group-focused theories are likely to increase their confidence and ability to conceptualize and implement interventions. Focal conflict theory, general systems theory, and the interpersonal approach make important contributions to the practice of group counseling and therapy. These frameworks clearly are more appropriate for group work than theories designed to understand clients in individual counseling and therapy settings. They share common themes that illuminate essential objectives, processes, and operational assumptions of group counseling and therapy.

Origin and Significance of Interpersonal Difficulties

Focal conflict theory, general systems theory, and the interpersonal approach have common assumptions about the origin and significance of interpersonal difficulties. First, each recognizes family-of-origin experiences as the most common source of interpersonal difficulties. These perspectives agree that interpersonal behaviors and perceptions of self and others are established as a result of interaction with significant others in families of origin. The intent of these interpersonal behaviors and perceptions is to obtain acceptance, develop and maintain positive self-perceptions, moderate anxiety, and maintain essential relationships. Early in life, these behaviors and perceptions become parts of individuals' personalities, form individuals' approaches to interacting with others, and persist into adult life. Often, the behaviors and perceptions developed in the family of origin interfere with individuals' ability to develop and maintain satisfactory relationships.

Interpersonal difficulties form as individuals attempt to meet their needs as children. Whitaker (1985) describes essentially the same process presented by Yalom (1995), although their ideas originated from different theoretical perspectives. H. Durkin (1981) discusses how family-of-origin systems influence the interpersonal boundaries of the individuals. That is, interaction with others, most commonly in families of origin, shapes how individuals interact and estimate their self-worth. When family-of-origin experiences do not meet the needs of individuals, individuals find ways of protecting themselves from emotional damage by developing dysfunctional interpersonal behaviors to meet their needs.

Yalom (1995), Whitaker (1985), and H. Durkin (1981) also agree that the patterns of relating formed at an early age persist into adult life. These patterns (interpersonal distortions, habitual restrictive personal solutions, or diffuse or impermeable boundaries) have a distinct influence on relationships and life satisfaction. Individuals, as Whitaker (1985) puts it, use solutions that usually originate in the family of origin "and remain important in adult life" (p. 204). There is also agreement that persons function as if they were in their family of origin throughout life even though circumstances are obviously different and their interpersonal behaviors are no longer useful.

The significance of difficulties in interpersonal relationships from the perspectives of focal conflict theory, general systems theory, and the interpersonal approach is that individuals can function only as effectively as they relate to others. That is, effective interpersonal functioning is the basis of mental health, and mental health concerns are viewed as interpersonal difficulties. Thus, therapeutic goals, whether they involve correcting interpersonal perceptual distortions, developing autonomous boundary functioning, or implementing enabling solutions, are all grounded in interpersonal relationships.

Relatedness of Members' Concerns

Each of the perspectives presented in this chapter indicates the relationship of members' concerns in two different contexts. First, to some extent, all members share common concerns. Second, the interpersonal issues that members demonstrate in their interactions in group are identical to the relationship problems members have outside the group.

Members become involved in groups because of interpersonal difficulties. These difficulties are manifested as dysfunctional interpersonal behaviors intended to meet relationship needs, moderate interpersonal anxiety, and maintain self-esteem. Thus, to some extent, all group members share each others' concerns. Shared disturbing and reactive motives, the isomorphic qualities of members concerns, and common "anxiety-laden issues" (Yalom, 1995) are seen as fundamental realities of the group social system.

Because all members' concerns are related, interventions or interactions that have an impact on one member are likely to affect other members. This premise should cause leaders to encourage all members to share their reactions to significant group events, such as noteworthy interventions, feedback exchanges, or corrective emotional experiences.

These perspectives also view the interpersonal issues, attitudes, perceptions, and behaviors that members demonstrate in group as consistent with those that members experience outside group. The concepts of isomorphism, habitual personal solutions, interpersonal perceptual distortions, and the group as a social microcosm share the contention that the interpersonal perceptions, apprehensions, and interactions of members both in and out of group are essentially identical. These premises mean that group interactions are significant and that helping members deal with the interpersonal issues they experience in group is highly relevant to meeting counseling or therapeutic goals.

Here and Now

Focusing on here-and-now interaction is indispensable. The solutions members negotiate to deal with shared disturbing and reactive motives, the restrictive habitual personal solutions used by each member, the isomorphic qualities of members' concerns, as well as interpersonal perceptual distortions all unfold in the context of here-and-now interaction. This assertion emphatically challenges the usefulness of dealing with members' reports of interpersonal concerns outside group.

In addition, interventions focusing on here-and-now interaction have a considerably more powerful effect on members than interventions aimed at helping members deal with problems they are not currently experiencing. Most important, here-and-now interventions are more likely to stimulate emotional expression and influence members' interpersonal perceptions and behaviors. In addition, because members enact their interpersonal difficulties in the here and now, interventions that improve how members interact in group ultimately help them become more effective in their relationships outside group.

Intervention Focus

Besides focusing interventions on here-and-now interaction, interventions need to focus on different levels of the group as a system: the individual, interpersonal, and group-as-a-system levels. Perhaps the greatest consistency in these approaches is the primacy of interpersonal interventions. Whether the intervention process involves identifying and correcting interpersonal perceptual distortions, opening or closing interpersonal boundaries, or identifying restrictive solutions and developing enabling solutions, the objectives are basically the same. Although focal conflict theory, general systems theory, and the interpersonal approach agree on the usefulness of individual interventions, they differ in their intent. General systems theory and focal conflict theory see individual interventions as a vehicle to intervene in the shared concerns of members and the group as a system. On the other hand, the interpersonal approach is not as concerned with the group as a system and is directed more toward dealing with an individual member's perceptual distortion.

Focal conflict theory, general systems theory, and the interpersonal approach agree that interventions focused on the group as a system are useful. Yalom (1995) sees group-as-a-system intervention (i.e., mass group commentary) as a means to optimize the effectiveness of the group environment but is the least enthusiastic about group-level interventions and warns against their overuse. The interpersonal approach does not articulate how interventions at the group-as-a-system level influence individual and interpersonal levels. General systems theory and focal conflict theory more clearly and completely describe the usefulness of group-as-a-system intervention and its connection with other levels of the group system. These two approaches see group-as-a-system intervention as a way to effect communication, influence individual members and subgroups, reveal and address shared concerns, define boundaries, and so on.

Members profit significantly when leaders are able to facilitate interpersonal learning. This conviction is predicated on theoretical assumptions and research that indicate that members learning from each other is far more powerful and memorable than learning from interactions with leaders (Yalom, 1995). Leaders' interventions, therefore, should emphasize interpersonal and group-as-a-system intervention. This perspective also suggests that interventions focusing on individuals should include efforts to involve other members. Individually directed interventions are potentially useful, but an overemphasis ignores the potent forces of interpersonal learning.

The Therapeutic Group Environment

The three perspectives describe a group environment that is most conducive to the therapeutic progress of members. Each approach indicates that leaders should establish a safe environment. Whitaker and Lieberman (1964) state this clearly: a "shared sense of safety is an essential condition for therapeutic progress" (p. 217). In general, there is agreement that leaders and members should communicate acceptance and caring. Desirable outcomes are also connected with members sharing the perception that participation is in their best interest. The establishment of a shared perception of safety in the group is one of the leader's more important responsibilities.

Interpersonal Objectives

These theories see interpersonal relationships as the origin of interpersonal difficulties and as the means to resolve these difficulties. Leaders who successfully enable members to improve their relationships in group will be successful in helping members make important changes in their lives. Leaders' objectives are thus to establish a group environment that supports interpersonal learning and to involve members in interpersonal learning processes.

Therapeutic Process

The perspectives presented in this chapter share some common ideas about the essential phases of group counseling and therapy. All seek to improve relationships in an interpersonal environment and include similar processes. In general, these perspectives agree that the group therapeutic process would include the following phases:

1. Individuals join counseling or therapy groups because of difficulties in their interpersonal relationships. These difficulties involve ineffective interpersonal behaviors, interpersonal communication problems, limiting interpersonal perceptions, and diminished perceptions of self-worth.

2. When members begin group, they interact using customary interpersonal behaviors. Over time, members' here-and-now interactions progressively reveal the ineffective behaviors, communication problems, limiting perceptions, and diminished perceptions of self-worth that have brought them to group.

3. Here-and-now interaction brings ineffective behaviors, communication problems, limiting perceptions, and diminished perceptions of self-worth progressively into members' awareness. Awareness is the product of interaction, observation of self and others, reflection, and feedback.

4. Members find that the dysfunctional behaviors and perceptions that have become increasingly ineffective in meeting their needs before coming to group are very ineffective in group and experience a range of emotional reactions.

5. A combination of increasingly uncomfortable emotions associated with not meeting interpersonal needs, building frustration with ineffective interpersonal behaviors, corrective emotional experiencing, consensual validation, and increasing confidence in the group's caring and support leads members to make decisions to change. At this point, members clearly understand that what they are doing is not working and that they need to do something differently.

6. When members decide to change, they become open to input, ask for input, and more openly share their emotions and experiences in the group. The input of others educates members about alternative interpersonal behaviors that could meet their needs more effectively.

7. Members experiment with alternative interpersonal behaviors, receive feedback to see how well these behaviors meet their needs, and affect other members.

8. As members continue to use and become adept with effective interpersonal behaviors, they experience satisfying relationships in the group.

9. As relationships with other members become more satisfying, members strengthen their perceptions of self-worth and alter limiting interpersonal perceptions.

10. As members become more proficient with interpersonal behaviors and satisfied with their relationships in group, they experience more satisfying relationships outside group. At the same time, perceptions of self-worth grow, and distorted interpersonal perceptions are corrected.

CONCLUSION

Leaders who employ theories designed for group counseling and therapy have distinct advantages over leaders who use theory designed for individual counseling or therapy. These advantages include having a means to simplify observation of group interaction, conceptualizing an effective group environment, understanding the processes and advantages of members learning from each other, and having a structure that provides a framework for conceptualizing interventions and intervention objectives. Each of these advantages is a clear reason why individual theories are deficient in the group setting.

Leaders whose practice utilizes these approaches are working on a solid foundation. The themes described in this chapter represent a "theoretical consensus" about group dynamics and how members change in the group setting. Leaders who base their practice on these themes lead with the knowledge that they are working with perspectives developed from group counseling and therapy research and the experiences of theorists who practice group counseling and therapy.

Leading Groups

Section 2 describes how leaders can use the principles and theories presented in Section 1 to lead groups. Chapter 8, "Organization and Operation," addresses the practical procedures and issues leaders confront as they design and implement their groups. The chapter offers practical and theoretically based ideas on planning, member selection, group composition, member preparation, operating guidelines, open group issues, coleadership, and leading solo.

Chapter 9, "Interactive Group Leadership," discusses essential leadership roles and functions and addresses the choices leaders have when considering their leadership style.

Chapter 10, "Basic Skills and Interventions," presents fundamental leadership skills for facilitating interpersonal learning and includes examples for the use of these skills. The chapter discusses leadership skills along with some important, theoretically grounded ideas leaders should consider when deciding how to intervene in their groups.

Chapter 11, "Developing Effective Group Membership Skills," describes the skills that members need to optimize their opportunities for interpersonal learning. The chapter describes skills for effective communication, self-disclosure, feedback, and experimentation and how leaders can help members develop these skills. In addition, the chapter provides leaders with a model for facilitating effective feedback exchange.

The primary emphasis of chapter 12, "Ongoing Leadership Tasks," is how leaders can build a productive group environment. The ongoing task of building a productive group environment includes helping members develop a group environment that can maximize their learning opportunities and chances of success.

Chapter 13, "Intervention Strategies," describes more involved leadership strategies. These strategies are designed to increase the effectiveness of groups as social systems. An especially important section in the chapter addresses how leaders can conceptualize and intervene in the social issues that emerge in their groups. The content of the chapter is the product of the author's experience as a leader and a supervisor of group counselors and therapists. Most of the content of the chapter has not appeared in the literature.

Finally, chapter 14, "Becoming a Group Leader," discusses the process of becoming a group leader. The chapter challenges leaders and prospective leaders to confront personal and professional issues involved in becoming an effective group leader.

CHAPTER 8

Organization and Operation

OBJECTIVES

After reading this chapter, you should be able to:

✔ Outline planning decisions and discuss the implications that the various types of counseling and therapy groups have for these decisions.

✔ Explain how to recruit, screen, and prepare group members and the importance of group composition.

✔ Describe essential group operating guidelines and how to implement them.

✔ Discuss how to manage open groups.

✔ Explain the benefits and issues associated with coleading and leading solo, how to work effectively with a coleader, and some supportive strategies for leading solo.

✔ Describe how to start and end group sessions.

✔ Discuss termination issues and strategies for termination.

INTRODUCTION

Leaders perform a number of tasks related to the organization and operation of their groups. Such tasks include group planning, member selection, group composition, using essential group guidelines, managing open groups, maintaining productive coleadership relationships, and terminating groups and members. By carefully performing these organization and operation tasks, leaders can form groups that function with minimal distractions. Groups function more effectively when leaders and members do not have to deal with the annoyances created by planning oversights, member selection and group composition errors, and the problems that emerge because of unstated policies.

PLANNING

Planning is the first step in developing a productive group. When a leader or coleaders decide to form a group, the decisions made about group size, type, duration, and composition set the tone for what will follow.

Planning Decisions

Group type, size, and duration are systemically related; decisions about one influence all the others. For example, a group scheduled to last eight sessions will not function effectively if it is unstructured, is open to new members after it begins, and includes a heterogeneous membership of 12. In this case, the group is most likely to be effective if it has moderate structure, a theme focus, and a homogeneous membership and is closed to new members once it commences. An example of this form of group is an 8-week group designed to develop assertiveness skills with 10 adults who have difficulty expressing anger. This group would provide didactic input and skill building designed to help members learn how to communicate needs and preferences effectively. Thus, as leaders plan groups, they should make a series of careful decisions that dictate the type, size, and duration of the groups they will offer. These decisions determine the potential effectiveness of the prospective group.

Leaders' first decisions involve assessing their resources. Such decisions include scheduling and space availability and the length of time leaders can commit to the proposed group. Leaders must clearly define their commitment when making time and scheduling decisions. Limited time and conflicting scheduling demands should cause leaders to question the wisdom of committing to a long-term or open-ended group. Leaders who decide that they can make a long-term commitment also need to guarantee the availability of a suitable physical space. Leaders are ready to make decisions about the type and size of their group once they have made time and scheduling decisions and determine they have space availability.

Leaders should plan groups that accommodate their resources. Leaders with limited time should consider shorter, more structured groups and recruit memberships that are more homogeneous. The principle here is that groups should become more theme focused and structured as time becomes more limited. Groups planned for 6 to 8 weeks, for example, are most likely to be effective if they include some structured experiences and instruction and are designed to serve a specific population of potential members. As available time increases, progressively less structured and more process-focused groups become better options.

As leaders plan their groups, they should be aware of alternative group types and formats. Besides ranging in duration, groups vary in terms of structure, openness to adding members, and membership size. Most groups are **time limited**, meaning that they have a predetermined concluding date, whereas more rarely occurring **open-ended** or **ongoing groups** have no predetermined conclusion.

Open-ended groups occur in settings such as treatment facilities that have groups scheduled on a year-round basis. Occasionally, open-ended groups operate in outpatient or private practice settings. **Long-term time-limited groups** commonly last from 30 to 40 sessions. Both open-ended and long-term time-limited groups tend to emphasize group process and interpersonal learning, are commonly unstructured, and tend to have heterogeneous memberships. Ideally, **heterogeneous membership** groups have members whose characteristics mirror the characteristics of the population of the community in which the group convenes. By mirroring the population, these groups enact the social microcosm (Yalom, 1995). In both long-term applications, members terminate before the conclusion of the group when they meet treatment goals. Consequently, these groups are commonly open to new members.

When time-limited groups convene for 20 to 30 weeks, leaders need to make careful decisions regarding group structure, group size, policy regarding openness to new members, and group composition. Although groups of this duration function effectively without a great deal of structure, leaders who form 20- to 30-week-long unstructured groups will be more successful with a homogeneous membership. A **homogeneous membership** means that members share characteristics, such as presenting concerns or demographic profiles. Unstructured process groups for college students dealing with relationship concerns or groups for midlife women considering a major lifestyle change are examples of time-limited homogeneous groups that can be highly successful. These groups, when closed to new members, are more likely to be effective.

Leaders of **time-limited groups** lasting 20 to 30 weeks may consider the addition of new members during initial group meetings, but only if the group is unstructured. Conversely, **structured groups** that feature a sequence of lessons or structured activities have a great deal of difficulty accommodating new members because new members will have missed interaction and content provided in missed sessions. This problem magnifies new members' feelings of being "outsiders." When considering the addition of new members, leaders should consider the interpersonal style of the potential members. Potential members who are reticent and highly anxious in interpersonal situations are not appropriate additions after initial sessions, given the time constraints of these groups.

Short-term groups lasting from 10 to 20 sessions require homogeneous memberships. Groups with homogeneous memberships are usually theme focused, meaning that a common characteristic of the group's members is the group's intervention objective. For example, a grief group designed to help members deal with grief issues includes members who are grieving; a social skills group designed to improve social skills is composed of members who have problems with social skills. Because of the short duration of these groups, it is essential that they remain closed to new members.

Leaders of short-term groups with specific learning objectives should consider the use of structure. Structured groups, as mentioned earlier, feature a planned sequence of lessons and structured activities, such as role plays and group exercises designed to meet specific learning objectives. Structure, however, should be balanced with time for here-and-now interpersonal feedback exchange. Even in shorter short-term structured groups with specific objectives, there are opportunities for interpersonal learning.

Brief groups last from 6 to 10 sessions and use specific learning activities and direct instruction to achieve group goals. For example, leaders of a group that has the objective of improving its members' relationships will plan to share specific information and use role play to practice skills. Because of their time limitations, leaders should close these groups to new members once they begin and should work only with homogeneous memberships (see Table 8.1).

The more leaders want to take the advantage of interpersonal learning, the more they should emphasize a process focus. To take advantage of such a focus, leaders need to think in terms of ongoing or longer time-limited groups with heterogeneous memberships, which can be open to new members. If less time is available, process-focused groups should be closed to new members and have homogeneous memberships. As available time increases, the need to close groups to new members and serve homogeneous memberships diminishes.

Leaders' decisions about the size of their proposed group depend on their previous decisions regarding resources and group type. In general, the literature recommends a range of 5 to 10 members for therapy groups (MacKenzie, 1990; Yalom, 1995). Gladding (1995) indicates that counseling groups are most effective when membership ranges from five to nine members. In groups that have fewer than five members, leaders become increasingly involved in order to encourage interaction. As time passes, because of leaders' increased levels of activity, interaction in groups with less than five members begins to resemble interaction in individual counseling or therapy (MacKenzie, 1990; Yalom, 1995). When membership becomes larger than 10, members lack sufficient time to work on individual concerns (Yalom, 1995). MacKenzie (1990) states that when group membership falls into the range of 15 to 20 members, leaders are unable to attend to individual needs, and the group develops a leader-centered format that closely resembles a classroom setting.

Table 8.1
Group Types and Formats

Duration	Structure	Openness to new members	Membership
Long term, open ended	Low	Open	Heterogeneous
Long term, time limited (30–40 sessions)	Low	Open	Heterogeneous
Time limited (20–30 sessions)	Low	Closed or open initially to select members	Homogeneous
Time limited (10–20 sessions)	Moderate	Closed	Homogeneous
Short term (10–20 sessions)	The longer the duration, the lower the structure, depending on goals	Closed	Homogeneous
Brief (6–10 weeks)	Moderate	Closed	Homogeneous

Ideally, counseling and therapy groups have a membership that ranges from 5 to 10 members. Yalom (1995) considers the ideal group size to be seven or eight members. MacKenzie (1990) considers the ideal membership to be five or seven members because groups that have an odd number of members are less likely to experience the polarizing effects of subgrouping. When making decisions about group size, leaders also should carefully consider their group's objectives and duration.

Brief groups that have specific objectives and include direct instruction can include as many as 10 to 15 members. This is because these groups will be leader centered (i.e., leaders provide information and directions) and do not depend heavily on interpersonal learning to meet group goals. Brief groups designed to include a focus on interpersonal learning are more effective when they include a membership that falls into the ideal range of five to eight members. Brief groups that become less leader centered are effective only with smaller group memberships.

Long-term time-limited closed groups function well with 8 to 10 members. Starting with a group of 10 is a good strategy if leaders anticipate members dropping out of the group and do not want to deal with assimilating new members. Table 8.2 offers some general guidelines for leaders to consider as they plan groups. It illustrates how group type, duration, and structure influence decisions to accept new members or to close the group to new members and suggests the number of members a group can effectively serve.

Another planning consideration is the length of group sessions. In general, group sessions last from an hour to 2 hours, an hour and a half probably being the most common length. When planning the length of a group's session, leaders should consider structure and objectives. Leaders also need to remember that members need time to transition from their daily interactions to the group environment. Groups that last an hour seem to end prematurely, whereas some groups lasting 2 hours seem excessively demanding.

A final consideration regarding length of group sessions and size of a proposed group relates to the ages and special needs of group members. When, for example, composing a group for children, leaders must consider their needs and developmental level. Think in terms of less—less not in terms of process but in terms of group size and duration. Gladding (1995) suggests that groups that last for 20 minutes may be very appropriate for members who are 5 or 6 years old. When planning groups for children and members with special needs, leaders need to explore relevant literature regarding appropriate group size and the duration of a group's sessions.

Recruiting Group Members

The decisions leaders make about the type, size, and duration of the group they are planning establishes whom to recruit for group membership. As stated previously, theme-focused and short-term groups serve a homogeneous membership predetermined by group objectives. Ongoing groups and longer time-limited groups, on the other hand, benefit from a more heterogeneous membership. Even so, in recruiting members for a long-term group, leaders need to articulate a general description of the clientele most appropriate for group membership. For example, leaders recruiting members for a long-term group may state that adults who are nearing termination of

Table 8.2
Group Type and Guidelines for Group Size

Group type, duration, and application	Structure	Open or closed	Members[a]
Long term, open ended Inpatient therapy group	Low	Open to selected new members as members meeting goals terminate	5 to 8
Long term, time-limited (30–40 weeks) Counseling or therapy group for a heterogeneous membership	Low	Closed after initial sessions[b]	5 to 8
Long term, time limited (30–40 weeks) Counseling or therapy group addressing eating disorders with an educational component	Moderate	Closed after initial sessions[b]	8 to 10
Time limited (20–30 weeks) Counseling or therapy group for members diagnosed with depression with an educational component	Moderate	Closed after initial sessions[b]	8 to 10
Time limited (20–30 weeks) A process-focused counseling or therapy group for people addressing relationship issues	Low	Closed after initial sessions[b]	5 to 8
Short term, time limited (10–12 weeks) A counseling group for adolescents dealing with divorce of parents	Moderate	Closed	6 to 10
Short term, time limited (12–20 weeks) A cognitive-behavioral group for depression	High	Closed	8 to 10
Short term, time limited (12–20 weeks) A process focused counseling group for members dealing with the loss of a partner	Low	Closed	5 to 8
Brief, time limited (6–10 weeks) Solution-focused group for members with relationship problems	High	Closed	10 to 15

[a]These are suggestions for adult members. Make adjustments for differing age-groups and population characteristics.
[b]Leaders should carefully screen members for inclusion after the group has commenced. Admission of new members needs to recognize group development issues.

individual counseling and want to improve the quality of their relationships are most likely to benefit from participation.

Leaders can use a variety of methods for announcing their groups and recruiting members. Whether leaders use their referral networks, advertisements, or clients already receiving services in their agencies, they should state the group's objectives and characteristics of appropriate members. In addition, leaders should state that they will interview prospective members before the onset of the group to ensure that the group is the most appropriate form of service. When announcing a group, leaders should also include information about scheduling, fee structure, duration of the group, and information that describes the nature of the procedures to be employed and the expectations of members' participation.

Member Selection, Group Composition, and Member Preparation

Member selection and group composition are critical determinants of group effectiveness. Invariably, however, group leaders working in educational and social service agencies comment on how they are required to include anyone referred to their groups. These leaders protest that they are unable to screen out individuals who are unsuitable for group membership. In contrast to this practice, group literature strongly insists that careful member selection and group composition decisions are both ethically necessary and critical to group effectiveness. Poorly composed groups will experience group development issues significant enough to negate their potential effectiveness.

Dies (1993) makes an important distinction between member selection and group composition. Group composition refers to the composite of the choices leaders make about members to be included in their groups. Member selection, on the other hand, involves a series of individually focused decisions. By focusing too heavily on individual decisions, leaders will make group composition errors. As leaders select members, they should be clear about the "big picture," or composite, of their decisions. For example, a leader who selects members for a group designed to improve relationships is likely to have problems if all the members chosen are withdrawn. Instead, this leader needs to be sure to include a mixture of withdrawn and outgoing members.

As leaders develop a plan for selecting members and composing their groups, they should carefully construct procedures to prepare members for group participation. Pregroup preparation is an educational intervention that explains what individuals should expect from group membership. It is widely recognized as instrumental to effective group functioning, especially in the early stages of group development. In addition, pregroup preparation is an ethical responsibility for group leaders.

Member Selection Criteria.   To comply with ethical standards and standards of practice, leaders must screen potential group members to determine their appropriateness for the group being offered (American Counseling Association [ACA], 1995; Association for Specialists in Group Work [ASGW], 2000a). Defining who is an appropriate member for a group is not a major issue in theme-focused short-term groups because the focus of theme-focused groups generally defines their memberships. In longer groups that stress interpersonal learning with a relatively heterogeneous membership, leaders need to consider selection criteria carefully. Leaders also need to understand that some individuals are clearly not appropriate for group counseling and therapy. Selection criteria for a group thus include qualifications for inclusion and exclusion.

Member selection studies have changed emphasis from diagnostic interviews to assessment procedures that stress the prospective members' ability to function and learn in an interpersonal environment (Dies, 1993). The ultimate aim of pregroup assessment is "establishing the optimal therapeutic 'fit' among the patient, the therapist(s), and the group system" (Dies, 1993, p. 487). Dies notes that although research has not developed highly reliable techniques for predicting success, it has offered a number of useful guidelines for the inclusion of potential members.

Dies (1993, pp. 488–489) discusses six assessment tasks for member selection: (a) intrapersonal diagnosis, (b) interpersonal assessment, (c) motivational appraisal, (d) goal setting, (e) evaluation of expectancies, and (f) initiation of the therapeutic alliance. In essence, Dies suggests that pregroup assessment should evaluate prospective members in terms of their ability to interact and benefit from interaction with others, their motivation for and expectations of treatment, and their ability to be helpful to others. Dies also remarks that member selection ultimately rests on leaders' clinical judgment.

Yalom (1995) also stresses the role of leaders' clinical judgement. He states, "If you discern a deeply rooted unwillingness to accept responsibility for treatment or deeply entrenched unwillingness to enter the group, you should not accept that person as a group therapy patient" (p. 235). Yalom also describes a number of criteria that suggest a person's appropriateness for group membership. First, it is essential to establish that the potential member's concern is interpersonal in nature. Yalom also lists characteristics of unsuccessful individual counseling and therapy clients who are good candidates for group work. Clients who require treatment that involves here-and-now interaction, interpersonal learning processes, emotional immediacy, spontaneity, and relationship-focused work are well suited for group therapy.

Salvendy (1993) also describes a range of criteria for member selection. His fundamental idea is that a person is appropriate for membership when that person demonstrates the ability to function effectively as a group member. He also suggests that leaders consider selection criteria that include motivation for treatment, freedom from scheduling conflicts, and the ability to be productively involved in feedback exchange. Because the problems best addressed in groups are primarily interpersonal, it is important to assess prospective members' commitment to improve their relationships and their motivation to be helpful to others (Salvendy, 1993).

Leaders' considerations of potential group members need to incorporate several essential criteria: the potential member's willingness and ability to engage in interpersonal learning processes, demonstration of problems responsive to interpersonal intervention, motivation for being successful in treatment, and commitment to improving relationships. Screening, however, ultimately relies on the accuracy of leaders' clinical judgment.

Criteria for excluding persons from group membership are irrelevant when leaders have developed adequate criteria for inclusion. Leaders, however, should consider a number of criteria for excluding members for greater specificity in their screening procedures. Exclusion criteria include difficulty managing stimulating environments, acute agitation, persistent hypervigilance and suspiciousness, inflexible denial, antisocial or sociopathic personality features, a schizoid interpersonal style, and pathology that requires intensive long-term treatment (MacKenzie, 1990). In essence, individuals who demonstrate pathology that precludes interpersonal treatment are unsuitable for inclusion in most group applications. Again, the best guide will be the clinical judgment of group leaders.

Conducting the Screening Interview.   Screening interviews provide the means for leaders to gather the information necessary to make decisions about potential members and group composition. These interviews are also the initial step in developing therapeutic relationships and preparing members for group work. Couch (1995) identifies four basic steps for conducting the screening interview: identifying needs, expectations, and commitment; challenging myths and misconceptions; conveying information; and screening. These steps organize screening assessment and initiate the member preparation process.

The first step involves interviewing prospective members about their needs for treatment, expectations about group process, and commitment and motivation for change. This stage helps prospective members clarify their concerns and treatment goals (Couch, 1995). From the leader's perspective, the most important aspect of this phase is to evaluate prospective members' commitment to change. Assessing commitment to change involves questioning prospective members about their motivation and acceptance of responsibility. Prospective members who are self-motivated as opposed to being coerced by others to seek treatment, believe that their participation will be productive, and believe that their participation and progress are their responsibility are ideal candidates for group treatment.

The second step identifies prospective members' assumptions about group participation. Couch believes that individuals who do not have experiences as group members tend to have misconceptions about what being a group member involves. Thus, leaders should listen for erroneous ideas about group participation when they conduct screening interviews. Once leaders identify erroneous assumptions, their goal is to correct these assumptions by offering accurate information. By doing so, leaders initiate the member preparation process.

Leaders provide prospective members with essential information in the third step of the screening interview. Essential information includes expectations for maintaining confidentiality, leaders' ethical obligations for breaking confidentiality (e.g., the requirement to inform authorities about child abuse), and the knowledge that it is impossible to guarantee confidentiality. Finally, leaders must provide informed consent. Section A.7.b.and c. of the ASGW's Best Practices Guidelines (2000a) defines informed consent as follows:

> Group workers provide in oral and written form to prospective members (when appropriate to group type): the professional disclosure statement; group purpose and goals; group participation expectations including voluntary and involuntary membership; role expectations of members and leader(s); policies related to entering and exiting the group; policies governing substance use; policies and procedures governing mandated groups (where relevant); documentation requirements; disclosure of information to others; implications of out-of-group contact or involvement among members; procedures for consultation between group leader(s) and group member(s); fees and time parameters; and potential impacts of group participation. (pp. 2–3)

After providing prospective members with essential information, leaders should obtain written consent from the prospective member or a parent or guardian if the prospective member is a minor. Leaders must clearly convey informed consent and confidentiality information, being certain that prospective members understand this information before their admission to group membership.

The final step of the screening interview involves assessing prospective members' suitability for group membership. Much of the information necessary to make a decision about a prospective member is the result of observation and questioning during the previous phases of the screening interview. Leaders, however, should not hesitate to ask the questions necessary to make informed decisions.

As leaders conclude screening interviews, prospective members should be informed if the group is not suitable for their needs and treatment goals. If another form of service is more appropriate, leaders should be prepared to provide necessary referral information. Members who are appropriate for the group and meet the leaders' needs for group composition should be given the necessary scheduling and location information. Members who are appropriate for the group but do not meet leaders' group composition needs should have several choices, including other forms of treatment, volunteering for a wait list (either for the next group or for admission after the group begins), or referral.

Group Composition.   In general, the more short term and issue focused a group becomes, the more homogeneous the group membership should become (Salvendy, 1993). Yalom (1995) essentially agrees, suggesting that group composition becomes less important when members share a common issue and the group becomes more structured. In contrast, long-term groups that depend on members' interaction and have an insight orientation probably are best composed with a more heterogeneous membership. In the case of longer-term interactively focused groups, composition becomes a critical concern for leaders (Yalom, 1995).

MacKenzie (1990) offers some specific recommendations for the composition of closed time-limited groups. MacKenzie believes that homogeneity is essential for a time-limited group. When members have common issues, they share common experiences and are thus able to develop group cohesion rapidly.

In groups relying on interaction as the primary learning modality, homogeneity of common issues is insufficient for composition decisions (MacKenzie, 1990). When members' interaction becomes important, leaders must also attend to "interactional variety" (MacKenzie, 1990, p. 100). **Interactional variety** emphasizes that group composition decisions should involve balancing members across a number of interactional types. MacKenzie suggests selecting members according to their role types (see chapter 2) to ensure that there is a balance of sociable, structural, and divergent members. The discussions of Schutz's and Bennis and Shepard's group development theories in chapter 3 provide alternative conceptualizations of personality types that also can be used to guide group composition decisions.

A final group composition principle is the "**Noah's Ark Principle**" (MacKenzie, 1990, p. 100). This principle holds that there should be no fewer than two persons of any description. Thus, there should be at least two members of any race, gender, ethnic origin, age-group, sexual preference, or religion.

Salvendy (1993) offers several additional broad principles for composing time-limited groups. First, group members should have a common tolerance for anxiety. A group composed of members who vary in their tolerance for vulnerability, for example, will be continuously conflicted over how personal to be during group interaction. Second, group leaders should consider several compatibility issues, one of which is the fit between members and leaders' styles. Members who demand structure and indicate the need for intensive instruction are not a good match for leaders who use less structured interactive approaches. Leaders should also consider members' compatibility. Groups composed of members who range widely in their "psychological mindedness" or motivation for treatment are not likely to interact effectively.

Group composition decisions, when made thoughtfully, can accelerate the development and the effectiveness of groups. Authors do vary, however, in their opinions about how to compose groups and even how concerned to be about group composition. Yalom (1995) believes that leaders should employ only the most general principles of balancing age and gender along with how energetically members might participate. Whitaker and Lieberman (1964) believe that it is crucial to select members who can tolerate similar levels of anxiety and vulnerability. Group development theorists (Bennis & Shepard, 1956; Schutz, 1966) contend that personality styles and how successfully members have confronted developmental issues are essential to making sound composition choices. There is no divergence, however, in authors' opinions that it is unacceptable to include members who are not suitable for participation as members.

Member Preparation.   Group counseling and therapy texts consistently advocate pregroup member preparation. Research on the effectiveness of member preparation, however, is not definitive. Both Dies (1993) and Piper (1993) state that the limited research describing the effects of member preparation on group outcome is not persuasive. Research, however, does establish that pregroup preparation has a number of important effects on member participation during initial sessions. These effects include improved attendance, reduced dropout rates, increased motivation, enhanced feedback exchange, and increased self-disclosure (Dies, 1993; Piper, 1993). Sklare, Keener, and Mas (1990) also point out that pregroup preparation reduces new members' anxiety during initial sessions, improves participation, and increases group cohesion and interaction. According to research and the consensus of authors in the field, pregroup preparation makes important contributions to group interaction.

Member preparation can be an integral part of the screening process with individuals or the focus of a group meeting held prior to the start of the group after screening and composition decisions have been made (MacKenzie, 1990). When preparing members for group participation, leaders can employ a variety of educational and experiential approaches to orient members to group membership. In performing preparation tasks, leaders should be careful not to initiate therapeutic work before the group commences.

The information to provide members in pregroup preparation includes expectations of group members (Couch, 1995; Levine, 1991; MacKenzie, 1990, 1994; Sklare et al., 1990), the role of group leaders (Couch, 1995; MacKenzie, 1994; Sklare et al., 1990), the group therapy process (Couch, 1995; MacKenzie, 1994; Sklare et al., 1990), group development issues (Couch, 1995; Dies, 1991; Sklare et al., 1990), essential group norms (Couch, 1995; Sklare et al., 1990), and how to get the most from group participation (Couch, 1995; MacKenzie, 1990, 1994; Sklare et al., 1990).

Pregroup preparation should address fears about group participation. By encouraging members to share their apprehensions about group membership and then addressing these fears, leaders help members lower their anxiety about becoming group members. Levine (1991) describes several common fears for new group members. Perhaps the most common fear is that confidentiality will be broken. To address this fear, leaders must acknowledge that although they cannot guarantee confidentiality, it is seldom a problem because members can choose what they disclose. This means that members make their choices about what to disclose on the basis of a growing mutual trust among members.

Other typical fears for new group members are being embarrassed by disclosing why they are joining the group and the feelings they are experiencing. In addition, fears of rejection and being intimate with others are common. To address these fears, leaders should reassure new members that most new members share these fears and they will deal with these fears as the group develops. Leaders should also indicate that group members work together to overcome these fears in order to instill hope (Levine, 1991).

When leaders integrate pregroup preparation into their individual screening sessions, they should keep three primary objectives in mind. First, they need to provide information about group counseling or therapy and describe what members should expect from group participation. Along with their verbal descriptions, leaders can provide printed materials designed to educate members about group counseling and therapy and the procedures used to help members change (e.g., interpersonal feedback, experimentation with new behaviors, consensual validation, and so on). Leaders should repeat this information freely during initial sessions to ensure members understand (MacKenzie, 1990). Second, leaders should elicit and address fears members may have about group participation (Levine, 1991). Third, potential members should be oriented to interpersonal learning, or, as MacKenzie (1994) puts it, members need to be primed for an interpersonal focus. Members are primed when leaders, during preparation, direct members to reflect on their significant relationships and describe the impact of these relationships on their lives. Leaders then point out how group process successfully addresses the impact of these relationships and elicits change.

Leaders who utilize group meetings for pregroup preparation have the same goals as individual screening sessions. Group preparation sessions, however, can employ experiential methods along with the instruction used to orient members in individual pregroup preparation sessions. MacKenzie (1990) suggests using structured experiences during pregroup meetings in which members first introduce themselves to orient them to what it will be like to self-disclose during initial sessions. Second, leaders ask members to express interpersonal goals (e.g., asking members to share one way that they would like to improve their interpersonal relationships) to orient members to interpersonal learning. Leaders process these experiences by initiating discussion of what these experiences were like for members and by describing how these experiences are similar to group interaction.

With either group or individual approaches, leaders need to ensure that new members clearly understand what to expect from group membership. It is critical that new members know how groups help members and how interpersonal learning processes provide this help. Finally, pregroup preparation should address the fears that individuals have about becoming group members and prime new members for interpersonal learning. The reassurance leaders provide reduces new members' anxieties and develops positive expectations about group participation.

ESSENTIAL OPERATING GUIDELINES

Leaders should implement several essential guidelines as they begin their groups. These guidelines should be part of the ground rules leaders present during a group's initial meeting and the information leaders discuss during screening and pregroup preparation meetings. These guidelines are prohibition of physical or psychological harm, confidentiality, limits on out-of-group socializing, and boundaries for leaders' relationships with members.

Prohibition of Physical or Psychological Harm

Group leaders should be extremely clear that members shall not harm each other. Leaders must unambiguously specify absolute prohibitions against verbal abuse and physical assault. Leaders also must clearly state that they will remove members immediately who harm others.

The prohibition of psychological harm is often an issue with members who lack the interpersonal and self-management skills necessary to express their anger appropriately. Leaders should be careful in selecting these individuals for group membership. When these individuals become verbally abusive, leaders must decide whether they should discontinue these members' participation in the group. Clearly, leaders should remove these members when they do not respond to feedback and instruction about more appropriate interpersonal behaviors and continue to be verbally abusive.

Confidentiality

Prospective members must understand the importance of confidentiality and the impossibility of guaranteeing it. During pregroup meetings, leaders also should inform members of the circumstances in which leaders are ethically and legally obligated to break confidentiality. Once the group begins, leaders must reiterate confidentiality policies and ensure that members understand these policies.

Confidentiality is essential for the development of a group's external boundaries and members' trust in each other. Leaders should encourage members to build trust incrementally. Members need to recognize that trust grows on the basis of their observations of others' reactions to disclosures that are progressively intimate. Chapter 11's discussion of self-disclosure as a membership skill provides useful suggestions for how leaders can present the idea of disclosing progressively intimate material to build trust. Once members trust each other, the issue of confidentiality subsides. In addition, the risk of members breaking confidentiality diminishes as members deepen their trust in each other and as group cohesion builds.

When presenting the requirement for maintaining confidentiality, leaders should state a confidentiality policy. This policy should clearly define what happens if a member breaks confidentiality. A policy stating that members will be immediately terminated from the group if they break confidentiality is recommended. By deciding on a policy before the group begins, stating and reiterating this policy in pre-group meetings and in the initial group session, and upholding this policy, leaders establish a clear boundary. Leaders should understand, however, that even in the case of clearly stated boundaries, circumstances find a way to make these policies feel ambiguous.

In contrast to a specific policy, some leaders, on hearing of a breach in confidentiality, will share that confidentiality has been broken with the group. They will then leave the matter up to the group, allowing members to decide the fate of the offending member. This approach places excessive pressure on the group and can be punishing for the member who has broken the group's confidence. Members, if given the responsibility for making this decision, confront their own concerns about exclusion and acceptability, causing the group to resurrect early group development issues. If members decide to allow the offending member to remain in the group, trust issues will emerge that can stall group progress. Leaders must take responsibility for dealing with a member who has broken confidentiality.

Limits on Out-of-Group Socializing

Clear boundaries must also be set for extragroup socializing, which occurs when members meet together outside of group meeting times. Leaders, while acknowledging that they cannot prevent extragroup socializing, should discuss the effects that such socializing has on group functioning.

Extragroup socializing has two prominent negative influences on group functioning. First, when members discuss their group experience outside the group, they avoid discussing issues in group that can be productive learning experiences for the entire membership. This takes energy from group interaction and may resolve issues in a nonproductive manner. For example, Jack has a strong reaction to Phyllis and discusses this reaction outside the group with Jane. If this discussion results in Jack being convinced by Jane to not share this reaction in the group (e.g., "Oh, her. Everyone has the same reaction"), Phyllis does not receive potentially valuable feedback, and Jack is deprived of an opportunity to confront one of his own concerns.

Extragroup socializing becomes a group issue when members develop relationships with each other outside the group and form a subgroup around a group issue. This form of subgrouping appears when members protect each other or present a unified stand on a group issue. An illustration is when two members meet outside the group because they share a similar reaction to having to share emotions in group. These members attempt to rescue each other from having to share emotions and unite to confront group pressure to share emotions.

Leaders should realize that extragroup socializing is inevitable, especially in longer-term groups. In spite of this, leaders should present the boundary that extragroup socializing is not acceptable, arguing that it reduces members' learning opportunities, lessens the energy of group interaction, and slows group progress.

Boundaries for Leaders' Relationships with Members

For ethical reasons, leaders must not have social relations with group members. Other interactions, however, are not as clear-cut. Leaders should set relationship boundaries with members for between-session processing, concurrent individual therapeutic relationships, and discussing members' conflicts with other members. Whenever leaders interact with members between group meetings, there is potential to interfere with group interaction and progress.

Between-group processing occurs when members initiate conversation or pose seemingly harmless questions to leaders about what occurred in a group session. Statements like "Well, that was certainly an amazing session" or questions like "How do you think I handled the way she attacked me?" can lead to counterproductive interaction. Interaction with members between sessions is counterproductive whenever it allows members to discuss any concern that can be handled in group. Because it is easy to become engaged in counterproductive conversation, leaders need to be clear about their boundaries and what interactions are most appropriate for the group. Conversations in which a member addresses an issue that concerns group interactions, other members, or interpersonal concerns are most appropriate for group sessions.

Concurrent individual therapeutic relationships with group members can be appropriate. Leaders, however, need to be clear that these relationships usually complicate their relationships with members and have several negative group outcomes. Members frequently view members who have individual sessions out of the group with leaders as having special relationships with leaders. Here, feelings of resentment and the belief that those seeing leaders are receiving special treatment emerge. Members seen as having a special relationship with leaders often find themselves in the difficult position of having to defend the extra time they have with leaders. Leaders are also in a difficult position, having to justify seeing a member outside group and to explain that seeing a member outside group is not offering that member "special" treatment. To add to these complications, leaders have to avoid sharing individual session material in group. Having to be careful not to share information that emerges in individual sessions in group interferes with leaders' spontaneity and choice of interventions. In addition, members seeing leaders outside group will invariably discuss their group experiences. Such discussion in individual sessions creates two problems: a blurring of the boundaries between the complicated member/leader and counselor/client dual relationships and the potential for resolving group issues outside the group. Because of these complications, leaders and members are better off not seeing each other in concurrent individual sessions.

Leaders should specifically state that they will not discuss what has occurred in group outside group. Often members are motivated to discuss their concerns with leaders out of group because they find the anxiety of directly addressing these concerns in group overwhelming. By discussing members' concerns out of group, leaders collude with members to avoid potentially powerful learning experiences. Leaders should understand the consequences of interacting with members outside group and avoid doing so unless circumstances, such as frank suicidal ideation, dictate.

MANAGING OPEN GROUPS

Groups open to new members present difficult challenges to group leaders and members. The addition of new members causes initial group development issues to recycle and negates leaders' efforts to establish functional external boundaries. The frequent addition of new members challenges ongoing members because they revisit issues related to developing trust and defining their role in the group. Because members revisit early group development issues, they are much less likely to face crucial group development issues that surface during later stages of development. Most authors (e.g., MacKenzie, 1990) agree that short-term groups should be closed to new members once they have commenced.

Leaders of groups face difficulties when unfortunate realities like agency policies or a rapidly changing patient census do not permit closing their groups to new members. Groups in settings that require the inclusion of new members are likely to experience the cyclic problem of including new members followed by group dropouts followed by more new members. These cyclic problems lead to groups that never seem to develop the cohesion necessary for productive interpersonal work.

Group Development Issues

When members' concerns about belonging and trust recycle, their opportunities to learn from interactions in a more highly developed group evaporate. This means that members will address issues related to belonging, trust, and depth of involvement when the group begins and will address these issues again each time a new member joins the group. Occasionally, members will become frustrated with their slow progress and angrily confront leaders for not making the group a place safe enough to express their concerns. In more structured groups, members will develop a sense of frustration about having to review information from previous sessions to bring new members "up to speed." Developmentally, groups that regularly accept new members die of arrested growth in initial stages.

Coping with Open Groups: Realistic Goals

Open groups are a major challenge for group leaders. The challenge is how to help members learn in a context that recycles early group development concerns. Unfortunately, the best answer, closing groups to new members, is unacceptable in some settings. To deal with members not being able to resolve and move beyond initial stage issues, leaders need to utilize a structured group approach and lower their expectations for what the group can accomplish.

A necessary compromise might be a structured approach that uses group activities and instruction in which each session's content and skills are independent of the content or skills developed in other sessions. These independent sessions are thematically related stand-alone "workshops." For example, a leader may develop a series of structured activities designed to enhance members' relationship skills. Sessions could include experiential exercises in clear communication, giving feedback, sharing feelings, communicating assertively, using responsible language, and other related activities.

Leaders who conduct groups that accept new members on a frequent basis need to lower their expectations for the depth of member involvement and the impact of interpersonal learning. Leaders must identify meaningful and realistic goals and believe that these goals offer members significant help in spite of the limitations of their group's open format. In addition, leaders should not abandon paying attention to process, identifying members' relationship issues, encouraging the use of interpersonal feedback, and providing opportunities to process members' interactions.

Ideally, leaders should not consider the inclusion of a new member when a group is dealing with critical developmental issues, such as a crisis in trust or the definition of external boundaries. In addition, leaders should consider the suitability of potential new members in terms of their treatment needs and interpersonal style. A potential member who struggles with being open with others and is not "psychologically minded" is not an appropriate candidate, especially for a short-term group nearing its conclusion or a time-limited group in its final 10 weeks.

COLEADERSHIP

Coleadership involves two group leaders in a supportive yet challenging relationship. Most authors believe effective coleader relationships have a powerful impact on group members and are an important tool for leadership training (Dies, 1994; Yalom, 1995). The literature reflects authors' preferences, as there is little evidence to support the efficacy of coleadership relative to solo leadership. Most authors prefer coleading to leading solo and encourage the use of group coleadership.

In general, the literature does not use as much ink pointing out the issues and the added demands associated with coleadership as it does in indicating the benefits of coleadership. Individuals considering coleading a group should not jump to the conclusion that coleadership is "easier," and they should make an informed decision about coleading. Included in this decision should be awareness of the benefits and issues of coleading and what is required to develop and maintain a highly effective coleader relationship. When considering a coleadership relationship, leaders also need to be clear about the impact of coleader relationship dynamics on group process.

Coleadership Benefits

In general, the literature agrees that coleadership offers specific benefits to both beginning and more experienced practitioners (Dies, 1994; MacKenzie, 1990; Roller & Nelson, 1993; Yalom, 1995). One benefit is the ongoing learning opportunity provided by coleader peer supervision (Roller & Nelson, 1993; Yalom, 1995). Another advantage is that coleaders have separate points of view that help them generate more intervention possibilities for difficult group issues, thus increasing the chance of success (MacKenzie, 1990; Roller & Nelson, 1993; Yalom, 1995). An effective coleader relationship also offers coleaders mutual support that includes acknowledgment for effective work. Acknowledgment leads to increased job satisfaction, provides emotional support, prevents burnout, and prevents feelings of isolation (Roller & Nelson, 1993; Yalom, 1995). Coleaders have the advantage of being able to perform complementary roles during group sessions. For example, while one leader intervenes, the other can monitor group reactions (MacKenzie, 1990; Yalom, 1995). In addition, coleaders can help each other examine reactions to group members that interfere with their effectiveness and ability to maintain objectivity (Roller & Nelson, 1993; Yalom, 1995).

Dies (1994), MacKenzie (1990), and Yalom (1995) describe benefits and issues encountered by group leaders in training who work with coleaders. When working with experienced leaders, leaders in training benefit from immediate feedback and the modeling of experienced leaders. At the same time, leaders in training invariably encounter feelings that they cannot possibly measure up to the competence of more experienced coleaders (Dies, 1994; MacKenzie, 1990; Yalom, 1995). In contrast, when coleaders in training lead with each other, they experience mutual support that diffuses some of the anxiety of learning to lead groups (Dies, 1994; MacKenzie, 1990; Yalom, 1995).

Coleadership provides a number of benefits for group members as well. When coleaders have a well-functioning, egalitarian relationship, their work together is a model for members who struggle in their relationships (Roller & Nelson, 1993; Yalom, 1995). In addition, female and male coleaders allow members to address family-of-origin issues and confront authority issues with persons of the opposite sex (MacKenzie, 1990; Roller & Nelson, 1993; Yalom, 1995).

Coleadership Issues

Issues surfacing in coleader relationships have a negative effect on group functioning. One of the most common issues is competition between coleaders (MacKenzie, 1990; Roller & Nelson, 1993; Yalom, 1995). Competition between coleaders surfaces in a variety of ways. Some examples are competition over who is the most "gifted" leader, who is most liked by members, who is "right," and who should "be in charge." When coleaders compete with each other, their groups often polarize (MacKenzie, 1990), splitting into factions and aligning themselves with one of the coleaders. Polarization around coleaders becomes a thorny issue when leaders disagree and members take sides.

Another issue related to coleader competition emerges when coleaders have conflicting theoretical orientations (Roller & Nelson, 1993; Yalom, 1995). Conflicting theoretical orientations create problems during group sessions when coleaders conceptualize interaction and necessary interventions differently. Between sessions, conflicting theoretical orientations make it difficult to plan for subsequent sessions because the leaders have different objectives. Before agreeing to form a coleader relationship, prospective coleaders should understand the need to use a compatible theory to conceptualize group interaction and interventions. Coleaders who believe in different theories will have to work very hard to develop a shared description of what is occurring in group and reach agreement on intervention objectives and strategies.

Closely related to conflicting theoretical orientations is confusion and poor communication during and between group sessions (Roller & Nelson, 1993; Yalom, 1995). Often, confusion and poor communication is evidence of a disagreement over how to conceptualize group interaction and interventions. During a session, confusion and poor communication often result in leaders using conflicting interventions that are confusing to members who have to shift topics abruptly and follow different lines of exploration.

Between sessions, poor communication leads to conflict and misunderstandings that, when not related to conflicting perspectives, are usually the result of coleaders not expending sufficient energy to communicate their perspectives clearly.

To maintain a collaborative relationship, coleaders must have clear relationship boundaries. Issues emerge when the coleaders have confusing, diffuse, or impermeable relationship boundaries (Roller & Nelson, 1993; Yalom, 1995). Coleaders with overly diffuse boundaries are reluctant to be honest with each other for fear of offending the other. When their boundaries are too diffuse, coleaders also will be reluctant to confront group issues that resemble the issues experienced in the coleaders' relationship (MacKenzie, 1990). Impermeable boundaries in coleader relationships are also unproductive, making effective communication highly unlikely. Consequently, issues that adversely influence coleader relationships cannot be addressed.

Coleading requires effective communication and coordination of efforts. These demands require coleaders to attend to their relationship. If the coleader relationship is not sound, coleaders will spend excessive energy attending to their relationship during group sessions. For example, coleaders who compete over whose conceptualization of group dynamics is most correct will focus on proving who is right during the group session. The result is that coleaders, at one time or another, miss important group issues (MacKenzie, 1990). An effective coleader relationship is critical if group interaction, not the coleader relationship, is to be the focus of the coleaders' attention during group sessions.

The literature maintains that only effective coleader relationships have a positive effect on groups (MacKenzie, 1990). Yalom (1995) offers sound advice when considering forming a coleader relationship: "You are far better off leading a solo group with good supervision than being locked into an incompatible cotherapy relationship" (p. 417).

Coleader Relationships and Group Issues

Groups led by coleaders experience the benefits of coleadership and the complications of the coleaders' relationship dynamics. Coleaders must acknowledge potential complications when they plan their groups. In particular, they should discuss how they want learning to occur.

When coleaders discuss how they want learning to occur in their group, they should discuss how members should be involved in group interaction. Coleaders who emphasize interpersonal learning as opposed to direct instruction as the primary learning modality will most likely agree that the quality of members' interactions essentially determines what is to be learned in their group. Coleaders who agree that members' interactions are essential need to evaluate how they are willing to communicate in their relationship.

In supervision, coleaders are often surprised when asked how the issues they describe in group interaction are transpiring in their relationship. Invariably, if the coleaders are honest, they will identify similar if not identical issues in their relationship. For example, coleaders who complain that members persistently avoid sharing emotions will acknowledge that they have avoided sharing emotions in their coleader relationship. Coleaders are commonly unable to help group members confront issues that they are unwilling to confront in their relationship.

Developing a coleader relationship requires a great deal of energy. First, each coleader must invest the energy necessary to ensure clear and complete communication. Second, coleaders should seriously commit to offering and receiving honest feedback. To do so, each coleader must be willing to approach difficult issues, such as one coleader's perception that the other is dominating interaction, is excessively judgmental, or is not open to hearing a different perspective. Third, effective coleader relationships require emotional honesty and openness. Each leader must be willing to develop a highly effective interpersonal relationship and encounter the emotions and awkward situations that this involves.

Working Together in and out of Group

When coleaders begin working together, they should develop a clear understanding of their working relationship in and out of group. Roller and Nelson (1993) contend that coleaders should explicitly address a number of factors as they initiate the process of developing their relationship. Relationship factors coleaders should discuss include theoretical orientation, preferred activity level and leadership style, leadership strengths and weaknesses, relationship issues that may potentially interfere, how they should communicate in group, and how they should support each others' interventions. Coleaders also should agree on out-of-group working relationship factors, including time for postgroup processing, planning time, supervision time, and most important a commitment to dealing with coleader relationship issues.

Postgroup Processing

One of the greatest advantages of coleadership is the opportunity for postgroup processing. Ideally, coleaders will spend time discussing their experiences during a group session immediately after the conclusion of the session (Dies, 1994). Postgroup processing involves coleaders discussing their experiences and perceptions of members' interactions and their work together. This time also should include the exchange of coleader feedback.

Planning Time

Planning involves making a number of decisions before the group convenes for the first meeting and making decisions between sessions about the following session.

Planning interventions and strategies requires coleader agreement on what needs to happen for the group to function most effectively. After coleaders agree on possible interventions and strategies, they need to agree on plans for working together in the next session. Planning time can be included in supervision, postgroup processing, or coleader tape review sessions. Coleaders should recognize the need to make plans and, at the same time, understand the need to be flexible enough to respond to changes in group interaction that dictate acting differently.

Supervision

Coleaders should seriously consider their needs for supervision. Some coleaders choose to obtain supervision, while others choose to review videotapes of their sessions, obtain occasional consultation, or depend solely on postsession processing. Whatever the choice or choices, coleaders should be aware of the advantages and limitations of each option.

Coleaders who choose supervision have several important advantages over coleaders who do not. First, supervision offers coleaders feedback about relationship issues of which they may be unaware. For example, coleaders may not be aware that they avoid confronting certain issues in their relationship or that one coleader defers to the other. Second, a supervisor offers coleaders conceptualizations of group interaction and interventions from the perspective of a person who is not involved in the group or in the coleadership relationship. Finally, the supervisor is a third party who can help coleaders resolve relationship issues.

The competence and courage of the supervisor are critical if coleaders are to benefit from supervision. Supervision from a supervisor who is unwilling to confront coleaders' relationship issues or who is not sufficiently knowledgeable about group theory and dynamics is likely to waste coleaders' time. Coleaders also will not profit from work with a supervisor who has limited knowledge of group work because of the supervisor's limited ability to help coleaders diagnose group issues, apply theory, and develop interventions. Conversely, supervision from a supervisor who is an experienced leader willing to confront coleader relationship issues and is expert in applying group theory and dynamics principles can be extremely productive for coleaders.

The next-best option to receiving competent supervision is reviewing group tapes. Coleaders who meet to process their group experiences and review the tape of a session shortly after the conclusion of a session can find this process productive. Prior to beginning the tape review process, coleaders should agree on the process of their review sessions. This agreement should specify what feedback to exchange, which theory to use to conceptualize group interactions, how to use session videotapes, and some form of session closure.

In addition, coleaders should consider the content of their tape review sessions. Possible content includes emotional reactions, perceptions, significant group events, the coleaders' working relationship, and impressions of members and their relationships. Agreeing to content and process avoids confusion and establishes a plan that ensures the sharing and processing of important information.

Coleaders should also set clear boundaries regarding feedback exchange during postgroup meetings. Coleaders who emphasize feedback regarding their interventions should be careful not to set limits that restrict feedback that can help develop their relationship. To be effective, coleaders need to process personal reactions to group events and each other. For example, a coleader who is angry with her coleader because he controls interaction will feel controlled and may withdraw unless she can process reactions with her coleader. Coleaders using the feedback model discussed in chapter 12 have a format that allows them to address personal reactions in a productive fashion. If coleaders elect to preclude personal reactions from postgroup sessions, they ignore issues that significantly influence their work together.

When coleaders plan postgroup processing sessions, they should discuss how they will use theory. A recommended process involves three steps:

1. Each coleader describes his or her perception of what occurred in group interaction.
2. Coleaders reach an agreement about the most significant events in group interaction.
3. Coleaders define these events in terms of the theory they are using.

Once coleaders have conceptualized interaction according to their theory, they should agree on some general goals for the next session. Examples of such goals can be as simple as working harder to direct members to address group focal conflicts or as complicated as developing a strategy to help members develop role flexibility. Once plans are complete, coleaders should attend to relationship building.

Coleader relationship building involves several important elements. First, coleaders should exchange feedback. Although coleaders often are hesitant to be completely forthcoming with their feedback, they are eventually better off by being completely open. Second, coleaders should completely process each other's feedback. Finally, coleaders need to agree on how to act on each other's feedback during the next group session.

Figure 8.1 describes a recommended process for postgroup processing and tape review sessions. When leaders have time, they can experiment with using the process during a single meeting. If time is limited, coleaders should process immediately after the session; reviewing the tape and relationship building can be done at another time prior to the subsequent session.

The effectiveness of coleaders' postgroup processing and tape review sessions depends on the effectiveness of the coleader relationship and the coleaders' knowledge and experience. Coleaders who experience issues related to conflicting perspectives, exchanging feedback, or communication are not likely to benefit from viewing tapes or postgroup processing; their relationship precludes it. In addition, inexperienced coleaders having limited understanding of group dynamics and theory will experience less substantial benefits from reviewing tapes.

Coleaders should use consultation when they reach an impasse in the groups they lead or become aware that they are having coleader relationship issues they cannot resolve. Coleaders who are unable to receive ongoing supervision should consider consultation in combination with postgroup processing and tape reviews. This can contribute significantly to coleader development.

Coleaders who do not receive supervision, review videotapes, process postgroup, or use consultation neglect opportunities to improve the quality of the

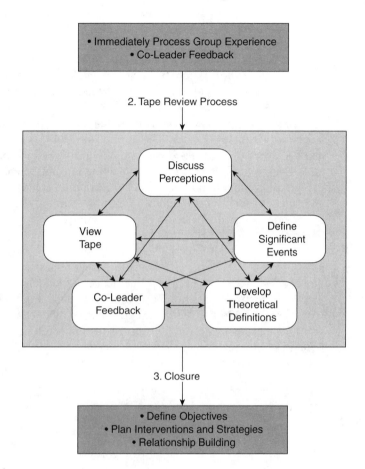

1. Initial Processing

• Immediately Process Group Experience
• Co-Leader Feedback

2. Tape Review Process

Discuss
Perceptions

View
Tape

Define
Significant
Events

Co-Leader
Feedback

Develop
Theoretical
Definitions

3. Closure

• Define Objectives
• Plan Interventions and Strategies
• Relationship Building

Figure 8.1
Recommended Postgroup Processing and Tape Review Session Process

groups they offer. Taking advantage of options to review group sessions is possibly less critical in highly structured short-term groups. Coleaders of these groups, however, should be clear that their groups will be more productive if they take time to reflect on their practice. Coleaders who attend to their relationship and take time to process sessions will inevitably provide more effective groups than coleaders who do not.

Dealing with Coleader Relationship Issues

Effective coleader relationships require commitment to resolving relationship issues because issues that remain unresolved in the coleader relationship invariably surface in group interaction. For example, coleaders who hesitate to exchange honest feedback invariably communicate, in some indirect way, this issue to group members. The result is that group interaction will begin to mirror the coleaders' issues.

An illustration of how coleaders' relationship issues influence group interaction occurred during a supervision session when coleaders complained how their group seemed to be stalled in its development and that members seemed to avoid exchanging "difficult but beneficial" feedback. The supervisor then asked the coleaders to share the "difficult but beneficial" feedback they have offered each other. The coleaders paused, then began to share some of the feedback they had been exchanging. The supervisor commented that it seemed that this feedback sounded safe and mostly complementary. The supervisor then asked the coleaders to share the feedback they thought about sharing but choose not to share. This conversation led to a discussion of the coleaders' fears about harming their relationship and being regarded as incompetent by the other coleader. Over the next several group sessions, after the coleaders began exchanging more frank and challenging feedback, group interaction became progressively more intense and feedback more "difficult and beneficial."

Because of the isomorphic connection between coleader relationship issues and group issues, coleaders need to explore their relationship frankly to determine how their issues "play out" in group interaction. Coleaders should also pay attention to group issues to see whether these issues are present in their relationship. Once such issues are identified, coleaders need to work diligently to resolve them. Coleaders will find that resolving relationship issues ultimately leads to the resolution of that issue in group interaction.

LEADING SOLO

Leading without a coleader avoids many coleadership issues and allows the fullest expression of a leader's personal style. Leading solo also means that the supportive processes available to coleaders are not immediately available. Without the support of a coleader, leaders are under greater pressure to define and understand group issues and intervene effectively. Solo leaders also have to manage the challenges and occasional attacks of group members without the support of a coleader. Thus, leaders who lead alone must attain higher levels of competence and self-confidence, which result from support, supervision, and experience.

Support and Supervision

Supportive relationships that encourage the exploration of emotional reactions and perceptions help leaders develop confidence in their ability to lead alone. In addition, leaders benefit from supervision when it includes exploration of personal reactions to group interaction and input designed to develop the skills and the conceptual abilities necessary to operate independently.

Colleagues who are experienced group leaders can offer developing leaders important support. Support differs from supervision in that support provides a nonevaluative mentoring relationship where the goals are to listen, offer suggestions, and provide encouragement to the developing leader. Receiving support from colleagues is especially critical when supervision is not available. Developing leaders benefit from discussing their impressions and emotional reactions to the groups they lead and from hearing the encouragement of an experienced and trusted colleague.

Supervision, on the other hand, is a formal hierarchical relationship that establishes roles and expectations for the supervisor and the group leader. Supervision is most commonly a regularly scheduled meeting in which a leader shows a group session videotape. During this meeting, the leader presents an overview of important interactions, a theoretical explanation of the interactions, a description and rationale for interventions, and specific requests for feedback and suggestions.

Supervision provides the supportive mechanism of helping leaders process their emotional reactions and perceptions and makes an active contribution to improving leaders' effectiveness. By watching tape and listening to how leaders conceptualize group interaction and intervene, supervisors can identify developmental needs for skills and theory application along with personal issues that interfere with leaders' effectiveness. Supervision also should help leaders identify what they do well and reinforce their progress. As Yalom (1995) points out, supervision "is the sine qua non in the education of the group therapist" (p. 515).

STARTING AND ENDING GROUP SESSIONS

Starting Sessions

Starting and ending group sessions involves leaders helping members make transitions. At the start of a session, leaders need to help members transition from their customary modes of social interaction to the intensive reflection and interaction of group members. Effective transitioning sets the stage for the work members do during the session. At the end of a session, leaders need to help members achieve "reentry," which helps members capture their learning and become reoriented to social interactions. Starting and ending sessions on time communicates clear leadership boundaries and signifies specific boundaries for starting and ending members' work.

The procedures for starting unstructured and structured groups are very different. In structured groups with specific learning objectives, leaders can begin simply by summarizing what was covered in the previous session and then describing what will be covered in the current session. In unstructured groups, leaders have to help members make the more difficult transition to here-and-now interaction.

Beginning any group's first session is simple because specific procedures are necessary. Here leaders review the group's purposes, procedures, and ground rules that were described in pregroup preparation and begin with a comment regarding members' getting to know each other. At this point, leaders can elect to use a structured approach that directs members to introduce themselves or to use a structured activity that involves more specific instructions. These beginning procedures should also be performed whenever a new member is added to the group.

Later sessions in unstructured groups are different because there is no specific content to cover other than reminding members about some of the preliminary comments made in the first session. As a session begins, leaders may elect to make a starting comment or simply observe how members interact. Making comments about beginning, however, are probably more useful in helping members transition, setting the stage for interpersonal work, and initiating interaction. Leaders can experiment with a number of opening statements to see what works best for the group they are leading. Several examples follow.

LEADER: "There seems to be some discomfort here and some uneasiness about how to get the group started tonight." (observation)

LEADER: "John, it looks like you're really uncomfortable right now. Tell the group what's going on with you." (observation and directive)

LEADER: "Who would like to start tonight?" (question to start the basic facilitation sequence)

LEADER: "How many of you are feeling scared about sharing what's going on with you? Talking about what scares you in here will be helpful." (question and directive)

Asking members to review a previous session or to discuss how they have applied what they learned in a previous session can also work. These approaches, however, are risky for several reasons. First, members can avoid here-and-now interaction by engaging in a historical review of the previous meeting. Second, members can shift to an out-of-group focus. Finally, members frequently respond to requests for reviewing previous sessions or discussing the application of group learning by staring blankly at the group leader; this is seldom helpful.

Ending Sessions

When ending a group session, leaders must remain aware of what is occurring in group interaction and the amount of time remaining in the session. Jacobs, Harvill, and Masson (1998) indicate that as a session approaches its end, all members should have the opportunity to share reactions to what has occurred during the group in order to promote cohesiveness. Also helpful is a process in which members are instructed to talk about what they have learned or what they have experienced during the session (e.g., predominant feelings, personal reaction to interaction, and so on) and not to interact with each other. This procedure provides members a process that marks the end of interpersonal work and transitions members to out-of-group interaction. Depending on the length of the session and the number of members, this process should take from 5 to 10 minutes. However leaders choose to end group sessions, they need to track the amount of time remaining and help members transition from interpersonal work to ending the session.

In transitioning from intensive interpersonal interaction to concluding a group session, leaders should let members know how much time they have left to work. For example, a leader might say, "You need to think about reaching some conclusion to your work. There's about 10 minutes left before we have to wrap up." An alternative procedure is for leaders to take charge of interaction in order to complete members' work. For example, "We have 20 minutes left. Jack, you were having a strong reaction to what Steve just said to you. Share your reaction with him in the form of feedback."

When interaction prior to a group's ending does not involve members in intense interaction, transitioning to the closing of the session is much easier. In this case, leaders might say something like, "We've got about 15 minutes left. So there's time to clarify impressions any of you might have about what happened tonight." This statement transitions to ending and attempts to keep members engaged in potentially useful interactions. With limited time remaining (i.e., 5 to 10 minutes), leaders should be careful not to initiate exchanges that might require more substantial interaction, such as initiating feedback requests and experimenting with new behaviors.

TERMINATION

Termination in some form is inevitable in all groups. Termination problems occur when members terminate prematurely or a group ends before its objectives have been met. Termination also signifies the end of the group or means that a member will not be returning. These endings have special significance for all members and leaders.

Premature Termination

Rice (1996) provides a useful context for understanding premature termination. When members join groups, they agree to continue as group members until they meet their counseling or therapy goals; this agreement is a treatment contract. Thus, members who leave a group before they meet their treatment goals or a short-term group before its conclusion break their treatment contract. Breaking a treatment contract signifies premature termination. The term **premature termination** can also identify a group that ends before its designated ending.

Most often, premature termination means that members choose to discontinue their membership because they perceive that the group is not meeting their needs. This perception is often associated with ineffective member preparation—members feeling threatened by the emotional demands of group membership or believing that participation is not helpful. Rice (1996) notes a variety of reasons members drop out of groups. Some members drop out when they have unexpressed anger toward leaders and when they feel unfairly attacked. In other cases, members fear their own anger, intimacy, or the anger of others. MacKenzie (1996) adds that members often terminate prematurely because of their reluctance to deal with their group's ending.

Whatever the members' reasons, premature termination represents a treatment failure. To reduce the probability of premature termination, leaders need to stress the demands and commitments necessary to be successful as a group member during pregroup preparation. Preparation by itself, however, does not guarantee that members will choose not to leave groups prematurely. In addition, leaders need to take steps to prevent premature termination and to make premature termination, when it occurs, a therapeutic experience for the remaining and departing members.

MacKenzie (1996) suggests a strategy for preventing premature termination. In time-limited groups, leaders should predict premature termination about four sessions before the group's end. By asking members whether they have considered leaving before the end, members are able to discuss premature termination as a group issue. This allows members to share their fears of ending the group and to deal with issues related to being abandoned by significant persons. Most important, discussing termination allows members to approach the issues and feelings associated with termination together.

Rice (1996) offers another suggestion for preventing premature termination that portrays the most essential factor for interventions designed to prevent premature termination. Rice believes that many members contemplate leaving groups prematurely because they perceive that they are misunderstood or believe that they are not receiving sufficient attention. When leaders convey the attitude that understanding why a member wants to leave is important and ask that member to share his or her feelings and thoughts about leaving, that member often chooses not to leave the group.

Gladding (1995) discusses two other approaches for dealing with premature termination that limit the impact of premature termination on the group. The first approach is useful when leaders become aware that they will have to leave the group before its termination. In this case, leaders should inform group members as soon as possible so that they can prepare for termination and have sufficient opportunity to express their immediate reactions. The second approach describes what leaders can do when they learn that a member plans to terminate prematurely. In this case, leaders invite the member to discuss their feelings in group. Gladding echoes Rice in his observation that these members frequently choose not to leave the group if they use the opportunity to discuss their feelings completely.

Gladding (1995) describes another premature termination scenario—a member leaving the group unannounced. When possible, leaders should ask the member to return to the group to share his or her reasons for leaving without exerting undue pressure. This meeting helps remaining members understand the departing member's reasons for leaving. Whether or not the member returns to share why he or she decided to leave the group, members need to deal with their feelings about the loss of a member. Leaders should listen for members blaming themselves for a member choosing to leave along with expressions of sadness over the loss. It is critical that members address these feelings fully.

Rice (1996) states that premature termination makes careful pregroup member preparation necessary. He also points out that predictors of members continuing in the group include members having recently terminated individual therapy and participation in concurrent individual therapy. Careful member selection and preparation and leaders' clinical judgment of who the best candidates are for group membership ultimately provide the most essential factors for dealing with premature termination.

Termination of a Group Member

When members meet their goals in an open-ended or a long-term group, it is time for them to terminate. This event has significance for the members who are leaving and for the members and the leaders who remain. Yalom (1995) notes that as a member nears termination, other members may attempt to influence the member to stay. Occasionally, the terminating member attempts to make leaving easier by making his or her presence uncomfortable for others or by suggesting a way to stay connected to the members he or she is leaving behind. In each of these scenarios, members are attempting to avoid the termination issues of loss and abandonment. When leaders inadvertently support members' attempts to avoid dealing with the termination of a member, they collude with members to avoid termination issues.

Klein (1996) describes seven tasks that leaders should perform when a member terminates an ongoing or a long-term group:

1. Encourage terminating members to discuss their thoughts about terminating in the group.
2. Help members review what they have accomplished and what treatment goals they have yet to accomplish.
3. Help the terminating member discuss what it has been like to be a member of the group and what it will be like to leave the group.
4. Encourage the terminating member to say good-bye to each remaining member and to the entire group.
5. Provide potentially useful referrals and help the terminating member make plans for what he or she will do after leaving the group.
6. Help remaining members explore their feelings about the meaning and experience of having another member leave the group.
7. Introduce, when appropriate, the prospect of including a new member.

When completing the tasks suggested by Klein, leaders should remain aware that terminating a member has significance for the remaining members. It is easy to forget that remaining members and leaders need to face difficult termination issues before they resume work. By resuming work as if nothing has happened, leaders and members avoid dealing with difficult feelings that are important to their development as persons. To address termination feelings adequately, leaders should allow members time to grieve the loss of an important person. It is also crucial that leaders of established groups ensure that members have dealt with their loss before a new member is included.

The Process of Ending a Time-Limited Group

Leaders initiate the termination of a time-limited group when prospective members have their initial contact with group leaders and leaders inform prospective members of the group's date of termination. Although termination and the realities of limited time are always present in these groups, members seem to lose awareness of the approaching ending. The group literature describes members' losing awareness of their group's ending as avoidance.

Avoidance of termination issues is common for members in groups that face ending or the loss of a member. Members avoid acknowledging the ending of their group for various reasons. Yalom (1995) describes members' avoidance as an attempt to manage the pain of separation. Yalom's views are consistent with the bulk of the group literature, which characterizes members' experiencing concerns connected to loss, abandonment, and grief (MacKenzie, 1996).

Termination issues in time-limited groups vary slightly from those faced in on-going groups (MacKenzie, 1996). Leaders should view termination as a tool that can accelerate members' progress in time-limited groups. Leaders of time-limited groups should carefully consider a strategy described by MacKenzie. To take advantage of this strategy, leaders should make certain that they maintain a closed group.

MacKenzie encourages leaders to initiate termination in their pregroup contact with potential members. During pregroup contacts, leaders should emphasize the time limitations of the group and that members will have to "get to work" early in the group if they are seriously concerned about meeting their goals. Leaders continue to remind members about the group's time limitations whenever the group meets. These reminders continue until the fourth session before the end of the group.

The fourth session from the end marks the time when many members terminate prematurely because they want to avoid termination concerns (MacKenzie, 1996). During this session, leaders need to ask members whether they are considering leaving the group before it ends. This discussion allows members to air their concerns about termination. Issues that commonly surface during this discussion include the idea that there is insufficient time, fears about separation, feelings about abandonment, and resentment about the group having to end. MacKenzie observes that as members discuss leaving, they often experience feeling closer to each other. As this discussion continues, leaders need to remind members that time is running out and that there is still time to reach goals.

Group literature (Gladding, 1995; Jacobs et al., 1994; Shapiro, Peltz, and Bernadette-Shapiro, 1998) describes leaders offering an invitation to members to address any "unfinished business" or interpersonal issues they have not completely dealt with before the group terminates. The fourth session from the end of a time-limited group, in addition to serving the purposes described by MacKenzie, is an excellent time to offer this invitation to group members.

Termination Sessions

In a group's final session, leaders need to accomplish a number of important goals. Leaders should conduct the final termination session as the culmination of a group termination process initiated at least four sessions prior to the ending. The termination process stresses the ending of the group and encourages members to meet their goals and to finish interpersonal work with other members.

The goals of the final session are to deal with the emotions members have about the termination of their relationships with one another, review and summarize what members have learned, and say good-bye. Leaders should structure the final group session in order to meet these goals by developing a plan that helps members move from being highly engaged to separate increasingly as the session progresses.

The final session can begin with leaders asking members to share feelings about terminating the group and their relationships with each other. Exchanging feedback during this phase involves the clear understanding that feedback will not initiate interpersonal work. Feedback during the final group session is a mechanism for sharing reactions and memorable impressions with each other.

Next, leaders become progressively more structured in their instructions as the session continues and direct members to share what they have learned and how they have applied this learning in their relationships outside the group. This phase is a "go-around" in which members take turns sharing but not interacting. Finally, members say their good-byes. This phase can include symbolic structured activities, such as exchanging symbolic gifts. Leaders, in planning and conducting termination sessions, need to be conscious of time limitations to accomplish termination goals.

Termination is an emotionally intense time for all members and the leader. The expression and sharing of emotions is heartfelt and significant for all. Termination signifies the end of meaningful relationships and thus is a sad time, but it is also a time for celebration.

CONCLUSION

The organization and operation of counseling and therapy groups involves careful planning and the use of procedures that increase the chances that a group will operate smoothly. Leaders who carefully plan, select, and prepare group members will minimize the potential problems that logistical issues or inappropriate or ill-prepared members will cause as the group progresses. Also, leaders who work to optimize the effectiveness of their coleader relationship or who seek needed support as solo leaders will ultimately have more satisfying leadership experiences and lead more productive groups. Finally, leaders who use procedures that recognize the needs of group members to start, conclude, and terminate group members and groups are most likely to meet the needs of group members as they transition in and out of their group experience.

Interactive Group Leadership

OBJECTIVES

After reading this chapter, you should be able to:

✔ Discuss core therapeutic factors and how to encourage their development.

✔ Explain essential leadership functions and how to perform them.

✔ Describe various leadership styles, their advantages and disadvantages, and a suggested interactive leadership style.

✔ Outline essential attitudes that facilitate effective leadership.

✔ Discuss important leadership objectives that stimulate the development of an effective group environment and effective interpersonal learning.

INTRODUCTION

The powerful influence that counseling and therapy groups have on their members is the consequence of immediate, congruent, and honest member-to-member interaction that occurs during the lives of these groups. These intense interactions most commonly occur in group environments where members experience the trust, safety, and support necessary to risk disclosing their emotions, perceptions, and reactions.

A number of factors contribute to the development of a group environment that promotes the learning of its members, including group composition, the setting in which the group convenes, the personal qualities demonstrated by group leaders, and the interactive norms established in the group. An environment that promotes learning is necessary but by itself is not sufficient for learning to occur. Members need to have the interactive skills necessary to communicate clearly, offer effective feedback, share emotions and perceptions, and present interpersonal challenges.

The presence of a facilitative group environment and effective group member interactive skills depends on the efforts of group leaders. If a group is to succeed, leaders must facilitate the establishment of effective norms and successfully teach members effective ways to disclose personal information, offer and receive interpersonal feedback, and participate in a collaborative learning environment.

TRUST AND GROUP BOUNDARIES

Central to a productive group environment is trust among group members. An important first step in building that trust is developing interpersonal and external group boundaries that promote members' learning. Interpersonal boundaries describe how openly members share emotions and perceptions with each other, whereas external boundaries describe the extent to which members' interactions focus on relationships within the group as opposed to events occurring outside the immediate group environment.

Members of successful counseling and therapy groups have interpersonal boundaries that allow them to share their experiences of one another and to learn from the sharing of other members. The presence of these boundaries is the outcome of leaders successfully executing their ongoing responsibility for facilitating the development of interpersonal boundaries. These boundaries are open enough to allow members to disclose emotions and perceptions and provide honest interpersonal feedback. In addition, leaders must ensure that these boundaries are sufficiently open to allow members to accurately hear, thoughtfully consider, and productively respond to the disclosures and feedback of others. The establishment of these boundaries depends on the amount of trust members have for one another.

Trust is most readily established when sufficient flow of immediate and authentic communication occurs between members. From the interactive perspective, trust is defined by how confidently members believe they can predict that others will respond usefully to their self-disclosures (Kline, 1986). In this context, useful responses refer not only to affirming, supportive, or sympathetic responses but also to growth-stimulating interactions, such as challenging, confronting, clarifying, or encouraging. Members base their predictions on observations of others' responses to prior self-disclosures and on observations of how members respond to each others' self-disclosures during group interaction. Perhaps the most significant basis for anticipating how others will respond to self-disclosures is each member's pregroup history of self-disclosure experiences. Members who have a long and difficult history of others responding negatively to their self-disclosures will be tentative to disclose and will often require direct encouragement. This tentativeness is common in members who have experienced painful criticisms, often in response to their disclosures as children by family members or peers. These members will need to develop a positive self-disclosure history in group in order to risk the disclosures necessary for growth and learning in group interaction. Such a history is developed in group when members are able to observe other members profiting from self-disclosures and feedback exchanges. The participation of these members often starts when they are encouraged to take "safe" self-disclosure risks.

The level of trust that eventually develops in groups influences the depth and content of members' self-disclosures. Trust is high in groups where members have routinely experienced helpful and positive responses to self-disclosure during group interaction. In such groups, members feel safer and tend to share more intimate personal information. As this sharing becomes common, members experience an increasing level of trust in each other, and the group develops communication norms that encourage immediate and intimate disclosures. These norms depend largely on group leaders' success in developing permeable interpersonal communication boundaries. Without boundaries that allow disclosure of sensitive personal information, it is unlikely that members will experience sufficient trust to profit from group membership.

Trust is a common concern of members in groups that experience early and ongoing resistance to here-and-now communication. This problem often shows itself in ongoing conversations about people and events that are external to the group and irrelevant to the group's objectives. These conversations indicate overly permeable external group boundaries. As leaders encourage the opening of interpersonal boundaries within the group, they must also promote the development of sufficiently closed external boundaries around the group. Such boundaries are necessary for the development of cohesion and a productive group culture. When sufficiently closed external boundaries exist, group interaction regarding events not specifically related to the purposes of the group or to the growth of its members is infrequent. A low level of trust in a group often results from leaders failing to establish sufficiently closed external boundaries. The longer groups continue to discuss external, safe, and mostly irrelevant content, the more members do not experience the benefits of here-and-now contact. The longer members avoid here-and-now contact, the more difficult it becomes to establish sufficiently closed external boundaries and permeable interpersonal boundaries.

DEVELOPING EFFECTIVE INTERACTIVE SKILLS

Establishing and maintaining effective interactive skills is an essential ongoing activity for group leaders. Instructing and reminding members to use interactive skills occurs during all phases of the group's life. The objective is that members will learn to use effective interactive skills without having to think about using them. Ideally, the use of such skills will become a group norm, and members will remind each other to use them.

At the beginning of groups, it is not sensible to expect new members to possess effective interactive skills. Thus, teaching members to communicate in the here and now and use responsible language are early tasks for group leaders. In the early phases of groups, leaders also have the crucial task of teaching members the skills for effectively giving and receiving feedback.

The level of trust and the communication boundaries that develop in group depend heavily on how effectively members use necessary interactive skills. Leaders will observe that as members continue to use effective interactive skills, trust increases because productive outcomes for member disclosures and feedback exchanges are more frequent and predictable. Consequently, interpersonal boundaries become more permeable, and disclosure norms evolve in a way that supports increasing levels of intimacy.

LEADERSHIP ROLE

Leaders who stress group interaction as the medium for members' learning use various skills, interventions, and strategies that perform essential functions and accomplish important objectives. In the following discussion, "skills" refer to specific leader statements, "interventions" refer to a sequence of skills used over a limited time, and "strategies" describe numerous skills and interventions used to address issues present in the group environment.

Factors Influencing the Leadership Role

Numerous factors influence how leaders perform the leadership role, including members' expectations for leaders, leaders' beliefs about how the leadership role should be performed, leaders' interpersonal needs, and the manner in which leaders interact with members. Leaders should be aware that group members' expectations define what group members believe leaders should do and strongly influence what leaders do.

During the initial stages of most groups, members will expect leaders to lower their apprehensions about group membership. These expectations usually include "Tell us exactly what we should do" or "Do whatever is needed to make our group less frightening." Whether or not these expectations are made clear in group interaction, leaders will feel pressure to comply. When leaders submit to this pressure, they will find themselves choosing not to make needed interventions. Later, as groups progress, leaders should be aware that group members' expectations will continue to influence what they do. Most leaders, for example, will become aware of expectations like "The members want me to ignore emotionally charged issues." If leaders comply with these expectations, their effectiveness is compromised because their interventions will begin to ignore emotionally charged issues.

The way in which leaders enact their leadership role is undoubtedly influenced by their beliefs about what leaders should do to be effective. Most leaders support common beliefs about effective leadership like "I should be honest, direct, and clear in my communications with the group." When leaders act according to beliefs consistent with effective leadership, they are more likely to be effective leaders. Ultimately, leadership effectiveness depends on leaders' behaviors being consistent with the beliefs that leaders know are necessary for effective leadership.

Problems occur when leaders' beliefs are inconsistent with effective leadership. When leaders consciously act on beliefs like "I must be involved in every interaction to ensure that learning takes place," they are consciously choosing to be ineffective leaders. In addition, when leaders are unaware of their beliefs about how they should function as leaders, their groups can be adversely affected. Acting on beliefs that are not in the awareness of leaders is especially problematic when these beliefs are not consistent with effective leadership. Leaders who are not aware that they are acting on beliefs that limit their effectiveness will not understand that they are inadvertently sabotaging the effectiveness of their groups.

The demands imposed by leaders' interpersonal needs also have a dramatic impact on their effectiveness as leaders. Leaders whose interpersonal needs are expressed by such ideas as "It is essential that everyone like me" when leading groups are likely to use members to meet their own interpersonal needs. Leaders who lead to meet personal needs abuse their roles as group leaders and use their position in group for their own purposes. All leaders should be highly invested in becoming aware of and understanding their own unmet interpersonal needs. Leaders must maintain awareness of these needs as they lead groups so that they can guard against interacting with members in order to meet these needs. Being aware of interpersonal needs also alerts leaders to times when they might choose to avoid interventions that are more difficult and to times when an intervention is designed to meet their needs. The most appropriate setting for leaders to confront their own interpersonal needs is in their own therapy and personal relationships, not in the role of group leader.

The way leaders interact with members as they attempt to meet their initial objectives is another prominent factor in how leaders enact the leadership role. Early on, members' expectations relate directly to the initial anxieties they experience when they join groups. Members often want leaders, because of their positions as "persons in charge," to fill such roles as caretaker, rescuer, teacher, or parent. Often leaders will experience a conflict between helping members become collaborative helpers and members' expectations that leaders should take care of them. It is also typical for members to blame leaders for the presence of anxiety and to expect leaders to eliminate the anxiety associated with self-disclosure and feedback.

Initially, leaders have the goals of modifying members' erroneous expectations for the group leaders and establishing expectations that are consistent with interactive group work. The process of clarifying member expectations is an important consideration for interactive group work because it defines how members will establish communication norms and develop interpersonal boundaries and establishes what members are responsible to do. Perhaps most critical to leaders, the process of interacting with members to clarify their expectations establishes what members will expect from leaders.

The manner in which leaders interact with members has important implications for members' expectations of leaders. For example, leaders who frequently interact with individual group members to solve interactive problems establish that leaders, not group members, are responsible for addressing interpersonal issues.

Unfortunately, members interpret this pattern of interaction as meaning that leaders do not view them as capable of addressing their personal concerns or interactive conflicts. Another common example is leaders who occasionally "take care" of group anxiety by accommodating interaction that reduces group tension. The paradox here is that these leaders contribute to the continuation of the group's anxiety by confirming members' fears about being unable to deal with difficult situations. In addition, leaders who rescue members from anxiety solidify members' beliefs that leaders are in charge of taking care of group anxiety.

Conversely, leaders who direct members to interact and challenge members to develop new ways to resolve interpersonal difficulties help members develop the belief that they can develop useful solutions to their problems. Groups that possess this belief have high energy levels, permeable interpersonal communication boundaries, frequent exchanges of feedback, and high levels of interpersonal learning. When members perceive that they can tolerate their own emotions and are able to respond productively to the emotions of others, they become increasingly capable of being autonomous and effective in interpersonal relationships. Leaders who direct members to interact and challenge members to develop new ways to resolve interpersonal difficulties develop group expectations that are consistent with the interactive approach. In general, leaders want to establish their roles as facilitators who are responsible for engaging members in interactions that stimulate their growth.

Establishing Therapeutic Factors

The promotion of essential therapeutic factors is integral to leaders establishing their leadership roles. Therapeutic factors refer to "crucial aspects of the process of change" (Yalom, 1995, p. 1). Corsini and Rosenburg (1955) initially conceptualized these factors as the result of their comprehensive review of research that described therapeutic processes in group therapy. Corsini and Rosenburg collected statements about the therapeutic elements of therapy groups, categorized them, and labeled the emerging nine categories "therapeutic factors." These factors were acceptance, altruism, universalization, intellectualization, reality testing, transference, interaction, spectator therapy, and ventilation.

Yalom (1970) made the next notable contribution to understanding therapeutic factors. He presented 11 factors that were the product of his research, clinical experience, and theoretical approach. These factors, which are remarkably similar to those presented by Corsini and Rosenburg, are instillation of hope, universality, imparting of information, altruism, the corrective recapitulation of the primary family group, development of socializing techniques, imitative behavior, interpersonal learning, group cohesiveness, catharsis, and existential factors. It is important to note that the factors listed by Corsini and Rosenburg (1955) and Yalom (1970) demonstrated the theoretical perspectives of the authors (e.g., transference and existential factors).

Bloch and Crouch (1985) used a research process similar to the one employed by Corsini and Rosenburg (1955). Bloch and Crouch reviewed the group therapy literature since the mid-1950s and developed a classification of therapeutic factors that indicated the themes and consistencies appearing in the research. Bloch and Crouch's goal was to generate conceptualizations of therapeutic factors that were independent of theory. Their research resulted in a more specific definition of the term *therapeutic factors*, a list of six discrete factors, and a cluster of additional factors. This text will use the factors presented by Bloch and Crouch (1985) because they depict concepts that have surfaced as themes across the group therapy literature and because they are the least theoretically biased.

Bloch and Crouch (1985) defined a **therapeutic factor** as "an element of group therapy that contributes to improvement in a patient's condition and is a function of the actions of the group therapist, the other group members, and the patient himself" (p. 4). Bloch and Crouch carefully differentiated therapeutic factors from "conditions for change and techniques" (p. 5). They stated that such conditions as having people in the group who are willing to participate and a therapist who uses various methods to conduct the group are prerequisites for the existence of therapeutic factors.

Bloch and Crouch (1985) presented the following factors and definitions:

Insight (self-understanding): "The basis of insight is that the patient learns something important about himself" (p. 28). This includes "learn[ing] how he comes across in the group, . . . learn[ing] about the nature of his problem," and "learn[ing] why he behaves the way he does and how he got to be the way he is" (p. 29).

Learning from interpersonal action: This is "the attempt to relate constructively and adaptively within the group, either by initiating some behavior or responding to other group members. . . . This factor operates when the patient tries out new, potentially positive ways of initiating behaviour with other group members . . . when the patient . . . tries out new potentially positive ways of responding to other group members" (pp. 70–71).

Acceptance and cohesiveness: These were grouped together. Acceptance depicts an individual's perception, whereas cohesiveness indicates a perception shared by group members. Bloch and Crouch regarded cohesiveness as a precondition for other therapeutic factors. More specifically, they indicated that acceptance is unlikely without group cohesiveness (attraction of the group for its members). Acceptance describes a member experiencing "a sense of belonging, warmth, friendliness, and comfort . . . feel[ing] valued by other group members, . . . value[ing] the support the group offers . . . feel[ing] cared for, supported, understood, and accepted by other group members, . . . feel[ing] unconditionally accepted and supported, even when he reveals something . . . he has previously regarded as unacceptable" (pp. 101–102).

Self-disclosure: This is the "act of revealing personal information to the group" (p. 128).

Catharsis: This is "an emotional release . . . which brings some measure of relief" (p. 162).

Guidance: This is "the imparting of information and the giving of direct advice" (p. 171).

Bloch and Crouch (1985) clustered the factors of universality (seeing similarities in self and others), altruism (helping others), vicarious learning (learning through observation), and installation of hope (perceiving that change is possible) because their study revealed insufficient depth in the research to support these factors as distinct. Despite the lack of research, the presence of these factors makes an important contribution to helping people change in groups.

Any conceptualization of these therapeutic factors ultimately is an oversimplification of the complicated and intertwined change processes that occur in therapy groups (Yalom, 1995). Therapeutic factors are "arbitrary constructs" (Yalom, 1995, p. 2) and are not independently existing entities. They are, in Yalom's (1995) words, "intricately interdependent" (p. 69).

INTERACTIVE THERAPEUTIC FACTORS

Therapeutic factors are systemically related in that it is impossible to examine one factor without considering its reciprocal relationships with other factors. For example, learning from interpersonal action cannot occur unless members self-disclose. Self-disclosure probably would not occur in sufficient depth if members were not experiencing the group as cohesive and feeling accepted. Accordingly, if self-disclosure, acceptance, cohesiveness, and learning from interpersonal action were not present to some extent, insight would be unlikely. The reciprocal relationship of these factors extends to universality, vicarious learning, installation of hope, and altruism. All the therapeutic factors depend on one another, and each factor is present only to the extent that other factors are operating.

Consequently, the interactive perspective regards therapeutic factors as more or less arbitrary "chunks" of a continuous interactive process. This perspective allows leaders to focus on establishing several of these factors, knowing that the other factors will be set into motion as a result. For example, if learning from interpersonal action occurs, members will become more hopeful about their own learning (installation of hope) and will perceive aspects of other members involved in the group's learning processes that they identify in themselves (universality). In addition, learning from interpersonal action probably cannot occur without members' self-disclosure (i.e., offering feedback, sharing personal reactions, and disclosing emotions), and that disclosure depends on that member experiencing some level of acceptance in the group. Consequently, the process of engaging members with each other is the most crucial objective because then therapeutic factors will emerge.

Because the interactive perspective focuses on managing interpersonal boundaries and facilitating members learning from each other, the most essential interactive therapeutic factors are learning through interpersonal action, acceptance, self-disclosure, and insight. Leaders whose interventions employ these factors as their basic leadership goals set the interactive process into motion. The development and implementation of therapeutic factors result from leaders performing essential leadership functions.

LEADERSHIP FUNCTIONS

Leadership functions are the tasks necessary to accomplish specific leadership objectives. In general, leadership functions establish an environment in which learning can occur. This environment is one in which members can learn from each other, develop flexible interpersonal roles and behaviors, learn about interpersonal relationships, experiment with interpersonal behaviors, and develop awareness, self-understanding, and insight.

Lieberman, Yalom, and Miles (1973) defined four primary leadership functions. They contended that "much of what . . . leaders do . . . can be subsumed under four basic functions: Emotional Stimulation, Caring, Meaning-Attribution, and Executive Function" (p. 233). Lieberman et al. were enthusiastic about their findings. They contended that these functions were "an empirically derived taxonomy for examining leadership in all forms of groups aimed at personal change, be they therapy or personal growth groups" (p. 235). Besides defining these functions, these authors described each as existing on a continuum from high to low utilization.

Emotional stimulation was "leader behavior which emphasizes revealing feelings, challenging, confrontation, revelation of personal values, attitudes, beliefs, frequent participation as a member in the group, exhortation, and drawing attention to self. Stylistically, stimulation represents the emphasis on the release of emotions" (Lieberman et al., 1973, p. 235). Emotional stimulation involves leaders in modeling self-disclosure and utilizing actions necessary to encourage members to disclose emotions.

Lieberman et al. (1973) depicted caring as both a function and a style. They described caring as "protecting, offering friendship, love, affection, and frequent invitations for members to seek feedback as well as support, praise, and encouragement. . . . leaders express considerable warmth, acceptance, genuineness, and a real concern for other human beings in the group" (p. 238).

Meaning-attribution is a process of conceptualizing or "cognitizing behavior—providing concepts for how to understand [group events] . . . and providing frameworks for how to change" (p. 238). When leaders conceptualize group events or offer educational input that conceptualizes group interactions, they are enacting the meaning-attribution function.

Executive function is a function that focuses on the administrative tasks of group leaders. Lieberman et al. (1973) defined this function as "behaviors such as limit-setting, suggesting or setting rules, limits, norms setting goals or directions of movement, managing time, sequencing, pacing, stopping, blocking, interceding, as well as . . . inviting, eliciting, questioning, suggesting procedures for the group or for a person, and dealing with decision-making" (p. 239).

More recently, authors have presented leadership functions that appear to be variations on the functions presented by Lieberman et al. For example, Gladding (1995) presents a discussion of both global and specific leadership functions. Throughout the life of their groups, leaders perform global functions, such as content and process functions. In general, Gladding refers to the attention leaders give to what is shared in group as the content function and the attention leaders give to the manner in which groups interact over time as the process function.

Gladding also describes other "main functions" of leadership. These functions have objectives that are more specific. He uses the functions presented by Bates, Johnson, and Blaker (1982) as an example. These functions include "traffic director," "modeler of appropriate behavior," "interaction catalyst," and "communication facilitator." For the most part, leadership functions presented in the literature are what authors believe are essential leadership objectives.

From the interactive perspective, theory shapes leadership functions. That is, theory shapes the conceptualization of group interaction, conceptualization forms leadership objectives, and objectives determine leadership functions. Leadership functions define how leaders use skills, interventions, and strategies in order to achieve the objective of each function. Interactive leadership functions are norm setting, boundary management, structuring, instruction, regard, languaging, and administration.

Norm Setting

Norm setting is an essential aspect of leaders' early activity. The norm-setting function demands that leaders structure the interactive environment of the group by helping members establish "rules" for interaction and participation. Examples of norms that leaders can implement early in the group are using personally responsible language, being on time, not talking while others are interacting, and giving direct feedback. Later, leaders can implement norms such as completing work before moving on (e.g., complete feedback exchanges or initiating experiments with new behaviors), honoring members' requests for ending feedback exchange, or checking feedback for consensus.

Leaders need to be aware that members may agree on how they should interact but may not act accordingly. For example, members may agree that they should not interrupt work that other members might be doing before they finish but regularly interrupt the work that might be occurring. Thus, the norm is "interrupt work," not "finish work." Because of this, leaders need to monitor group interaction to see whether norms that hinder group effectiveness are present. A discussion of the strategies and interventions leaders can use to identify and stop norms that block effective interaction appear in chapter 13.

Norm-setting work involves a continuum of leaders' actions that range in authority styles from authoritarian to democratic. Examples of such actions include presenting norms that are useful to the group and asking the group to implement the norms, presenting norms to the group and enforcing them, or involving the group in a discussion of what they believe the rules for interaction should be and involving them in enforcing these rules. Enforcing a norm also involves leaders' actions that range in authority from identifying behaviors that break a norm and directing members to conform to that norm to asking the group to identify the norm that is operating and to discuss how it contributes to members satisfying their needs.

Before initial group meetings, leaders should carefully consider and select several norms that they believe are crucial for effective group functioning and commit to establishing these norms. Leaders who attempt to establish an excessive number of norms will find that enforcing these norms is very labor intensive. Attempting to implement "too many" norms distracts leaders from performing other necessary functions and diminishes their effectiveness. The "right" number of norms depends on leaders' carefully considered choices of indispensable norms. In any circumstance, leaders should commit to implementing the norms they present to the group. Presenting a norm and not bothering to enforce it is an inconsistency that will erode leaders' credibility.

It is best to think of norm setting as an additive process. Leaders should develop several important norms early. Then, when members implement these norms without prompting, leaders can consider developing additional norms when necessary. Groups, as a product of their interaction, develop additional effective norms (i.e., rules for interaction that promote the interpersonal work of the members) after some early norm-setting work by leaders. Groups will also develop counterproductive norms (i.e., rules for interaction that block the interpersonal work of the members) that will require ongoing intervention.

The way in which leaders perform the norm-setting function has implications for the behaviors that members expect from leaders and what members perceive about how they should interact with each other. Table 9.1 describes a number of approaches leaders can use to establish group norms and some resulting member expectations. The manner in which leaders perform this function affects the group environment, the issues that surface, and the group's eventual effectiveness.

Boundary Management

The boundary management function requires leaders to attend to communication content and process. This function involves the direct actions that leaders take to facilitate open interaction among members. These actions encourage members to develop interpersonal boundaries in the group that permit the sharing of emotions, perceptions, attitudes, beliefs, and assumptions about others' motivations. Boundary management often involves directing members to disclose their emotions to each other and share their perceptions of other members:

LEADER: "Sharon, tell Vince the emotions you are feeling toward him now."
LEADER: "Rob, tell Jean what you think her silence is about."

Boundary management also involves establishing external group boundaries to promote interaction that emphasizes the interpersonal relationships within the group. External boundaries define what and how much communication occurs in the group about events external to the group. This essential leadership function establishes a group culture that has communication boundaries different from those that operate in social systems outside the group. The boundaries that leaders establish in a group create the group's unique culture and feature here-and-now interaction that includes emotional content. This communication is also open, honest, immediate, direct, and related to the goals of the group.

To establish effective external group boundaries, leaders help members develop an awareness of how participation in the group differs from their experiences outside the group and how this "difference" makes participation in the group valuable and meaningful. Some ways to meet this objective are leaders' comments that describe such helpful group processes as sharing emotions and questions that direct

Table 9.1
Leadership Function Performance and Role Establishment, Norm Setting

Behaviors	Group expectations
Leaders establish norms and intervene whenever the norms are violated.	Leaders are responsible for enforcing norms and correcting members' behaviors.
Leaders observe the enactment of nonproductive norms by members, ask members how it affects them, and then ask members to develop a norm that could work better.	Leaders identify issues and facilitate group problem solving.
Leaders ignore counterproductive norms.	Leaders have no expectations regarding establishing or developing effective procedures and the way the group operates is okay.
Leaders present norms and then intervene inconsistently or not at all.	Leaders are not serious about norms, interventions can be ignored, and the group can interact however it wants.
Leaders establish norms and intervene by involving the group in making choices about these norms.	Leaders provide rules, the group makes choices about what works best, and leaders involve the group in problem solving.
Leaders establish norms and intervene by using "try on" norms (see norm intervention discussion).	Leaders identify blocking norms, encourage norms experimentation, and involve members in making decisions about what works best.
Leaders present several essential norms early in the group and work diligently to enact and enforce them. Leaders also identify counterproductive norms that develop as the group continues and replace them with norms that are more productive.	Leaders have essential rules for the group and intervene when necessary to help the group become more effective.

members to describe how participation in the group differs from typical interactions outside the group. Leaders who hear member statements like the following have an indication that effective external group boundaries have been established.

"I couldn't wait to get here this week. I just had to find some people whom I could be honest with and would tell me, honestly, how they feel about me."

"I can say stuff in here that I just can't say anywhere else."

"When we really get into a conflict in here and actually resolve it, that blows me away!"

Examples of other approaches that can help develop effective boundaries include directing or asking members who have shared emotions with each other to describe to the group what that experience was like for them. In addition, members who have observed the honest and immediate sharing of emotions and perceptions can be asked to discuss their observations as well as the feelings that surfaced in them as they watched. It is usually helpful to bring the effects and benefits of productive emotional exchanges to the attention of the group. By highlighting how group interaction works, leaders build effective group boundaries.

Sometimes leaders will find that boundary development is elusive. As a group develops, leaders will often observe a "dance of intimacy" as members experiment with being emotionally immediate and then retreat by closing their boundaries. Leaders should understand that members are especially vulnerable after intense, emotionally charged experiences. Members, consequently, will often close their boundaries, reflect on and give meaning to their work, and consider changing. If members remain persistently vulnerable, they are less able to give meaning to their interactions or make useful choices about changing their behaviors because they are not able to think clearly. In such cases, leaders can help members close their boundaries temporarily to reflect on their experience. To do this, leaders can ask the member to think about his or her experiences and temporarily withdraw from group interactions to reflect on these experiences. Alternatively, leaders can direct other group members to not interact with a member to allow that member an opportunity for reflection.

Table 9.2 gives examples of various approaches to boundary management and some of the resultant group expectations and reactions.

Structuring

When leaders direct and specifically shape how interactions occur, they are performing the structuring function. This function involves giving members instructions about how to interact in order to facilitate interpersonal learning. The most common examples are directing interaction in feedback exchange, directing interaction to teach communication skills, and establishing interactive procedures for problem solving or conflict management. The structuring function also includes giving instructions for structured procedures, such as opening or closing rounds.

Structuring is a directive function that can be used whenever circumstances demand that members interact in a structured manner (i.e., sequentially with specific directions for interaction). Such circumstances are those that dictate that clear communication between members is essential. Occasionally, these circumstances involve leaders making the decision that the extent of the emotional involvement of certain members prevents them from interacting effectively. More frequently, the decision to structure interaction occurs when it is essential for communication to be clear, effective, and complete. Such structuring is appropriate when involving members in feedback exchange or when members' interactions are demonstrating communication problems.

In addition, structuring is a useful way to manage time when members are not likely to have an opportunity to contribute if interaction is not structured. Closing rounds are a good example of this application. In this case, leaders instruct members to share a specified type (e.g., emotions, learning that occurred, or thoughts) and amount (e.g., a number of words or a sentence) of ideas about what occurred during a group session. These instructions should also direct members not to share their reactions with each other. Thus, all members have a chance to contribute in a limited time.

Table 9.2
Leadership Function Performance and Role Establishment, Boundary Management

Behaviors	Group expectations
Leaders frequently involve individual members by direct means (e.g., reflecting feelings, questioning, directing them to share, and so on) and directing others to respond.	Leaders are responsible for bringing feelings into interactions, and members are to wait until they are called on.
Leaders direct members to interact with each other and share perceptions and emotions. Leaders also process interactions with the group and offer observations about interactions.	Leaders establish interaction boundaries, facilitate interaction, and help members learn from each other.
Leaders do not intervene to encourage sharing of perceptions and emotions or the exchange of reactions to group events.	Leaders do not expect the exchange of perceptions and emotions or reactions to group events.
Leaders terminate feedback exchanges or emotionally charged interactions.	Leaders are caretakers, intervening because members cannot take care of themselves.
Leaders instruct members how and when to terminate feedback exchange and give members who receive feedback the responsibility for doing so.	Leaders facilitate learning and believe that members can take care of themselves.
Leaders check with members, only as necessary, about saturation in feedback exchange.	Leaders support members when it appears that they need it.
Leaders engage individual members by using questions and other counseling skills, such as reflecting feelings, paraphrasing, and confrontation, and rarely make an effort to connect members with each other.	Members should interact with leaders because leaders do not expect meaningful member interaction, and leaders believe that members can learn only from leaders.
Leaders stress interacting in the here and now, "convert" external discussions into discussion of issues occurring in the group, and illuminate the learning processes that occur in the group.	Leaders expect the group to be different and more helpful than external social systems, the group is a place to learn, and members are expected to interact meaningfully and directly.

Table 9.3 gives examples of structuring interventions and potential member perceptions and expectations that form as a result.

Instruction

Instruction is an active and directive leadership function that has the objective of teaching members skills or concepts that can facilitate their learning. Examples of this function are teaching members effective interactive skills, such as giving and receiving feedback, making direct requests, and paraphrasing what others say to ensure effective communication. Instruction also includes teaching group members how, if, and when to transfer the new behaviors learned in group to outside environments and relationships.

Table 9.3
Leadership Function Performance and Role Establishment, Structuring

Behaviors	Group expectations
Leaders direct feedback exchange between two members and direct the feedback receiver to check with other group members for consensus.	Leaders expect certain procedures to be followed in feedback exchange processes and direct these exchanges so that members can learn.
Leaders structure opening rounds by presenting specific procedures to follow.	Leaders have procedures for involving members that save time but are sometimes awkward because they do not allow interaction.
Leaders interrupt an interaction where it is obvious that those engaged are becoming overwhelmed by their emotions and structure it so that these members can continue their work and make sense of it.	Leaders intervene to enable members to learn from their experiences and provide safeguards that prevent members from "losing it."
Leaders structure a problem-solving process so that all members have an opportunity to contribute.	Leaders believe it is important to involve members in developing ideas that can make the group work better and have procedures for doing so.
Leaders intervene to structure interactions persistently before members have an opportunity to engage each other (i.e., learn from the process of interaction).	Leaders have a specific way for members to interact, control how and what members share in the group, and do not trust members to interact productively.
Leaders structure interactions in the group on an ongoing basis by introducing a series of structured experiences.	Leaders will tell members how to interact and what the content of those interactions will be.
Leaders ask two members involved in a heated exchange to paraphrase what the other member has said before sharing their reactions.	Listening and hearing what others are saying is important, and leaders will intervene when this does not happen.

Teaching members about transferring their learning is important because members may not fully understand the effects that changes in their interpersonal behaviors might have on their relationships. Members could be at risk for damaging their relationships without specific instruction or consultation on how to select behaviors for transfer to their social environments and how to introduce new behaviors into their out-of-group relationships.

Leaders can use the instruction function when needed at any time during the life of the group. However, this function should not be overused in groups designed to involve members in learning from each other. Leaders should be aware that the most essential objective for this function is to help members develop interactive skills; to facilitate interaction. These skills are necessary for members to learn how to become effectively engaged with each other as active, not passive, learners.

Leaders who extend instruction to frequent or extended philosophizing or academic discussion are likely to observe a progressively disengaged group. Such a group is the product of norms that develop largely as a result of leaders' conceptual

Table 9.4
Leadership Function Performance and Role Establishment, Instruction

Behaviors	Group expectations
Leaders provide early instruction regarding effective feedback exchange and communication and assist members in becoming proficient with these skills (e.g., prompting or instructing).	Leaders present skills for effective interaction and believe in the need for them. In addition, leaders ask members to communicate effectively and create anxiety as a result.
Leaders provide early instruction regarding effective feedback exchange and communication and then enact an inactive or observational role.	Leaders know about effective interactive skills but are not serious about members needing or using them.
Leaders offer instruction about the generalization, application, or experimentation of learning in the group to outside the group.	Leaders help members to "take their learning home." What members learn in the group has application elsewhere.
Leaders do not offer instruction about the application, generalization, or experimentation of group interaction skills outside the group.	Members are on their own to figure out how to apply in-group learning elsewhere and/or what members learn in the group has no practical purpose.
Leaders lecture about group process, philosophize about learning and changing, and carefully describe what they believe members need to know.	Members should listen and learn from leaders. Sharing ideas and intellectualizing about their experiences are what is expected.

conversations. When leaders observe a disengaged group, they should carefully reflect on the extent to which their interventions have focused on conceptualizing group interaction or have had a cognitive focus. Leaders who overuse the instruction function become characteristically cognitive in their interactions with group members. This style supports closed boundaries and contributes to members closing their boundaries.

Table 9.4 gives examples of leaders' instructional behaviors along with resultant group perceptions and expectations.

Regard

Regard involves leaders demonstrating certain attitudes and actions in their interactions with members. These attitudes and actions are as follows:

1. Genuineness: Believing in the importance of being real and congruent in relationships and acting accordingly
2. Acceptance: Believing in the inherent worth of others and demonstrating unconditional acceptance of them
3. Empathy: Valuing and expressing an understanding of the internal emotional experiencing of others

Whereas Rogers (1961) regarded empathy, genuineness, and acceptance as necessary and sufficient conditions for change, the interactive approach contends that the demonstration of these qualities alone is not enough. Leaders must also perform the interactive leadership functions necessary for members to interact effectively and learn from one another.

Nonetheless, it is essential that leaders effectively demonstrate these qualities; otherwise, groups are not likely to develop a climate conducive to learning. Leaders who do not consistently communicate empathy, genuineness, and acceptance will observe that members fear criticism, demonstrate facades, and struggle with the expression of emotions.

Regard is consistent with the ideas presented by Leiberman et al. (1973) regarding their caring function. They stated that it is important that "leaders express considerable warmth, acceptance, genuineness, and a real concern for other human beings in the group" (p. 238). Leaders' goals in performing this leadership function are to demonstrate humanness and a real concern for the welfare and the learning of group members. This does not mean that leaders should support avoidance of anxiety or avoid confronting ineffective interpersonal behaviors; rather, it means that they should communicate honestly and show sincere concern while challenging members to confront fears, develop awareness, and initiate change.

Table 9.5 gives examples of leaders' actions that communicate and do not communicate these conditions, along with the resultant group expectations and perceptions. These behaviors, like most other leader behaviors, exist on a continuum; there are many degrees of expression for each of these elements.

Table 9.5
Leadership Function Performance and Role Establishment, Regard

Behaviors	Group expectations
Leaders are appropriately and congruently open in presenting perceptions and emotions.	Leaders can be trusted because "we know who they are" and "we know where we stand."
Leaders do not share their reactions or emotions.	Leaders are evaluative and distant, their motivations are uncertain and questionable, and group interaction is scary.
Leaders consistently encourage the expression of emotions, reflect demonstrated emotions, and make empathic statements.	Expressing and experiencing emotions is expected and acceptable. It is important to understand and accept the emotions of self and others.
Leaders either do not encourage the expression of emotions or are inconsistent in directing members to present emotions.	It is okay and expected that emotions are kept hidden and that understanding emotions is "not that important" in this group.
Leaders directly communicate their acceptance of members as persons by differentiating persons from their behaviors.	Leaders value and accept members and care about members as persons. Members are acceptable although they have behaviors that need changing.
Leaders are critical of members and their behaviors and do not differentiate members from their behaviors.	Leaders evaluate and judge members. It is very risky to disclose personal information.

Languaging

The languaging leadership function is similar to the instructional function in that it presents concepts to the group. The difference is that the languaging function describes specific events that have occurred in the group, focuses on members' perceptions and experiences, and is not a skill-building process. The languaging function expands Lieberman et al.'s (1973) conceptualization of meaning attribution from a process of "cognitizing behavior—providing concepts for how to understand [group events] . . . and providing frameworks for how to change" (p. 238) to constructing language about effective learning processes. Although the meaning-attribution goal of creating frameworks for change is similar to the objectives of languaging, the interactive languaging process is different. The basis for the languaging function is the social constructionist principle that languaging about solutions helps solve problems, whereas languaging about problems makes them real and maintains them (Becvar, Canfield, & Becvar, 1997).

The languaging function includes a continuum of activities that range in the extent of leaders' and members' involvement. At one end of the continuum is leaders' input, or leader languaging, that does not involve group discussion. Examples of leader languaging include process commentary, educational input regarding a group event, and educational input about interaction. At the other end of the languaging function continuum is member languaging, examples of which include discussion about how the group solves problems, the positive impact of a facilitative norm, and interactions that resulted in members' learning effectively.

To facilitate member languaging, leaders involve members in discussing group events to describe and label what worked. Events that have worked are the interactive processes that have successfully facilitated the growth of the group and its members. Leaders initiate member languaging until the group begins to do it on its own.

The member languaging process can be used once interactions that work have occurred. At this point, leaders initiate a conversation that directs members to describe what worked. This conversation can include members presenting observations, describing interactions, discussing outcomes, sharing emotional and cognitive reactions, and labeling what worked. Following are examples of leaders' statements designed to initiate the languaging function.

LEADER: [Gesturing to the entire group] "What did you observe that worked just now?"

LEADER: "I'd like group members to describe what you just saw happening."

LEADER: "What did you all see happen as a result of Sally sharing her emotions?"

LEADER: "How are you all reacting to what just happened?"

LEADER: "What does the group want to call what happened in Art and Connie's interchange?

LEADER: "It seems that it would be useful to name what happened so that we can do it again when we need to."

Languaging that is initiated with such statements causes members to increase their awareness of, accept responsibility for, and understand what they did that worked.

If members understand what they did that worked, they can function more effectively because they know what to do and have ownership of it.

Member languaging about what works also magnifies the confidence that members have in the helpfulness of the group. These conversations build group cohesiveness because group members increasingly believe in the power of the group to affect the lives of its members positively. When leaders effectively facilitate member languaging, members will increase their trust and involvement in the group.

Leader languaging occurs when leaders explain group events that work. Languaging at this end of the languaging continuum is more consistent with the meaning-attribution function described by Lieberman et al. (1973). This form of intervention helps members conceptualize group events and develop a framework for change. Typically, leader languaging seems to have much less impact than member languaging because members do not participate in a languaging process that involves them in developing concepts to describe what they have experienced. In addition, leader languaging reinforces the perception that leaders are the experts. This perception places the responsibility for learning on the shoulders of leaders and limits the potential of group interaction.

Leader languaging, however, does have some useful applications: It is time efficient and can heighten member awareness. When leaders use languaging interventions to present concepts that describe what works, members focus their attention on interactions that work. In addition, leaders can use languaging when the primary intention is to bring an interaction or pattern of interaction to the attention of the group. This is the case when leaders point out a norm (e.g., "The group seems to have agreed that everyone should be listened to."). Leaders will usually not see the group make an immediate change in how it interacts as a result of this intervention. Instead, leaders should operate with the hope that heightened awareness, on its own, can result in the group learning how to operate more effectively.

Whenever possible, leaders should use terms developed during member languaging processes. Members feel some attachment to the terms they generate in their languaging interactions, as such terms are significant and meaningful to them, and they are much more likely to fully understand their meaning. Terms that leaders introduce in their languaging interventions are less likely to be significant or understandable to members.

Table 9.6 gives examples of various forms of languaging interventions, along with potential member perceptions and expectations.

Administration

Leaders perform the administrative function when they conduct business that pertains to the practical aspects of group management. Examples of the more mundane aspects of this function include scheduling sessions, selecting a location, and setting the length of sessions. Also included are two procedures that are vital to a group's ultimate effectiveness: pregroup screening and orientation.

Pregroup screening is essential because ineffectively composed groups will seldom become useful therapeutic modalities (Yalom, 1995). Usually, screening

Table 9.6
Leadership Function Performance and Role Establishment, Languaging

Behaviors	Group expectations
Leaders offer "educational" commentary.	Leaders are responsible for offering concepts that define or describe group events because they are experts.
Leaders offer concepts during interpersonal exchanges so that the members involved have words to use to describe and attach meaning to their interactions.	Leaders offer concepts to help members develop a vocabulary for group events. Leaders are here to help and guide our understanding, and they are the experts.
Leaders engage members in languaging about a group event that worked.	Leaders facilitate the construction of a group vocabulary to describe "what works."
Leaders language about members' behaviors by telling members what their behaviors mean.	Leaders are experts who are in charge of telling members what they are learning and experiencing.
Leaders language about enabling solutions (see focal conflict theory).	Leaders are group process experts who present diagnostic comments that stimulate anxiety and point out effective solutions to the group's anxiety.
Leaders present restrictive solutions to focal conflicts and engage members in "languaging" about enabling solutions.	Leaders generate anxiety by identifying issues and engaging members in defining solutions.

involves an interview of each prospective member by a leader or leaders (Gladding, 1995). The screening interview involves assessing a person's readiness to profit from participation in a counseling or therapy group. Piper and McCallum (1994) list a number of characteristics that are useful to assess in the screening interview: a minimum of interpersonal skill, motivation for treatment, positive expectations of gain in therapy, current psychological discomfort, an interpersonal problem, commitment to changing interpersonal behavior, susceptibility to the group influence (moderate approval-dependency), and a willingness to be of help to others.

Pregroup orientation is also an important contributor to group effectiveness (Yalom, 1995). Leaders can conduct this orientation during the initial group meeting after members have been screened or, most appropriately, with prospective members during screening interviews. Pregroup orientation should include information that describes the processes, techniques, and interactions that will probably occur during the group along with the potential risks for emotional or psychological stress. Orientation information should present leaders' theoretical perspectives, areas of expertise, credentials, and experience as group leaders.

Table 9.7 gives examples of various administrative function actions, along with potential member perceptions.

Table 9.7
Leadership Function Performance and Role Establishment, Administration

Behaviors	Group expectations
Leaders define a contract for meeting times and establish other housekeeping rules in collaboration with group members.	Leaders define and apply "administrative" rules when the group agrees to them.
Leaders revise contracts with group members whenever group members are dissatisfied.	Leaders submit to group pressure and need to make group members happy.
Leaders present specific parameters for meeting times, how or whether they are to be contacted outside the group, session times, and other housekeeping rules and are not open to negotiation.	Leaders are serious about maintaining rules for group operation and have firm boundaries. Leaders are not flexible or sensitive to member needs.
Leaders are inconsistent in how they present, enforce, apply, or interpret group parameters, housekeeping rules, and so on.	Leaders are not certain about what they want and what they expect from group members. Members "should guess what makes leaders happy."
Leaders define essential "administrative" rules and form others in collaboration with group members.	Leaders have certain essential expectations and are open to negotiate other administrative rules.
Leaders perform in a professional manner, selecting only members appropriate for the group and advising members about what to expect from group participation.	Leaders are professional, ethical, and competent. Members are initially less anxious because they are advised about what to expect.

LEADERSHIP FUNCTIONS: LEADER BELIEFS AND MEMBER ATTITUDES

When leaders perform the various leadership functions, they have to make numerous choices about the content and purposes of their interactions. Leaders simplify these choices if they make the objective of engaging members in interaction with each other the most important priority. This objective is grounded in the belief that people, if given the proper environment and the necessary interactive skills, learn best from each other.

A major benefit of engaging members with each other is that it results in members developing attitudes that positively influence participation and learning. As a result of being engaged with each other, members learn from each other. Consequently, members develop the attitude that they are responsible for the amount and depth of their participation and, as a result, what they learn. Additional "learning attitudes" develop as members experience productive outcomes to group interactions. Members become increasingly confident that they can trust other members to be acting in their interest as productive outcomes occur. The attitudes of being personally responsible for learning and trusting the intentions of other members lead members to become increasingly honest and immediate in their interactions.

LEADERSHIP STYLE

When establishing their leadership roles, leaders must be clear about the group environment they want to establish. As leaders develop this environment, they should be aware that the way they interact with members will establish how members perceive them and their role. Leaders' approaches to developing the environment they believe is most consistent with members' learning is a very significant contributor to groups' effectiveness. Leaders whose styles are ineffective will limit their groups' effectiveness even if their efforts are intended to develop an effective group environment. This section will focus on leadership style and the ways leaders interact to achieve objectives and will discuss potential reactions of group members to a range of leadership styles.

Lewin's (1944) classic research depicted leadership style on a continuum of authority that ranged from authoritarian to laissez-faire. Hansen, Warner, and Smith (1980) described a variety of leadership styles on leader-centered to group-centered, autocratic to anarchistic, and directive to nondirective continua. From the interactive perspective, leadership style exists on authority, activity, and personal involvement continua. The authority continuum refers to leaders' characteristic style of making and implementing decisions and beliefs about who is responsible for what happens in group. The activity continuum refers to the frequency and duration of leaders' interactions. Finally, the personal involvement continuum refers to the extent to which leaders become personally involved in group interactions.

Leaders' customary manner of interacting with groups informs members about what they should do. For example, leaders who characteristically do not disclose emotions, continuously conceptualize interactions, and frequently enforce group norms inform members that they should interact cognitively and wait for leaders' directions. Leaders' styles define how members perceive leaders, the behaviors members expect from each other and leaders, and ultimately the atmosphere and interpersonal issues that surface in the group.

The Authoritarian, Democratic, and Laissez-Faire Continuum

The authority continuum ranges from authoritarian, to democratic at the midpoint, and to laissez-faire. This continuum depicts leaders' beliefs about who is responsible for making and implementing decisions: leaders only, leaders and members in collaboration, members only, or no one. This continuum reflects leaders' beliefs about who is competent to make and implement decisions.

Regardless of the style leaders demonstrate, authority issues will emerge in groups. Leaders' authority styles shape the emotional intensity or subtlety in which authority issues emerge and are "played out." The following discussion will address this developmental reality.

Authoritarian leaders "feel that the group members, by themselves, are not able to develop the necessary insights or group behaviors that will bring about the necessary changes" (Hansen et al., 1980, p. 389). These leaders believe that without their expertise, members would be lost. Accordingly, these leaders believe that members do not have the capacity to understand their problems adequately, gain insight without explanation, or function as members without ongoing direction. Therefore, authoritarian leaders are not likely to develop a group where members can learn effectively from each other.

Nevertheless, leaders must recognize that authoritarian leadership behaviors are essential in numerous situations. For example, the early implementation of such norms and boundaries as "owned" language, complete feedback exchanges, finishing work before moving on, here-and-now communication, and sharing feelings require consistent prompting. In addition, leaders need to be authoritarian in situations that require decisive action, such as enforcing norms that involve the safety and well-being of members.

Members have characteristic responses to leaders who are persistently authoritarian. Dependent members (Bennis & Shepard, 1956), who typically want others to direct them or solve their problems, will initially enjoy authoritative leadership. This is because the interactions of authoritarian leaders allow them to follow directions about how to participate. These leaders' interactions minimize the risks of participation because dependent members are not responsible for developing their abilities to solve problems independently or act autonomously. Counterdependent members (Bennis & Shepard, 1956), who have a pattern of challenging authority, will rebel against leaders who continuously attempt to direct their behavior. Independent members (Bennis & Shepard, 1956), who base their opinions about authority on what actually happens, will not have an immediate reaction to an authoritarian leader. Instead, they will wait to experience how well their needs are being addressed before deciding how to react to authoritarian leaders. Once dissatisfied, they are likely to challenge the authoritarian leader.

Leaders who use authoritarian styles should carefully examine their interpersonal needs. In the group environment, these needs mark a desire to avoid the rejection of group members and the accompanying fears of intimacy. By controlling interaction, leaders do not have to fear the potential rejection associated with revealing themselves to members. In most groups, these interpersonal concerns will mirror the experiences of members as they struggle to engage one another openly. If leaders share these concerns and use leadership styles that defend themselves from these fears, groups are likely to stall. This is because members' and leaders' fears will permit only a superficial level of intimacy.

Democratic leaders use collaborative actions that engage members in decision making and carrying out group responsibilities. Hansen et al. (1980) state, "The democratic leader uses clarification, synthesis, feedback, and evaluation of process as the chief tools. The aim of this leader is to involve members to such an extent that each participant contributes to the welfare of other individuals in the group. . . . The democratic leader works in cooperation with the group in establishing goals, directions, and procedures" (p. 389). Democratic leaders believe that members have the ability to learn and grow. These leaders know that group members, given the proper conditions, are capable of learning from each other and developing self-understanding and insight.

The behaviors and attitudes of leaders using the democratic leadership style are, for the most part, consistent with interactive principles and procedures. Issues surface, however, when leaders do not feel free to use authoritarian interventions. Such interventions are occasionally necessary when members of a democratic group make decisions that can retard the development of a facilitative group environment. For instance, when members agree that sharing "negative" emotions is not appropriate for group interaction, leaders need to intervene authoritatively. Purely democratic leaders who allow members to make and act on the decision to not share "negative" emotions will have to wait until members experience the limitations of this decision. Once members' interactions indicate a problem with their decision, leaders can initiate a renegotiation of the "sharing negative emotions" rule. This is a waste of time in groups intended to be therapeutic.

Purely democratic leaders develop operating procedures in collaboration with group members. As soon as members agree to procedures, they are responsible for implementing and cooperating with the procedures. Leaders are then responsible for observing members' compliance with the procedures they have agreed to and facilitating the renegotiation of these "rules" when members agree that the "rules" are not helpful.

The time and energy necessary to conduct a group in this manner often results in truly democratic groups becoming bogged down in process; that is, such groups have to use time that could be devoted to members' personal work to reach agreements about how the group should operate. If group goals are not to study decision-making and problem-solving processes, then the situational use of authoritative interactions is necessary to perform leadership functions. Members who participate in groups led by democratic leaders tend to have ownership for what transpires in their groups. Nevertheless, participation in democratic processes is probably not an adequate reason for the implementation of a purely democratic approach.

The interaction of purely democratic leaders and group members is also an important consideration. Leaders who use an extensively democratic style should be clear that a strong need for acceptance does not excessively influence their choice of style. Leaders who are concerned about acceptance can use democratic problem-solving and decision-making procedures to avoid confronting members to reduce the risk of rejection. If relational issues are not interfering, leaders must be clear about the extent to which their approach is consistent with group objectives. Time spent dealing with issues that surface naturally in group interaction is more consistent with members' interpersonal lives than is their participation in democratic group processes.

Although it would appear that democratic leaders would avoid authority issues, this is not the case. Dependent members (Bennis & Shepard, 1956), looking for protection and direction, often consider democratic leaders as abnegating their responsibilities for directing group. Counterdependent members (Bennis & Shepard, 1956), regardless of leaders' attempts to give the group the responsibility for itself, will assign responsibility to leaders and challenge leaders' competence. Finally, independent members (Bennis & Shepard, 1956) will respond most favorably to the democratic leadership style, initially seeing the sharing of responsibility as an opportunity to learn. Should group interaction become unproductive, however, even independent members can become disgruntled.

Laissez-faire leaders do not participate in the development of group procedures, norms, or boundaries. The laissez-faire style is difficult to describe as a leadership style because leaders employing this style assume no responsibility for the direction, content, or processes of their groups. These leaders do not actively participate in directing group interactions, and their involvement resembles that of group members (Hansen et al., 1980).

The laissez-faire leadership style is generally inconsistent with the interactive approach because laissez-faire leaders are not actively involved in developing a facilitative interactive environment. At times, however, observing the group and reflecting on what is occurring in group interaction can be useful, as when leaders are not certain about what is occurring or they want members to struggle with an issue to elevate group anxiety. Observation and reflection are also useful when an intervention fails. In this case, leaders can profit from observing and reflecting to clarify what is going on in the group. This "pause" allows leaders to gain some emotional distance from a failed intervention before reengaging with group members. Leaders should avoid using a passive observational style for any extended time.

Members who experience leaders who persistently employ a laissez-faire style, regardless of their personality styles, will have authority issues with laissez-faire leaders. These reactions stem from leaders' nonperformance of necessary leadership functions. Essentially, laissez-faire leaders are never there when anyone needs them.

Hansen et al. (1980) point out that laissez-faire leaders often have strong needs to be liked. By being more members than leaders, they try to gain the approval and acceptance of the group members. Laissez-faire leaders choose not to interact in a way that best serves their needs to gain the approval of group members.

Interactive Authority Style.   Although interactive group leaders will use behaviors found in all three leadership styles, the behaviors and attitudes characteristic of the democratic leadership style are essential. Especially important is the attitude that members have the resources that allow them to learn from each other and eventually learn to function autonomously. However, at times leaders must actively direct group interaction or observe and reflect. In general, though, the interactive approach vigorously disagrees with the attitudes characteristic of the authoritarian and the laissez-faire approaches.

Interactive group leaders use behaviors consistent with the various leadership styles, depending on circumstances. For example, early in groups, members need to acquire interactive skills, and groups need to develop and use facilitative interactive norms. To accomplish these objectives, leaders are active and directive. Later, when norms are operational and members have developed effective interactive skills, leaders can use more observational and democratic procedures. Just as leaders work with group members to be flexible in their interpersonal roles, developing a wide range of interpersonal behaviors and resources to draw on as circumstances dictate, leaders must be flexible in how and when they enact aspects of the various authority roles.

Active Versus Passive

To perform interactive leadership functions effectively, leaders actively participate early in the group. The goals of this activity are to establish effective interaction norms, develop effective interpersonal skills, and manage interpersonal and external group boundaries. Later, as members demonstrate increasing self-sufficiency, leaders should become progressively less active. Ultimately, however, leaders' involvement depends on what is transpiring in the group. For example, leaders, observing group interaction, may become highly active when a feedback exchange is incomplete or when a member is scapegoated for the introduction of conflict in an otherwise peaceful session.

The term **active participation** generally describes leaders who frequently participate in group interactions. In some cases, highly active and authoritarian leaders actively share their knowledge because they believe that their expertise is necessary for effective group work. Therefore, active leaders establish a communication pattern in which they become the hub of group interaction. This form of active leader participation eventually creates more intense authority and dependency issues. In other cases, active leaders participate to establish group norms and ground rules, develop permeable interaction boundaries, structure group interaction, and direct members to interact with each other. Despite these admirable intentions, this approach also creates authority and dependency issues as members experience a "demand" for open interaction. However, in this case, these issues are necessary steps toward group autonomy.

When considering the persistently active leader, it is important to consider two potential interpersonal issues. These issues often surface in leaders who are persistently active in conceptualizing group events or lecturing. Frequently, these leaders are apprehensive about emotional intimacy and rejection. In this case, leaders' activity blocks intimacy in the emerging relationships within the group. Because of the ongoing conceptual activity of these leaders, members continue to stay engaged with each other, but at a conceptual level. Members' interactions will eventually mirror their leaders' interpersonal fears.

Passive leaders usually believe that minimal interaction with members is essential for group effectiveness. Although occasionally observing and reflecting on group interaction is useful, the usefulness of an ongoing passive observational approach is doubtful. In some cases, passive leaders believe that minimal participation offers members an opportunity to explore their projections and transference relations with leaders. More commonly, passivity indicates leaders' interpersonal concerns and stimulates the development of distrust in leaders.

Leaders who employ a passive approach to group involvement should be clear about where they stand regarding several interpersonal issues, including fears of being rejected or of being perceived as incompetent. When these fears are present, leaders tend to believe that by not being actively involved in the group, they can maintain safety, that is they can maintain safety by remaining hidden. Paradoxically, members often criticize this leader for being distant and judgmental.

Interactive Activity Style.   In the context of interactive groups, leaders' activity depends on what is going on in the group. Active participation, as well as more passive observational and reflective leader involvement, can be appropriate given what is transpiring in the group. Because of this, leaders should self-monitor their activity on an ongoing basis. Habitually passive participation cannot be responsive to what is occurring in the group because intervention is eventually required in all groups. At the same time, habitually active participation deprives members of learning opportunities that are not available when leaders are doing "all the talking." To lead groups effectively, leaders must have an activity level that is responsive to the needs of the group—active or more passive as necessary. Monitoring activity level is especially important in coleadership situations where coleaders are struggling to have equal airtime or are competing for the attention of the group members.

Personal Involvement and Technical Skills

Interactive group leaders need to balance leading as technicians who expertly use skills, interventions, and strategies with leading as persons who disclose genuine personal reactions and emotions. By being extensively involved as either one of these, leaders limit their effectiveness, because the extensive use of either approach creates member expectations that limit the potential for productive group outcomes. Leaders need to be adept at using interventions and comfortable sharing personal reactions. Most important, leaders need to be clear about the implications of participating too heavily in either mode.

Group members learn to trust each other as the consequence of exchanging increasingly intimate self-disclosures over time. As members become increasingly intimate and learn that other members accept them, they develop a sense of trust and safety. Leaders retard this process when they rely heavily on using technical expertise and avoid sharing personal reactions. Often, leaders who use this approach are anxious about how others perceive them. These leaders find that using a leadership style that heavily emphasizes technical expertise abates this anxiety. However, this style has its problems.

Leaders who rely heavily on technical expertise hear reactions from members that describe interacting in group as a very scary experience. Often, these reactions involve members attributing their fears of interacting with each other to leaders whom they perceive as distant, manipulative, and judgmental. Often members, because they do not have information about the personal reactions of leaders who rely on their technical expertise, do not trust these leaders and assign critical or judgmental characteristics to them. Members in groups led by technicians often come to believe that "because we don't know who you are and don't know where you stand, we believe you are judging us and rejecting us as persons."

In contrast, leaders who are persistently personally engaged experience a very different array of group reactions. Initially, these reactions include being liked and admired by members. This helps leaders who are apprehensive about their relationships with group members feel more comfortable. However, as groups proceed, this role becomes progressively confusing to members.

Members' confusion about personally engaged leaders' roles is the outcome of the ambiguous messages sent by these leaders. Ambiguity emerges because the personal involvement of leaders blurs the difference between the roles of members and leaders. Members become confused about what behaviors to expect from leaders and begin to expect leaders to use essentially the same behaviors members use. These expectations are especially problematic when leaders are in a situation that demands the use of authority. For instance, personally engaged leaders, who have interacted like other members, confuse members when they use very unmember-like authoritarian interventions to establish boundaries or protect a member from harm. Leaders who rely heavily on personal engagement to avoid challenges and gain acceptance ultimately face heated leadership challenges in situations where it is necessary to direct the group.

Leaders who use personal disclosure to develop a close bond with members will often find themselves in an awkward position when they attempt to perform leadership functions. In essence, leaders, once their participation begins to resemble that of members, create member expectations that do not support the utilization of the leaders' expertise or authority. Leadership dilemmas experienced by leaders who use excessive personal engagement are consistent with the boundary issues enmeshed parents face when they attempt to carry out family rules with their children.

Interactive Involvement Style.   Using a leadership style that balances technical expertise and personal involvement is essential. Leaders must demonstrate regard for the experiences of members and be transparent enough to allow group members to know them as persons. At the same time, leaders need to use interventions that are necessary to establish effective interpersonal boundaries and confront group issues. The proper balance of these leadership dimensions requires the judgment of leaders based on what is occurring in the group at the time. Leaders' emotional disclosure is usually not useful in a feedback exchange that requires the performance of the structuring function. Conversely, using techniques to address members' fears may not be as useful as an emotional disclosure that demonstrates understanding of members' fears.

The Interactive Leadership Role

The interactive leadership role is grounded in theoretical assumptions that establish leadership objectives. These objectives include the following:

1. Interacting and intervening in a manner that implements therapeutic factors conducive to interpersonal learning
2. Forming members' interpersonal communication boundaries that allow the sharing of emotions and perceptions
3. Establishing external group boundaries that sustain group environments that promote interpersonal learning and cohesion
4. Composing a normative structure that encourages interaction, self-disclosure, feedback exchange, and experimentation with new interpersonal behaviors
5. Providing structure to ensure learning and members' languaging solutions
6. Teaching members communication and feedback skills that facilitate learning

This perspective suggests how leaders can accomplish group objectives, and the actions leaders perform to meet their objectives. These actions include leadership func-

Figure 9.1
Leadership Role

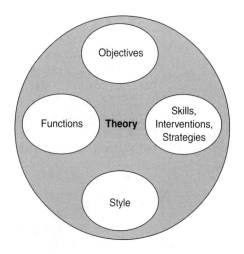

tions; skills, interventions, and strategies; and leadership style (see Figure 9.1). Leadership style, in particular, has significant implications for the group environment, the members' expectations of leaders, and members' perception of their responsibilities for learning.

As leaders gather experience, they should reexamine their beliefs about how interaction helps group members. Changes in these personal beliefs modify how leaders perform interactive leadership functions. When leaders are clear about these modifications, they can experiment with small changes in their leadership approach to see what works best for them. By using this experimentation process, leaders can develop their most congruent and helpful leadership approach. Leaders who participate in this process are much more likely to sustain their enthusiasm and ongoing development as group leaders. Leaders will find that they are most effective when their leadership is consistent with their experiences and beliefs.

CONCLUSION

Essential attitudes and objectives can reduce the complexity of the group leadership task. The following list summarizes these ideas:

1. Direct members to interact with each other. This means that the leadership role focuses on the facilitation and orchestration of interaction.
2. Establish and reinforce the personal responsibilities of members for learning and interacting congruently.
3. Help members develop interpersonal boundaries that allow the communication of feelings and the disclosure of perceptions.
4. Challenge the group to develop here-and-now norms and sufficiently closed external group boundaries.

5. Strike a balance between technical expertise and presence as a person. Leaders cannot develop an effective learning environment without establishing their presence as an open, authentic, and direct person.

6. Engage members in identifying avoided interactive concerns and work diligently to involve the group in confronting and resolving them.

7. Continuously demonstrate the attitude that members and not leaders are the primary source of therapeutic change.

8. Act with confidence in the belief that members are capable of dealing effectively with difficult, emotionally charged interpersonal issues.

CHAPTER 10

Basic Skills and Interventions

OBJECTIVES

After reading this chapter, you should be able to:

✔ Outline affective, behavioral, and cognitive objectives for basic skills and interventions.

✔ Describe intervention levels and their importance.

✔ Discuss the timing, balance, and intensity of interventions and their implications for skill and intervention use.

✔ Describe basic skills and interventions and learn how to use them.

✔ Explain why basic skills and interventions occasionally do not work and what to do when this happens.

INTRODUCTION

The skills and interventions leaders use are most effective when they establish a safe group environment and mobilize the powerful forces of group interaction. This premise is grounded in the conviction that members learn most effectively when they learn from each other. From this perspective, the leaders' role is to facilitate increasingly intimate here-and-now self-disclosures, honest feedback exchange, appropriate risk taking, confrontation, experimentation with alternative interpersonal behaviors, and members' efforts to change. Leaders' responsibilities also include protecting members from harm, providing a cognitive structure to make sense of group interaction, offering only necessary educational input, modeling effective interpersonal behaviors, and helping members process group events.

Basic skills are leaders' most fundamental response to group interaction. These skills are simple statements designed to facilitate interaction and help members focus on specific aspects of group interaction. *Basic interventions* are leader statements that involve a sequence of basic skills. In general, these interventions use a basic skill to illuminate a specific aspect of interaction and an additional basic skill or set of skills to facilitate interaction. Basic skills and interventions are the tools leaders use to perform their various functions (see chapter 9).

All skills and interventions address one or more levels of the group system: the group as a system, subgroups, or individual group members (See Figure 10.1). Effectively used skills and interventions help leaders meet several important global objectives: encourage affective experiencing and expression, provide a cognitive structure, and change, encourage, and direct members' interactive behaviors.

Leaders should use skills and interventions with an awareness of timing, balance, and intensity. Knowing when to intervene is as critical as selecting and knowing how to use a skill or intervention. Poorly timed interventions are ineffective. Conversely, even clumsily presented skills or interventions can have a positive outcome if they are well timed. Balancing the focus of interventions is also important. Continuously stressing a particular level and objective has an adverse effect on interaction and the group environment. Leaders also should be aware of the intensity of their interventions. Interventions that are excessively or insufficiently intense can slow a group's progress. When leaders are clear about what they want to accomplish, level, objective, timing, balance, and intensity lose their apparent complexity.

Figure 10.1
Intervention Levels and Objectives

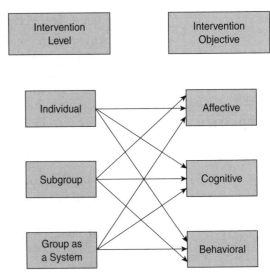

AFFECTIVE, COGNITIVE, AND BEHAVIORAL OBJECTIVES

Learning in groups is most effective when it includes emotional experiencing, cognitive understanding, and experimentation with alternative behaviors. Members who experience and express emotions are most likely to encounter their most limiting personal concerns and to receive meaningful feedback. Learning to effectively express and experience emotions also frees members to become more self-accepting, honest, and spontaneous in their relationships. Affective experiencing alone, however, is not sufficient for change.

Members need to develop a cognitive structure that defines their experience and leads to conceptualizing desired changes. The usefulness of a cognitive structure is especially evident in effective feedback exchange where members are able to conceptualize the impact of unsatisfactory habitual interpersonal behaviors and define desirable alternative behaviors.

Affective experiencing and cognitive understanding must be coupled with opportunities to develop more effective relationship behaviors. These behaviors emerge from feedback exchange and experimentation directed toward developing healthy and more satisfying relationships with other group members. The process and ultimate goals of interactive group counseling and therapy are experiencing and expressing emotion, developing a cognitive framework that leads to understanding and insight, and learn more personally satisfying and relationship enhancing behaviors.

Affective Objectives

Experiencing and expressing emotions are critical objectives because they are prerequisites for members learning and changing. Meeting affective objectives requires work at each level of the group system. At the group-as-a-system level, leaders strive to develop a normative structure and group culture that supports and expects the expression of emotions. Subgroup- or interpersonal-level objectives focus on leaders promoting the expression of emotion in members' relationships in the group. At the individual-member level, leaders meet affective objectives by helping members learn to openly share and value their own emotional experience.

Leaders also encourage members to experience and share emotion to help open interpersonal communication boundaries (MacKenzie, 1990). Once members' boundaries are open enough to share and experience emotions, they become more intensely involved in interaction. When members are emotionally involved, they are more likely to experience interactions that lead to change (Yalom, 1995). Emotionally involved members are more intensely engaged with one another, more open to receiving and sharing feedback and confronting and being confronted, and more likely to experience affect-laden interactions that lead to meaningful change. Members have met affective objectives when their interactions include open, spontaneous, and honest expression of emotions. At this point, leaders have an indication that members are cohesive and perceive the group as a safe environment.

Cognitive Objectives

Experiencing emotion "opens the door" to change. Experiencing emotion by itself, however, is not sufficient for change (Yalom, 1995). Members must develop a cognitive structure in order to understand their emotional experiences. This cognitive structure takes shape when members receive feedback, language about productive group events, and process here-and-now interactions. Cognitive objectives are, in general, the language or information members require to understand and attribute meaning to their interactions and relationships and develop solutions that lead to change.

At the group-as-a-system level, cognitive objectives encompass the information members need to optimize their learning. This information includes how to exchange feedback, how to communicate more effectively, and what to do to develop more effective interactive norms. Group-level objectives also include languaging about group events that have productive outcomes. Interpersonal cognitive objectives include relationship-specific information that helps members conceptualize relationship issues and define the behaviors and attitudes necessary to address these issues. Leaders define cognitive objectives at the individual level by what individual members need to understand their relationship problems, here-and-now experiences, and behaviors necessary to make desired changes. Depending on a leader's theoretical preferences, cognitive objectives at all intervention levels can include identifying and challenging thinking, assumptions, and attitudes that limit members' interpersonal effectiveness.

Leaders need to be cautious about how actively they work to meet cognitive objectives. Excessive cognitive input, as described in chapter 9, encourages members to disengage and communicates a message that can lead to leadership role problems. An emphasis on cognitive objectives also risks establishing norms that prioritize content over affect. These norms conflict with meeting crucial affective objectives and frustrate efforts to open interpersonal boundaries. In addition, poorly timed cognitive input drains energy from emotionally charged and meaningful member interaction.

Educational Input.   In general, educational input is appropriate when information is imperative to facilitate interaction and change. Information designed to help members interact effectively, such as basic listening skills and how to most effectively give and receive feedback, is useful if its presentation is correctly timed.

When considering offering educational input, leaders should acknowledge several major cautions. Excessive educational input contributes to members becoming dependent on the leader and viewing the leader as a sanctified expert. It also risks developing or maintaining group norms that support uninvolved cognitive conversation. Finally, it must be connected to what is occurring or has recently occurred in interaction to be meaningful for members. For example, a discussion about effective feedback exchange has a far greater impact on members when they have shared an experience with ineffective feedback than a lecture that is not related to a shared experience.

Educational input is required in several circumstances. Leaders are obligated to provide information necessary for the well-being of the group members (e.g., discuss safe sex when members talk about being sexually active). Leaders also have the ethical responsibility, at the beginning of the group, to reiterate informed consent information and to discuss their ethical responsibilities.

Languaging.   Languaging is a process that describes and names solutions to members' problems that have emerged during group interaction (see chapter 9). Languaging has the goals of increasing members' confidence in the helpfulness of the group, creating concepts that describe effective learning processes, and emphasizing interactions that lead to effective learning. Because languaging is a discussion of group processes that lead to effective outcomes, it encourages members to become more focused on solutions. Such focus disrupts members' tendency to obsess about problems. Obsessing on problems or maintaining a problem focus maintains problems and decreases the probability of change. Languaging is both a cognitive process and an objective that conceptualizes helpful interactions so that they can be repeated.

Processing.   Processing, along with languaging, is an essential ongoing leader task and a vital tool for meeting cognitive objectives. Leaders process group events to help members reflect on and learn from here-and-now interaction. This self-reflective loop (Yalom, 1995) allows members to discuss what has immediately occurred or is occurring in the here and now in order to make sense of it and, potentially, develop insight. Processing is discussed in detail as an aspect of leaders' ongoing responsibilities in chapter 12.

Behavioral Objectives

Members learn most effectively when they: (a) receive feedback about interpersonal behaviors, (b) discover effective alternative behaviors, (c) experiment with alternative behaviors, and (d) incorporate into their relationships the alternative behaviors that work best for them. These outcomes are most likely achieved when behavioral objectives are met at the group-as-a-system, interpersonal, and individual levels. At the group-as-a-system level, behavioral objectives involve establishing norms that develop a facilitative interactive group environment (see chapter 2). These norms support feedback exchange and experimentation with alternative behaviors. Interpersonal-level objectives focus on identifying and learning more effective relationship behaviors. For example, two members might learn that they could improve their relationship by not contradicting each other persistently and by looking for ways to agree with each other. Objectives for the individual level are met when members conceptualize their personal objectives in terms of relationship behaviors. For example, a member who learns that he or she comes across critically to other members might find that experimentation with listening skills designed to deepen understanding achieves a more desirable reaction from others.

Change is possible when members identify and understand the impact of behaviors that interfere with their relationships and receive input from others about potentially more effective relationship behaviors. Behavioral objectives are met when members have experimented with alternative relationship behaviors and find the behaviors that both enhance their relationships and meet interpersonal needs. Focusing on relationship behaviors also helps members alter their perceptions of self and others. By focusing on behaviors, members learn to think in terms of "behaviors that do not work" instead of attributing what goes wrong in relationships to their own relative worth and that of others.

Change.   Significant change demands identifying critical interpersonal concerns, understanding and insight, emotional experiencing, meaningful involvement with others, and the use of more effective behaviors in members' relationships. The process of change begins when members experiment with new behaviors and continues as members receive feedback about the effectiveness of their experiments. The change process progresses as members make choices about which of their experimental behaviors best meet their needs and most effectively enhance their relationships and concludes when these behaviors become an integral part of how members act in their relationships in and out of group. The implication of this change process is that, whenever possible, leaders need to help members identify and learn about the effects of their counterproductive habitual interpersonal behaviors and experiment with potentially more effective interpersonal behaviors.

Ongoing feedback about the effectiveness of experiments with new behaviors is an important step in members choosing to change. Feedback provides information that allows members to learn behaviors that can improve the quality of their relationships. When a member receives feedback that experimental behaviors work for others, that those behaviors achieve what the member wants, and that those behaviors are personally viable, the member can then make choices about maintaining those behaviors in his or her relationships. For example, Al experimented with a number of ways to express disagreement. After a number of experiments, Al got feedback that others understood his point of view and felt that the way he stated his point of view invited them to engage in a discussion about their differences. This is what Al wanted, and he felt comfortable using these behaviors. He then decided to make these behaviors a habit in all his relationships.

INTERVENTION LEVELS

Groups are social systems composed of individual, subsystem (or interpersonal), and group-as-a-system levels. All interventions and skills that leaders use address one or more of these levels and have an impact on all levels. Regardless of the level addressed, interventions and skills should be used to engage members with one another. The manner in which the intervention is made and the target of the intervention are less important.

Individual-Level Skills and Interventions

Probably the most overused and least effective skills and interventions are those directed toward individual members. Leaders who overuse individual-level skills and interventions fail to engage members sufficiently with one another. Thus, they fail to utilize members' interactions, the most powerful source of learning and change. Leaders employ a disproportionate number of individual-level communications for many reasons. Some of these are artifacts of individual counseling and therapy training, inadequate group leadership training, and the interpersonal fears and needs of leaders.

Interventions and skills directed toward individual members are, however, occasionally necessary to involve and support a member's participation. At the same time, these skills and interventions should be used with awareness of associated dangers. The most obvious danger is overuse. Overuse of individually focused skills and interventions risks establishing norms that define leaders as experts in charge of each member's change and that encourage a passive membership. Passive members are much less likely to help each other and develop meaningful relationships in the group. Expert leader roles and passive membership sabotage powerful interpersonal learning processes. By staying aware of the effectiveness of members' interactions, leaders are in a position to address these dangers. Clearly, even a marginal overuse of individually focused skills ignores the purpose of group work and destroys the potential of interpersonal learning.

Subgroup (or Interpersonal) Skills and Interventions

Subgroup (or interpersonal) skills and interventions should be foremost in the minds of leaders. Skills and interventions aimed at members' relationships are a major priority because helping members develop healthy and satisfying relationships is the most essential purpose of group counseling and therapy. Interpersonal skills and interventions have the objectives of promoting interaction, initiating feedback exchange, opening interpersonal boundaries, challenging habitual restrictive solutions, confronting interpersonal perceptual distortions, initiating and completing interpersonal learning processes, and initiating changes in members' relationships. The bulk of "the work" that members do occurs at the interpersonal level.

Group-as-a-System Skills and Interventions

Skills and interventions that address the entire membership have the intent of dealing with issues experienced by all members. One of the most prominent goals of group-as-a-system-level skills and interventions is to establish norms that make the group an effective learning environment. These norms, discussed in depth in chapter 2, promote safety, cohesion, and acceptance. Group-level interventions are also used to confront issues that block the group's progress. These interventions identify and direct members to deal with shared concerns and focal conflicts. By identifying shared concerns and focal conflicts, group-level interventions can noticeably elevate the anxiety present in the group. As is true for individually directed interventions and skills, overuse is a danger. Leaders who overuse group-level interventions are often perceived as distant or impersonal (Yalom, 1975), and members respond to the overuse of group-level skills with anger and resentment directed toward leaders. The careful use of group-level skills and interventions, however, is indispensable because it can greatly enhance members' learning and group effectiveness.

INTERVENING: TIMING, BALANCE, AND INTENSITY

The goal of members interacting therapeutically is the basis for making decisions about when, how often, and how powerfully to intervene. Although concrete guidelines are impossible, the following discussion will offer some ideas that can be useful when making intervention decisions. Leaders will gain a sense of timing, balance, and intensity with experience.

Timing

Timing is crucial. When considering an intervention, leaders should remember that members' interactions often attempt to manage anxiety. These attempts consist of solutions that include avoidance and denial, maintaining open external group boundaries, clinging to closed interpersonal boundaries, or disconnected cognitive discussion. Although these solutions normally require robust interventions, interventions are not always advisable.

When groups first meet, leaders should be careful, as interventions that confront members' anxieties directly and attempt to develop enabling solutions may make anxiety overwhelming and produce a defensive membership. Later in the group, however, these interventions can be highly productive. Consequently, knowing when to raise members' anxiety is a major factor in considering when and how to intervene. As a rule, leaders are encouraged to increase anxiety, but never to the extent that it destroys members' perception of safety.

When members are interacting productively, leaders should feel free to develop enabling solutions and frustrate restrictive solutions. At this point, members have developed a sense that the group is a safe environment and that they can face uncomfortable anxiety. Interventions that significantly escalate anxiety should not be used before members have developed the skills and attitudes necessary to manage intense emotion, at which point leaders can directly address focal conflicts and more risky boundary issues.

Regardless of a group's stage of development, before intervening, leaders need to consider when anxiety might become overwhelming and thus members' sense of safety threatened. When anxiety is high and it appears that interaction may shut down, leaders should consider using temporary "escape hatch" restrictive solutions. Such solutions allow members to maintain their sense of safety in the group. Either by ignoring restrictive solutions or by introducing one, leaders can manage the group's anxiety. The following examples show how a leader can lower a group's anxiety by introducing an "escape hatch" restrictive solution.

LEADER: "Well, we've been dealing with some really scary stuff tonight. I'm wondering how everyone's deodorant is working?"

LEADER: "Wow! I think it's time we all take a deep breath. It seems like we can all be proud of how we faced some difficult issues today."

Knowing when to intervene is one of the most difficult decisions for beginning group leaders. Generally, interventions are helpful whenever it is necessary to bridge members who are not interacting, initiate feedback exchange, and establish a facilitative group environment. Important interventions that require more sensitivity to timing are modifying ineffective communication behaviors, identifying and modifying interpersonal perceptual distortions, helping members and the group develop effective external boundaries, and encouraging the development of autonomy. Interventions that are critical to group effectiveness and require even greater sensitivity to timing include challenging restrictive solutions and identifying focal conflicts, developing enabling solutions, and confronting. These lists do not include all possible interventions leaders can make. The essential point is that interventions that produce increasingly greater anxiety require increasingly greater sensitivity to timing.

One circumstance requires no consideration for timing: Leaders must intervene whenever a member has the potential of being harmed. Although confrontation and challenging are important and the expression of anger and other emotions is healthy and inevitable, interactions intended to do harm are unacceptable. Whenever it is clear that a member may be harmed, leaders must intervene immediately and forcefully. These interventions should establish clear boundaries that prevent damaging interactions. Accordingly, leaders must carefully monitor interactions with members who are in jeopardy of becoming scapegoats. These members frequently risk being the target of critical or hostile interaction.

Leaders should carefully consider when to intervene in relation to an intense group interaction. Ordinarily, leaders should not intervene when members are engaged in an intense interaction and the interaction promises to have a productive outcome. It is especially important not to intervene to preempt members' attempts to deal with emotionally intense issues if these attempts show promise of progress.

Emotionally intense interactions need to conclude with the interacting members having openly shared, communicated effectively, clarified their concerns, and understood how to address their relationship concerns. As emotionally intense interactions progress, leaders should intervene only when necessary to help conceptualize the meaning of the emotional expression and the events associated with the expression. It is also prudent to intervene during emotionally intense interactions whenever members are clearly having communication problems.

Leaders should monitor their interventions to ensure that they are not developing the habit of intervening whenever interaction becomes intense. This pattern of intervention communicates that members are incapable of being self-sufficient. Leaders who find they have this tendency should look carefully at their own tolerance for emotional expression. Anxiety associated with members' emotional expression should be addressed with leaders' supervisors, in consultations with other professionals, in debriefing with coleaders, or in their own counseling or therapy.

In general, the timing of interventions becomes more critical as groups continue. Attempts to intervene whenever needed to develop a facilitative group environment early in the life of a group usually pay off later when the group becomes progressively more self-sufficient. However, leaders who continue to intervene whenever it seems necessary will limit the effectiveness of their groups. These groups will lack creativity and spontaneity, be dependent on leaders for ongoing direction, and are much less likely to develop autonomous boundaries. Members need to have opportunities to become self-sufficient. Allowing members to struggle with group and interpersonal issues is the first step in members discovering that they have the necessary resources to confront their issues.

Balance

Balance describes how leaders distribute their interventions in terms of form, objective, level, frequency, and amount. *Form* describes the types of skills or interventions used. *Objective* includes the affective, cognitive, and behavioral goals of each intervention. *Level* describes the part of the group system an intervention addresses—individual, interpersonal, or the group as a system. *Frequency* refers to how often leaders intervene and to how long they speak when they intervene. Balanced interventions incorporate various forms and objectives directed at various parts of the group system. Balance also means that leaders talk much less than group members.

Leaders' interventions attempt to meet affective, cognitive, or behavioral objectives. Interventions focused excessively on any of these areas have an adverse affect on groups. Leaders should remain aware of their overall objectives and attempt to strike an appropriate balance in their intervention objectives.

Affective interventions have the purpose of opening interpersonal boundaries and promoting intimacy in members' relationships. Leaders who stress affective interventions too heavily challenge members' perceptions of safety. Steadily repeated affective interventions, regardless of how sensitively presented, may close members' boundaries instead of opening them. At the same time, leaders need to persist with affective interventions to open boundaries and encourage affective expression. This persistence should be paired with careful observation of members' reactions to these interventions. When members become defensive, it is time to back off for a while. In addition, when members appear to react defensively to affective interventions, the exploration of these reactions with the entire group can be very productive.

Cognitive interventions are most effective when they are connected to the immediate affective experiencing of group members. Cognitive interventions, timed in this manner, help members understand interaction and develop insight. Overly frequent cognitive interventions, however, can be disastrous. These disasters usually are associated with excessive educational input or prolonged conceptualization of group interaction. The goals of cognitive interventions are to provide members with enough concepts to understand what is occurring and what needs to happen to initiate change. Any more than this defeats the purpose of group interaction.

Languaging or processing group events are productive cognitive interventions. Leaders can feel freer to language or process than provide educational/cognitive input. Still, however, leaders should monitor members' reactions to all cognitive interventions. An indication that cognitive interventions have been overused is when members become disengaged and stay with cognitive discussion.

Behavioral interventions have the purpose of helping members develop more effective interpersonal behaviors. It is almost always appropriate to challenge or direct members to experiment with new behaviors. In addition, feedback exchanges are never complete until the members receiving feedback have defined an experimental behavior to try or until feedback senders have clarified their perceptions of the receiver's behavior.

Interventions also should be balanced in terms of level. Leaders who direct interventions exclusively at one level of the group system undoubtedly are missing essential interactive material. An extensive focus on individual interventions most likely will fail to utilize the group's therapeutic potency. An excessive number of these interventions result in members looking to leaders for help. By doing so, members are not utilizing interpersonal learning. In terms of group-as-a-system interventions, members perceive leaders who overly stress group-as-a-system interventions as detached and insensitive. Consequently, these leaders are often unsuccessful in developing the perception of safety in the group environment. If any level of intervention is to be stressed, it should be the interpersonal level. Learning in groups concerns learning how to have more effective relationships. Members who become effective in their relationships in the group setting are most likely to develop more satisfying relationships outside group.

As a rule, leaders should use individual interventions only as a means of involving a member with other members. Group-as-a-system interventions are most useful when leaders have the goal of identifying and challenging focal conflicts, shared themes, and norms and roles that do not promote effective interaction. Because interpersonal interventions stress members' relationships, they are seldom inappropriate. In general, however, the quality and amount of interaction that follows an intervention determines its effectiveness.

When considering intervention balance, keep in mind the goal of facilitating the development of a self-sustaining group. Members respond to frequent leader interventions by withdrawing and waiting for the leader to tell them what they need to do. These members become passive, quickly lose their energy, and take less responsibility for their own learning. Optimal frequency of leader intervention is demonstrated when groups become self-sufficient. This usually means that at the beginning of the group, leaders intervened frequently enough to facilitate the development of effective interactive norms, focused on teaching members interactive skills, and effectively promoted members becoming personally responsible for learning. Members of these groups do not depend on their leaders because they have learned how to learn effectively from each other.

Leaders should also consider the duration of their interventions. Lengthy interventions are detrimental because they direct members' attention away from interaction to listening to the leader. This requires that members shift from active participation to passive listening. Interventions should attempt to maintain or energize interaction. In general, leaders should always strive to make their interventions as short as possible. Direct, concise interventions have greater impact and maintain members' contact with each other.

Intensity   *Therapeutic pressure*

Intensity refers to how high an intervention raises members' anxiety. More intense interventions face disturbing motives and reactive motives directly by naming them. These highly intense interventions may direct members to act on disturbing motives, thus directly confronting their reactive fears. The least-intense interventions direct the group away from disturbing motives and reactive fears and serve as restrictive solutions that dramatically reduce members' anxiety. By developing an appraisal of the group's tolerance for anxiety, leaders can develop a sense for how intense their interventions should be.

It is not useful for the group environment to have either an insufficient or a consistently uncomfortable amount of anxiety. If anxiety is too low or too high, the group will be ineffective. When anxiety is excessive, members will persistently attempt to implement restrictive solutions and withdraw. If anxiety is too low, restrictive solutions are operating. Leaders should allow restrictive solutions only when anxiety is suddenly intolerable or chronically excessive (Whitaker & Lieberman, 1964). These "escape hatch" restrictive solutions can reestablish a sense of safety within the group when anxiety has been overwhelming. Leaders have to decide which restrictive solutions avoid issues and should be confronted and those that are responses to overwhelming anxiety and should be ignored.

BASIC SKILLS AND INTERVENTIONS

Listening Skills

Listening skills are fundamental to individual counseling and therapy (Ivey, 1994; Young, 1992). The most basic of these skills are statements designed to encourage interaction and ensure effective communication between leader and members. By accurately restating the affective or cognitive content of members' statements, leaders can be confident that they understand members' communication and are stimulating introspection. Basic skills also include open-ended questions, beginning with "how" or "what" (Ivey, 1994). Open-ended questions encourage members to share or expand on their thoughts and emotions. Closed questions, another basic skill, begin with "do," "are," or "have" (Ivey, 1994). These questions confirm understanding and close down interaction.

More advanced listening skills confront discrepancies in members' actions, emotions, or verbalizations; increase immediacy in the relationship; and probe more deeply into members' emotions and thinking (Ivey, 1994). More advanced skills help members gain a fuller understanding of their thoughts, emotions, and behaviors. These skills also promote more intense relationships and can initiate change.

Listening skills are composed of statements and questions. In the group context, leaders should use listening skills to involve individual members with one another, not to initiate extended interaction with a particular member. Examples of useful listening skills applications include using a question to involve a member in interaction, restating what a member has said to ensure others understand, making a statement that identifies the emotions associated with a member's experience, and asking a member about a reaction to another member's statement or a group event.

There are two important uses of listening skills. One is to initiate the basic facilitation sequence and other interventions. The other is as a set of skills to teach members. When members learn these skills, the effectiveness of their communication increases dramatically.

Directives

Directives are leader statements that instruct members to participate in a specific way. Directives are the most efficient way to connect or redirect interaction and initiate members' experimentation with alternative behaviors. This skill can halt a member's prolonged verbalization that blocks productive interaction or moves the group away from productive interactions. Finally, directives can instruct a member to offer feedback or share information, reactions, or emotions with the group, a particular subgroup, or a particular member. Examples of directives include the following:

LEADER: "Michelle, you've been talking for a while. Stop now."
LEADER: "John, say 'I' instead of 'we'."
LEADER: "This concerns Sally. Say that directly to Sally."
LEADER: "Rick, before we move on to your topic, we need to let Steve finish. Steve, continue."
LEADER: "Jill, you've received lots of feedback. Tell the group to stop when you've had enough."
LEADER: "Let Susie finish before you jump in."
LEADER: "Stay with the feelings you're having now."

Members who are working on clarifying their interpersonal boundaries are helped when they develop directive skills. Leaders can direct members to use directives like the following:

LEADER: "Tell them what you want."
LEADER: "You can tell other members when you've had enough feedback."
LEADER: "You're in charge of defining your own boundaries in here. Tell the others what you want them to know."

Experimentation with directives allows members to practice and experience what it is like to establish clear boundaries. Some examples are as follows:

BILL: "I want you to stop telling me how I should act."
JEAN: "Tell me how you feel about me."
STEVE: "I want you to give me some feedback."
DAVE: "Roz, stop asking me those questions. I feel like you're intruding on me."
ARTHUR: "I'm done."

Directives that target the entire group are very effective management tools. Group directives are simply statements to the entire group that instruct all members about desirable behaviors. These directives can be used to manage communication, promote the establishment of facilitative norms, or manage the group's boundaries:

LEADER: "Be here on time. The group starts at 8:00 sharp."
LEADER: "When members say they want to stop receiving feedback, stop giving it."
LEADER: "When you have a strong reaction to another member's behaviors, it's a good time to give that member feedback."

Observation

Observation involves watching and listening to interaction and making a statement about what has been seen and heard. Observation includes statements about members' nonverbal expressions, what members say or do in a specific interaction, or patterns in a member's interactions. A more sophisticated form of observing involves looking for process. Observing process involves reflecting on the probable purposes of members' interactions. For example, does a particular member appear to be intimidating, controlling, manipulative, or acting out a victim's role in attempting to get what he or she wants?

Sharing observations is an effective way to increase members' awareness of their interpersonal behaviors, which is important because most individuals interact in their social environments with a limited awareness of their interactive behaviors. Thus, most people have no understanding of what they are doing that blocks meeting their interpersonal needs. When members hear observations of their behaviors, they become aware of these behaviors. With awareness, members can consciously use a behavior and observe how others react. If the reaction is not what members want, they can choose to experiment with different behaviors.

Leaders can share observations when a member is having a noticeable reaction and is not verbalizing the reaction. Observations can also be made when a member appears to be disengaged. Observations should be simple statements that, as much as possible, avoid overly interpreting a member's behaviors. The observation "Pam, you're wrinkling your brow and setting your jaw. It looks like you're having a reaction to what Michelle has just said" avoids the overinterpretation of a member's behaviors. Empathically generated statements about the feelings a member appears to be experiencing can be included with observations when a member is not sharing these feelings: "Pam, you're wrinkling your brow and setting your jaw. You look angry."

Leaders sharing observations of members' interactions helps members develop more effective interpersonal behaviors. By sharing an observation of interaction, leaders identify relationship issues and can then initiate experimentation with alternative relationship behaviors. Interpersonal observations should contain an objective description of what leaders have seen or heard. This "interaction snapshot" includes identification of specific verbal and nonverbal behaviors. The following are examples of various interpersonal observations:

LEADER: "Steve, when you respond to another member's suggestions, you say, 'Yes, but.'" (observation of verbal behavior)

LEADER: "Rob, when you waved your fist in Cheryle's face, she jumped back." (observation of behavior and consequence)

LEADER: "Dave, after you said 'I don't care what you say,' several group members sat back in their chairs." (observation of verbal behavior and consequence)

Leaders should promote observation as a membership skill. When members share observations of each other's behaviors, all members increase their potential for learning. In addition, observation is an essential aspect of feedback exchange. Effective feedback includes observations of specific behaviors or words so that feedback receivers can understand what they are doing that leads to others' reactions.

Leaders should look for opportunities to involve members in sharing their observations:

LEADER: "I'm going to stop what's going on now. Group, what exactly do you see going on in Kevin and Bill's discussion?"

As members share observations, leaders should help members offer specific and objective observations. Members should understand that observations are not interpretations of the meaning or intention of a member's verbal or nonverbal behaviors. Interpretations presented as observation commonly produce defensive reactions. The following examples compare an objective observation and an interpretation offered as an observation:

LUCILLE: "You're trying to scare other members." (interpretation)
LUCILLE: "You're shaking your fist and talking very loudly." (observation of verbal and nonverbal behaviors)

Observations of the group as a system are important ingredients for several interventions. The simplest form of group observation increases the group's awareness of how it interacts. Observations can also identify counterproductive or productive group norms. Finally, observations of group interactions can initiate languaging:

LEADER: "Whenever the topic of emotions comes up, every member leans back in their chair and looks at the floor." (observation to increase awareness of interactions)
LEADER: "It seems like everyone in here follows the same rule. When conversation becomes intense, it's time to change the subject." (observation of a limiting group norm)
LEADER: "Everyone seems to be learning something very important in here this afternoon. What do you all think it is?" (observation and invitation to language)

The Basic Facilitation Sequence

The basic facilitation sequence is a series of skills designed to elicit input and engage members with each other. This sequence follows a simple progression.

1. *Elicit:* Use a listening skill to elicit a member's sharing relevant to current or recent group interaction.
2. *Clarify:* If needed, use a question or a statement to clarify what the member has said.
3. *Connect:* Use a question or statement to generate member to member interaction if other members do not respond spontaneously.

The basic facilitation sequence invites interaction. Frequently, however, members have the tendency to address the leader instead of each other. In these cases, leaders need to add a fourth step to the facilitation sequence and *redirect*

Figure 10.2
Basic Facilitation Sequence

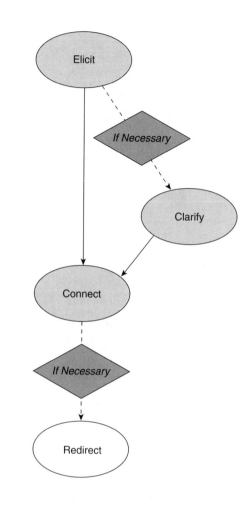

interaction so that members speak with each other. Figure 10.2 depicts this sequence and its various options.

Examples of the basic facilitation sequence follow. The first example shows an elicit and connect sequence, and the second shows an elicit, clarify, connect, and redirect sequence.

Example 1

LEADER: "Wanda, you look very angry. What's going on?" (elicit)
WANDA: "I'm really annoyed with Dave."
LEADER: "Tell Dave what you're annoyed about." (connect)

Example 2

LEADER: "Terry, you're having a reaction you're not sharing." (elicit)
TERRY: "Something just happened that really bothers me."

LEADER:	[Gesturing to the whole group] "Tell us what you're reacting to." (clarify and connect)
TERRY:	[To the leader] "Matt just gave Jill some feedback that I don't buy."
LEADER:	"Terry, you need to be saying this to Matt. Tell Matt." (redirect)

These examples show how individually directed interventions are transformed into interpersonal exchanges by using the basic facilitation sequence. Member-to-member interaction should be the goal for all individually focused interventions and skills.

Bridging

Bridging (Ormont, 1990) is an interpersonal intervention that seeks to establish and develop emotional connections between members. Bridging should be used whenever members do not spontaneously connect with one another. Although bridging is useful throughout the life of a group, it is especially important during the initial stages of group development. Here, bridging has the goal of establishing member-to-member interaction and connecting as norms.

Leaders use bridging at its most basic level to involve members who share issues, cognitive and emotional reactions, defenses, or perspectives in interaction. A more sophisticated use of bridging involves identifying the underlying theme in interaction and including all members in discussing how the theme impacts them. Creating a bridge between members requires initiating a conversation between them about what they share that is happening in the here and now.

Ideally, bridging eventually involves all group members with each other (Ormont, 1990). The objective of involving members is based on the premise that members can effectively help and support one another. In addition, by connecting members, leaders help members learn that they do not have to be alone when they confront their struggles. Bridging also contributes to the development of increasingly intimate self-disclosure, unconditional acceptance, cohesiveness, and universality. As an additional benefit, bridging can increase members' understanding and empathy in their relationships. Ormont (1990) describes three basic forms of bridging.

Open Bridge.   An open bridge is an open-ended request for a member's reaction to a group event. This type of bridge does not pursue a specific topic; instead, it opens interaction to new topics:

| LEADER: | "Louise, what do you think is going on with Richard?" |

This question creates a bridge between Louise and Richard and raises other members' awareness of Richard's reactions. Ormont (1990) points out that the member responding to this bridging question "discloses his own feeling as well as the person he is conjecturing about" (p. 8).

Directed Bridge.   A directed bridge specifies the topic of the bridge:

| LEADER: | "John, do you see that Janis is angry about what you just said to her?" |

This bridging question is presented to John for several reasons. These include bringing Janis's feelings into the group's awareness, helping John create a bridge with Louise, and involving John in an interaction that can increase his sensitivity for the effects of his communication.

Bridging About an Interaction.   This bridge involves using the observations and perceptions of a member to help other members become more aware of their interactions:

LEADER: "Jerry, what do you see going on between Diana and Bill?"

In this example, Jerry was asked this bridging question because his earlier interactions had demonstrated similar issues. By including a member who has had similar experiences, the leader increases the impact and depth of the bridge. Here, Jerry can share experiences and what he did to address the issue being experienced by Diana and Bill. Any member who observes an interaction can be involved in this type of bridge, with an intention similar to the open bridge, that is, to open interaction to a broad range of reactions. This form of bridging is also useful in identifying and resolving relationship issues.

It may be necessary to employ the basic facilitation sequence when using bridging questions (i.e., elicit, clarify, and connect). This sequence is useful when clarification of a member's response to a bridging question is needed or when it is necessary to redirect a member's response. The following examples depict how bridging can be used in conjunction with the basic facilitation sequence:

LOUISE: "I am really scared to talk about my feelings in here. I'm just not used to sharing my feelings with anybody."

LEADER: "Rhonda, I noticed that while Louise was talking, you were nodding as if you were agreeing with what Louise was saying about being afraid of sharing feelings." (observation and directed bridge)

RHONDA: [To the leader] "I know exactly what she . . ."

LEADER: [Interrupts] "Rhonda, speak directly to Louise." (redirect)

RHONDA: "OK. Louise, I know exactly what you mean. I'm not used to sharing my feelings, either. It scares the h— out of me."

At this point, the leader has several options: wait to see what develops between Louise and Rhonda, direct Louise and Rhonda to talk more about their shared fear, or bridge to other members. If the leader sees others reacting nonverbally, the leader can follow up if Louise and Rhonda bog down:

LEADER: "I'm seeing other members reacting to what Louise and Rhonda are saying about being afraid of sharing their feelings. Who would like to share the feelings you're having when you think about sharing feelings in here?" (observation and directed bridge)

Another common application of bridging involves connecting members who have shared consistent reactions or similar concerns during the life of the group. This is a powerful way to connect members who can use each other's support:

IAN: "I am really getting uncomfortable with having to share my feelings when I give feedback. It really shouldn't be that important."

LEADER: "Dave, you shared this very same concern last week. Tell Ian where you are with that now." (directed bridge and connect)

If the leader is interested in expanding on Ian's concern and hearing the reaction of other group members to what Ian has said, the leader can bridge to another member. This intervention can be repeated to generate the participation of additional members whenever desired:

LEADER: "Jeff, what are your reactions to what Ian has said?" (open bridge)

Leaders can also bridge to the entire group by not selecting a particular member. When bridging to the group, the leader gives members the choice to share or not share. This approach is useful when the leader believes that a topic will create excessive anxiety if a specific member was identified for the bridge. The risk in presenting this type of bridge is that no one will respond:

LEADER: "I'm wondering who would like to talk about how uncomfortable it is to talk about being sexually attracted to another member." (directed bridge to group)

If group members do not respond or if the leader believes that sharing is unlikely, a direction to share can be used to involve members who seem to be having the strongest reactions to the interaction:

LEADER: "Dan, you look like you're having a very strong reaction to Rhonda and Louise's conversation. Share with them what's going on with you." (open bridge and connect)

Ormont (1990) discusses uses of bridging that impede interaction. First, it is inappropriate to use bridging as a way for a leader to avoid being challenged. Second, leaders should refrain from bridging to a member who is unlikely to share useful information. Finally, it is not productive to bridge when several members are interacting meaningfully and including other members in the interaction would be distracting.

Confrontation

Confrontation is a variation of observing that can be used as an individual, an interpersonal, or a group-as-a-system intervention. Confrontation is the observation of discrepancies in members' behaviors. Young (1992) describes five areas of incongruities where the use of confrontation is appropriate:

1. When incongruities exist between verbal and nonverbal behaviors (e.g., member talks about being sad with a smile)
2. When a member's self-perceptions and those of others differ (e.g., a member's self-description of being an unacceptable person when others admire and like the member)

3. When what a member says he or she will do and what he or she actually does are inconsistent (e.g., a member says he or she will participate more frequently and stays withdrawn)
4. When what a member wants and the reality of their concern and history are incompatible (e.g., a member wants to have an intimate committed relationship when he or she is closed to others' input and has a history of failed relationships)
5. When two of a member's verbal messages are contradictory (e.g., a member says he or she wants feedback, then says he or she is not interested in other's perceptions)

Confrontations can be powerful tools that initiate change, or they can elicit defensive reactions. Carroll, Bates, and Johnson (1997) and Donigian and Malnati (1997) agree that the intentions and attitudes of leaders making the confrontation largely determine the impact of the confrontation. A confrontation offered with respect, caring, and sensitivity is likely to be effective, whereas a confrontation made in anger with the intention of hurting or demeaning another person is likely to obtain a defensive and potentially harmful reaction.

As members begin to use confrontations, leaders should monitor their use. Confrontations that attack or are not sensitive to the reactions of the member receiving the confrontation should be preempted. Helping members learn how to make caring and sensitive confrontations is an important goal for group interaction and ultimately an effective relationship skill.

Confrontations have the goal of increasing awareness and initiating change. Change resulting from confrontation involves a member learning to develop consistency in words and actions. This change helps a member become more congruent and communicate more honestly in relationships. Members who change successfully in response to confrontation will often hear that others perceive them as more honest and trustworthy than they had earlier. This change in perception is related to members losing the trust of other members because their words and actions had been inconsistent.

Leaders should make confrontations with the goal of member-to-member interaction. Usually this means that confronting a member should lead to feedback exchange. After a confrontation, the reactions of the member receiving the confrontation should be elicited and clarified, and other members should be invited to offer feedback. The following dialogue illustrates this sequence:

LEADER: "Laurel, you say you aren't happy with what you're getting out of group and that you're bored. It worries me that that's your experience. But, at the same time, you haven't participated very much, and you haven't shared anything that you want to work on." (confrontation of inconsistency of words and actions)
LAUREL: "I am bored."
LEADER: "You're bored, and you choose not to participate actively?" (reiteration of earlier confrontation)
LAUREL: "I see what you mean."

LEADER: "Yep, you're boring yourself. As a way to start being 'unbored,' would
             you like to get some feedback about how other members are reacting
             to you?" (confirm openness to initiation of feedback exchange)
LAUREL: "What the h—, I might as well start now."
LEADER: "I saw several of you reacting to the conversation Laurel and I were
             having. Laurel wants to get started, so how about some feedback for
             her?" (observation and question to initiate feedback exchange)

Interpersonal confrontation objectives focus on issues emerging in members' relationships. One of these objectives is to point out incongruities between verbal and nonverbal behaviors (e.g., members express concern for each other while they avoid eye contact). Another objective is to observe the discrepancy between what members say they will do and what they actually do in their relationships (e.g., members agree to be more emotionally expressive with one another and then avoid contact). An additional objective is to identify contradictions in verbal messages (e.g., first members say they want feedback from another member, then they say they are not interested in what the other has to say).

Interpersonal confrontation also involves the observation of destructive interaction patterns that choreograph many relationships. Three commonly observed destructive patterns include manipulation—"Come here, go away"—and sadomasochistic setups (Nicholas, 1984). To intervene effectively in these patterns, leaders need to recognize that relationship issues are relationship issues, not an individual's issue. Relationship issues involve all parties concerned, not just the member who appears to be the victim or the cause of the problem. Thus, for example, a member who manipulates another member needs to find another member who is willing to be manipulated.

Manipulation is often observed in group interaction. Usually, it takes the form of one member setting conditions for what it takes to have or maintain a desired relationship and another member willing to submit to those conditions. For example, one member may literally say or imply to another, "If you want to get close to me, you have to always agree with me." When the other member agrees to operate by these rules and acts accordingly, that member has agreed to be manipulated.

Manipulation appears in numerous variations that affect communication and feedback exchange. A commonly observed scenario is when a member presents as being extremely vulnerable and lets others know how criticism "just devastates me!" Other members, who would never want to devastate anyone, then withhold any feedback that has the slightest hint that a behavior has an undesirable effect. In this scenario, group members were willing to be manipulated to avoid being responsible for the devastation of another person. Confrontation of manipulation should include an observation of the manipulation and the payoff for the member who agrees to be manipulated. This confrontation can be directed either to the member doing the manipulation or to the member agreeing to be manipulated:

LEADER: "So, Joseph, let me see if I have this right. If you do exactly what
             Nancy wants you to do and don't do what you want to do, you'll be
             happy?" (confronting the member agreeing to be manipulated)

LEADER: "So, Nancy, if Joseph does exactly what you want him to do, he'll be the one you want to have a relationship with?" (confronting the member doing the manipulation)

"Come here, go away" is also a frequently observed interaction pattern. This destructive pattern involves the participation of two or more members who express a desire to be close or intimate with one another. At the same time, however, these members are uncertain about intimacy. This ambivalence translates into verbal expressions of wanting intimacy and nonverbal behaviors that are inconsistent with this request. For example, Larry and Joe express their attraction to each other and say they want to get more intimate with each other. As they discuss this "shared desire," their nonverbal behaviors appear defensive—arms crossed over their chests and leaning away from each other. Thus, their verbal behaviors say "come here," but their nonverbal behaviors say "go away." Confrontations of this interactive pattern should initiate experiments with consistent verbal and nonverbal behaviors. The following examples show an interpersonal confrontation and an individual confrontation used to set up an interpersonal experiment:

LEADER: "Larry and Joan, you both say how much you want to develop a more intimate relationship, and at the same time both of you are using body language that says 'go away.'" (confrontation of discrepancy in interpersonal behavior)

LEADER: "Linda, you've heard from other members that, while you say you want a close relationship with Fred your nonverbal behaviors say keep away. I'd like you to try an experiment, if you're willing, and let us know how it feels. Open your posture by unfolding your arms and uncrossing your legs, look directly at Fred, and say, 'I'd like to be a close friend of yours.'" (restatement of confrontation and challenge to experiment with consistent behaviors)

Nicholas (1984) describes another interpersonal relationship pattern that should be the target of confrontation. This pattern, the sadomasochistic setup, is somewhat similar to manipulation but has a more damaging outcome. The sadomasochistic setup involves one member (the sadist) who asks another member to be vulnerable (the masochist). Once the masochistic member complies by being vulnerable, the sadistic member criticizes, belittles, rejects, or in some way hurts the "vulnerable" masochistic member. While the masochistic member complains about being hurt, that member continues to participate willingly in a relationship pattern that continues to cause pain.

For example, Minnie tells Joe, "Joe, I really care about you. If you would be more open and intimate with me, we could have a wonderful relationship." Joe responds by sharing feelings that are very sensitive for him. Minnie then criticizes Joe for sharing "unimportant and meaningless" feelings. Later, Minnie repeats her request, and Joe complies again and is hurt again. In this example, Minnie could easily be described as the "bad guy." It is important to note, however, that Joe, who seems to be the "good guy," willingly complies, although he will be hurt again. This pattern, much like other interpersonal patterns, recycles. Even leaders who are experienced and knowledgeable about destructive relationship patterns may not identify these patterns until they have been repeated several times. Confrontation of both members is definitely indicated when a sadomasochistic setup is identified. These confrontations initiate ongoing feedback and experimentation with these members. Both of the following confrontations might be used:

LEADER: "Joe, you complain about Minnie hurting you, and at the same time you continue to allow yourself to get set up to get hurt. She asks you to open up, you do, and you get slammed."

LEADER: "Minnie, you tell Joe you want to be close to him and ask him to be open with you. When he does, your words belittle him and reject him. You ask for a relationship, then slam the door in his face."

Interpersonal confrontations should use the same skills and conditions that lead to effective individual confrontations. As is the case with individually directed confrontation, interpersonal confrontation uses observations that identify contradictions and discrepancies in actions and words. Leaders need to remember that a goal of confrontation is to initiate behavior change. Confrontations that result in defensive behaviors are not useful, whereas those offered with respect and sensitivity are most likely to succeed.

Challenges

Challenges focus on motivating members to use new interpersonal behaviors. Challenges, although related to directives, differ from directives because they offer members a choice about using new behaviors or taking risks. Challenges range in intensity from comments that suggest experimental behaviors to more direct comments that "strongly recommend" experimental behaviors. Leaders vary the intensity of their challenges on the basis of the amount of anxiety they want a challenge to create. Challenges can encourage risk taking that involves boundary-opening self-disclosures designed to increase the intimacy in relationships.

Because challenges direct members to interact, they usually do not require follow-up connecting or eliciting skills, which are needed only when members do not respond to a challenge. Before challenging a member, leaders should be clear that members are in charge of choosing how they are going to interact. A challenge should always be presented as a choice, and members should not be pressured or coerced into performing challenges. Follow-up questions or directions that explore members' choices are, however, appropriate and important.

Challenges that promote experimentation can be implemented by leaders to follow the confrontation or feedback members have received or, in the absence of these, as an invitation to experiment with new behaviors. Examples of leaders' challenges follow. The first two follow feedback, and the last two are leader-generated experiments made in the absence of feedback:

LEADER: "Richard, you just got some feedback that suggested some behaviors you can use to look angry when you feel angry. If you are ready, since you seem to be really annoyed with Gracie, you can try now with Gracie." (challenge as feedback follow-up)

LEADER: "Jeff, you just heard several people suggest that looking at them and smiling when you were telling them that you cared about them might work better than looking at the floor. I'd like to see you smile and tell Susie how you feel about her. [Pause] Jeff, I know you can do this and it's risky for you. Perhaps you could do it now or wait a while before you do it. What's your choice?" (challenge as feedback follow-up emphasizing choice and acknowledging risk)

LEADER: "Michelle, if you're interested, I'd like you to try an experiment. Here it is. Whenever you hear another member act like they expect you to go along with what they say without asking you, try saying something like, 'I'm not a doormat; you have to ask me first and give me a good reason why I should agree with you.'" (leader-generated challenge)

LEADER: "Francis, here's an experiment for you. You can try it when it seems useful. The experiment is, when you get feedback you didn't ask for, say, 'When I want your feedback, I'll ask for it.'" (leader-generated challenge)

Challenges that encourage risk taking can also follow confrontation or feedback exchange or initiate a leader-generated experiment. The goals of risk-taking challenges are to increase members' involvement in their relationships. This is an intentional way to influence members to open their interpersonal boundaries and abandon habitual solutions that keep members isolated. Here are a few examples of risk-taking challenges:

LEADER: "Ed, it seems that you might find a particular experiment useful. You can try it a couple of times tonight and let us know how it works for you. Here it is. When you hear someone say something that makes you feel even a little sad, say to that member, 'I felt sad when I heard you say that.'"

LEADER: "Nancy, when you have a strong reaction to what another member says, I'd like you to try something different than screaming. If you're willing, I'd like you to say, 'I'm scared because I'm not sure I understand what you are saying. Please help me understand what you are saying.'"

Leaders should experiment with challenges to find an approach that works best for them. Some leaders believe they need to offer a rationale for their challenges. Other leaders prefer not to, stating instead to the member being challenged that once the member has experimented several times, they want the member to share what they have discovered while doing the experiment.

Relationship challenges initiate experiments for members with various degrees of involvement in specific relationships. These challenges can follow feedback or confrontation or initiate a leader-generated experiment:

LEADER: "Joe and Nancy, if you two are willing, here's an experiment for you. Nancy, when Joe starts to share his feelings with you, stop him and say, 'Sharing your feelings with me will only get you hurt.' Joe, when Nancy says she wants you to share your feelings with her so that the two of

you can have a relationship, I want you to try saying, 'I'm not interested in being hurt.'" (challenge to try a leader-generated experiment,
follow-up on earlier confrontation)

LEADER: "Randy, you and Ann haven't developed much of a relationship with
each other yet. The two of you have not really interacted at all. Here's
an experiment I'd like you to try, if you're willing. During the next
three sessions, observe each other from time to time, and when you
have a reaction, share it or, better yet, share some feedback. I'd like
each of you to do this at least twice a session." (leader challenge to try
a boundary-opening experiment)

Challenges directed at the group as a system are the same in form and content
and are directed at the entire group for the same reasons as those directed at individual members or relationships. Group-directed challenges encourage the group
to experiment with different norms or different communication boundaries. These
challenges are parts of more complicated intervention strategies described in
chapter 13.

Communication Clarification

Leaders use communication clarification whenever members' interactions demonstrate communication problems. As described in chapter 12, communication problems include bypassing, inference making, polarizing, and signal reactions (Tubbs,
1992). The objectives for communication clarification are to clarify members' intended messages and ensure understanding. Improving communication has important implications for how effectively members interact and, most critically, for the
usefulness and potency of feedback exchange.

Communication clarification interventions can include observations, listening
skills, directions, and feedback exchange. Communication clarification is a process
that begins by stopping interaction that demonstrates a communication problem,
continues by describing the observed communication problem, and then concludes
by directing members to use more effective communication skills.

Leaders can involve members in addressing communication problems by stopping an interaction that demonstrates a communication problem and asking members to share their observations of the interaction. This approach supports previous
interventions designed to develop communication skills and involves members in
monitoring each other's communication skills. A variation of this intervention involves interrupting an interaction that has communication problems and directing
members to give the interacting members feedback about how they have been
communicating.

Leaders should ensure that members receiving feedback about communication
problems learn more effective communication behaviors to use in their interactions.
Once the interacting members have defined more effective communication behaviors, these behaviors should be used immediately. This process involves three steps.
First, the leader directs the interacting members to repeat their interactions, this time
using effective communication behaviors. Second, the leader asks the interacting

members to discuss their experience using the communication behaviors. Finally, the leader directs the group to offer feedback on the communication behaviors. An example follows:

LEADER: "Steve, you and Del have been having some problems communicating with each other. The two of you got feedback that you might try experimenting with, repeating what you heard the other one say before you respond. As I recall, you two started by disagreeing about sharing the feelings you were having about other members in here. I'd like you to start over. This time try using the feedback you got." (summary and direction to experiment with alternative behaviors)

After Steve and Del have experimented with the alternative behaviors:

LEADER: "Del and Steve, how did repeating what the other said work for you?" (question to elicit reactions)

Del and Steve share reactions, after which the leader directs them to interact with each other briefly about their experience of each other when using the experimental behaviors:

LEADER: "Group, what feedback do you have for Del and Steve?" (question to initiate feedback exchange and bridge)

Another application of communication clarification involves improving a member's ability to communicate effectively. Although this is an individually focused intervention, its intent is to improve interpersonal relationships. When members demonstrate a pattern of communication problems, leaders can offer feedback or direct the group to offer feedback that identifies the problematic communication behaviors and develops effective communication skills.

Communication clarification as a group-as-a-system intervention has the goals of improving the communication skills of the entire group and developing facilitative communication norms.

Contracting

Contracting is an interpersonal intervention that can be used to follow up feedback exchange, confrontation, communication clarification, or any other intervention that addresses the relationship behaviors of two or more members. Usually, contracting involves two members in an agreement but can also involve other members, even the entire group. Contracting is an agreement that specifies an experimental behavior, the circumstances in which to apply it, and an interaction to promote that behavior. From a leader's perspective, contracting involves members in helping each other change. Contracting distributes responsibility for monitoring how members progress toward their goals. Distributing responsibility helps build norms that establish a shared responsibility for change; this increases members' involvement in interpersonal learning. Contracting engages members, helping to establish how members can assist each other and open interpersonal boundaries.

Contracting performs a number of useful support functions. It helps members follow through with developing new interactive skills. Contracting can involve members who manage their boundaries effectively in helping members who have difficulty managing their boundaries learn more effective boundary management skills. In addition, contracting can facilitate the ongoing monitoring and observation of members' behaviors. Contracting is very useful when several members are working on developing the same behaviors. By developing a contract for members to encourage each other to use a behavior, leaders do not have to monitor these members closely. At the same time, the members who participate in the contract experience offering and receiving support. In addition, when members monitor each other's behaviors and continuing experimentation, they become more personally responsible for their changes.

Leaders initiate contracts by identifying or acknowledging a member's or members' goals. Once goals are described, the leader asks the member or members involved whether they would like help in achieving their goals. When members agree, other members are involved, and an agreement is developed. Leaders can promote this process by suggesting that support might increase members' chances of reaching their goals. Contracts need to be clear and uncomplicated. Leaders should avoid developing contracts that involve multiple behaviors or complicated sets of circumstances in which to perform the contract.

Contracts are agreements between members to provide support for ongoing experimentation, to remind or challenge each other to use experimental behaviors, or to encourage risk taking. These ongoing agreements can involve members skilled in the use of particular behaviors in helping other members become proficient with that behavior. Contracts can also challenge members to use experimental behaviors when it is uncomfortable to do so.

The following dialogue illustrates how a leader can initiate a contract after feedback exchange:

LEADER: "Joseph, it seems like you've decided that there are times when it might be useful for you to close your boundaries when Nancy struggles with her feelings. Am I right about that?" (summary and question to ensure understanding)

JOSEPH: "Yeah, I know I need to sit back, shut up, and let her have her feelings and not think that I'm in charge of how she feels."

LEADER: "It seems like that might be scary for you." (reflection of feelings)

JOSEPH: "That's for sure! I can't deal with her pain."

LEADER: "So allowing her to have her feelings will be difficult. Would you like some help with that?" (restatement to ensure understanding and a question that invites the initiation of a contract)

JOSEPH: "I can use all the help I can get!"

LEADER: "I want you to decide who you think can help you best. This is the person who can best let you know when it's time to sit back and, maybe, get more comfortable with letting Nancy act and feel hurt when she needs to. Now, ask." (direction, contract initiation, and connect)

JOSEPH: "Scott, can you help me out? You seem to be OK with people having their feelings."

SCOTT: "Sure, Joe, what can I do?"

LEADER: "Tell Scott exactly how you want him to help you out." (direction to ensure understanding)

JOSEPH: "Scott, just tell me to 'chill out'! When Nancy starts to melt, look my way and tell me to 'chill out' if I look like I'm ready to rescue her."

Contracting involves the leader more intensely when the leader directs another person to offer help and specifies the help to offer. This strategic move is used to involve two members who are closed to each other or to ensure that a member who will follow through with a contract is involved. A variation here would be to ask Joseph to develop a contract with the entire group.

Contracts are simple to initiate in cases where members share the same experimental behavior. This form of contract also bridges two members:

LEADER: "Dave, it seems that you have decided that sharing your emotions is an important goal for you in the group. Sandy, that's your goal, too. How do you two think you could help each other meet your 'sharing feelings' goals during our sessions?" (summary and question to initiate contract and bridge)

There are many ways to develop and initiate contracts. The essential pieces of contracts and their initiation are specific behaviors and clear agreements between members about when and how they will support each other's changes. Leaders, as they experiment with using contracts, will find many strategic uses and diverse ways to initiate and shape interpersonal and group-as-a-system contracts.

Boundary Setting

Boundary setting is a specific set of interventions that help leaders perform their boundary management function (see chapter 9). These interventions involve helping members define their communication and relationship boundaries and move toward more autonomous functioning. Boundary-setting interventions are designed to help members make better choices about when and how much to open or close their boundaries.

Boundary-Opening Interventions.   Boundary-opening interventions are helpful for members who have boundaries that are not permeable enough for them to develop healthy relationships or benefit from interpersonal learning. These members are emotionally unexpressive, detached, and closed to feedback. Boundary-opening interventions have the goals of helping these members become more receptive, open, and emotionally available. Such interventions encourage the development of various behaviors, including expressing emotion, self-disclosing appropriate and relevant personal information, asking for and using feedback, giving effective feedback, sharing reactions to group interactions, expressing concern for other members' struggles, and offering and asking for interpersonal support.

Boundary-opening interventions require the use of observations and confrontations to increase awareness, exploratory listening skills to engage members with closed boundaries with others, and directions and challenges to initiate behavior change. An example of a boundary opening intervention follows:

LEADER: "Jack, you haven't shared much and haven't asked for any feedback." (observation)

JACK: "Your point is?"

LEADER: "I get the point that you'd like me to leave you alone. At the same time, you're looking vulnerable and sounding angry." (confrontation and attempt to invite disclosure)

JACK: "What of it?"

LEADER: "Jack, I'm not going anywhere, even though you want me to back off. I'd like to know what's scaring you so much?" (listening skill to explore reaction and invite interaction)

JACK: "Leave me alone. This is making me really uncomfortable."

LEADER: [To the group] "I wonder what the rest of you are seeing going on here?" (leader invites group interaction to keep others engaged and possibly to bridge with Jack)

WARREN: "I know what it's like to be scared to share what's going on with me. Jack, the only way to make it easier is sharing your feelings and finding out you can survive."

PHYLLIS: "Warren is right, Jack. You're making it hard for yourself by hiding. What do you think we'll do to you—help you or something?"

JACK: "I am getting really mad now . . ."

LEADER: [Interrupts] "Jack, you look terrified, not mad." (confrontation)

JACK: "OK, d—— it! I'm scared, and you guys are ticking me off. I didn't want to let you see how scared I am."

LEADER: "Jack, I've got an experiment that could make this easier for you. I hope you'll do it at least two more times before the group ends in 45 minutes. The experiment is to make a feeling statement to another member when you have an emotional reaction to what they say. If two times is too scary, do it just once. Anybody want to help Jack with his experiment?" (challenge to use a boundary-opening behavior and invitation for a support contract)

This example shows how a leader could challenge a defensive member with closed boundaries to be more open. The use of a challenge and the invitation for a support contract reflect the leader's sense of the member's fearfulness about trying on a very uncomfortable behavior.

In many cases, members with rigidly closed boundaries are very resistant to boundary-opening interventions. These members require patience and will become engaged in interaction only after they have built significant trust in the group and become less fearful of not being able to defend themselves when vulnerable. These members create trust issues in the entire group and have great potential for becoming scapegoats.

Boundary-Closing Interventions. Boundary-closing interventions are useful whenever members demonstrate diffuse or excessively open boundaries. Members with diffuse boundaries are overly concerned about others' feelings, avoid taking responsibility for their own emotions, are inordinately compliant, and constantly attempt to gain approval. Boundary-closing interventions have the goal of developing behaviors that lead to personal autonomy. Such behaviors that members can experiment with include allowing others to experience intense emotions, stating opinions that differ from those of others, expressing anger, saying no to requests, and taking responsibility for their own emotions.

Boundary-closing interventions utilize listening skills, observations, confrontations, challenges, and directives. Exploratory listening skills engage members with diffuse boundaries in dialogue about their behavior. Observations and confrontations develop awareness and motivate change in relationship behaviors. Challenges are useful when members experience boundary-closing behaviors as highly threatening. Leaders can use directions when experimental behaviors are not excessively risky or when a member seems unlikely to respond to a challenge. The following is an example of a boundary-closing intervention:

LEADER: "Sandra, whenever another member starts to share their feelings, you jump right in. When you do, you change the subject or tell the person having the uncomfortable feeling not to get upset or listen to anything that upsets them." (observation)

SANDRA: [To the leader] "You're scaring me. You could be nicer. [Pause] Is there something I can do to make you happy with me?"

LEADER: "You think I'm upset with you now, and you want to make me happy so you won't have to be scared." (immediacy)

SANDRA: "You are such an incredible leader. What can I do to be a better member?"

LEADER: "I want you to do an experiment. I know you will because you want to be a good group member. Here it is. Disagree with me now and three more times with other group members during this session." (direction)

In this example, the leader uses the member's need to please as leverage to involve a member with diffuse boundaries in a boundary-closing experiment. Disagreeing is boundary closing because it defines a member's opinion and differentiates that member from others.

Requesting Input

Leaders request input by using questions or directions when reactions to group interaction, suggestions for alternative behaviors, ideas for problem solving, personal history that relates to current interaction, or other forms of information can facilitate progress. Other examples include asking or directing members to share the expectations of group membership with a new member, members to describe their experiences with experimental behaviors outside the group, or a member to describe his or her experience with a shared concern.

When asking members for informational input, leaders need to be very cautious. Asking for information directs the group into conceptual conversation and away from meaningful interaction. Thus, leaders should request information only when essential. In addition, to eliminate potential detours to cognitive conversation, directions that move interaction back to the here and now should quickly follow informational input. The following are examples of leader statements that elicit information:

LEADER: "I'd like you all to share with Tom what's expected from members in this group—the expectations you have for each other and how we go about learning in here."

LEADER: "Joe, you were going to try on some different relationship behaviors after our last session. Could you share how they worked for you?"

LEADER: "Diane, you have been working on making some changes that are very similar to those Lucy has just started to face. Would you share with her what it has been like for you to make these changes?"

Requesting input can generate possible approaches to conflict management or potential solutions for problem solving. In terms of managing conflict, this intervention is appropriate when members are involved in nonproductive conflict, which occurs when there is an impasse in interaction that consists of an argument that repeatedly covers the same issues. When leaders observe that conflicts between members are becoming circular conversations, they can intervene with a request for input. This intervention involves the use of an observation and a directive or question:

LEADER: [Interrupting and looking at the group] "Wanda and Susie seem to be covering the same issues over and over again and are going nowhere. I'm wondering if any of you have some ideas about other ways they might approach their disagreement." (observation and request for input)

The most useful application for requesting input follows feedback exchange. When a member has received feedback but has not identified an experimental behavior, the leader can follow the feedback exchange by requesting input. This follow-up involves asking or directing the entire group or selected members to generate ideas about experimental behaviors:

LEADER: "What ideas do you all have about some behaviors for Scott to try on?" (question requesting input)

LEADER: "Jim and Cindy, give Scott some ideas about some different behaviors to try on." (direction for input)

Structuring

Structuring interventions are the specific procedures that leaders use to perform the structuring function (see chapter 9). Structuring shapes the interaction of group members and uses observations and directives. Observations about interaction and directives to reshape interaction are the basic structuring sequence. Structuring is used to teach feedback and communication skills and to manage interpersonal or group interaction. Managing group interaction can shape interactive norms or control heated interaction. Structuring interpersonal interaction is a management tool intended to ensure understanding. The following examples provide illustrations of how leaders can initiate structuring interventions:

LEADER: "Wow! You folks are really feeling some intense emotions, but most of you are sharing at the same time. I'd like you to speak one at a time so each of you can be heard." (observation and direction)

LEADER: "Marie, your feedback didn't include exactly what Betty was doing to cause your reaction. Restate your feedback and include what exactly Betty was doing." (observation and direction)

LEADER: "Ronnie, you and Janet are making statements that defend your points of view. I'm not sure that you two are really hearing what the other is saying. Continue to share your reactions with each other. This time repeat what you heard the other person say before you give your opinion." (observation and direction)

Once members have finished participating in structured interactions, leaders should direct the interacting members to discuss their experiences. This reaction-sharing phase can highlight what worked in the structured interaction. Using a direction starts this phase. The direction to share reactions often leads to languaging about what has worked in the interaction:

LEADER: "Betty, Marie included some specific behaviors in her feedback to you. Tell us if and how that worked differently for you." (observation and direction)

BETTY: "When she told me what the specific things were that I was doing, I didn't feel attacked, and I knew what I did that got her upset."

LEADER: [To the group] "What happened here that was helpful for Betty?" (question to initiate languaging)

WHEN BASIC SKILLS AND INTERVENTIONS DO NOT WORK

Leaders need to question the effectiveness of their skills and interventions when they are not successful. Besides poor timing, interventions are ineffective for several reasons. A common one is inaccurate diagnosis of interactive problems. Interventions can also be ineffective because they fail to address or appreciate members' fears. Leaders who have not accurately identified focal conflicts or boundary issues or defined members' shared fears may continue to intervene using similar interventions. When these persistent interventions are based on an inaccurate assessment of group issues, leaders often become increasingly baffled about why the group is not cooperating.

When leaders are uncertain about why their interventions are ineffective, they need to reassess the goals of their interventions. Occasionally, leaders can experiment with not intervening as a method to understand more accurately what is occurring in the group. Not intervening when intervention is apparently called for is an excellent diagnostic tool, especially for beginning leaders who are often overwhelmed by the complexity of their role.

Not intervening allows leaders to observe interaction and more clearly define existing norms and their impact on interaction. By not intervening, leaders also can gain a better idea of what members' motivations are for not responding to an intervention. Withholding interventions can also allow leaders an opportunity to diagnose focal conflicts or to determine whether the group has become overly dependent. Not intervening also encourages members to assume more responsibility for group interaction and norm development and maintenance. Leaders who choose not to intervene in order to diagnose interaction should be careful. This diagnostic process does not release leaders from their responsibilities.

CONCLUSION

The skills and interventions presented in this chapter are fundamental for facilitating interactive groups. Whenever leaders use these skills and interventions, they must maintain awareness that their goal is for members to interact and learn from one another. These fundamental skills and interventions are needed to perform leaders' ongoing tasks and responsibilities. The ongoing tasks of leaders and strategies designed to deal with problems in group interaction are discussed in the following chapters.

Developing Effective Group Membership Skills

After reading this chapter, you should be able to:

✔ Outline the membership skills necessary for effective group functioning and interpersonal learning.

✔ Discuss how and when to teach effective communication skills to group members.

✔ Explain how to identify communication problems as well as effective and ineffective communication.

✔ Describe effective and ineffective forms of self-disclosure.

✔ Discuss how to encourage effective self-disclosure.

✔ Outline the necessary components of effective feedback exchange and experimentation.

✔ Explain how to teach and structure feedback exchange.

✔ Discuss how to initiate and monitor experimentation.

INTRODUCTION

Learning how to interact effectively is critical for members of groups that emphasize interpersonal learning. The effectiveness of members' interactions depends on the development of several essential membership skills. As members develop these membership skills, leaders will observe that the frequency and quality of members' learning increases. These skills include effective interpersonal communication skills, self-disclosure, feedback exchange, and experimentation.

Because members need to have certain skills to benefit from interpersonal learning processes, leaders have the goal of helping members become skilled interpersonal learners. As members become skilled, they become increasingly self-sufficient and are able to learn with increasingly less active leader intervention. As members become self-sufficient, leaders are able to attend more fully to observing interaction dynamics, shared concerns, and impediments to group development. These observations are the basis of accurate leader interventions that eventually have the greatest impact on group interaction and members' learning.

The most crucial component of interpersonal learning is members having the skills necessary to give and receive feedback. Giving and receiving feedback works best when members have the communication skills needed to clearly present and understand the feedback they are given. Communication and feedback exchange skills, however, do not necessarily lead to change. To change, members must define new behaviors to experiment with and develop in group and then incorporate the new behaviors that have worked in group into their relationships outside group.

Training members to use communication skills increases the quality of feedback exchange. When members paraphrase and question to ensure understanding and reflect feelings to communicate awareness of others' emotional experiences, they have the skills necessary to participate meaningfully in interpersonal learning. In addition, as members self-disclose to share their immediate experiences and establish emotional connections, the group progresses as a highly effective learning environment.

Members' use of effective communication skills creates an environment that increases opportunities for interpersonal learning. In addition, effective communication, along with meaningful self-disclosure, is the foundation for the development of trust. When members trust each other, their fears of rejection diminish. Consequently, an atmosphere of safety develops, and members become less concerned about interpersonal risks.

EFFECTIVE INTERPERSONAL COMMUNICATION

Interpersonal communication is the "process of creating meanings in the minds of others. These meanings may or may not correspond to the meanings we intend to create" (Tubbs, 1992, p. 212). Members make progress as they learn how to communicate their experiences and perceptions effectively and understand the meanings of others' communications. In essence, effective communication allows members to exchange information that helps them learn.

When attempting to facilitate effective communication in groups, leaders should be mindful that cultural differences do exist. Ivey, Ivey, and Simek-Morgan (1993) offer an important example: "The expression of emotions . . . may be totally inappropriate and alien for some Asian-Americans and Native-Americans" (p. 9). They emphasize that counselors should evaluate the appropriateness of their interventions for individuals from different cultures. Cultural differences are certainly a factor that leaders must always keep in mind. Nevertheless, leaders should be extremely reluctant to abandon the idea that it is essential that members learn how to understand each other and that members using effective communication skills is the way to ensure that this happens.

Guidelines for Effective Communication

Effective communication is the shared responsibility of members who both send and receive messages. Johnson and Johnson (2000) indicate that because communication is interpersonal, it involves both a member effectively sending a message and another member effectively receiving the message. The guidelines Johnson and Johnson describe are relevant for group environments that focus on interpersonal learning. Leaders may use these guidelines as they guide group interaction, as content for discussion during pregroup orientation meetings, or as ideas they can infuse into the interventions they use to address communication problems.

Sending.   Effectively sent messages have eight characteristics (Johnson & Johnson, 2000). These characteristics increase the chances that others will understand and respond nondefensively to the messages they receive:

1. Members should "own" their statements by using the pronouns "I" or "my." Using these pronouns demands that members assume responsibility for their statements. Those who receive an "owned" statement are more likely to believe it. Consider the following statements: "You get sad when you get ignored" and "I feel sad when you ignore me." Although these statements can express the same meaning, the member who offers the latter statement expresses him- or herself more clearly. Making owned statements of emotion also connects speakers more meaningfully with their own experience.
2. Members need to include necessary information and make statements specific. Partial or vague statements increase the chances of miscommunication. By omitting information, speakers increase their chances of being misunderstood. The member who states, "When you do that, it upsets me and I feel differently about you," offers the receiver insufficient information. If the receiver of this message does not ask what "that" and "feel differently" mean, he or she can only assume what the sender means. The consequence of these assumptions is that the receiver will draw erroneous conclusions about his or her behavior and relationship with the sender.
3. Members need to send congruent messages to be believable. Members perceive others whose verbal and nonverbal behaviors do not agree as insincere. A common example of incongruent messages is members who state that they are angry while they smile. Members who receive incongruent messages will be confused, not understanding which part of the message to respond to, the words, or the smile. Believable and accurately heard messages are most likely when members match their verbal and nonverbal behaviors.

4. Members should repeat parts of their messages to increase the chances of being heard and understood. Members communicate effectively when they restate a point clearly and succinctly. Others will also understand that the point is important to the speaker.

5. Members should ask for verification from the receivers of their messages in order to clarify their communication and improve their interactive behaviors. When receivers respond to verification statements like "Tell me what you heard me say," senders can determine whether they have been heard accurately. When members are frequently misheard, it is useful for them to explore what happened to cause the miscommunication. Questions like "What did I do to make it difficult for you to hear what I said?" can be used to initiate this exploration. Responses can help members develop greater awareness of how their style of verbal and nonverbal communication affects their relationships with others.

6. Members should use terms that are understandable to the receiver. Members who use terms that are convoluted, jargonistic, metaphoric, or abstract are often misunderstood. When members communicate in this manner, receivers are less likely to hear a message specifically related to the sender's intentions. Receivers may also experience the embarrassment of having to admit they do not understand what the sender is trying to say. Leaders should encourage all members to use words that others will understand. Leaders need to ask members to translate easily misconstrued language into clear and specific terms. This process often has a powerful effect on both the speaker and the receiver, leaving little room for misunderstanding.

7. Whenever possible, members should include words that describe the emotions they are experiencing. The messages that offer the clearest indication of the sender's intentions include statements of emotion. Receivers who hear "I'm really hurt by what you've said" will have a clear understanding of the sender's message. On the other hand, receivers who hear "I can't believe you said that" are left to wonder whether the sender is angry, joking, sad, or hurt. In this case, if others do not guess the sender's feelings accurately, a miscommunication occurs.

8. When members react to the behaviors of other members, they should specifically identify those behaviors and not attach evaluative terms. Members should also avoid interpreting the meaning or motivation of these behaviors. A nonevaluative message that does not interpret the motivations of others is less likely to elicit defensive reactions. For example, the statement "You did that stupid grin again, you're just trying to confuse me" will probably elicit a defensive reaction. Conversely, the statement "When you finished talking you smiled. I'm not sure how to respond to you" allows receivers to develop awareness of the impact of their behaviors and provides an opening to talk about their intentions.

Receiving.   Effectively receiving others' communications requires effort. This often means that leaders will need to monitor interaction to ensure that members hear each others' messages accurately. Johnson and Johnson (2000) offer three guidelines for effectively hearing the messages of others:

1. To ensure that they hear a message accurately, members should restate both the information and the emotions shared by the sender. These restatements should be made in the receiver's own words and should not include an evaluation of

the message, attach or remove information, or draw conclusions about the motivations behind the statement.

2. The effectiveness of responses to a sender's statements increases when receivers state their perception of the sender's emotions. These statements should be tentative and owned as the receiver's perceptions.

3. After receivers have paraphrased and shared their perceptions of a sender's emotions, a negotiation process begins that has the objective of reaching agreement about the meaning of the message. Receivers initiate this process by making statements like "I think you're saying that . . . " or "I believe you mean . . . "

Teaching Communication Skills

This section describes specific communication skills that leaders can teach members and presents some suggestions and examples of how to teach these skills. The skills included in this section are reflecting feelings, paraphrasing, and questioning. These skills help members learn from each other and communicate more effectively in their daily lives.

Reflecting Feelings.   Ivey (1994) describes elementary reflection of feelings as noticing another's emotional expression, then stating the observed emotional expression to the person. Reflection of feelings can note overtly expressed feelings or be a statement of a member's perception of another's feelings. Reflections use emotion words, such as *angry, happy, hurt, scared, sad, empty,* and *lonely.*

STEVE: "Well, I had to say something to her because who else was going to say anything?"

BILL: "You look angry." (reflection of observed feelings)

or

BILL: "No one saying anything is really scary for you." (reflection using an imagined feeling)

Leaders should encourage members to use reflections in several instances:

1. When members are having emotional experiences and are not recognizing these experiences

2. When a member attempts to understand another member and does not include an effort to understand the other's emotional experience

3. When two members are having emotional reactions to each other but are not stating their feelings

Teaching members to reflect each others' feelings helps members "put words" on the emotional connections they are experiencing. "Putting words" on emotional connections brings these connections clearly into awareness and increases group cohesion. Directing members to use reflections is one of the most fundamental ways to help members open their communication boundaries:

LEADER: "Dave, it seems that you and Jill are experiencing some emotions here and you're not sharing them. Try this. Tell Jill what you understand her saying and add how you think she is feeling to your statement."

DAVE: "Jill, you're telling me to stop being late, and you're angry."

Paraphrasing.   Ivey (1994) describes paraphrasing as persons stating in their own words what they have heard another person say. This restatement should include key words the other has said and should attempt to be a shorter statement than the one made. By shortening the restatement, the paraphrasing member can focus on what he or she perceives to be the most important aspects of the other member's communication. Paraphrases ensure that members accurately hear each others' words. After hearing a paraphrase, members can indicate how well the paraphrasing members have stated what they have said:

STEVE: "Well, I had to say something to her because who else was going to say anything?"

BILL: "You say things when you don't know who else will."

STEVE: "Yeah, somebody had to."

Paraphrasing is an important first step in helping members understand and act on feedback. Leaders should teach members to paraphrase to clarify understanding of any important communication and as an initial response to receiving feedback. After members paraphrase, if they still do not understand the feedback they have been given, they can ask questions to gain further clarification. Directing a member to paraphrase is also useful when members' emotional responses to each other do not seem consistent with the words they are using.

When a member's reaction to what another member has said seems inconsistent with the statement made, it is often because of a misunderstanding. Members involved in emotionally charged interactions can occasionally benefit from accurately paraphrasing what others have said before sharing their own reactions. The following example shows how leaders can teach members to use a paraphrase to clarify interaction:

CINDY: "I don't know where I stand with you, Art. You seem to be trying to keep me away."

ART: "Cindy, you don't seem to care about me."

LEADER: "Art, I'm not sure you understood what Cindy was saying. Say to Cindy in your own words what you heard her say."

ART: "You basically said I'm a real jerk and you don't care for me."

CINDY: "No, Art, that's not what I said."

LEADER: "Cindy, say what you want to say to Art. Art, before you respond, say what you heard her say in your own words to see if you heard her accurately."

Questioning.   Leaders should teach members to use questions to confirm understanding, ask for clarification, and request information from others. There are two basic types of questions: open and closed. Closed questions can be answered in only a few words (Ivey, 1994) and usually start with the words *are* and *do*. Closed questions are especially useful for verifying understanding:

STEVE: "Well, I had to say something to her because who else was going to say anything?"

BILL: "Are you saying you're in charge of saying things when no one else will?"

STEVE: "Well, someone has to say something."

Open questions (Ivey, 1994) encourage others to describe their thoughts and feelings more fully. Open questions usually start with the words *what, how,* and *could:*

STEVE: "Well, I had to say something to her because who else was going to say anything?"

BILL: "What do you think will happen when no one says anything?" or

BILL: "What are you thinking when no one says anything?"

Leaders need to teach questioning skills to members when it appears that they are making assumptions or do not understand other members' communications. Be cautious when encouraging the use of questions because members often will substitute questions for feedback and more honest and direct statements. When this happens, leaders should direct them to offer feedback or make a direct statement:

SALLY: "Ken, what are you trying to do when you argue with me?"

LEADER: "Sally, it seems that you have some feedback for Ken. Restate your question as feedback."

SALLY: "Ken, when you argue with me by giving me fact after fact, I assume you're trying to control me, and that really ticks me off!"

Leaders teach members to use communication skills so that they can communicate effectively. The objective is to help members communicate their awareness of others' emotional experiences, establish emotional connections, and ensure and deepen understanding. By paraphrasing and questioning, members develop their understanding of information others share. When members use reflection of feelings, they experience what it is like to be more intimate in their relationships and understand others at the most meaningful level.

The Timing and Teaching of Communication Skills.   Ironically, the skills and processes necessary to ensure effective communication have liabilities. First, learning and using effective communication skills requires considerable effort. Second, using communication skills, especially before members use them fluidly, can reduce the spontaneity of group interaction. Third, when these skills are first used, interactions feel artificial. Finally, developing these skills can become a more significant focus of group time than the issues that concern the group's members. Because of these issues, leaders need to consider carefully when to direct members to use effective communication skills.

Leaders should teach members to use communication skills whenever they are involved in an interaction that has communication problems. This does not mean that leaders should stop their groups and teach all members communication skills, as this does not address the problematic interaction sufficiently to demonstrate respect for the members involved. Rather, leaders should stop the members who are having trouble communicating, instruct the members involved, and immediately direct the involved members to apply the skill in their interaction as other members observe. Leaders should make every effort to make this instructional intervention as brief as possible.

From a timing perspective, teaching members to use communication skills has far greater impact when members are encountering communication difficulties. The motivation for learning communication skills is far greater when the skills are associated with an immediate need. In addition, teaching particular members to use communication skills when they need the skills is a learning experience observed by the entire group. When members demonstrate how effectively the skills work in their interactions, the entire group observes and learns vicariously how to use the skills and what the skills accomplish.

Communication Problems

When members communicate ineffectively, experiences can be potentially destructive. Ineffective communication creates a group climate of distrust and competition (Gibb, 1961; Johnson & Johnson, 2000). Distrust and competition are the outcomes of members perpetuating communication problems by not employing the necessary skills to interact effectively. Evidence of ineffective communication in a group includes the following:

1. Members making and not verifying their interpretations of the meaning of others' statements
2. Interaction that includes assumptions about the motivations of others
3. Frequent conflicts that appear more semantic than substantive
4. Members having emotional reactions to others that seem inconsistent with the content of their interaction
5. Conflicts that escalate with increasingly intense member statements and emotional expression regardless of the importance of the issue
6. Misunderstandings about expectations that lead to emotional reactions
7. Members using language that causes others to have immediate and intense negative reactions
8. Members agreeing on an issue when it is clear that they do not understand what each other means
9. Disagreements emerging over issues when members actually agree but do not know it because they are using different words to say the same thing.

As leaders help members learn to communicate more effectively, they must be aware of some basic problems in communication and be ready to intervene. Members understand communication when they accurately hear the meaning of the messages they receive. Often members do not understand the messages they receive as the sender of the message intended, and at times the words used cause strong reactions. Frequently, misunderstandings and emotional reactions are the result of basic communication problems. Tubbs (1992) describes four common problems in interpersonal communication: bypassing, inference making, polarizing, and signal reactions.

Bypassing.   Bypassing is a common cause of misunderstanding in interpersonal communication. This occurs when the sender and the receiver assign different meanings to a word or phrase that they use in their interaction. Tubbs (1992) identifies two instances of bypassing. One occurs when persons have different meanings for a word or phrase and the other when persons using different words express the same thought.

A consequence of bypassing is that group members may be agreeing on a point but do not know they are. This results in a conflict connected not to the point members have but rather to the words being used. Intense disagreements can occur when members actually agree. Leaders need to help members state the meanings of the words and phrases that are key to their contentions. Members are often surprised to discover they are using different words to say the same thing and are actually agreeing.

Bypassing also happens when members use a word or phrase and agree with each other when they really disagree. This occurs when members attach a different meaning to the words they use. Leaders will commonly see members agreeing on how they will interact and later react emotionally because others have not lived up to their agreement. Leaders should frequently check with members who agree to clarify what each believes they are agreeing to.

Inference Making.   Inference making occurs when members make assumptions about the motivations behind others' communication. These usually erroneous conclusions shape the interpretations a member makes about the meaning of others' interactions. Leaders will commonly observe inference making when members have a reaction to each other that does not seem to fit with the content of their interaction. These "out of proportion" reactions are often related to the assumptions made about others' intentions. When leaders observe a receiver of a communication having a disproportionate reaction, it is useful to explore the receiver's assumptions about the intentions of the sender. Asking the sender to state his or her intentions should follow this.

Polarizing.   Polarizing occurs when members have intense disagreements and exaggerate their perspectives. As one member overstates his or her point of view, the other, in order to make his or her point as powerfully as the other, does so as well. The effect of these reciprocal exaggerations is that the persons involved get farther away from possible agreements.

When leaders observe polarizing interactions, they can ask the disagreeing persons to restate what the other has said before stating their own point of view. This procedure reduces the emotional intensity of the interaction and results in clearer communication (Tubbs, 1992). By lowering the intensity and increasing the clarity of communication, the resolution of disagreements is far more likely.

Signal Reactions.   Tubbs (1992) states, "All of us learn to react to certain verbal and nonverbal stimuli in some strong and predictable ways" (p. 238). Occasionally, group members use certain phrases or words that have a dramatic effect on interaction.

Signal reactions are the strong emotional reactions that commonly follow the expression of these words and phrases. Words and phrases that produce signal reactions include profanity and terms that denote strong cultural, gender, racial, or religious biases. Other instances of signal reactions include phrases like "I've tried that and it doesn't work," "You don't get it, do you?" or "What do you know about my problems?"

When signal reactions occur, leaders should direct members to discuss how these words or phrases affect them and initiate feedback exchange. When members use terms that indicate insensitivity to differences, leaders must intervene to address the damaging effects of the words and confront the associated prejudices.

By addressing communication problems and strategically teaching communication skills, leaders increase group effectiveness. First, by helping members communicate more effectively, opportunities for learning increase, and these opportunities are more productive. Second, effective communication increases the level of trust members experience in the group. Finally, the group environment increases in safety because communication problems are resolved. Each of these outcomes contributes to group development and the establishment of an effective learning environment.

Self-Disclosure

"Client self-disclosure is the process by which clients intentionally and voluntarily discuss [personal] information" (Kline, 1986, p. 94). In groups, this sharing includes personal information others are not likely to know unless the disclosing member shares it. Self-disclosure implies that members perceive the content of their disclosure as sufficiently intimate that they would not openly disclose to it everyone (Culbert, 1973; Jourard, 1971; Pearce & Sharp, 1973).

Counseling and therapy groups cannot function as productive learning environments without self-disclosure. Porter and Mohr (1982) described the role of self-disclosure: "Until individuals have had (and used) opportunities to reveal how they see and do things, they are not likely to receive information that will help them decide whether they want to make behavioral changes" (p. vii). In addition, meaningful self-disclosure allows group members to check out their perceptions, engage in feedback exchange, develop relationships with others, and accept themselves more fully (Yalom, 1995).

Members who avoid self-disclosing often fear rejection. Contrary to this is the corrective emotional experience of members disclosing what they perceive as the unacceptable aspects of who they are, only to find that others do not reject them. As members offer progressively intimate disclosures, they learn that acceptance based on the facades they use to gain approval is hollow. A significant part of the healing process in groups is members experiencing others' acceptance in spite of their own imperfections. This cannot occur without self-disclosure.

There are many important reasons for self-disclosure in groups that focus on interpersonal learning. Some of these reasons are as follows:

1. Experiencing acceptance
2. Making emotional connections with others

3. Learning how to develop increasingly intimate relationships
4. Sharing personal experience related to the immediate content of group interaction to connect with others and make information available so others can learn (feedback)
5. Offering reactions and emotions in order to obtain support, feedback, and cognitive input
6. Reality testing cognitive reactions and experience
7. Learning how to take interpersonal risks and tolerate the anxiety associated with these risks
8. Learning how to be congruent in interpersonal relationships

Effective Self-Disclosure.   Effective self-disclosure initiates and sustains interaction. When members express their immediate emotional and cognitive reactions, they learn from each other and become increasingly intimate. Self-disclosure of "my experience of you right now, as we look at each other" is one of the most personal forms of interpersonal expression. As members approach this level of intimacy, they discover the powerful impact of interpersonal learning.

Effective self-disclosures are the product of a member choosing to disclose. Because of this, leaders need to be especially aware of how groups pressure individual members to disclose. Ideally, group participation helps members develop awareness of their thinking and feeling, and understand the potential risks involved in disclosing thoughts and emotions and how to make a conscious choice to disclose. This process has important implications for the relationships that members have outside the group.

When members coerce others to disclose, the process of members choosing to disclose is short-circuited. Leaders have to decide whether members encouraging a member to disclose are coercive or supportive of that member's learning. When a member resists encouragement to self-disclose, leaders should explore the reluctance rather than push for a disclosure.

Effective self-disclosure develops trust and increasingly intimate interaction. As members share progressively intimate information, they develop confidence that they can predict how others will respond to their disclosures. Trust builds as members have productive experiences with their disclosures. As trust builds, the group becomes a safer place to disclose increasingly intimate information. This trust-building process occurs most readily when disclosures include immediate emotional and cognitive reactions.

Finally, effectively communicated self-disclosure is most potent. Self-disclosures that include "owned statements," feelings, specific information, congruent statements, understandable language, and nonevaluative terms are most effective.

The following example demonstrates how a leader might encourage the use of self-disclosure and the impact of effective self-disclosure:

HUCK: "You don't understand me. I just want you to give me some attention."
DAVE: "Stay away from me, leave me alone. I don't want you to hurt me."
LEADER: "Huck and Dave, the two of you are not communicating what your fears and emotions are. Try sharing what you're feeling and what you're fearing the other will do."

After a long pause:

HUCK: "I'm really feeling scared, like I'm doing something wrong or unacceptable. All I want to do is be your friend, but I'm afraid that you'll just ignore me."

DAVE: "Huck, I'm afraid you'll hurt me somehow. I'm scared that if I allow you
to get close to me that you'll want more from me than I can offer."

Defensive Self-Disclosure.   Defensive self-disclosures isolate the discloser from
others in the group. Members who fear making themselves known to others commonly make these disclosures, which include content that keeps others at a distance.
Some commonly observed types of defensive self-disclosure include distancing,
shocking, expressing painful vulnerability, and monopolizing.

Distancing self-disclosures persistently focus on differences to establish interpersonal boundaries that exclude others. Members making these disclosures imply
that others cannot possibly understand or appreciate their experiences. For example, "I feel so lonely in here because no one can possibly understand me and what
I've been through. You can't even begin to know how to help me!"

When a member persists with distancing disclosures, other members have angry
reactions and withdraw their attention. When leaders observe a member using a pattern of distancing disclosures, they should state their observations. Most important,
leaders should urge other members to share their reactions to the distancing disclosures and help distancing members address their interpersonal fears.

Shocking uses intensity as a means of keeping others away. Members who use
shocking may offer stories of horrible trauma, be extremely intimate, or express extremely intense emotions when these disclosures are inconsistent with group interaction norms. Shocking occurs commonly in initial stages of a group when members
disclose overly personal information before other members have developed a sense
of safety or trust. Later, shocking more commonly happens as intense emotional expressions or disclosures that exceed the group's norms for intimacy. Leaders should
confront members who use shocking as a defense. This intervention should incorporate feedback from members who are having profound reactions to the shocking
disclosures.

Expressing painful vulnerability is an overstatement of emotional fragility. Members who use this defense present themselves as extremely fragile. These disclosures
suggest that virtually any interaction would devastate them. The message communicated by this defense is "Stay away from me, unless you want to destroy me." Other
members will commonly withhold their reactions and feedback from the fragile
member and attempt to reassure or protect this member. Leaders identifying a member's use of this defense should offer observations about this member's behavior and
the reactions of other group members. For example, "Lucy, it seems that the more
you tell others how fragile you are the more you keep them away" or "Telling Steve
how frightened you are seemed to push him away. Seems that you're more afraid of
being close than you are of being hurt." The intervention goal is to involve the "fragile" member. Even if this member is actually experiencing painful emotions, engaging with others and learning how to obtain and respond to interpersonal support is
crucial.

Monopolizing controls other members. As long as a member controls conversation, that member controls the group. Monopolizing occurs when individuals present a very prolonged, usually personal narrative. This narrative is difficult for other members to interrupt because it contains sensitive material and the monopolizing member will not stop talking. Monopolizing members usually use prolonged storytelling to avoid intimacy and the intensity of interpersonal contact.

Although self-disclosure is essential, it can be counterproductive. Leaders, as they listen to self-disclosures, need to stay aware of process, that is, the objectives of members' self-disclosure. Leaders should definitely consider intervening when a member's self-disclosure causes others to retreat. This involves initiating a feedback exchange process where others share the impact of the disclosures.

Encouraging Effective Self-Disclosure.   Encouraging self-disclosure is important throughout the life of most groups. Often, especially when disclosure is risky, leaders need to direct members to disclose how they are currently experiencing each other. Self-disclosures in the context of here-and-now interaction commonly involve members sharing the emotions they experience in response to other members' verbal and nonverbal behaviors.

Leaders can follow the direction to self-disclose with an invitation to exchange feedback. Following up with an invitation to exchange feedback is most useful when the interacting members have not shared enough to have learned from the interaction. When members exchange disclosures that allow them to learn and make emotional connections, leaders should allow interaction to continue without intervention:

LEADER: "Dave, you seem to be having an emotional reaction to what George is saying. Share that emotion with him."

DAVE: "George, I'm really angry with you."

GEORGE: "Oh, really?"

LEADER: "Dave, give George some feedback about what he is doing that angers you."

Self-Disclosure and the Interactive Group Environment.   Self-disclosures that communicate immediate emotional experiences are very powerful. These disclosures increase intimacy and enhance members' perceptions of connection. When members share a full range of immediate emotional reactions, it is an indication that their group is developing as an effective learning environment.

Interpersonal learning requires self-disclosure. Learning depends on members sharing their emotional reactions and perceptions of others' behaviors. In addition, self-disclosure is indispensable for a group environment that features mutual trust and acceptance.

Feedback

Feedback is a form of self-disclosure in which members offer their emotional and cognitive reactions to others regarding their behaviors (i.e., words and actions). Feedback exchange is one of the most important learning processes in interactive groups.

Unfortunately, many people describe feedback as positive or negative, which places a value on the content of the feedback. Negative, or corrective, feedback indicates that the sender reacts negatively (i.e., dislikes, disapproves, detests, and so on) to the receiver's behavior, whereas positive feedback indicates that the sender reacts positively (i.e., likes, approves, admires, and so on) to the receiver's behavior. When leaders or members describe feedback as positive or negative, members who receive negative feedback get the message that they are doing something wrong. This perspective impedes feedback exchange, as most members are reluctant to evaluate others because they worry about damaging their relationships. In addition, the feedback format "When you ———, I feel ———" attaches a value to the receiver's behavior. For example, "When you talk loudly, I feel scared" assigns responsibility to the loudly speaking person for another member's emotions and implies that the person talking loudly should change his or her behavior if he or she wants the sender to feel differently—a form of emotional coercion.

From the interactive perspective, effective feedback is simply data; it is neither positive nor negative. Feedback is not an evaluative process intended to correct or compliment; rather, it is members sharing their reactions to others' behaviors. Members who receive feedback have the freedom to make choices about changing or continuing their interpersonal behaviors in light of the information provided by the feedback.

To be complete, feedback must involve a statement of the interpretations the member giving the feedback has about the behaviors of the member receiving the feedback. Interpretations should be included because they are closely associated with the sender's emotional reactions to the receiver's behaviors. For example, when a member interprets another's behaviors as intimidating, they will be afraid. This perspective emphasizes the interpretations of the person giving feedback and the intentions of the person receiving the feedback.

When feedback statements include owned statements of senders' interpretations of receivers' behaviors, feedback has a different tone. A person hearing "When you talk loudly, I feel scared because I assume you are trying to hurt me" is less likely to feel evaluated and more inclined to discuss his or her intentions. This is because the addition of an owned interpretation removes the implication that the behavior should change. Instead, this form of feedback moves the conversation to the examination of how members interpret other members' behaviors. When this occurs, the leader can initiate a discussion with the person receiving the feedback about his or her intentions.

Feedback exchanged in this manner also becomes a process in which members who give feedback can learn how their assumptions about others' behaviors affect their relationships. This occurs when the interpretations of others in the group are different from the interpretations of the member giving the feedback and do not match the intentions of the receiver. At this point, the sender of the feedback has a chance to examine how his or her interpretations of others' behaviors affect his or her relationships in and out of group. This examination occasionally leads to members gaining insight into the origin of their interpretations. For example, a terrified member who interprets another member's loud voice as dangerous could learn how family-of-origin experiences explain his or her fear of others' anger.

Effective Feedback.   Effective feedback includes the following:

1. Presentation of immediate observations and reactions to a pattern and not an isolated occurrence of a behavior.
2. Specific descriptions of behaviors and/or words used by the feedback recipient.
3. An owned statement of the assumptions and interpretations being made about the motivations and purposes of the receiver's words and/or behaviors.
4. Disclosure of the feelings experienced by the feedback giver. An effective feedback statement is "You changed the subject and looked away from me. When you did that, I assumed you were afraid and trying to avoid me. Right now, I feel sad about that."

Effective feedback exchange is complete only when the member receiving feedback has defined alternative behaviors for experimentation. This occurs when other members agree about the impact of the receiver's behaviors, the receiver recognizes that his or her behaviors are not getting the desired result, and the receiver chooses to experiment with different behaviors. The following example demonstrates this:

LEADER: "Beth, it seems like many group members are having a similar reaction to your teasing. They seem annoyed by it and want to avoid conversations with you. I guess that that's not what you want to happen."

BETH: "I'm only teasing to make friends. I want all of you to like me."

LEADER: "So, what you're doing to make friends isn't working in here."

BETH: "No, it's not! This really sucks. Now I understand why I felt like nobody in here liked me."

LEADER: "Maybe you could get some ideas from the group about some different ways to start relationships with them."

BETH: "OK, you folks have some ideas for me?"

RHONDA: "Wow, Beth, I didn't know you were trying to be friends with me. For me, making friends starts with showing interest in me and sharing what's going on with you."

This interaction continues until the group has offered Beth some ideas about different behaviors and Beth agrees to experiment with some of them. Beth's experimentation continues until she gets the results she wants and other members perceive her behavior as she intends.

Ineffective Feedback.   Ineffective feedback is a delayed reaction to another member's behaviors. Instead of focusing on specific words or behaviors in nonevaluative terms, ineffective feedback includes conclusions made about the intentions of the person receiving the feedback, characterizes and evaluates the person, and implies an understanding of the member's motivations (Mead, 1977). "Last week, you were nasty! You obviously wanted to hurt Steve" is a clear example of ineffective feedback. Ineffective feedback is likely to create misunderstanding, be based on untested assumptions, be evaluative, be used to punish, initiate angry exchanges, and use value-laden terms that illicit emotional reactions. If ineffective feedback continues, the group environment will deteriorate. Members will learn to distrust each other and regard feedback exchange as a damaging process. Whenever leaders recognize ineffective feedback, they must intervene.

Feedback and the Interactive Group Environment.   Members learn the most when effective feedback exchange flows freely. When members exchange feedback, they learn about the impact their interpersonal behaviors have on others. Members also learn how their interpretations of others' behaviors affect their relationships in and outside the group. As members examine their interpretations, they acquire insight into the origin of their interpersonal behaviors and relationship problems.

Teaching Feedback Exchange

Teaching members to give effective feedback involves directing members to interact, share perceptions, and offer immediate emotional reactions. Teaching feedback skills is most effective when members have compelling reactions to each other and struggle with how to share and respond to these reactions. Leaders can begin by teaching feedback skills to a member involved in sharing reactions with another. This individualized approach to teaching skills helps a member learn how to interact more effectively with another member while other members observe. The intention is not to involve a single member in a prolonged leader intervention but rather to initiate skill development for the entire group.

As groups progress, members will continue to need coaching with feedback exchange. Continued coaching, whenever needed, reinforces members' learning about feedback skills. Thus, more formal skill instruction is seldom necessary. When effective feedback exchange behaviors become group norms, members will take over the coaching process by prompting each other to use feedback skills. When members assume the coaching role for each other, leaders can be less heavily involved in monitoring feedback exchange.

The Process of Teaching Feedback Exchange.   When leaders identify a member who has a need to give feedback, leaders ask the member about his or her reactions to another member. If these reactions are persistent and not a one-time reaction to an unusual behavior, leaders should proceed. Once leaders confirm that the member reacting to another's behaviors is willing to learn a different way to share reactions, leaders begin the teaching process.

Leaders begin the process of teaching feedback exchange by directing the member involved to state the specific behaviors and/or words that initiate that member's reactions. Next, leaders ask the member to state his or her assumptions about the intentions of the words and/or behaviors that the other member uses. Next, leaders direct the member to share the emotions experienced when the other member uses those words and/or behaviors. Finally, leaders direct the member to put all these components together in a statement made directly to the member who is to receive the feedback.

Initially, the process of teaching feedback exchange skills requires the sequential teaching of very specific skills. The ultimate goal is that feedback exchange skills become norms monitored by group members. The following illustration tracks how a leader would initially teach feedback exchange skills:

LIZ:	"Robert, you just don't understand. You can't control me that way."
LEADER:	[Interrupting] "Liz, you seem to be having some definite reactions to Robert."
LIZ:	"I am!"
LEADER:	"I'm wondering if these reactions have been going on for some time?"
LIZ:	"Yes, I just got to the point where I had to say something."
LEADER:	Would you like to give Robert some feedback that could help both of you." (confirm willingness to give feedback)
LIZ:	"I guess so, but I kinda thought that's what I was doing."
LEADER:	"Feedback needs to have three parts for it to work. First, tell us exactly what Robert is doing that you're reacting to." (teach and direct)
LIZ:	"Well, lots of stuff. He's trying to convince me to do things his way."
LEADER:	"What exactly is he doing to convince you?" (question to specify behaviors)
LIZ:	"He keeps giving me all these reasons to do something I don't want to do. He keeps going and going and going and doesn't seem to listen to me."
LEADER:	"What do you mean when you say he doesn't listen to you?" (question to further specify behaviors)
LIZ:	"He won't stop when I ask him to."
LEADER:	"OK, let's see if I've got this right. Robert keeps on giving you reasons to do something you don't want to do even though you ask him to stop." (paraphrase to confirm understanding)
LIZ:	"Yes!"
LEADER:	"The second part of feedback has to do with what you believe Robert is trying to do, your assumptions about the intentions of his words and behaviors. So, when he gives you these reasons and won't stop, what do you assume he's trying to do?" (teach and direct)
LIZ:	"It feels like he's trying to control me, to act the way he wants me to act. Like my way isn't right."
LEADER:	"OK, so he keeps on giving you reasons to do something even though you ask him to stop and you assume he's trying to control you." (paraphrase to confirm understanding)
LIZ:	"Yeah."
LEADER:	"Liz, you seem to be having an emotional reaction to Robert. Your emotions are the third part of feedback. Tell us what your emotions are when you assume Robert's trying to control you." (teach and direct)
LIZ:	"He annoys the h—— out of me!"
LEADER:	"Now, Liz, say this to Robert. Tell him what he's doing, what you think he's trying to do, and how you feel when this happens." (direct and connect)
LIZ:	"Robert, when you keep on giving me reasons to do something even though I tell you to stop, I feel like you're trying to control me and that I'm unacceptable the way I am."

LEADER: "And your emotional reaction . . ." (prompt)
LIZ: "Yeah, when you do that, you really tick me off!"

When the next opportunity for feedback exchange occurs, the leader abbreviates this process by asking members to share feedback and using prompts to ensure that the components of effective feedback are included. After a number of exchanges, members will begin to initiate the process of feedback exchange and coach each other. Members' participation in initiating and monitoring feedback exchange increases as leaders take a progressively less active role in feedback exchange. Leaders should feel free to encourage members to take charge of feedback exchanges by directing members to assume responsibility for this role.

Teaching Members to Receive Feedback

Effective feedback requires the member receiving the feedback to use some necessary skills and demonstrate several important attitudes. These skills and attitudes include effective communication skills, knowing how to use the perceptions of other group members to validate the feedback, openness to hearing and understanding feedback, and the willingness to give and receive feedback. In addition, feedback exchange is complete only when the receiver has defined alternative behaviors for experimentation. Teaching members to effectively exchange feedback, define experimental behaviors, and experiment with these behaviors are crucial ongoing leadership tasks.

When members learn how to receive feedback effectively, they usually become less defensive and more open to hearing it. Teaching members to receive feedback is the second step in teaching feedback exchange skills. When leaders teach a member to give feedback and the feedback has been given, leaders then must teach the member who has been given the feedback how to receive it. Occasionally, while teaching a member to give feedback, it may be necessary for the leader to direct the feedback receiver to listen and not interrupt the feedback giver.

A number of attitudes and actions are needed to receive feedback effectively (Mead, 1977):

1. Effectively receiving feedback means that receivers should *listen* intently to the words of feedback givers. Feedback receivers who stop listening to the feedback to prepare a response will not hear the feedback accurately.

2. Once sent, feedback receivers should *paraphrase* the feedback to ensure that they have accurately heard and understand the feedback. By ensuring that they have accurately heard and understand feedback, receivers reduce the possibility that they are making assumptions about the meaning of the feedback. Receivers listen more intensely when they understand they are responsible for accurately paraphrasing feedback. Leaders should coach members who are unclear about the meaning of the feedback to ask clarifying questions.

3. Once feedback receivers have accurately paraphrased the feedback, they should check for *consensus* with other members. Checking for consensus determines whether other members share the feedback giver's perceptions. If other members do not have similar perceptions, leaders can explore the perceptions of the member

who has given the feedback. Occasionally, when feedback is not validated by group consensus, members who have given the feedback should either receive feedback or begin to look at their own possible perceptual distortions.

4. It is important that members who receive feedback retain *autonomy*. Members are not obligated to change their behaviors simply because they have received feedback. Nonetheless, feedback that has been validated by group consensus often implies, in the minds of group members, that behavior change should follow. Leaders need to be cognizant of this implication because it means that group members may pressure feedback receivers to change. Leaders must protect members' freedom to make choices about change.

If a member does not change in response to ongoing feedback, leaders need to explore both the group's needs to change the member's behaviors and the member's reluctance to change. Occasionally, the group's need to change a member's behavior is an indication that a feedback receiver is frustrating the group's solution to a focal conflict or evidence that the member is breaking an important norm or role expectation.

Teaching feedback receiving skills thus involves coaching members to listen, paraphrase, check for consensus, and retain autonomy. When members decide to change behaviors, leaders instruct them to ask for alternative behaviors and help them set up experiments with selected behaviors:

ROBERT: "Liz, I'm really hurt that you don't think I care about you."

LEADER: "Robert, before you respond more to Liz, I'd like you to say to Liz what you heard her saying to you. This is the first thing you should do when you get feedback." (direct, connect, and instruct)

ROBERT: "Liz, you said that I don't care about you and that all I want you to do is to act the way I want."

LIZ: "That's not it. I don't think you heard what I said."

LEADER: "Liz, give Robert your feedback again. Robert, I want you to listen carefully. When Liz is done, I want you to say back to Liz what you heard her say." (direct and connect)

Liz repeats her feedback and Robert accurately paraphrases it.

Involving the Group in Feedback Exchange

Teaching members to give and receive feedback is not limited only to the members involved in the exchange. Feedback exchange is a group event that affects and involves all members. Besides learning feedback skills through observation, other group members learn about the effects of certain behaviors, validate feedback, and offer input about alternative behaviors.

The group's active participation in feedback exchange begins after a member has received feedback and has accurately paraphrased it. At this point, leaders direct the member who has received the feedback to ask other members to validate the feedback. Once feedback is validated and the receiving member decides to change behaviors, the group is involved again. At this time, the group participates by helping the feedback receiver develop alternative experimental behaviors. Once the receiver selects an experimental behavior, the group continues to participate by offering ongoing feedback on the experimental behaviors. Thus, the entire group actively participates to support both the feedback exchange and the experimentation processes.

The role of members in validating feedback is to develop consensus about the accuracy of the feedback. Consensus, in this case, means that members who have not been directly involved in the feedback exchange share a common perception of the feedback receiver's behaviors. To validate feedback, leaders direct the member who has received feedback to ask the other members whether their perceptions agree with those shared by the member giving the feedback:

LEADER: "Robert, it's important to check out feedback with other group members to see if they have similar perceptions as Liz. Ask the others how they see it." (instruct, direct [consensus], connect)

ROBERT: "Does anybody else have the same reactions that Liz does?"

LESLIE: "Robert, I couldn't put my finger on my reactions to you until now. What Liz said totally fits with my reactions. I feel like I have to do things your way or you'll badger me."

TED: "When you try to convince me to see things your way, I just tune out. I can't handle the intensity of your arguments. I just say to myself, 'There he goes again.'"

LEADER: "It seems like most of the other members agree with Liz's feedback. We'll stop now. Robert, what are you learning from this?" (seeing members agreeing with Leslie and Ted, the leader cuts off conversation that could be damaging to Robert)

During the feedback validation process, leaders should allow members to add reactions that may provide more information to the feedback receivers:

JANICE: "Robert, I agree with the feedback. Something that's a part of what you do is the tone of voice you use when you offer your reasons. From the way you sound, I assume you believe you know what others need to know. It's part of what's annoying to me."

Leaders also need to guard against receivers becoming overloaded by feedback. **Feedback overload** occurs when receivers become overwhelmed by the amount of information they are hearing and/or become overwhelmed by the emotions they experience as a result of the feedback. To profit from feedback, receivers need to develop a clear idea about their behaviors and the effects of these behaviors. This task becomes overwhelming when the diverging points of view of other members, necessary to clarify feedback, include more information than the receiver can manage. Thus, they become confused, and the impact of the feedback is lost. In addition, when members become extremely emotional, they stop hearing feedback. As feedback is validated, leaders must monitor receivers for overload and remember that the validation process is for the benefit of the feedback receiver, not an opportunity for members to dump their frustrations on another member:

LEADER: "Robert, you've been hearing a lot from other members about their perceptions of you. You think you could say what their main reactions are?" (boundary setting and question to monitor understanding)

ROBERT: "I could at first, but it's getting confusing. I've heard so much that I'm not able to keep it all straight."

LEADER: "OK, let's stop now and see if we can pinpoint exactly what others are reacting to." (direction)

Another problem arising during the validation process occurs when members begin to give new feedback that addresses behaviors not included in the original feedback. Leaders need to prevent the introduction of new feedback during the feedback validation process. Such feedback confuses receivers and reduces the impact of the original feedback. Leaders should limit feedback validation to the words and/or behaviors included in the original feedback:

AL: "Robert, I agree with the feedback you got. There's also this other thing you do that . . ."

LEADER: "Stop there, Al. This is something you can take up with Robert later. Right now, we're dealing with Liz's feedback. Robert, tell the group what you're hearing so far." (boundary set and direct)

ROBERT: "I've heard a lot from almost everyone in the group. It's beginning to get confusing."

LEADER: "Robert, it seems that others agree with Liz's feedback. This may mean that your behaviors are not working the way you want. It's up to you now to decide if you want to change your behaviors." (summarize and direct)

ROBERT: "I don't want people to see me as controlling and judgmental. I guess I need to do something different."

Members' involvement is also very important at the conclusion of feedback exchange and validation. When feedback receivers indicate that they want to experiment with new behaviors, the collective creativity and knowledge of members is used to help receivers define alternative behaviors. To generate alternative behaviors, leaders direct feedback receivers to ask the entire group or selected members for possible alternative behaviors. Figure 11.1 illustrates the process leaders use to teach group-effective feedback exchange skills.

EXPERIMENTATION

Experimentation with new behaviors is the primary objective of feedback exchange in interactive groups. Members who experiment with new behaviors take advantage of the opportunity to receive ongoing feedback that helps refine new interpersonal behaviors in a supportive environment. Feedback exchange makes information available, but it does not necessarily lead to changes in behaviors, attitudes, or emotions. Experimentation is the key.

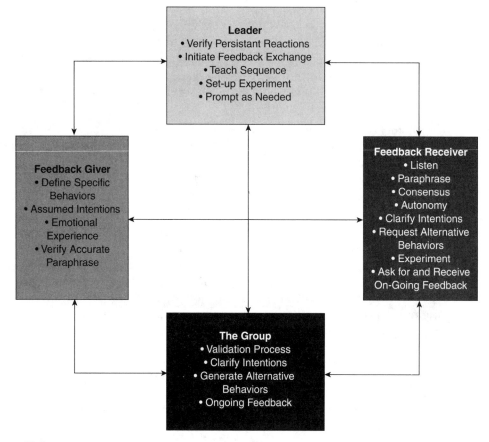

Figure 11.1
Teaching Feedback Exchange Skills

Members experiment with new behaviors when they decide that their behaviors do not achieve the interpersonal results they want. Figure 11.2 shows the disclosure-feedback-experimentation cycle in detail. The process begins with self-disclosure. As members interact, they react to one another.

Members use feedback exchange to share their reactions. At this point, members discover how well their interpersonal behaviors get the results they want. For example, members who want to develop relationships with other members may get feedback that confirms or disconfirms that their behaviors invite closer relationships. If members then want to develop behaviors that are more likely to get the interpersonal results they want, they ask for input about alternative experimental behaviors. Once members get some ideas about different behaviors, they can experiment with the behaviors they select.

Feedback and experimentation continue so that members can refine new behaviors until they get the interpersonal results they want. At any time during the experimentation process, members can decide whether their experimental behaviors

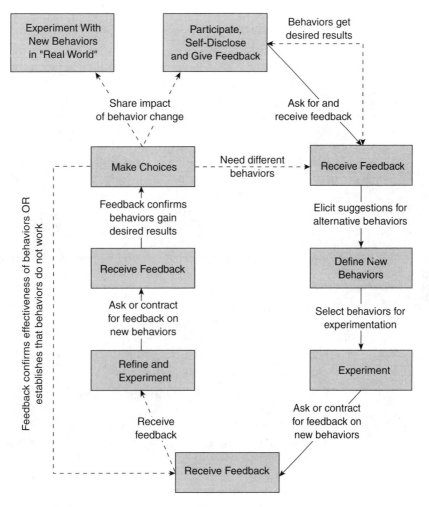

Figure 11.2
The Disclosure-Feedback-Experimentation Cycle

are congruent with how they want to view themselves and how they want to be perceived by others. If they are not, the group helps generate different experimental behaviors. Then experimentation resumes until members get the results they want.

Finally, members, in consultation with the leader and the group, make choices about using the behaviors developed in group outside group. Leaders should periodically help members explore how they experience the impact of their experimental behaviors. Frequently, this exploration is a process that leads to additional insight and refining the experimental behaviors.

The disclosure-feedback-experimentation model focuses on members' interpersonal behaviors, but it is not behavioral to the extent that it ignores a complete range of experience. Experimentation leads to behavioral, attitudinal, and emotional change. Leaders need to involve members in conversations with each other as they experiment and eventually incorporate new behaviors. In particular, it is essential to initiate conversations with members that focus on the emotional aspects of their experience. As members share their experiences with each other, they commonly describe how faulty assumptions have constricted their relationships (e.g., "I never thought I could just ask" or "I could disagree and others could get mad, and I felt like I didn't have to please them!"). The process of experimentation uses an initial behavior focus that attempts to initiate change in all facets of members' experience.

To begin the process of developing alternative behaviors, members need first to clarify their intentions and develop experimental behaviors others see as more consistent with those intentions. Leaders can begin this process by asking feedback receivers what they were attempting to accomplish by using the behaviors identified during the feedback exchange. In cases where a member's intentions are inappropriate, leaders need to help that member explore those intentions with other members. In general, inappropriate intentions are associated with behaviors that violate boundaries, manipulate, or harm others in any way.

The process of generating alternative behaviors influences the entire membership. The behaviors produced during this process offer all members ideas about more effective interpersonal behaviors. Ideally, following several repetitions of this process, norms develop that support the generation of alternative behaviors after feedback validation. Eventually, leaders will only need to prompt members to generate these behaviors.

The following example demonstrates how a leader clarifies a member's intentions and helps generate experimental behaviors:

LEADER: "Robert, what did you want to communicate to Liz?" (question to clarify intentions)

ROBERT: "I don't want Liz to get hurt. I thought I could give her reasons that would convince her to be more cautious about what she shares. I wanted her to know that I care about her and want her to be happy. This is something I've been struggling with for a long time."

LEADER: "Robert, to learn other ways to communicate what you intend to communicate, you'll need to make a specific request for input. What exactly is it that you're not getting across that you want to get across?" (instruction and question to explore intentions)

ROBERT: "I want people who I care about to understand that I care about them."

LEADER: "Ask the rest of the group for some ideas about what you could do differently to help others understand that you care about them." (direct and connect)

ROBERT: "Can anyone give me some ideas about what I can do to help you understand that I care about you?"

As members offer suggestions for different behaviors, leaders monitor interaction for excessive input that could overload the receiver and listen for consensus in the suggestions. When members inundate receivers with suggestions or begin to offer irrelevant suggestions, leaders should conclude the process of generating alternatives. When there are several viable suggestions, leaders direct receivers to choose a behavior that makes the most sense to them for experimentation. Remember that when members generate alternative behaviors, all members are hearing suggestions about potentially useful interpersonal behaviors:

LEADER: "Robert, you've heard a number of good suggestions. Which one do you think might work for you?" (boundary setting to conclude generation of alternative behaviors and direction to select a behavior for experimentation)

ROBERT: "Well, Sally's idea to say that I care and that I'm available for support and not say what the other person should do seems like it would work. It would be hard to do, but I think I could do it."

LEADER: "OK, you want to experiment with saying that you care and are available for support instead of supplying lots of reasons." (paraphrase to confirm understanding and to initiate experimentation)

ROBERT: "That's right."

Once behaviors for experimentation have been identified, leaders can structure an initial experiment. This helps the member working with an experimental behavior to "try on" the behavior. To "try on" a behavior, the leader coaches the member through an initial experiment that involves the member using the experimental behavior in an interaction that initiated the feedback exchange. If the behavior gets the results the member wants and other members react positively to the behavior, the member "trying on" the behavior then uses it in ongoing experimentation during group interaction.

A leader-developed feedback contract with selected members or the entire group facilitates ongoing experimentation. The purpose for using a feedback contract is to involve the group in monitoring experimental behaviors and giving feedback about the effectiveness of the experimental behaviors. The processes of receiving feedback (i.e., listen, paraphrase, validate, and autonomy), generation and selection of alternative behaviors, and the initial "try on" experiment are completed once ongoing experimentation begins. As experimentation continues, ongoing feedback is used to refine experimental behaviors so they become increasingly congruent and effective. When experimental behaviors are ineffective, alternative experimental behaviors are generated, selected, and employed. Occasionally, the experimentation process reveals concerns of the experimenting member that were not initially confronted. For example, it may become clear that Robert's "caring" for Liz disguised Robert's rigid expectations for others' behaviors or the projection of his own fears on to Liz:

LEADER: "Robert, you want to say that you care and are available to give support instead of attempting to get others to do what you want." (paraphrase to ensure understanding)

ROBERT: "Yeah, that's what I want to try."

LEADER: "Before you do this on your own, let's try an experiment to be sure you're on the right track. Try doing this with Liz to see how it works." (set up "try on" experiment and direct)

ROBERT: "Liz, I didn't know that I could just say . . ."

LEADER: [Interrupting] "Just say it." (direct and connect)

ROBERT: "Liz, I want you to know that I care about you. I'm scared you might get hurt. If you want my support, I'm here to give you whatever kind you want."

LEADER: "Liz, give Robert some feedback about how what he said worked for you." (direct and connect)

Liz offers feedback, and other members describe their reactions to Robert's experimental behaviors.

LEADER: "OK, Robert, do you like how you came across enough to keep experimenting on your own in group?" (question to explore and confirm ongoing experimentation)

ROBERT: "You know, that was really scary, but I like that Liz and the others understood what I wanted to communicate."

LEADER: "Robert, it's useful when you're learning a different behavior to get some ongoing feedback about how well the behavior is working. Sometimes you can change it to work better and feel more natural for you. To do this, you need to make a feedback contract with other group members." (instruction and direction to set up ongoing experimentation and feedback contract)

Robert, with the leader's prompting, develops a feedback contract with the entire group.

CONCLUSION

When members communicate effectively, self-disclose, exchange feedback, and experiment with new behaviors, they become highly skilled group members. Skilled group members achieve the greatest benefits from group participation. These benefits include corrective emotional experiences, interpersonal insight, improved interpersonal boundaries, and changes in the habitual personal solutions that limit their satisfaction in relationships.

CHAPTER 12

Ongoing Leadership Tasks

After reading this chapter, you should be able to:

✔ Discuss the leadership tasks that are necessary to perform throughout the lives of groups.

✔ Describe essential processing skills.

✔ Explain how to maintain a group environment that promotes members' learning.

✔ Outline a frame of reference and the strategies that lead to members sharing a perception of safety in the group.

✔ Discuss how to protect members from harm.

✔ Explain how to ensure individuals' chances of success as group members.

✔ Describe how to monitor group interaction for focal conflicts.

INTRODUCTION

Developing a facilitative group environment and facilitating interpersonal learning are ongoing leadership tasks. Leaders intervene during a group's initial stages to develop a facilitative environment and use the same types of interventions throughout the group's life to maintain the quality of the group environment. Similarly, the interventions leaders use to facilitate interpersonal learning are not limited to a particular group stage. Leaders intervene to facilitate interpersonal learning from the start and continue until the group's final meeting.

When performing the ongoing tasks of developing a facilitative group environment and facilitating interpersonal learning, leaders should be aware that these tasks are systemic. This means that the interventions leaders use to develop a facilitative group environment also influence the quality of interpersonal learning and that interventions used to enhance interpersonal learning affect the quality of the group environment (see Figure 12.1).

Because the group environment and interpersonal learning are systemically related, leaders could focus their interventions on either developing the group environment or facilitating interpersonal learning and probably be successful. However, leaders should balance their interventions between developing a facilitative environment and facilitating interpersonal learning. By balancing their interventions, leaders can deal more directly with members' needs and group issues.

When leaders observe that the group environment does not support interpersonal learning, they can focus on facilitating effective interpersonal learning. Leaders will find that as members observe and experience productive interpersonal learning, the group environment will become more facilitative. When leaders recognize that interpersonal learning is not productive, they can closely observe the group environment to determine what shared concerns, restrictive solutions, boundary issues, or blocking norms are slowing interpersonal learning. When leaders accurately diagnose group environment issues and effectively intervene, interpersonal learning becomes more frequent and productive.

When leaders are unsuccessful at helping members become proficient interpersonal learners, they should consider the group environment. Often, members' ineffective use of interpersonal learning and group membership skills has nothing to do with how successfully leaders have taught or how well members have learned these skills. Rather, it very often is the consequence of obstacles in the group environment, including norms that preclude the expression of emotions, restrictive solutions that allow members to avoid sharing impressions, and shared fears of evaluation and judgment.

To maintain a facilitative group environment and facilitate interpersonal learning, leaders must perform a range of ongoing tasks. Such tasks include processing,

Figure 12.1
Systemic Relationship of
Interpersonal Learning and
Group Environment
Interventions

optimizing the group's facilitative qualities, establishing a shared perception of safety, protecting members from harm, and increasing individual members' chances of success.

PROCESSING

Processing is a set of interpersonal learning tasks that direct members to share, reflect on, and more fully understand their here-and-now experiences. It is a group discussion about members' experiences of a group interaction or series of interactions. Although processing takes a number of forms, it should initiate interaction that identifies interaction processes and increases members' understanding of these processes.

Processing and languaging are closely related. Languaging, a form of processing, directs members to define and give meaning to interactions that have led to learning in the group. The overall function of processing, however, is more general, as it includes discussing emotionally charged interaction, identifying issues in interaction, and initiating discussion of interactions that have had an impact on group members. Leaders begin processing by doing the following:

1. Initiating discussion designed to describe, define, and understand any effective group interaction
2. Sharing observations and beginning discussion of issues occurring at the group-as-a-system level
3. Starting a discussion of members' reactions to group interactions members have either experienced or observed
4. Directing members to discuss experiences in structured activities in order to conceptualize and generalize learning

The common element unifying processing tasks is the goal of helping members understand and attach meaning to what has immediately occurred during group interaction.

The processing tasks of leaders are very similar to the learning processes described by Yalom (1995), who referred to the process of helping members reflect on their experiences and develop a cognitive framework to understand these experiences as the "self-reflective loop." The self-reflective loop is a sequence of events that involves members having open, honest, here-and-now interactions with each other and then reflecting on these interactions to understand, conceptualize, and gain insight. In addition, leaders' processing task of sharing observations and/or beginning discussion of issues occurring at the group-as-a-system level is similar to leader process commentaries described by Yalom.

Processing Skills

Processing generally involves stopping the group after a significant interaction or series of interactions and directing members to discuss their emotional and cognitive reactions. Once members share their reactions, leaders direct them to reflect on these reactions and conceptualize what their reactions mean to them. The outcomes associated with processing are that members develop insight into interpersonal behaviors, define desired changes, connect on an emotional level, develop language to describe what works, conceptualize personal and shared concerns, and reality test reactions. When members share emotional and cognitive reactions, they also feel more closely related and less lonely.

Well-timed processing provides members learning opportunities. Leaders can start processing at almost any time during a group session to highlight a significant group event. Processing is not appropriate, however, if it diverts members' attention from interactions such as productive intense emotional interactions, feedback exchange, or the confrontation of a member's behaviors. Leaders should be clear, when they begin processing, that they have the intention of deepening members' learning and not avoiding their own emotional reactions to group interaction. In addition, leaders can process what is occurring in group to "buy time" when they are in doubt about what to do next. Commonly, when leaders are in doubt, so is the rest of the group. Although sounding facetious, the expression "When in doubt, process" is not far from the truth.

The processing approaches described here are not exhaustively comprehensive; rather, they illustrate how processing can be used in various situations. As a rule, processing should immediately follow group interactions that produce reactions that leaders believe members need to discuss. Leaders who believe that virtually all interactions are significantly meaningful will probably overuse this intervention. On the other hand, leaders looking for profound events to process will probably underuse this intervention.

Leaders' judgment about the possible benefits of processing determines when to process. When leaders believe that processing could produce important learning or help members sort out their reactions to a significant group event, they should process. At the same time, leaders should be careful to begin processing only when the interaction they want to highlight is at a point where it could be interrupted. Processing is useful at the following times:

1. When interaction defines an issue that retards group interaction (e.g., members are focusing on external events or are avoiding expressing emotions)
2. When an intense interaction between several members has had an emotional impact on others and they are not discussing it (e.g., members are avoiding the expression of emotion that is related to their shared fears or that addresses the group focal conflict)
3. When members are participating in interactions that pose a threat to a member (e.g., a member is being scapegoated)
4. When members are avoiding giving feedback to a member whose behaviors are having an adverse effect on interaction (e.g., a member is monopolizing interaction and other members watch passively)

Leaders should not begin processing when it would terminate meaningful interaction. The primary exception occurs when leaders believe that an interaction is becoming harmful to the group or the members involved in the interaction.

Helping Members Share Reactions.   Processing engages members in sharing their reactions to a group event. To help members do this, leaders simply stop interaction and use a direction or a question that initiates a discussion of an event members experienced and members' reactions to it. The following are some examples of how leaders might initiate processing of a group event:

LEADER: "Let's stop here. What did you all just see happen?"

LEADER: "I want to hear how each of you is reacting to the interaction that George and Debbie just had."

LEADER: "Something just happened that quieted down the entire group. Who wants to start talking about it?"

LEADER: "Whew, that was intense. I want you all to share the emotions you are feeling now. Terry, you start."

LEADER: "I see many of you reacting to what just happened, but you're not saying a word. All of you seem very uncomfortable. Something happened that we need to talk about. Who wants to start?"

Helping Members Conceptualize Concerns.   When members identify and label their concerns, they can identify what they want to change. Helping members conceptualize their concerns, however, usually requires a shift in most leaders' thinking. Instead of being devoted to the idea of defining what is wrong, leaders should think in terms of solutions to problems that are not working. When leaders see members having difficulties interacting with others, they are observing members' failed solutions (Watzlawick, Weakland, & Fisch, 1974). Most typically, members struggle with failed solutions to the problem of interpersonal anxiety. For example, the member who withdraws from interaction does not have the problem of being withdrawn; instead, this member's solution of being withdrawn is not working. As other group members attempt to become involved with the member, the greater the member's anxiety, and the more the member withdraws. As the group doubles its efforts to involve the member, the member continues to use withdrawal. Withdrawing fails to lower the member's anxiety because the other members will only increase their attempts to "help" the member become involved. Withdrawal fails because it only invites other members to try harder.

During interaction, group members commonly develop norms organized around reducing anxiety. Interaction thus moves from solution to solution in an attempt to minimize the anxiety created by the demand to interact honestly, openly, and congruently. When members find solutions that lower their anxiety, members perceive interaction as safer. These solutions, however, work only temporarily, as members are not developing solutions that allow them to confront the issues that create their anxiety (e.g., being rejected, ignored, or judged). When members decide that "talking about anxiety" is the means to lower anxiety and solutions that "avoid anxiety" are failed solutions that do not work, the group can effectively address the interpersonal concerns shared by all members.

When leaders help members conceptualize failed solutions to the demands of group interaction, members are in a position to develop solutions that work. These solutions involve a range of interpersonal behaviors that improve the quality of group interaction and contribute to improving the quality of members' relationships outside the group. Consistent with the principles of the languaging leadership function, leaders should first direct the group to discuss what is not working so that the group can develop the language to describe the failed solution. The following examples show how leaders can initiate the processing task of helping members conceptualize their concerns:

LEADER: "There's something going on right now that's not helping the group talk about what's happening. What do some of you think is getting in our way now?"

LEADER: "It looks like the group has come up with a way to keep it safe in here. Who can say what it is?"

LEADER: "Every time the group gets close to dealing with how scary it is to interact in here, something happens to shut down the conversation. Let's talk about what it might be."

LEADER: "It looks like the group has bought into the idea that it can be totally safe in here. When interaction gets scary, something happens and we go nowhere. Let's talk about what we're doing to keep us stuck."

Helping Members Define Change.   Processing is also a way to help members define changes they want to make. This processing intervention is an important follow-up to conceptualizing concerns. The following are some examples of how leaders can help members define change as an aspect of processing:

LEADER: "It seems that you all understand that changing the subject when someone gets uncomfortable is not working in here. What do you all think you can do that would work better?"

LEADER: "I think we should talk about ways to interact that you all believe would help you learn."

LEADER: "What have you all noticed that helps us learn from each other?"

Helping Members Develop Insight.   Although processing occasionally leads to insight, leaders should not believe that it is within their power to offer members insight. Developing insight is impossible as an intentional leader activity; most commonly, it is accidental. However, insight does emerge when members understand how the interactive behaviors they use during certain group interactions mirror situations and behaviors that have occurred in their past. For example, a member becomes aware that he reacts angrily whenever he is not involved in group discussions. As the member reflects on his reactions, he remembers how sad and lonely he felt when his older siblings did not include him in their activities. He also remembers that if he acted very angry, they would pay attention to him and include him.

Processing also can lead to insight when members discuss motivations for the interpersonal behaviors they use during particular interactions. As members discuss their motivations for interpersonal behaviors, they may describe an "aha" experience. When members have this experience, they suddenly become aware of how and why certain interpersonal behaviors developed. They have developed interpersonal insight when they become aware of the motivations for their interpersonal behaviors. Members who make these discoveries might say, "So that's why I do that!"

Leaders who make it a point to direct members to discuss the motivations behind their behaviors may help members develop insight:

LEADER: "Don, what did you want to happen when you challenged Kathy?"

LEADER: "I'm wondering, Mary, what you're getting from taking care of the other members."

Although it is quite likely that members will not be aware of the reasons for their behaviors, asking members to reflect on their motivations enhances awareness. Occasionally, enhanced awareness over time can lead to insight.

Developing insight is not something leaders do. Leaders can only make conditions right for the development of insight by processing group interactions and directing members to discuss motivations. Insight happens serendipitously; virtually any statement made during the processing of group interactions can lead to members gaining insight.

OPTIMIZING THE GROUP'S FACILITATIVE QUALITIES

Leaders' ongoing environmental tasks have the overall objective of optimizing the facilitative qualities of the group. To reach this objective, leaders focus on developing enabling solutions, building a shared perception of safety, protecting members from harm, increasing members' chances of success, and monitoring group interaction for focal conflicts and themes.

Supporting Enabling Solutions

An essential leadership task is establishing and maintaining a group environment that optimizes each member's chance of having a successful group experience. Leaders are most likely to achieve this objective if they can successfully encourage members to develop and implement enabling solutions. If leaders do not do so, restrictive solutions, in all likelihood, will dominate interaction. Groups dominated by restrictive solutions greatly diminish members' opportunities for interpersonal learning and chances of success.

Leaders should always expect the emergence of restrictive solutions. At the beginning of groups, as the expectation of sharing personal information becomes clear, members are uncertain about the consequences of initial interactions. To combat the anxiety generated by this uncertainty, group members devise restrictive solutions.

During a group's initial interactions, while group members are developing restrictive solutions to manage their anxiety, most group leaders are trying to "get their groups off to a good start." To do so, many leaders encourage members to follow ground rules that advocate open here-and-now interaction. Ground rules that advocate such interaction are, in essence, attempts to prescribe enabling solutions (e.g., share your immediate emotions, honestly state your reactions). Unfortunately, attempting to establish ground rules that promote enabling solutions have serious limitations. Regardless of what leaders attempt to prescribe, members will devise restrictive solutions; they respond first to their fears, not to leaders.

With experience, leaders discover that the most useful strategy is to install ground rules that satisfy ethical standards and expect restrictive solutions. By expecting restrictive solutions and not attempting to establish ground rules that challenge members' perception of safety, leaders are in a better strategic position. For example, by attempting to install ground rules, like share immediate feelings and stay in the here and now, leaders directly challenge members' initial fears about the consequences of interaction (e.g., offending others and being rejected). On the other hand, by diligently asserting the need for confidentiality and anticipating members needing to work out how open they can be with each other, leaders can proceed directly to dealing with interpersonal concerns.

Leaders who install only ethically necessary ground rules are in a better position because they do not have to determine why ground rules that prescribe how to interact are ineffective. From a strategic perspective, promoting ground rules that are destined to fail erodes members' confidence in leaders, sets up early leadership challenges, and leads to power struggles over how members should interact. By installing ethically necessary ground rules and expecting restrictive solutions, leaders can be ready to identify restrictive solutions as they emerge and intervene to frustrate their use.

Identifying and Frustrating Restrictive Solutions

To initiate the process of establishing enabling solutions, leaders must first identify restrictive solutions. This involves careful observation of group interaction. Although leaders can easily observe some restrictive solutions, most are not obvious.

Restrictive solutions are used by group members whenever group members covertly or overtly agree that interaction creates too much anxiety. The most obvious forms of restrictive solutions are those that result from overt agreements. Such solutions are usually products of group discussions that judge some aspect of group interaction as unnecessary or harmful. For example, members may reach a very quick consensus that interaction should always focus on each others' strengths and not on weaknesses because "It just isn't productive for us to talk about negative stuff."

The most difficult focal conflicts to identify are those created covertly. In chapter 2, the discussion of group norms described how obstructing norms develop from a process of covert negotiation. The covert processes that develop restrictive solutions and those that develop obstructing norms are identical. In fact, when restrictive solutions become long-term patterns in group interaction, they have become obstructing norms. For the most part, however, restrictive solutions come and go as members continue to negotiate and then renegotiate the most effective means to manage anxiety.

Identifying covertly developed restrictive solutions involves observing interaction for patterns. These patterns are often associated with interaction that seems to approach an issue, only to take a sudden detour to safer topics. For instance, members discussing how interaction could be improved by including members' expressions of emotions suddenly become sidetracked into a discussion about how demanding members' jobs have become.

Restrictive solutions are also present when there are obvious issues in group interaction and members do not speak about them. An example of unspoken issues occurs when several group members do not participate and none of the other group members mentions their nonparticipation. Another example is when members are obviously having strong emotional reactions and others avoid mentioning their emotional display. In both cases, the observed patterns narrate what group members do to avoid interactions that could elevate anxiety. What members are doing to avoid interactions that could elevate anxiety are restrictive solutions.

Once leaders identify restrictive solutions, they should intervene. When confronting restrictive solutions, leaders need to think in terms of a series of interventions because members diligently cling to restrictive solutions that allow them to avoid anxiety. Numerous interventions are also necessary because members are adept at generating a new restrictive solution to replace a solution that no longer spares them from anxiety.

The most effective approach to interfering with the effectiveness of a restrictive solution is to verbalize the disturbing motive and the reactive fears. By doing so, leaders influence members to develop enabling solutions and frustrate members' restrictive solutions. Repeated verbalization of disturbing motives and reactive fears is successful over time because leaders continue to state aloud the issues members want to avoid and members are unable to avoid them. When leaders successfully elevate anxiety to the extent that members cannot ignore disturbing motives and reactive fears, the restrictive solution fails. When a restrictive solution fails, members are most open to considering an enabling solution. The following are examples of leader statements that initiate the process of frustrating restrictive solutions:

LEADER: "You all seem intent on talking about how tired you are. It seems that you might make more progress if you'd talk about how scary it would be to share how you feel about each other."

LEADER: "The longer you concern yourselves with how Scott handles feedback, the longer you avoid talking about how scared you are to be ignored."

LEADER: "I wonder how talking about the last meeting helps you deal with being afraid that you'll be hurt by another group member if you share how you really feel."

Group leaders can also frustrate members' attempts to develop restrictive solutions during interaction. When leaders determine that members' discussion has the goal of developing a restrictive solution, leaders should direct discussion toward the disturbing motive and reactive fears. As leaders do so, they should also help members see how a restrictive solution will not satisfy their needs:

LEADER: "So how does giving only positive feedback help you all deal with being afraid to be real with each other?"

LEADER: "I don't get it! How does talking about issues at home help you all talk about how scared each of you are that another member will find something wrong with you and cause you pain?"

Whitaker and Lieberman (1964) believed leaders' errors in developing group environments usually occur when leaders choose not to intervene when they have identified a restrictive solution. An additional crucial error occurs when leaders do not notice the emergence of a restrictive solution. In both cases, by not intervening or not identifying a restrictive solution, leaders support the continuance of a restrictive solution. Leaders must make supporting the use of enabling solutions a priority, meaning that leaders continuously observe group interaction to identify restrictive solutions and diligently intervene to develop enabling solutions. See the earlier discussion of focal conflict theory for more information.

ESTABLISHING A SHARED PERCEPTION OF SAFETY

A necessary condition for meaningful interpersonal learning is members sharing the perception that participation in group interaction is safe. When members believe it is safe to take risks and engage in emotionally intense interactions, the group becomes a powerful learning modality. Taking risks and engaging in emotionally intense interactions, however, is very inconsistent with most members' perceptions of what they need to do to stay safe.

Most members begin groups with boundaries and habitual solutions that do not support interaction that leads to interpersonal learning. At the beginning, members commonly attempt to protect themselves from interpersonal harm by hiding. When members hide, they avoid expressing reactions and emotions, which allows them to control the amount of anxiety they experience. Staying hidden, however, is a solution that does not allow members to develop relationships, gain acceptance, overcome loneliness, establish emotional connections, or experience congruent interactions. Although staying hidden is a solution that does not work, those who use it experience less anxiety despite the fact that they are miserable. Being hidden, especially if it becomes a group norm, creates interpersonal boundaries that obstruct interpersonal learning and threatens the facilitative capacity of the group environment.

When groups first convene, members commonly reach consensus that the group is a risky place to share personal information. To cope with this risky environment, members usually negotiate avoidance as the best way to stay safe. Consequently, members avoid meaningful interaction, support each others' avoidance, and develop the perception that avoidance leads to safety. This perception is persuasive because staying hidden allows members to manage their anxiety. The outcome is a hidden membership that shares a perception of safety in an environment members perceive as threatening.

A real sense of safety occurs only after members have confronted their fears and engage in conflict (see chapter 4). To confront their fears, members must risk interacting with others in a more open and intimate way than they are accustomed. Members become secure in their perception of safety when they witness and experience productive interpersonal learning. As mentioned earlier, interpersonal learning and the facilitative nature of the group environment are systemically related. As one develops, so does the other.

There are steps leaders can take to facilitate the development of a shared perception of safety in their groups. Developing safety begins with leaders' group composition choices (Whitaker & Lieberman, 1964). When groups are composed of members who diverge dramatically in their interpersonal boundaries and tolerance for anxiety, developing safety is nearly impossible. Developing safety is nearly impossible because members with permeable boundaries are likely to share personal information that threatens members who are protective of their impermeable boundaries. Differences in boundaries, or **boundary incompatibility**, results in a group divided between members feeling frustrated that sharing is not open and members feeling threatened by what others want to share. In addition, when members have a varying tolerance for anxiety, solutions that satisfy the needs of some members are either excessively threatening or stifling for others.

Groups composed of members with similar boundaries and tolerance for anxiety are more likely to develop interactive norms that ultimately lead to safety. Boundaries that permit members to share concerns, reactions, and emotions along with a common tolerance for anxiety allow members to interact honestly without creating excessive anxiety or threatening the perception of safety in the group.

Safety further develops when enabling solutions allow members to speak openly and deal directly with their interpersonal fears. That is, interpersonal boundaries become progressively more open as members risk disclosing. When members' productive learning experiences are witnessed by the membership, these boundaries become even more open, the perception of safety increases, and the group environment becomes progressively more facilitative. As the group becomes more facilitative, a shared perception of safety builds.

A shared perception of safety, however, is never permanent. As groups continue, leaders and members will conflict over how to approach and resolve members' relationship issues. Such conflict occurs because leaders have the objective of helping members learn how to manage relationship issues and members' have the desire to avoid uncomfortable anxiety. Leaders thus face the reality of having to balance urging members to confront relationship issues and maintaining a shared perception of safety.

When deciding to challenge attempts to avoid relationship issues, leaders must weigh their goal of confronting relationship issues against the goal of maintaining a shared sense of safety. When maintaining this balance, leaders should consider two factors. If leaders believe that members' avoidance of difficult group issues is an "escape hatch" for intolerable anxiety, they may choose not to confront members' avoidance. This action involves ignoring members' avoidance and supporting members' efforts to redevelop the shared belief that group interaction is safe. Some possible ways leaders can support and initiate escape hatches are as follows:

LEADER: "Let's shift topics now. What are some of the interactions that happened tonight that you learned from, and what did you learn?"

LEADER: "The tension in here is intense! Rick, say more about what you've been learning."

If, on the other hand, leaders believe that members are avoiding difficult issues they could successfully resolve, they should challenge members' avoidance.

Successfully intervening to challenge members' avoidance depends on leaders identifying what members are avoiding and continuously frustrating members' attempts to shift discussion to safe topics:

LEADER: "Jim and Art still have not talked about their anger with each other, and the group seems willing to let that slide."

LEADER: "Terry, Jill, Matt, and Alan, I'm very confused about why you're talking about work. The four of you are just fuming! You four are having some strong reactions, and you're sitting on them."

It is not useful for the group environment to have a consistently uncomfortable level of anxiety. Groups with a high level of anxiety will become ineffective because members shift their attention from interpersonal learning to closing their interpersonal boundaries and negotiating how to make the group reasonably safe. To be sensitive to members' perception of safety, leaders should assess the level of anxiety present in their groups by observing members' nonverbal behaviors and the content of interaction. When anxiety is excessive, leaders should shift or allow members to shift discussion to less threatening "escape hatch" topics on a **temporary** basis. Escape hatches, carefully and sparingly employed, can support a shared sense of safety in groups.

PROTECTING MEMBERS FROM HARM

Closely associated with developing a shared perception of safety is protecting members from harm. When members understand that they can depend on leaders to protect them from harm, their confidence that the group is safe increases. In her discussion of the responsibilities of group leaders, Whitaker (1985) emphasized leaders' roles in establishing safety:

> Persons in groups are supported in feeling safe enough to take risks if they can hold on to the sense that there is one person in the group who retains sufficient understanding, strength, courage, and disinterest to handle acutely difficult situations and emergencies should they arise. (p. 382)

To establish the perception of safety, leaders should be alert to situations that harm members and preempt them. There are several situations that lead to member harm: members pressuring other members, members in isolation, and group boundary problems. Members pressuring other members refers to situations in which group members coerce other members to engage in behaviors that those members do not wish to perform. This also refers to situations in which members blame a member for group issues. Members in isolation includes occasions when members do not share intense emotional reactions they experience in group or make choices about using behaviors observed in group outside the group without first discussing them during group. Group boundary problems concern both the group's internal interpersonal boundaries and its external boundaries.

Members Pressuring Other Members

Members pressuring other members occurs when group members pressure another member to conform to their requirements. Interactions that illustrate the pressure to conform occur when members attempt to convince another member to participate more actively, to take risks, or to receive and act on feedback. Although these attempts can be very beneficial for the pressured member, there is a point at which pressuring to conform becomes damaging.

Defining when pressure to conform becomes damaging is critical. Defining this point is difficult because leaders will often find themselves "sucked" into being on the side of the members who are doing the pressuring. For example, leaders want all members to be actively involved in feedback exchange. When group members pressure a member to be more actively involved in feedback exchange, leaders will find themselves supporting the members' efforts to involve the pressured member.

Members urging another member to be involved is not necessarily negative; in fact, it can be very positive. When pressuring becomes coercive or abusive in any way, however, leaders should intervene to support the pressured member's choices about participating in feedback exchange and address other members' apprehensions about that member not being involved.

Other unacceptable instances of pressuring a member to conform are more easily identified. Some of the more obvious cases include demanding that a member share personal information, agree with a group decision, or interact in a way that is unacceptable to that member. Leaders should be assertive in supporting members' rights to make their own choices unless these choices involve harm to self or others.

Leaders need to be alert to the possibility that a member who does not conform to the expectations of others will experience negative consequences. One consequence is a member being blamed for the anxiety other members experience. The process of group members coming to regard a member as the cause of their anxiety is especially well explained in focal conflict theory.

The focal conflict perspective describes circumstances in which individual members are blamed for other members' anxieties. One of these cases occurs when a member enacts a restrictive solution and the group is attempting to implement an enabling solution. Another circumstance occurs when a member enacts an enabling solution and the group is attempting to implement a restrictive solution. In each case, the noncomplying member will be pressured to conform. If the noncomplying member does not conform, other members often blame that member for the group's problems. This is an indication that a member is at risk for becoming a scapegoat. The following scenario is an illustration. Mike insisted that he would not share his emotions during the group (represents a restrictive solution). Other members had just concluded dealing with the issue of sharing emotions. They decided that sharing feelings was necessary because it would help members connect and would make the group a safer place (represents an enabling solution). As Mike and other members interacted, it became clear that there was a growing opinion that Mike was holding the group back. Interaction grew in its intensity, and anger was the prevalent emotion. Finally, one member stated, "Mike, if it weren't for you, we could actually get something done in here. We'd be better off if you weren't a member of this group."

Members become scapegoats when they do not comply with the other members' solutions to focal conflicts. Noncomplying members are seen as the reason group-developed solutions are not working the way group members had hoped. When members are scapegoated, other group members often become abusive and criticizing, blaming the scapegoated member for problems in group interaction. Scapegoated members, especially those who are emotionally fragile, will feel rejected and can be devastated by the harsh comments of other members. If leaders are not aware of the scapegoating process and fail to intervene, scapegoated members can be harmed.

Leaders should be alert to problems that involve coercion and scapegoating. Once leaders identify coercion or scapegoating, their interventions should be decisive and clear. These interventions should focus on the group and not on the member being pressured or scapegoated. In each of the following examples, the leader interrupts conversation that pressures or scapegoats a member:

LEADER: "It seems that sharing emotions is important and that trying to talk Mike into it is not helping you do that. I'd like all of you who want to share your feelings to go ahead and share them. Certainly, Mike's not trying to stop you."

LEADER: "Most of you believe that sharing emotions is important, and so do I. It's time we start doing it. Who wants to start?"

LEADER: "It seems that sharing your feelings and not knowing that everyone would reciprocate is scary. We should talk about that fear. Jessie, you can start."

Members in Isolation

Members in isolation pose very difficult problems for group leaders, especially in two primary situations: when members have profoundly disruptive experiences and when members use behaviors outside group that they have observed in group. The issue in both cases is that members are not disclosing their intentions or experiences in group, so leaders can be totally unaware of what is happening. The goal for leaders in dealing with members in isolation is to do all they can to prevent problems.

When members experience an emotionally intense reaction to a group interaction and do not share it, they cannot be helped to process their experience. Thus, they are much less likely to develop an understanding of their experience or draw on the support capacities of the group. Besides having to deal with intense feelings in isolation, a possible implication is that a member may leave the group and be at risk for harming themselves or others.

Members who decide to use behaviors they have observed or experimented with in group in regular social settings without first discussing the use of these behaviors may be at risk for damaging their relationships. Customary social interactions, even those in primary relationships, commonly do not involve the openness or honesty found in the interactions of members in effectively functioning groups. Members who choose to interact with significant others as they have with other group members will shock unprepared significant others. Irreparable harm is possible in relationships that are not based on openness and honesty. A member who confronts an employer as she would another group member, for example, may lose her job.

To prevent the problems that isolated members experience, leaders need to accomplish several objectives related to what members should share in group. By establishing and maintaining the norms "share reactions, especially strong ones" and "never try a behavior outside group before discussing it in group," leaders take a step toward preempting potential problems. Leaders should also carefully scan group members, especially after emotionally intense interactions, to read their nonverbal reactions. Members who are not sharing their reactions should be strongly encouraged to enter group interaction to process their reactions. In addition, members experimenting with alternative interpersonal behaviors should be cautioned to discuss the possible implications of using these behaviors in their relationships before using them outside the group.

Group Boundary Problems

Potentially harmful boundary problems surface at the internal and external boundaries of groups. Internal boundary problems include verbal and physical assault and coerced self-disclosure. External boundary issues include breaches in confidentiality and the inclusion of inappropriate members.

Examples of unacceptable interpersonal boundaries occur when either verbal or physical assault harms members. When leaders screen new members, present group ground rules, and develop group norms, they must state explicitly that verbal or physical assaults are unacceptable in the group environment and clearly indicate the consequences of these assaults.

Clearly, leaders must immediately eliminate from the group individuals who physically assault or seriously threaten another member with physical assault either in or out of group. Group members should never have to consider the possibility that another member may physically attack them. The presence of a member who threatens physical assault or actually assaults another member totally undermines leaders' efforts to establish an environment of safety.

Verbal assaults are not always as clear-cut as physical assault in terms of leaders' actions; verbal assaults present room for interpretation. In some cases, members learning how to express anger may not have the interpersonal skills necessary to verbalize anger in a productive manner. Instead, these members tend to be verbally abusive. Clearly, these members can benefit from feedback and experimentation with behaviors that more appropriately communicate anger. Leaders must judge when a member has the ability and the skills to share anger productively but instead chooses to remain verbally abusive and when a member's inappropriate expression of anger unfairly limits other members' opportunities for learning.

When leaders believe a member will continue to be verbally assaultive or abusive in spite of feedback exchange, they must remove that member from group. On removing a member from the group, leaders should speak with the individual involved outside group to discuss that member's removal from the group. During this discussion, leaders should also be prepared to provide appropriate referrals. Once leaders remove a member, they need to process the member's removal thoroughly in group.

External boundary problems include breaches in confidentiality and the inclusion of members who are inappropriate for group work. During screening interviews and the group's initial meetings, leaders should emphasize the importance of confidentiality and explain their ethical and legal responsibilities in terms of confidentiality. When members breach confidentiality by discussing information other group members have disclosed outside the group, leaders have several courses of action.

Some leaders may stipulate during screening and initial meetings that members breaching confidentiality will be immediately dropped from the group. This stipulation presents the clearest boundary for members and contributes to external group boundaries that enhance members' perceptions of safety and trust. Other leaders might devise a way for members to confront a member who has broken confidentiality and give group members the responsibility of deciding to retain or remove that member. There are several major issues connected with this approach. First, by giving members responsibility for deciding whether a member should remain in group, leaders send members an ambiguous message about the responsibilities of their role. Later, if leaders need to make a decision about removing or including a new member, the members will not understand why they have suddenly lost one of their responsibilities. Second, when members are permitted to remain in the group after breaking confidentiality, members' perceptions of trust and safety will always be insecure. Finally, asking members to decide who should be in or out of the group places members in the difficult position of having to make a reasoned decision about a person who they may have grown close to and who has betrayed their trust.

Including an individual who is inappropriate for group work is an external boundary problem that can be precluded by careful screening. In addition to the criteria presented earlier in the discussion of leaders' administrative function, leaders should carefully consider a prospective member's history of treatment and current mental status. As leaders screen individuals for inclusion in their groups and decide not to admit an individual, they should be aware of referral sources that might offer services that are more appropriate. Finally, during screening interviews, leaders should understand that they are making choices about group composition. Points made in the discussion of developing a shared perception of safety and those made in chapter 3 regarding members' personality styles are especially important considerations.

ENSURING INDIVIDUAL MEMBERS' CHANCES OF SUCCESS

An essential ongoing task of leaders is ensuring that every member has opportunities to have a successful group experience. Successful group experiences occur when members have enough opportunities for interpersonal learning to make their group experience useful. These opportunities occur when members self-disclose emotions and perceptions, give and receive feedback, and experiment with new behaviors.

On the other hand, when members participate superficially or do not participate at all, they are unlikely to have a useful group experience. To ensure that members make the most of their opportunities, leaders must intervene to address the factors that prevent members from participating in meaningful interaction.

Focal conflict theory (Whitaker & Lieberman, 1964) conceptualizes how members use customary interpersonal behaviors or habitual personal solutions to avoid the anxiety associated with group participation. When members' habitual solutions interfere with opportunities for learning, leaders should identify the events that lead to the use of these solutions. In other words, when a member uses a defensive interpersonal behavior for an extended time, leaders should identify what is occurring in the group that may be causing that member to be uncomfortably anxious.

Once leaders have identified the situations in which a member uses a habitual solution, leaders can use several interventions. One of these involves interfering with what the group is doing to evoke a member's anxiety. A group may be dealing with issues that a member finds especially threatening, or the group may be unreasonably challenging a member to change his or her behaviors. Whenever leaders recognize that the group is challenging one of its members unreasonably as a way to address its own anxiety, leaders must intervene by frustrating or blocking the challenge. For example, a leader could make the following intervention when the group is unreasonably challenging one of its members to withhold anger:

LEADER: "It seems that the group is having a hard time dealing with Jim's anger. Sue, perhaps you can talk about what it's like for you to experience anger in here."

When leaders judge that a member's habitual solution is a response to a reasonable challenge by other group members, leaders use a different intervention, the goal of which is to frustrate the member's habitual solution. For example, when members are challenging a member about not being open to feedback, leaders might say the following to frustrate a member's habitual solution:

LEADER: "Michelle, several members have attempted to give you feedback and have tried to talk you into receiving it. You've been quite angry with them and have told them you don't want to hear it. It seems that your anger hasn't worked because they keep after you to receive some feedback. Go ahead and ask the group for some input about a more effective way to say no."

Habitual solutions are most problematic when members use them to avoid interactions that could lead to interpersonal learning. For example, members who use anger to shut down productive interactions or refuse to listen to feedback are using habitual solutions that block opportunities for interpersonal learning. At the same time, other group members lose opportunities for learning because of the time and energy they invest in trying to persuade these members to participate productively. While struggling to involve members using habitual solutions in interpersonal learning, other members also avoid their own learning because attempting to change a member's habitual solution allows members to avoid self-disclosing and exchanging feedback.

To ensure that members' habitual solutions do not block opportunities for learning, leaders should share their observations of habitual solutions with the group. If observations, subsequent confrontation, and feedback from others do not help engage the member using habitual solutions in interpersonal learning opportunities, leaders need to examine the group as a system.

When examining the group as a system, leaders should try to determine how a member's continued use of a habitual solution supports how the group operates. For example, a member refusing to be involved sustains a group system organized around avoiding the anxiety associated with participation. This happens when a group focuses its energy on trying to include a member who refuses to be included. By using group time to convince a member to participate who refuses to be convinced, the group is able to avoid talking about their fears of participation. As long as the member refuses, the group system of interaction and avoidance continue.

By observing how a member's role operates in the group system, leaders can better understand how other group members are actually supporting the member's continued use of a habitual solution. These observations also provide leaders with important information about the shared fears of group members. When observing a group to see how a member sustains a group system, leaders may find it useful to consider the following questions: "What is the group's pattern of interaction?" "How does this member's behavior help the group continue this pattern?" "What shared fears are members attempting to avoid?"

Leaders should consider interventions that target both the member using the habitual solution and the entire group. Interventions that address both these targets are probably the most effective way to deal with a group system that supports a member's continued use of a habitual solution. When using these interventions, leaders should not expect immediate results. Such results are not likely because these interventions attempt to reorganize a group system so that all members can experience learning opportunities. The success of interventions designed to reorganize a group system requires repeated attempts to frustrate how the system operates. In other words, what the system is organized to do (e.g., avoid feelings) does not work because leaders continue to frustrate how it operates (e.g., direct members to talk about feelings). Following are some examples of how leaders might initiate interventions to change members' patterns of using habitual solutions and to address group systems that maintain the use of habitual solutions:

LEADER: "It seems that each of you is really invested in helping Sandy stay angry. Tell me what would happen if she wasn't ticked off."

LEADER: "It seems that each of you is really invested in helping Sandy stay angry. Go ahead and interact the way you would if she weren't angry."

LEADER: "You all have worked really hard to involve Jim in the group. He refuses to, so perhaps it's time to move on. Who wants to begin?"

LEADER: "You know, Bill, if you would do something different, the rest of the group might actually have to take some responsibility for making sure different points of view are shared."

Interventions that challenge a member's habitual solution involve modifying that member's interpersonal boundaries and addressing his or her interpersonal perceptual distortions. Once members elect to abandon their habitual solutions and not replace them with other ineffective habitual solutions, they are likely to open their boundaries to more meaningful interaction. In the process, members encounter perceptual distortions that have led them to stay closed to others. For example, Joe kept his feelings to himself (i.e., his habitual solution) because of his experiences with his father, who would criticize him for sharing his feelings. When Joe witnessed other members sharing feelings without criticism, he decided to open his boundaries sufficiently to allow him to express his feelings in group.

Monitoring Group Interaction for Focal Conflicts and Themes

Removing impediments to interpersonal learning often involves identifying focal conflicts and group themes that interfere with meaningful interaction. Group themes and focal conflicts are impediments to interpersonal learning because they represent what members attempt to avoid. When leaders identify group focal conflicts and themes, they have insight into the dynamics of group interaction and can define intervention objectives.

Stock and Lieberman (1962) described various clues that help leaders identify focal conflicts and group themes. These clues include group interaction content, the way members interact, and members' nonverbal behaviors. In focal conflict terms, a group organizes around the avoidance of anxiety created by various interpersonal issues. Avoidance of an interpersonal issue influences the content of group interaction and impedes interpersonal learning. Consequently, the avoidance of an issue organizes the content of interaction, and the content of a group's interaction reflects its current focal conflict.

By accurately identifying the theme in group interaction, leaders are able to identify elements of the focal conflict. For instance, as group members interact regarding how they should participate, leaders might hear a theme in members' discussion that suggests they share a fear of being criticized. This theme identifies the reactive motive (i.e., fear of criticism), which is a potential target for intervention. The leader in this example could offer one of the following interventions presented in increasing intensity:

LEADER: "You all seem to be suggesting that you might be criticized in here. Let's talk about how scary it is to be criticized."

LEADER: "Being criticized can really hurt. John, you start. Tell us what it would be like for you to be criticized by another member."

LEADER: "Francis, you and other members seem to be fearful that you may be criticized. Tell the member you think is most likely to criticize you why you think that member would criticize you and how you would feel if that happened."

Any discussion members have about circumstances outside the group is an additional clue regarding the current focal conflict. From the focal conflict perspective, all content included in group interaction is in some way related to the focal conflict being experienced within the here-and-now of group interaction. For example, discussion regarding how the press has wrongfully accused a member of the community can be relevant to fears members have about other members drawing inaccurate conclusions about them in group.

Leaders should frustrate the continuance of extensive externally focused conversation, as such conversation is a very common means to avoid the anxiety of directly addressing a group issue. However, before shifting conversation back into the group, leaders should first listen for a theme in the conversation that is relevant to group interaction. When shifting conversation back into the group, leaders should relate the theme in the discussion to members' here-and-now experience in the group. Regarding the current illustration, the leader might say the following:

LEADER: "Let's switch our focus slightly. It seems you all need to talk about what it would be like for other members to get the wrong idea about you."

Leaders can be confident that members are talking about issues related to a focal conflict by observing the way members respond to the content. Clues to look for include nonverbal and affective reactions, the energy and pace of interaction, and the emotional tone of the discussion. When, for example, members are uncomfortably shifting about in their chairs, not looking at each other, and talking rapidly and anxiously, their discussion is probably getting very close to verbalizing the focal conflict.

In addition, leaders should consider the context of the group discussion. For example, an abandonment theme in interaction content might be explained by the fact that the group is about to conclude or that the leader is about to go on vacation. The group leader needs to attend to context clues in order to understand group themes, connect these themes to focal conflicts, develop interventions, and then intervene.

CONCLUSION

The ongoing leadership tasks described in this chapter have the singular goal of optimizing members' opportunities for learning. By helping members communicate effectively and exchange feedback in a productive manner, leaders are on their way to reaching this goal. When leaders also successfully confront group environment issues that slow learning, members are likely to have productive learning experiences, and leaders will attain their goals.

Intervention Strategies

OBJECTIVES

After reading this chapter, you should be able to:

✔ Discuss how to use intervention strategies for confronting obstructing group norms and implementing facilitative group norms.

✔ Describe intervention strategies designed to deal with interpersonal and relationship issues and how to use them.

✔ Explain "problematic" member roles from a focal conflict perspective.

✔ Outline intervention strategies for addressing "problematic" member roles and how to use them.

✔ Discuss the dynamics of social/diversity issues and how they emerge during group interaction.

✔ Describe how to use intervention strategies to address social/diversity issues in counseling and therapy groups.

INTRODUCTION

Intervention strategies are sequences of interventions made over the course of a session or several sessions to improve the facilitative qualities of the group environment and encourage member change. Intervention strategies may involve a number of interventions focused on specific ongoing objectives (e.g., developing a group's normative structure). Other intervention strategies may have objectives that require a session or several sessions to accomplish (e.g., helping members change their roles and improving certain aspects of their relationships).

Leaders use intervention strategies once they have observed group-as-a-system interaction patterns that impair group productivity or identify the need for changes in some members' patterns of interpersonal relationships. These patterns include obstructing norms, interpersonal and relationship issues, problematic member roles, and social issues that emerge in group interaction.

OBSTRUCTING NORMS

Obstructing norms are patterns in interaction that support behaviors that are inconsistent with group objectives. Ordinarily, these interactive patterns hinder effective communication, feedback exchange, experimentation, and the development of a facilitative group environment. Examples of obstructing norms include implicit rules for interaction, like sharing compliments and not feedback, discussing thoughts and not feelings, and interrupting others when what they are sharing causes anxiety (see chapter 2).

From the focal conflict perspective, obstructing norms are restrictive solutions members use to avoid confronting the anxiety produced by disturbing and reactive motives. Restrictive solutions become obstructing norms when members use them for extended periods of time and these solutions become a pattern in group interaction. Leaders need to remember that obstructing norms develop subtly and are initially difficult to recognize. For leaders to recognize obstructing norms, they must identify the pattern of interaction that slows group progress. By reflecting on the reasons behind ineffective group interaction, leaders can then identify the disturbing and reactive motives that members are attempting to avoid. For example, whenever a member begins to express emotions, other members change the subject. Whenever leaders observe an obstructing norm, they should intervene; otherwise, they allow obstructing norms to become a more entrenched interactive pattern that becomes increasingly resistant to change.

Once leaders identify obstructing norms and choose to modify them, they can choose from an array of interventions. These interventions include implementing new ground rules, observing the obstructing norm, observing and directing the group to discuss the obstructing norm, experimenting with a helping norm, or confronting the obstructing norm. Whichever interventions leaders choose to use, they must remember that they are intervening in a social system. Such intervention means that members must understand the problems associated with an obstructing norm, be clear about the benefits of implementing a helping norm, and commit to and follow through on working with other members to change "the rules" of group interaction. Successful norms interventions occur only when facilitative norms replace obstructing norms. Norms interventions are energy intensive but can have a profound impact on the quality of group interaction.

Implementing New Ground Rules

Implementing new ground rules is frequently effective and is often the simplest norms intervention. This intervention, however, does require considerable energy on the part of leaders to ensure the implementation of the new ground rule and often does not address the dynamics that cause the development of obstructing norms. Leaders should use this intervention sparingly and attempt to implement a new ground rule only infrequently. This is because a leader-implemented ground rule requires that leaders attend to monitoring and directing the implementation of the new ground rule. Leaders who attempt to implement new ground rules and do not monitor their implementation fail to follow through on this intervention, and the new ground rule will be unsuccessful. In addition, members will begin to question the importance of the new ground rule and the earnestness of leaders' interventions.

Leaders can consider implementing a new ground rule whenever they observe a problem in group interaction that suggests the presence of an obstructing norm. The objective for implementing a new ground rule is to create a norm that will improve group interaction. This intervention differs from the essential ground rules that leaders implement at the onset of the group to protect members and define the external boundaries of the group (e.g., confidentiality, no abusive behaviors, and so on). To intervene, leaders simply point out the problem in interaction and direct members to follow a new ground rule:

LEADER: "It seems that most group members have developed a pattern of saying 'we' when they are really talking about their own point of view. From now on, each of you need to say 'I' when you present your own perspective."

LEADER: "Whenever a member begins to describe how they feel, they are cut off, and the subject is changed. We need to adopt the ground rule that members expressing their feelings should be allowed to complete their expression before anyone else speaks."

These examples depict how leaders can attempt to legislate new group norms by directing members to use them. These interventions require ongoing leader monitoring to be successful, which involves redirecting interaction:

LEADER: "Jeff, repeat what you said. This time remember to use 'I' instead of 'we.'"

LEADER: "Judith, stop. Let Randy finish saying how he's feeling."

Observing Obstructing Norms

As mentioned before, identifying norms that obstruct group effectiveness is usually a difficult task. Most group norms develop subtly and often escape leaders' awareness. When leaders identify obstructing norms, however, a useful initial intervention is simply to identify the obstructing norm. This intervention is most effective in mature working groups because it is necessary only to raise members' awareness. In mature groups, members will understand the intervention and will often develop more facilitative norms independently. In less mature groups, where members experience intense anxiety when facing difficult disturbing and reactive motives, this intervention is much less effective. Leaders who share their observations of obstructing norms in less mature groups will often observe members ignoring the intervention.

The objective of the observing obstructing norms intervention is to help members become aware of norms that block effective interaction. The outcome of this intervention in mature groups can be highly productive. In less mature groups, leaders can be satisfied when this intervention performs an educational function. The trick in less mature groups is ensuring that members actually hear the intervention and, at least, reflect for a moment on the norms that guide their interaction. Examples of this intervention follow:

LEADER: "It seems the rule the group is following now is to change the topic whenever the issues get too intense."

LEADER: "The norm the group is using to deal with disagreements is to ignore them."

LEADER: "Everyone in the group seems to have forgotten that sharing feelings is important."

Sharing an observation of a group's obstructing norm identifies a restrictive solution members have developed to avoid anxiety. Observing a group's obstructing norm will raise anxiety if members actually discuss it. In less mature groups, in particular, leaders should repeat this intervention and direct members to discuss the obstructing norm to have maximum impact.

Observing and Directing Members to Discuss Obstructing Norms

This intervention is a follow-up to leaders sharing their observations of obstructing norms and substantially increases the effectiveness of observing obstructing norms in most groups. Here leaders follow identifying a norm that obstructs group effectiveness with asking or directing members to discuss how the obstructing norm blocks the group's effectiveness. Leaders can add the step of directing members to reach a consensus about a norm that would be more effective and develop an agreement to use the more effective norm. Although this intervention is effective, it can be quite time consuming. At worst, a protracted discussion of an obstructing norm can serve as an alternative restrictive solution if the discussion becomes excessively cognitive. Thus, leaders need to make a decision about using this norms intervention based on the group's purpose, needs, and time limitations.

Some examples of observation and direction to discuss an obstructing norm are the following:

LEADER: "It appears that whenever a member shares their feelings, the group responds by changing the subject. Tell me what you all think about how changing the subject is helping you make progress in this group."

LEADER: "I've been observing how group members have been giving feedback, and it looks like there's a rule that whenever a member asks for feedback, others take turns giving compliments. Let's talk for a moment about how well this is helping you all learn in here."

Examples of how leaders can use observation and direction to discuss an obstructing norm and add the additional direction to reach consensus on a more effective norm follow:

LEADER: "It appears that whenever a member shares their feelings, the group responds by changing the subject. I want you all to talk about how that's getting in your way and come up with a different way to handle your feelings."

LEADER: "I've been observing how group members have been giving feedback, and it looks like there's a rule that whenever a member asks for feedback, others take turns giving compliments. You all need to talk about this for a while and decide on what you believe is a more productive way to exchange feedback."

The direction to reach consensus on a facilitative norm to replace an obstructing norm can also be a separate intervention that follows a group's discussion of the obstructing norm. A covert leader strategy here is to frustrate a group's restrictive solution. The rationale for this sequence of interventions is that the longer a leader involves members in discussing a restrictive solution (obstructing norm) and enabling solutions (facilitative norms), the more likely it is that members will face disturbing and reactive motives. The combination of sharing observations of obstructing norms, directing members to discuss these norms, and directing members to develop more facilitative norms is powerful because it sustains members' focus on issues that they want to avoid. Avoided issues, when discussed in a progressively open fashion, lead to members facing difficult interpersonal issues and developing more effective interpersonal behaviors.

Experimentation with New Norms

Norms experimentation involves a mixture of leader-directed interventions and member participation to develop norms that are more effective. This intervention is usually very productive in less mature groups, where interventions that more directly involve members in confronting restrictive solutions may excessively threaten homeostasis. This intervention also spreads the responsibility for the development and implementation of facilitative norms to members. Because all group members and the leader share responsibility for the development and implementation of a facilitative norm, it requires less energy on the part of the leader and develops a more democratic group atmosphere.

Norms experimentation is, however, a complicated intervention that requires time for implementation and follow-through. Five steps are required:

1. Leaders identify a pattern in group interaction and ask members whether they would like to try an experiment.
2. Leaders suggest a norm to experiment with, carefully describing when to use the norm and the interactive behaviors involved.
3. The leader contracts with the members to use the norm for a specified period of time (e.g., the rest of a meeting or several meetings). This period is the "experimentation period." The contract includes the agreement that members will commit to monitoring each other's interactions to ensure that all members are using the norm. The contract should also include the understanding that the experimental norm can be renegotiated if it is too disruptive.

4. The experiment begins, and members remind each other to use the behaviors included in the norm.

5. At the end of the experimentation period, leaders initiate a discussion of how well the norm worked. This discussion has the goal of deciding to continue or discontinue the use of the norm.

Here is an example of how a leader might implement a norms experimentation intervention:

LEADER: "Something I've noticed is that members who are sharing their feelings are frequently cut off by others who either change the subject or interrupt to reassure the one expressing their feelings that everything is OK. Would you all like to try an experiment?"

Members usually are uncertain what "trying an experiment" means and are curious about what the leader is asking. At this point, the leader moves to the second step:

LEADER: "What I'm asking you to do is to consider experimenting with a different way of interacting. I'm suggesting that whenever another group member shares his or her feelings, each of us allows that member to finish, then, before changing the subject or reassuring that member, respond to what that member has shared. Are you all willing to try this experiment?"

Group members are usually willing to try the experiment and still are not sure of what the leader is asking:

LEADER: "Here's what the experiment will involve. First, let's try the experiment for the rest of this session and during the next time we meet. At the end of our next session, we will talk about how our experiment worked and if we want to continue to not interrupt or reassure and instead respond to a member's feelings before moving to another topic or issue. I'd like to ask each of you to commit to reminding each other to use these behaviors whenever someone does not use them. We can always talk about these behaviors if they disrupt what we're doing too much. Everyone agree? Any questions?"

Once the leader has clarified what is involved in the norms experiment, members begin using the new behaviors as an experiment. Usually, members require only minimal prompting by the leader to monitor the experimental behaviors. Ideally, monitoring norms experimentation by members involves simply identifying the behaviors another member is using and reminding that member to use the experimental behaviors. It is important that these reminders not have a judgmental tone. Reminding each other to use the experimental norms behaviors is also an opportunity for members to practice feedback exchange. On occasion, reminders to use behaviors associated with an experimental norm escalate the anxiety of members who would rather avoid interactions that involve the experimental norm behaviors. This is an opportunity to explore the apprehensions of these members. At the end of the experimentation period, the leader summarizes what has happened and initiates a discussion of the experimental behaviors:

LEADER: "Well, we've completed the experiment. I got the impression that it was
              scary at first and then, as we got more accustomed to using the experi-
              mental behaviors, that some good things started to happen. I want to
              hear how the experiment went for each of you."

After members share their experiences with the experimental behaviors, the
leader processes their experiences. If the norms experiment was successful, the
leader asks whether members would be willing to continue to use and remind each
other to use the experimental behaviors:

LEADER: "If you are willing, I think we should make our experimental behaviors
              a part of how we interact in this group. Would you all be willing to
              continue using these behaviors and to remind each other to use them?"

At the conclusion of successful norms experiments, members are usually willing
to continue using the experimental behaviors. Resistance to using the new behaviors usually expresses itself when members "forget" to remind each other to use the
behaviors. Commonly, these behaviors become norms, and the need for reminders
decreases.

Confronting Obstructing Norms

Confronting obstructing norms is essentially the same as identifying restrictive solutions that have become "permanent fixtures" in group interaction. This approach
to intervening with obstructing norms involves challenging members to consider
their interactive behaviors in the context of their expressed objectives for group
participation. When using this approach, leaders must be careful not to judge
members' interactions by conveying that they are inappropriate or inadequate.
When leaders convey judgment of members' interactions, it is often an indirect expression of leaders' frustration. Leaders should be clear about their reactions to
group interaction before using this intervention. When frustrated about group interaction, leaders should consider offering clear and specific feedback to group
members.

Examples of how leaders can confront obstructing norms follow:

LEADER: "Help me understand why you all continue to block the expression of
              your fears in here when you've all stated that you need to confront
              your fears to reach your goals."
LEADER: "It seems like you all are still trying to avoid exchanging feedback
              even though you all have agreed several times that it's essential that
              you do it."
LEADER: "When members agreed to supporting the expression of each other's
              feelings, I thought you were interested in doing it, not discouraging
              each other's sharing, as you are all doing now."

Confronting obstructing norms calls attention to problems in group interaction
forcefully. As discussed previously, identifying obstructing norms may be sufficient
to change norms in mature groups. In less mature groups, confronting obstructing
norms is an effective way to elevate members' anxiety. Elevating members' anxiety

by confronting obstructing norms can be an effective way to frustrate the benefits members experience by using a restrictive solution.

Confronting obstructing norms is a more intense intervention than simply observing obstructing norms. A potential pitfall in using this intervention is that members could perceive these confrontations as judgments of their participation. Confronting obstructing norms is probably most useful when leaders determine that the intensity of their norms interventions are not sufficiently challenging to gain members' attention. A challenge that follows members not acting to change a norm they have committed to change is a powerful reminder and a means to elevate members' anxiety.

Norms Interventions: Final Considerations

Leaders make norms interventions with the intention of changing group social systems, which requires changes in all members' interactions and the expectations members have about each others' participation. Successful norms interventions are thus not solely dependent on the effectiveness of leaders' interventions. Success requires members' cooperation. When members choose to avoid experimenting or following through on changes in group norms, leaders' only recourse is to be diligent about sustaining a sufficient amount of anxiety to make the enactment of obstructing norms less comfortable. That is, when members avoid the implementation of new norms, all leaders can do is to call attention to the obstructing norm and persistently call members' attention to the disturbing and reactive motives that obstructing norms attempt to avoid.

INTERPERSONAL AND RELATIONSHIP ISSUES

Members come to groups because of problems in their interpersonal relationships. Thus, leaders should expect members to experience inevitable struggles in establishing, developing, and maintaining their relationships in group. In fact, leaders should regard the relationship issues that surface in group as important opportunities to address members' most critical concerns in living as they occur during the process of here-and-now group interaction. However, some relationship problems occurring between group members may be particularly resistant to leaders' interventions and limit the group's effectiveness, for example, members who persistently engage in protracted arguments or members who repeatedly rescue another member. Relationship problems that are resistant to intervention can pose particularly difficult barriers for group progress because groups rely on members' relationships as the medium of change.

According to the group counseling and therapy theories discussed earlier, members' relationship issues emerge as distorted interpersonal perceptions, ineffective boundary functioning, or restrictive habitual personal solutions. These interpersonal problems are observed in members who isolate themselves from others, defend themselves from meaningful involvement, attempt to control the content of interaction, and develop enmeshed or fused relationships. The interventions described in this section are two possible approaches for dealing with these interpersonal problems.

An additional issue to consider when dealing with interpersonal problems is whether an interpersonal problem is a role problem. Role problems are particularly resistant to interpersonal interventions because roles are an integral part of the group's social system and require interventions that involve the entire group. It is highly likely that when interpersonal interventions do not work, it is because the group supports the continuation of problematic interpersonal behaviors associated with a member or members' roles. Thus, the interventions described here are first steps designed to change interpersonal behaviors. When these interventions are not effective, role interventions and possibly group norm interventions can be more effective.

Interpersonal Boundary Interventions

Interpersonal boundary interventions involve the leader in directing members with excessively closed boundaries to share information that they have withheld. For example, a leader may ask or direct members to share their emotions or offer feedback. Interpersonal boundary interventions also involve directing members to withhold information that leads to overinvolved or fused relationships with other group members. This may occur when a leader directs a member not to rescue another member from the experience of sharing painful emotions. Members with overly diffuse boundaries may also benefit from sharing information that more clearly defines their boundaries with other members. In this case, interventions may include directing members to experiment with assertive language, disagree with others, or ask for what they want.

Opportunities to use interpersonal boundary interventions occur as members interact. In some cases, these interventions attend to issues emerging in particular relationships. In other cases, these interventions are useful when particular members demonstrate relationship problems in all their relationships with other members. Such interventions are useful in developing the relationship of two members or helping a member in all of his or her relationships in the group.

The following are some examples of interpersonal boundary interventions. First, let's look at boundary interventions with relationships that demonstrate excessively closed boundaries:

LEADER: "Art, tell Sharon how you feel."
LEADER: "Sally, you seem to be reacting to what Beth is saying. Give her feedback about the reactions you're having to what she is doing."
LEADER: "Mark, you and Michael really have strong reactions to each other. I'd like each of you to tell the other what you think he is trying to do."

Now let's look at boundary interventions with relationships that demonstrate excessively open boundaries:

LEADER: "Colleen, you seem to agree with almost everything Jack says. Tell him how you disagree with him."

LEADER: "Gina, you really seem to want to get along with me. I want you to
             know that I only get along with people who disagree with me and state
             different points of view."

LEADER: "John, before any of the other members shares their reaction to what
             just happened, I'd like you to say what you think."

LEADER: "Gina, tell Yvonne how your point of view differs from her point of
             view."

Interpersonal Contracts

Interpersonal contracts are a useful follow-up to interpersonal boundary interventions and experimentation with new behaviors and occur as one of the final elements of a feedback exchange process. The objective of interpersonal contracts is to continue a member's use of new interpersonal behaviors. By doing so, a member is in a position to continue to receive feedback and develop the effectiveness of new behaviors.

Interpersonal contracts employ the following steps:

1. The leader initiates the contracting process by asking the member or members (in the case of a relationship focused intervention) whether they are willing to continue the use of new interpersonal behaviors.

2. The leader, if the member or members agree to continue, asks whether the member or members would like some assistance in continuing the use of the behaviors. Often, it is useful to frame this step as an inquiry about whether a member or members would like to receive support from other members in continuing to develop new ways of interacting in the group.

3. If the member or members are willing to receive support or help to continue the use of the new interpersonal behaviors, the leader initiates the contract.

4. To initiate the contract, the leader secures an agreement with other group members or a particular member to participate in the contract. This agreement involves making a commitment to remind and encourage the member or members developing the new behavior to use the new behavior whenever it is useful. One way of doing this is to ask the member or members using the new behaviors to identify a member who they would like to help them and ask that member to act as a support person.

Another option involves the leader strategically selecting a member to participate in the contract. For example, if the contract involves helping a member to use "I language," the leader can ask a person who struggles using "I language" to act as the support person. Alternatively, the leader can ask a member who is especially effective using "I language" to act in the support role.

A fourth option is to involve the entire group in the support role. By doing so, the leader can also consider this contract as a means of norms intervention. For example, asking the rest of the group members to remind a member to ask for what he or she wants is a way of reinforcing the idea that all group members should use this interpersonal behavior.

The following is an example of how a leader might use an interpersonal contract with a member developing a new interpersonal behavior:

LEADER: "Joan, when you were direct and told Todd to not boss you around, it looked like it worked for you. What was it like to be that direct?"

JOAN: "It was really scary at first, and when he backed down, it felt really good, like I had some power."

LEADER: "Is being direct by saying how you feel and what you want in your relationships in here something you want to continue?"

JOAN: "It's a little scary, but I'd like to."

LEADER: "How would you like to get some support from another group member to help you continue working with being direct?"

JOAN: "Oh, I'm not too sure, I don't know what . . . "

LEADER: [Interrupting] "Be direct with me. What do you want?"

JOAN: "That's right, OK. Yes, I want support."

LEADER: "Great, Joan! I'd like you to directly ask another member to remind you to be direct when you need to be direct but forget. This person will be your support person."

Joan asks Ruth, and she agrees.

LEADER: "Ruth, are you clear about what Joan is asking you to do?"

RUTH: "She wants me to remind her to be direct when she needs to be but forgets."

LEADER: "Joan, tell Ruth if that's what you want."

At this point, after the agreement is clear, the contract is in place. The leader can invite the members involved to modify or terminate their contract whenever it is unnecessary or when it does not appear to be working. Interpersonal contracting is a very versatile intervention, and leaders should use their imagination to create variations. Interpersonal contracting can be as useful for the support persons as it is for the member or members receiving support because it also maintains their awareness of the behaviors in the contract.

PROBLEMATIC MEMBER ROLES

Members come to groups because of interpersonal difficulties and interact with other group members using the interpersonal behaviors that express these difficulties. Eventually, the way in which a group member interacts with other members can become problematic for the entire group. These problems usually involve group members expending an excessive amount of energy in trying to change the behaviors of the "problematic" group member. Often, these problems arise when a member fails to meet the expectations "that they should be respectful of others, cooperative, responsive, grateful for help, and do what they say they will do" (Kottler, 1994, p. 4). Problematic members are often described as resistant (Kline, 1990) and defined in terms of specific roles (Yalom, 1995). In general, the literature agrees that members assume problematic roles when their interactions appear to block productive interaction and they are assigned responsibility for ineffective group functioning (Kline, 1997).

When confronting a "problematic role," it is important to consider both basic group dynamics principles and group counseling and therapy theory. In terms of group dynamics, roles are a structural property of a group's social system. That is, each group member enacts a role because of the expectations of all the other group members and occasionally the inadvertent expectations of the group leader. Thus, to change a member's role, interventions must always address the expectations of the other group members.

Theory and group dynamics conceptualizations are very similar. From the perspective of focal conflict theory, problematic roles are deviant-enabling or deviant-restrictive members who demonstrate habitual personal solutions that cause other members considerable anxiety. Systems theory regards a problematic role as a structural part of a group's social system. Both these theoretical perspectives recognize problematic roles as functionally related to the interactions of all group members.

It is important to remember that members come to groups because of difficulties in their interpersonal relationships. Frequently, these difficulties cause other members and leaders problems. In addition, individuals who are not appropriate for group membership cause problems in group interaction. Realistically, even the most brilliant sequence of leader interventions may not have a meaningful impact on the interactions of individuals inappropriate for group membership. On the other hand, members who are appropriate for group membership can benefit from thoughtful interventions. The objective for conceptualizing interventions, however, is not to always think specifically of helping a member who is causing problems to change behaviors. Rather, the objective is to think in terms of identifying and helping the members who can benefit from intervention. Usually, this means first looking at the issues being experienced by other group members.

Conceptualizing Problematic Roles

Focal conflict theory provides a framework for conceptualizing problematic member roles and identifying leaders' intervention targets. One intervention scenario surfaces in the case of a deviant member who represents a restrictive solution. A deviant-restrictive member uses a habitual personal solution that interferes with a group-developed enabling solution. For example, a deviant member who fears interpersonal intimacy will react strongly or withdraw from interaction when other members have begun to share their feelings about each other. At other times, the deviant-restrictive member may attempt to persuade other members to discontinue their sharing. Either the withdrawing or the convincing reactions of the deviant-restrictive member can be problematic for the other members because other group members will begin to direct their attention to involving the restrictive member or convincing the restrictive member to participate in the group's enabling solution. By focusing on the deviant-restrictive member, group members deprive themselves of opportunities to participate in more productive interaction. This situation is also problematic for the deviant member because of the pressure and the frequent anger that other members direct toward the deviant-restrictive member. Deviant-restrictive members risk becoming scapegoats if leaders are not sensitive to members building criticisms of the deviant-restrictive member.

The other intervention scenario involves a deviant member who represents an enabling solution. The deviant-enabling member threatens other group members because his or her interactive behaviors often frustrate the successful use of the restrictive solution members have developed to avoid anxiety. For example, in a group where members have decided that it is important to avoid the expression of anger, a member who persists in expressing his or her anger will become a problem for the other members. In this case, other members will attempt to convince the deviant-enabling member to cease his or her expressions of anger or try to ignore the deviant-enabling member's expressions of anger. These responses slow the progress of the entire group because of the time and energy members devote to changing or ignoring the behaviors of the deviant-enabling member. In reality, the interpersonal behaviors of the deviant-enabling member represent an enabling solution, and the efforts of the other group members are inconsistent with group progress.

Intervening with Problematic Roles

An important first step is to recognize what is occurring. A role problem usually occurs when members appear to be investing considerable energy in convincing a member to act correctly (i.e., go along with a group-developed enabling or restrictive solution). More pronounced and serious role problems occur when members openly criticize another member for how that member participates. For example, a group has spent 25 minutes trying to encourage a member to stop sharing his or her feelings. Another example occurs in a group that has tried repeatedly to involve a member who has withdrawn from participation. By conceptualizing role problems in focal conflict terms and by seeing role problems as group problems, leaders can involve group members in potentially productive interaction.

In the case of a deviant-restrictive member, leaders will observe group members trying to influence the deviant-restrictive member to engage in interactions that are more productive. An example of this situation occurs during feedback exchange processes. Leaders will notice a member who does not seem receptive to feedback about a behavior that is legitimately problematic. Usually, this member refuses, rejects, deflects, or ignores other members' efforts to offer him or her feedback. Other examples of role problems with a deviant-restrictive member include members attempting to convince the deviant-restrictive member to share his or her feelings or members trying to persuade a deviant-restrictive member to stop criticizing others. In these cases, leaders need to think how they can support the enabling behaviors of other group members and not focus on the behaviors of the deviant-restrictive member.

To initiate role interventions with deviant-restrictive members, leaders must first assess what is occurring in group interaction. Instances when intervening are necessary include those times that the group persistently uses feedback and argument to pressure a deviant-restrictive member to engage in a group-developed enabling solution. A common illustration of where intervening may be useful includes times when group members have invested considerable energy in attempting to persuade a member to share his or her emotions or participate more actively. The deciding criteria is if the group is investing so much time and energy in attempting to convince a member to engage in their enabling interactions that they avoid participation that takes advantage of these enabling interactions. For example, a group that spends time trying to encourage a member to be more involved in feedback exchange is unlikely to spend much time involved in feedback exchange.

Leaders' assessments of the interactions members use to convince a deviant-restrictive member to use their enabling solutions may determine that group members are using the deviant-restrictive member as a way to avoid participating in an enabling solution. That is, by investing time and energy in attempting to change the deviant-restrictive member, members avoid more anxiety-provoking interaction. For example, members trying to convince a member to share his feelings are often avoiding sharing their feelings with each other.

When leaders see members using a deviant-restrictive member to avoid anxiety or participation in their enabling solution, leaders should intervene:

LEADER: "The longer you all try to talk Bob into hearing your feedback, the longer you avoid exchanging feedback that can help you learn. Steve, you've been responding to something Sylvia is doing. Perhaps you can give her some feedback."

LEADER: "Let's change what we're doing. We've spent some time talking to Bruce about what he needs to do differently in here. Now it's time to move on. Jim, what would you like to do to improve your relationship with other group members?"

LEADER: "You all seem to be spending lots of time working on Elizabeth to be the way you all want her to be instead of doing what you need to do to learn in here. Randy, maybe you can tell Rita what you want from her."

Interventions that focus on deviant-restrictive members should focus on the other group members when it is clear that the deviant-restrictive member is not receptive to feedback. The objective is to support the enabling solutions of the other group members. By focusing on enabling solutions, leaders put pressure on the deviant-restrictive member indirectly, without a high risk of scapegoating that member. The deviant-restrictive member will then face increasingly high levels of anxiety produced by attending a group that does not support his or her use of a restrictive habitual personal solution.

Often, when a group begins to invest energy attempting to influence a deviant-enabling member, it will appear that the group is responding to a threat. Frequently, this threat appears when members confront or challenge a deviant-enabling member for doing something unacceptable in the group. In the case of a deviant-enabling member, the members' efforts usually are to censor that member's enactment of an enabling solution. For example, leaders commonly will observe members attempting to shut down a member's efforts to exchange feedback, express emotions, or share intimate connections with other members. Attempts to shut down a deviant-enabling member often include comments that communicate "You need to keep those feelings to yourself," "Why do you have to be so angry," or "You're not fitting in, you need to stay positive."

When intervening, leaders need to support the deviant-enabling member. Interventions should focus on supporting the enabling behaviors of the deviant member, protecting the deviant member from pressure to use the group's restrictive behaviors, and helping group members look at the fears associated with the deviant-enabling member's behaviors. The following examples depict leader interventions that accomplish these objectives. First, let's look at supporting the enabling behaviors of a deviant member:

LEADER: "Jack, I really like the way you spontaneously share your feelings."
LEADER: "Jerry, perhaps you can give some of the other members some ideas about how you build up the courage to be direct and honest."
LEADER: "You know, Dot, other members seem to have difficulty with you wanting more openness in your relationships with them. I want to support you in achieving that in here. Anything I can do to help you out?"

Now let's look at protecting the deviant-enabling member from group pressure:

LEADER: "Jeff, I'd like you to talk about what it would be like for you to share your feelings in here before you try to talk Jack out of doing it."
LEADER: "Jerry's honesty and directness has really upset you, Phyllis. Can you share what makes this so frightening for you?"
LEADER: "Linda, you really want Dot to back off getting closer to you. What do you have to lose?"

Now let's look at directing the group to explore their reactions to the enabling behaviors of a deviant member:

LEADER: "You folks really react each time Jack puts his emotions out there. Dean, what's going on in you when Jack shares his feelings?"
LEADER: "Most of the group seems to be having some trouble dealing with Jerry's directness. Let's take a look at what makes this so scary for you. Jesse, you are having some noticeable reactions. What's so scary for you?"
LEADER: "It really seems that Dot hits a nerve in all of you when she asks for more sharing. What's so scary about that? John, you start."

The interventions directed toward the behaviors of a deviant-enabling member are designed to frustrate a group's restrictive solutions. Members who are courageous enough to use enabling behaviors should receive support, and other group members should be guided to examine their surfacing fears. The only exception to this strategy is when a member's enabling behaviors may be so threatening that they cause the group overwhelming anxiety. This requires leaders' best judgment. In this circumstance, the deviant-enabling member should receive feedback about their choices of when to use their enabling behaviors. These members need to examine how to know when it is the best time to use their enabling behaviors and examine how to be more sensitive to when others are ready. Typical examples of members who are ineffective in their use of enabling behaviors are those who disclose intensely personal information before they have developed relationships with other members and members who use self-disclosures to distance themselves from others.

Leader Precautions When Intervening with Problem Roles

Problematic member behaviors include the behaviors of a member who is inappropriate for group membership or the behaviors of a member that threaten other group members. Clearly, the first problem stresses the need for careful group composition decisions. In the case of the second problem, leaders need to be aware that there are several serious pitfalls.

When groups deal with members who do not go along with group-developed enabling or restrictive solutions, leaders are easily seduced into aligning with group members' perspectives. When groups pressure deviant-restrictive members to use more enabling solutions, their actions are consistent with leaders' goals and easy to support. For example, it is easy for a leader to be seduced into supporting the group when they challenge a member to stop being critical. When members pressure deviant-enabling members to "back off" their enabling behaviors, leaders often support members' actions inadvertently because the enabling behaviors might also be threatening to the leaders. For example, leaders who are tentative about sharing emotions in their relationships can easily align with group members' efforts to censor the emotional expressions of another member. Thus, leaders must be sensitive to and very aware of their own reactions to deviant members and to the potential to scapegoat deviant members.

To monitor the extent to which leaders' personal issues intrude in their interventions with problem members, leaders should assess the intensity of their emotional reactions. Intense emotional reaction may indicate that leaders' personal issues are interfering with their interventions. Leaders should confirm their reactions with observations they make about group interactions. Then, just as in feedback exchange, leaders should identify the words and behaviors "problem" members are using. Finally, leaders should frankly consider whether they can make an intervention that is not judgmental or excessively influenced by their own personal issues (Kline, 1990).

Considering the removal of a member from the group is the final option when dealing with a problem member. This option is appropriate for members whose needs cannot be met in the group. Other members who are appropriate for membership, however, can also be candidates for removal. After direct feedback and group-focused interventions have proven ineffective, leaders should determine whether the problem member's behaviors will be an ongoing obstacle to the learning of other members. If the member does not respond to interventions and significantly distracts members from productive interaction, leaders should remove the member. In these cases, removal is the absolute last option. Leaders are ethically bound to refer members they remove from their groups to more appropriate treatment options. As a final note, leaders who have experienced the process of responsibly removing a member from their groups are very strong advocates for careful member screening.

CONFRONTING SOCIAL ISSUES

Counseling and therapy groups exist in the context of broader social systems. Because of this, counseling and therapy groups cannot escape the influences of these broader systems. This is especially true when counseling and therapy groups have external boundaries that allow information to flow, when necessary, between the group and its external environment. These external boundaries are essential to allow the transfer of changes members make in group to members' relationships outside the group. That is, all groups, to be relevant to the lives of their members, must have external boundaries that do not totally isolate them from the world in which they exist. One important implication of these boundaries is that the social issues occurring in the social environment also occur in counseling and therapy groups.

The Nature of Social Issues in the Group Context

From the systems perspective, all parts of a social system have isomorphic qualities. This means that group interaction inevitably demonstrates the social issues present in the group's social context. Thus, issues related to ageism, racism, sexism, and intolerance of others with handicapping conditions, different religions, cultures, and sexual orientations emerge in some form during group interaction.

Many group leaders, however, can probably describe instances when diversity issues did not emerge and were not relevant to group interaction. These descriptions are understandable but are not defensible. They are understandable because members and leaders often want to avoid the anxiety involved in confronting diversity issues. Such avoidance is common when leaders and members prefer avoiding conflict, confronting their own biases, and dealing with the fears they associate with owning their own prejudices. Such descriptions are not defensible because diversity issues are always present in counseling and therapy groups just as they are in the broader social context.

When the diversity issues present in a group are not blatant, members and leaders tend to ignore them. From the focal conflict perspective, confronting diversity issues in most counseling and therapy groups is a disturbing motive that leaders and members alike would rather avoid. The reactive motive is fear that conflict will emerge and individuals will have to admit and confront their own biases and prejudices. Commonly, the focal conflict associated with these fears operates subtly and is undetected or ignored. Thus, diversity issues become a secret in most groups that members and leaders covertly agree to keep. Diversity issues often stay out of awareness unless leaders bring these issues to the attention of group members.

Identifying and confronting diversity issues is an important responsibility of group leaders. Fulfilling this responsibility requires commitment and the courage to be proactive. Being proactive means that group leaders find a time during the lives of their groups to direct members to confront the biases and fears related to being citizens of a world populated by diverse individuals and groups. Being courageous means bringing up and sustaining a discussion of a focal conflict that is difficult to confront.

Confronting Diversity Issues in the Group Context

Leaders can use a reactive approach to confronting diversity issues by confronting these issues whenever they emerge during group interaction. Leaders, however, are encouraged to assume a proactive stance by identifying and confronting diversity issues before they emerge. Although either a reactive or a proactive approach can be effective, the pitfall associated with a reactive approach is that leaders might never find the "right time" to address diversity issues. The most important principle is that leaders involve all members in exploring the diversity issues that impact their lives and their relationships with others. Ideally, leaders should be able to say that they have addressed diversity issues in all the groups they have led.

Confronting diversity issues as they emerge in group interaction is essential. Dealing directly with diversity issues is a proactive process that reflects leaders' commitment to confronting biases that limit and harm persons. The process of linking group interaction to diversity issues is one that requires careful timing. Premature introduction of diversity considerations is a possibility. The following scenario illustrates a relatively common group issue and a premature leader intervention.

> Jean has been talking about how the male members of the group have been treating her like the group mascot. She perceives that the male members placate, patronize, and dismiss the importance of her contributions. Her interactions with the male members are intense and emotional. As Jean becomes increasingly clear about her boundaries and her emotional expressions become more clear, the group leader interrupts. "It seems that Jean is talking about some really important issues. What gender issues are you all seeing?"

In this example, the group leader is premature in directing members to discuss gender issues. This direction is premature because it preempts interactions that are likely to be extremely productive. Leaders should be careful to allow members to confront the diversity issues that operate in the group at a personal level before introducing the risk of leading the group to a disconnected intellectual conversation. The more personal and emotionally connected the confrontation of diversity issues are to the here and now of group interaction, the more powerful they are. Consider the following example with different leader intervention timing.

> Jean has been talking about how the male members of the group have been treating her like the group mascot. She perceives that the male members placate, patronize, and dismiss the importance of her contributions. Her interactions with the male members are intense and emotional. As Jean becomes increasingly clear about her boundaries and her emotional expressions become more clear, the group leader encourages Jean to give the male members some specific feedback about her reactions to the way they are treating her. As the feedback exchange nears completion, the leader involves the other women in the group. "As Jean has been sharing her experiences, I've noticed the other women in the group reacting intensely to what's been going on. I want to hear your reactions." After their sharing, the leader involves the male members in processing their reac-

tions with the goal of increasing their awareness of how they relate to the women in the group. Then the leader states, "You all know that what we're dealing with in here limits the quality of our lives out of the group as well. Let's talk for a moment about how we can use what we've become aware of in here and outside of group."

In this scenario, the leader uses group process to complete the emotionally charged relationship work that is necessary for the group to operate effectively. Then, using this energy, the leader involves all the members in conversation that increases awareness and identifies different ways of interaction, both in and out of the group. This process is most meaningful for members and does not save members from confronting the biases present in their immediate relationships in the group. Although this scenario deals with gender issues, the process described is equally relevant to other diversity issues that might emerge.

Leaders who are sensitive to diversity issues can also use their observations of group interaction to confront difficult issues. These observations, as described previously, should be connected to members' relationships in the group and not to an intellectualized discussion of "issues out there." The following scenario is an example of how a leader could do this:

LEADER: "Don, I've noticed that there seems to be something different about the way group members relate to you. They seem to be careful how they talk to you; they seem to be walking on eggshells. Is this something that happens often to you as an African-American male?"

DON: "Sometimes it's not as noticeable as it is in this group."

LEADER: "Don, tell the other members how you feel about this and how you'd like them to interact with you."

(After Don has shared.)

LEADER: "What's going on? It looks like most of you are feeling sad and ashamed. We need to talk about this."

The process described in this scenario attempts to keep the issue connected with the interactions and emotional experiences of the group members in the here and now. Opportunities like the one in this scenario are opportunities for powerful learning experiences. Although educational input can be productive, it should occur as a follow-up to members' immediate interactions.

CONCLUSION

The successful use of intervention strategies can change a group's culture. Changes in a group's culture change the way members relate to each other. These interventions are often difficult and complicated but at the same time are critical. Leaders' first priority is to shape group interaction so members can learn from one another. Group cultures that do not support feedback exchange, meaningful interaction, and the confrontation of social issues that impair members' relationships are unlikely to provide members with meaningful experiences.

CHAPTER

14

Becoming a Group Leader

OBJECTIVES

After reading this chapter, you should be able to:

✔ Discuss the emotional and intellectual demands of group leadership and the personal impact these demands have on group leaders.

✔ Describe how leaders' personal issues impact their ability to lead groups and the importance of leaders having experiences as group members.

✔ Explain how group leaders' knowledge of group dynamics, group theory, and interventions impact their ability to lead groups and the importance of attaining and integrating knowledge into a personally congruent leadership style.

✔ Discuss the importance of developing a personally congruent leadership style.

✔ Describe the significance of experience as a group leader and learn some ways to gain experience as a leader.

✔ Explain the essential nature of leaders' ongoing personal development and a way to plan for this development.

✔ Discuss the significance of leaders developing and maintaining awareness of various personal boundaries.

INTRODUCTION

The emotional and intellectual challenges of leading groups confront leaders throughout their careers. Leaders will continue to experience the challenges of being apprehensive about their abilities and the emotions stirred by seeing their relationship concerns play out in the interaction of group members. In addition, all leaders will experience the challenges of conceptualizing individual and interpersonal concerns, define themes in group interaction, and develop appropriate interventions. Becoming and being a leader includes inevitable emotional and intellectual challenges.

To become effective group leaders, individuals must acquire knowledge and experience as group leaders and members and participate actively in their own ongoing personal development. Minimally, group leaders must understand theory and group dynamics principles and develop an array of personally congruent skills and interventions. In addition, leaders are best prepared for the demands of group leadership when they have experienced meaningful growth as group members. Leading with different coleaders and leading groups that include diverse members in various settings also will enhance group leaders' development. Leaders should, whenever possible, take advantage of opportunities to interact with other group leaders and supervisors. Finally, leading groups is highly rewarding and personally demanding. To deal with the personal demands of leadership, leaders must attend to their own physical and emotional well-being.

EMOTIONAL CHALLENGES

The intensity of their emotional reactions usually surprises leaders during their initial leadership experiences. Beginning leaders in particular should understand that it is common to be anxious about intervening competently, experiencing emotional reactions to group interactions, and hearing the emotion-laden concerns of members. Still, awareness does not rescue beginning leaders from the intensity of their experiences. It is important, nevertheless, that group leaders not lead groups with the erroneous assumption that they should be immune to emotional reactions. Instead, leaders should be clear that "therapists are entitled to the same range of human emotions and reactions as anyone else" (Levine, 1991, p. 55).

Leaders' emotional reactions to group interactions are normal. In fact, leaders' emotional reactions are an important barometer of what members are experiencing and an essential aspect of leaders engaging members genuinely. To be able to use their emotions to help them lead groups, developing leaders must accept and tolerate their own emotional reactions. Leaders who accept and tolerate their emotional reactions can then learn to value emotions as a meaningful connection with the experiences of group members.

Leaders who are comfortable with their own emotional reactions are able to reflect on their emotions in order to understand members' experiences more fully. Thus, when a leader is aware that he or she is sad about a group interaction, he or she can make an intervention like "I'm sensing sadness in the group about what Mary just said. Who would like to share their sadness with Mary?"

Leaders who reflect on their emotions to initiate emotion-stimulating interventions can help members who struggle to make connections. At times, interventions based on leaders' reflections of their own emotional reactions can stimulate movement from disconnected cognitive discussion toward members making more intimate connections. These interventions often lead to connections that are possibly the fullest expression of understanding members can offer each other.

Weiner (1993) reinforces the importance of leaders developing comfort with their emotions and the emotions of group members. To lead groups that stress members' interaction effectively, leaders must be sensitive to their groups' "emotional undercurrents" (p. 86). He goes on to state that "the interpersonal group leader also needs to tolerate and to deal with intense emotions and emotional interchanges that result from dealing with here-and-now interpersonal relationships" (p. 86).

Group leaders who shut off or deny awareness of their own emotional experiences deny themselves a valuable way to understand members' experiences and help members make meaningful contact with each other. Eventually, members will not trust leaders who attempt to deny their own emotions, as members will perceive these leaders as emotionally distant and aloof. Shutting off or denying awareness of emotions are defensive tactics used by leaders who tend to view their own emotions as unacceptable. Generally, these leaders fear that their emotions will overwhelm them and cause them to lose control.

Inevitably, the fears of leaders who deny or shut off their emotions become realities. These leaders eventually witness several unfortunate outcomes. Some experience overwhelming emotions because intense group interactions inevitably overcome any attempt to shut down or deny emotions. These leaders are overwhelmed because their often-rigid personal requirements for maintaining emotional control are unattainable, and their fears of losing emotional control are coming true. The experiences of leaders who have rigid requirements for emotional control are especially terrifying when their requirements for emotional control preclude experiencing even the slightest anxiety.

Leaders who fear their own emotions and the emotions of others will eventually direct members' interactions away from potentially productive topics. These leaders divert members from issues that elicit their own emotions because these issues cause reactions that make them aware of their own emotional vulnerabilities. Inevitably, leaders who cannot accept or tolerate their own emotions will deprive group members of meaningful opportunities to confront difficult issues. Unless they are willing to begin their own therapy, leaders who have rigid requirements for not experiencing their own emotions or who fear others' emotions are not appropriate candidates for the role of group leader.

Leaders who cannot accept or tolerate their own emotions often attempt to deny and hide their emotional reactions. These leaders are unlikely to conceal their emotions successfully because members are very sensitive to the emotional tone of leaders' reactions, interventions, and nonverbal messages. Invariably, leaders who believe they can suppress their emotional reactions unwittingly communicate their emotions to group members. Members will question leaders' sincerity when they witness leaders attempting to hide their emotions. In addition, members interpret leaders' attempts to hide emotions as a message that expressing emotions is inappropriate. Finally, members will have angry reactions to leaders who deny and attempt to hide their emotions and at the same time encourage members to express their emotions. Leaders attempting to mask their own emotional reactions eventually lose their credibility and send confusing indirect messages that emotions should be denied. Ultimately, leaders cheat members when they attempt to hide or deny their emotions.

The leadership role does not require leaders to be an emotional "blank slate." Rather, the leadership role involves being a guide who helps members find, develop awareness of, and understand their emotional worlds. To fill this role, leaders must be tuned into members' emotions and be emotionally congruent at the same time. Wright (2000) contends that leaders must develop "thoughtful awareness and tolerance of affective states and to clarify what is the essence and deep structure to what we inevitably communicate" (p. 195).

Shapiro, Peltz, and Bernadette-Shapiro (1998) discuss an another important aspect of leaders' emotional experiences during group sessions. They believe that by maintaining awareness of their own emotions, leaders can be clearer about their motivations as they make interventions. They argue that individuals act more commonly on their emotions than on their thoughts. Because of the power of emotions to initiate action, they reason that group leaders' interventions are most commonly an indication of their emotional reactions to interaction rather than their appraisal of interaction. Thus, leaders who are not fully aware of their emotions will make interventions that are likely to be emotionally motivated and not based on a clear understanding of what is transpiring in the group.

In addition to maintaining emotional awareness, Shapiro et al. present two leader attitudes that significantly benefit leaders who are emotionally aware: "1. My feelings are an accurate and in-depth index of group process. 2. Whatever I feel is a result of something that is going on in the group" (p. 140). Leaders who acknowledge and develop comfort with their emotions are most likely to maintain awareness of their emotional reactions during group sessions. Emotional awareness offers leaders an extremely important medium for developing an understanding of group interaction and connecting with members' experiences.

LEADERS' PERSONAL ISSUES

A major leadership problem occurs when leaders do not understand how their personal reactions to group interaction influence their interventions. When unrecognized, leaders' personal issues and beliefs related to personal and sexual relationships could have an inadvertent and adverse influence on how they choose to interpret group interaction and intervene. Maintaining awareness in these areas is essential if leaders are to be clear that their interventions respond to issues surfacing in group interaction and not their personal biases and interpersonal issues.

Because leaders are not immune to personal concerns, they must develop and maintain an awareness of how their personal concerns influence their perceptions and interventions. This is critical for group leaders because of the power of group interaction to evoke relationship concerns. Levine (1991) describes six personal characteristics that reflect developmental issues and interpersonal needs. He claims that these characteristics are critical areas of concern for group leaders. These areas are self-reliance and dependency needs, comfort with authority, acceptance needs, comfort with others' emotional expression and the leader's own emotions, comfort with intimacy and capacity for intimacy in the leader's own relationships, and comfort with separation. Levine believes that leaders' experiences and learning in these areas derive from experiences in their relationships and families of origin. Leaders who are not aware and have not achieved some resolution with these developmental issues are likely to attempt to meet their needs when they lead groups. In addition, leaders who have not adequately resolved these issues will have the tendency to direct members away from important interactions that mirror these concerns because of the discomfort they experience as these issues surface.

Rosenberg's (1993) discussion of the necessary qualities of a group therapist presents ideas similar to those of Levine. Her ideas reflect the complexity of leaders' relationships with members and the potential for countertransference to affect group process adversely. From her perspective, leaders must be aware of their emotional reactions and their needs for expressing emotion and experiencing intimacy. Rosenberg also stresses that leaders must develop understanding of their needs in the areas of control, dependence, and love and sex. In order to understand, develop awareness, and monitor these needs, leaders commonly need therapeutic experiences as clients.

Horwitz (2000) also describes how leaders' needs adversely affect group members' progress. He believes that individuals who lead groups in order to maintain or enhance their self-esteem are likely to slow members' therapeutic progress and will probably damage members. Leaders who use their interactions with members to maintain or inflate their self-image as highly effective and caring therapists are not likely to risk making interventions that could lead to negative reactions or criticism. These leaders are likely to give preferential treatment to members who are complimentary and intervene in a punishing way with members who are not. In pronounced cases, leaders who attempt to satisfy narcissistic needs encourage members to be complimentary about their remarkable skills and impressive insights. By intervening in a way designed to maintain their self-esteem, these leaders avoid interventions that could challenge their abilities and make interventions that increase the chances that members will hold them in high regard. Interventions motivated by personal glorification are one of the clearest indications of leaders using groups unethically to meet their own needs.

"Unless the leader is self-aware, there is an ever-present danger that her personal conflicts, inadequacies, and needs, instead of those of the members, will guide group interventions" (Shapiro et al., 1998, p. 118). To guard against this danger, leaders must maintain a high level of self-awareness and participate in experiences that deepen their self-understanding throughout their careers.

KNOWLEDGE

In addition to the personal aspects of group leadership, leaders face intellectual demands. Intellectually, group leaders must have the knowledge necessary to conceptualize group interactions and utilize this understanding to develop interventions that benefit group members. Simply obtaining the knowledge necessary to conceptualize group interaction, however, is insufficient. Leaders must systematically integrate knowledge of theory and personal perspectives into their practice (Bascue, 1978). Integrating knowledge into practice requires "emerging therapists [to] face themselves by identifying, evaluating, and refining their own beliefs rather than just adopting some existing group theory and attempting to conform to it" (p. 452).

Group leaders must have a sufficient knowledge base to understand group interaction and define objectives for the group environment and members' interactions. This knowledge base, at a minimum, includes an understanding of group counseling and therapy theory and group dynamics principles. Leaders who understand theory and group dynamics can apply these principles to organize and conceptualize group interaction, after which they can develop and use interventions that lead to meaningful changes in members. In addition, after experience and reflection, leaders should eventually articulate personally congruent theory, skills, and interventions.

Leaders must also have a rudimentary understanding of group dynamics. Understanding how norms and roles develop as a product of group interactions is critical. This understanding points the way for interventions designed to develop a group environment that supports risk taking and experimentation. Leaders who do not comprehend these rudimentary principles do not understand and may not be aware of either productive or counterproductive patterns that emerge in members' interactions. When leaders do not understand fundamental group dynamics principles, they do not have a sufficient understanding of group interaction to know how to structure interventions to modify blocking norms or help members develop role flexibility.

A working knowledge of an appropriate group counseling or therapy theory is also essential. Without an appropriate theory (see chapter 5 for the characteristics of an appropriate theory), leaders will find the complexity of group interaction overwhelming. Leaders using a theory designed for individually focused counseling or therapy or those functioning without a theory suffer a serious disadvantage. These leaders have no guidance regarding what aspects of interaction are important or unimportant, no guiding concepts that can help them understand interactions, and no model to guide interventions (Shapiro et al., 1998).

EXPERIENCE

A grossly underemphasized area of experience in counseling accreditation standards and counseling and group therapy certification criteria is requirements for leaders' formative experiences as group members. Although counseling training standards (Council for Accreditation of Counseling and Related Educational Programs [CACREP], 2000) require a group experience for counseling trainees, they offer no guidelines for the type, quality, or intensity of these experiences. In the area of group psychotherapy, the American Group Psychotherapy Association does not require experiences as group members for entry into the organization's clinical membership status. In addition, the more stringent standards for certification as a Certified Group Psychotherapist (CGP) do not stipulate experience as a group member. This is also true for the entry-level National Certified Counselor (NCC) and advanced-level certification for the Certified Clinical Mental Health Counselor (CCMHC) counseling certification.

Contrary to certification and accreditation requirements, the vast majority of writers in the field of group counseling and psychotherapy strongly emphasize the need for prospective leaders to have experiences as group members in their training. These authors agree that formative experiences as group members are necessary for trainees to become competent practitioners. Yalom (1995) describes indispensable benefits of group participation for leaders in training:

> You experience the power of the group—the power to wound and to heal. You learn how important it is to be accepted by the group; what self-disclosure really entails; how difficult it is to reveal your secret world, your fantasies, feelings of vulnerability, hostility, and tenderness. You learn to appreciate your strengths as well as weaknesses. You learn about your own preferred role in the group. Perhaps most striking of all, you learn about the role of the leader by becoming aware of your own dependency and your unrealistic appraisal of the leader's power and knowledge. (pp. 518–519)

Shapiro et al. (1998) also address the need for leaders in training to have experiences as members. From their perspective, group leaders can begin to understand the powerful effects of group membership only when they have had experiences as group members: "Unless a leader can empathize with the intense pressures and fears of membership, his understanding of members will be subsequently diminished. Group leaders must understand group phenomena affectively and sensorially as well as intellectually" (p. 172). Day (1993) succinctly states the need for leaders in training to have their own therapeutic experiences: "The more they [leaders] know themselves, the deeper they can look into others and the more they can appreciate the complexity of the group" (p. 665).

Leaders who have experienced meaningful growth as group members have an unequivocal advantage over leaders who have not; they understand the experience of change from the perspective of a group member. Not only can leaders who have had productive experiences as members fully understand what members of their groups experience, but they can also be more honestly committed to the power of group interaction to produce meaningful change. Leaders who have not had productive experiences as group members cannot congruently advocate members' participation and cannot interact with members with the same conviction or enthusiasm as leaders who have had productive experiences. Developing leaders should reflect on questions answerable only from the perspective of experience. These questions are "Can I fully understand what it is like to be a member?" "Do I have a reservoir of experience as a member that allows me to connect emotionally with members' experiences in the groups I lead?" and "Can I honestly and congruently encourage members to participate in a process in which I have chosen not to participate?"

Another experiential element of developing as a group leader is taking advantage of opportunities to lead groups in different settings with a variety of members.

Leaders who have a broad range of experiences have encountered greater variations of group dynamics, issues in interaction, and member characteristics and concerns. Varied experiences encourage leaders to become more flexible in their style, better able to adapt to varying group dynamics, and more open to understanding differences and unique interactive issues. Leaders who compile most of their experiences in one environment run the risk of developing a narrow, stereotypical set of expectations for group dynamics and member concerns. Leaders who have a narrow range of experiences are also not likely to develop a full range of diagnostic skills and interventions. Consequently, leaders with a narrow range of experiences develop a narrowly defined set of anticipations about what members need and what group development issues will emerge. Over time, limited anticipations cause leaders to miss important group content and cause them to be less flexible in their ability to adjust their intervention and diagnostic skills to diverse memberships and issues.

While leading groups in different settings with different members broadens leaders' experiences, so too does leading with different coleaders. Leaders benefit from opportunities to work with different coleaders for a number of reasons. First, it demands that leaders clarify their relationship concerns with each coleader. This reclarification process helps leaders maintain awareness of how their relationship concerns influence their interactions with group members. Second, it provides leaders with an opportunity to observe alternative interventions and leadership styles. Finally, it offers leaders the opportunity to process group events, receive immediate feedback, and reality test reactions to group members, with leaders operating from a variety of experiential perspectives. Work with coleaders also prevents isolation.

As leaders gain experience, they will eventually encounter the problem of isolation, which occurs when leaders encounter the problems of having no one with whom to process their leadership experiences, reality test their impressions, or explore the effectiveness of their interventions. When isolation persists, leaders become stagnant in their development because they do not enrich themselves by hearing new ideas and varying perspectives or the challenges posed by others to sharpen their conceptualization or diagnostic skills. Isolated leaders operate on untested assumptions about their style and effectiveness. Although group leaders can partially deal with isolation by reading, attending workshops and conferences, and reflecting on their practice, they are still isolated. Interaction with other group leaders and supervisors about their perceptions of interaction in the groups they run, the influence of their own relationship concerns on their leadership, and effectiveness of their style and interventions are critical for leaders' ongoing development.

PERSONAL DEVELOPMENT

It is extremely important that group leaders attend to their own needs as persons, especially in terms of their own relationships. As described earlier in this chapter, leaders' relationship needs have the potential of adversely influencing the decisions they make about interventions. In the most problematic form, leaders who are unaware of problems in their relationships can use group interaction to meet their own relationship needs. Leaders must maintain awareness of their own relationship needs as they lead and should take necessary measures to attend to problems they experience in their relationships. Day (1993), Horwitz (2000), Levine (1991), Rosenberg (1993), Shapiro et al. (1998), Weiner (1993), and Yalom (1995) strongly suggest that leaders and leaders in training attend to their own relationship needs either in therapy groups, in peer supervision groups, or even in individual therapy.

Because of the demands of group leadership, leaders should allow themselves adequate time to reflect on their lives and practice. Group leadership can be exhilarating and is often very gratifying. It can also be frustrating, and it always demands considerable physical and emotional energy. Leaders should be aware of the physical and emotional demands of leadership and attend to these needs.

Possibly the most effective way for group leaders to understand their interpersonal boundaries, maintain awareness of their emotions and interpersonal behaviors, and clarify their beliefs about relationships and the experiences of others is to participate as members of peer supervision or therapy groups. The group therapy literature repeatedly emphasizes ongoing peer supervision groups as a means for group therapists to maintain and further develop awareness of their own countertransference and narcissistic issues. Horwitz (2000) describes the benefits of effective peer supervision groups: "When functioning optimally, such groups provide the opportunity to expose one's anxieties and self-doubts to a few trusted fellow professionals" (p. 233). Other avenues for maintaining awareness of personal boundaries and clarifying relationship concerns are in counseling and therapy groups led by master practitioners.

PERSONAL LEADERSHIP STYLE

Shapiro et al. (1998) add an additional personal objective to the process of becoming an effective group leader. As leaders gain experience and competence, their ongoing development demands that they develop a personally congruent leadership style: "The best method for any person is one that reflects his or her personal values and nature" (p. 119). A personally congruent leadership style is ultimately the most effective. Leaders who mimic others' leadership style, use programmed skills, or depend on structured techniques abandon the power of personal contact and isolate themselves from the lives of their groups' members.

To support the evolution of a leader's personal leadership style, a relevant theory is required. Group leaders who engage in thoughtful and reflective practice eventually develop a theoretical perspective that reflects their assumptions about group interaction and accommodates their leadership style. Beginning with theory relevant to group work is the first critical step.

THE PERSONAL BOUNDARIES OF THE GROUP LEADER

Leaders' personal boundaries define how they participate in their groups as leaders and persons. These boundaries vary from one leader to another, depending on personal style. However, some parameters hold true for all group leaders. First, leaders must interact with group members in a way that helps members learn. Second, leaders must never prioritize their personal needs over the needs of members. Two other boundary concerns also require specific discussion. These areas require reflection and are not as concrete as the first two boundary areas. One boundary involves leaders' views about the use and limits of power, authority, and responsibility in the leadership role. The other centers on leaders' awareness of their own personal biases related to gender, racial, religious, and cultural issues.

Power, Authority, and Responsibility

An important boundary is the product of leaders' beliefs about the limits and extent of their power to influence what occurs during group sessions (Whitaker, 1985). Whitaker comments that leaders often possess unrealistic assumptions about their real power to influence group members. She also discusses how leaders' beliefs about their power can lead to frustration and even to a desire to abdicate the power they actually have to influence group members.

Occasionally, leaders will develop the impression that they influence members too easily and wish that they did not have as much power as they believe they have. Whitaker (1985) offers a perspective on power that challenges this wish: "Part of a [leader's] responsibility is to acknowledge and use his powers to further his purposes" (p. 378). Realistically, the only power leaders have is a function of their role. Role-related power involves convening groups and establishing and maintaining group membership. In addition, leaders have power because the leadership role requires them to be "in charge" of directing interaction. In the group room, leaders' power derives from their ability and success in directing group interaction in a way that influences member change.

Coupled with directing interaction, leaders also have power because of their knowledge and ability to observe the group from a different perspective than members. By sharing observations and using observations to formulate interventions, leaders can bring into awareness issues members wish to avoid. This means that leaders become influential because their knowledge allows them to identify disturbing and reactive motives. By intervening in a way that causes members to confront disturbing and reactive motives, leaders have the power to regulate the amount of anxiety present in the group room.

The power leaders possess is essentially limited to role-associated parameters: the power to direct interaction, the power to form and convene the group, the power to include and exclude members, the power to use their knowledge and observational perspective to identify issues, and the power to regulate anxiety. Beyond these parameters, the power leaders actually have to influence members to change is extremely limited.

Whitaker (1985) succinctly identifies the boundaries of leaders' power: "The only power the leader has while a group is in session is over his [or her] own behaviour" (p. 376). Leaders have the power to choose the content of their interventions, to confront or ignore issues, and to collude with or frustrate restrictive solutions. Leaders do not have the power to change members; they only have the power to increase the chances that members will choose to change. Thus, leaders who become disappointed because they have not successfully altered the way members interact are probably acting on an erroneous assumption about the extent of their power to change members. In general, any power that leaders have to encourage members to make decisions that lead to important changes should be used to its fullest.

Whitaker (1985) describes the boundaries of leaders' responsibility as "an obligation or duty to do everything he [or she] can, to the best of his [or her] ability, to work towards his [or her] overall purpose of utilizing the group for the benefit of the members" (p. 378). Given that leaders are responsible for ethical behavior and meeting standards of practice, leaders should examine the realities of group practice when defining the boundaries of their responsibilities. Although having power to influence the outcomes of their groups, leaders do not have the power to determine group outcomes.

Whitaker (1985) points out that leaders' "behaviour in the group is only one of a number of factors which influence outcome, and it is not necessarily the most important one" (p. 379). In terms of responsibility, this means that leaders are responsible to behave in ways that are most consistent with productive group outcomes. This also means that leaders have a responsibility not to act in a way that can cause the group to be "unhelpful or even damaging to individual members" (p. 379). Leaders do have the power to harm group members and have an ethical and moral responsibility to refrain from doing so.

Leaders must carefully examine their beliefs about the realistic boundaries of their power and responsibility. Leaders who feel that they have the power and the responsibility to change others should carefully examine these beliefs. Leaders who believe they can change others and are responsible to do so are likely to view members who do not change "when they are supposed to" as noncompliant or resistant and regard themselves as failed group leaders.

Wright (2000) describes group therapists who believe that they have the power to change members. Leaders who share this belief often have a need to see progress and to regard themselves as the most important person in their members' lives. Members of the groups led by leaders with these needs and beliefs are likely to experience leaders' wrath if they do not respond the way these leaders desire. Leaders who function with these needs and beliefs lead ineffectively and will eventually harm members.

Gender, Racial, Religious, and Cultural Issues

Rosenberg (1993) extends the discussion of leaders' boundaries: "Group therapists must also be aware of their social ideals and religious values, so that they can realistically set boundaries of their own behavior and respect the boundaries of the group members" (p. 652). Clearly, leaders' boundaries must not reflect personal biases that can harm group members. Leaders are ethically and morally obligated to confront their own personal biases and issues relevant to gender, racial, religious, and cultural diversity. The discussion of how multicultural and racial issues affect therapeutic relationships has been especially evident in counseling literature.

Many authors believe that the first step a counselor or therapist should take in working with clientele from diverse cultural, racial, religious, and sexual orientation perspectives is to gain clarity about their own beliefs, feelings, and assumptions. Lee (1991) stresses that counselors should be fully aware of their own heritage as well as the biases they have that might interfere with how effectively they can help others. Yu and Gregg (1993) emphasize that the process of developing awareness demands that counselors uncover potential "blind spots" relative to diverse clientele: "Counselors should recognize they may unknowingly harbor biases and prejudices toward members of specific ethnic groups. They need to be willing to work through these issues before true therapeutic work can begin. If they cannot do so, a referral may be necessary" (p. 91). D'Andrea and Daniels (1997) extend this conversation to group leaders. Competent group leaders must "examine their own assumptions, biases, and feelings concerning diverse cultural-racial groups . . . consider the way these assumptions/biases/feelings might affect their interactions with group members . . . [and] be aware of the ways in which the group members' assumptions, biases, and feelings about culturally-different persons may influence the group process" (p. 106).

The Association for Specialists in Group Work (ASGW, 2000b) articulates essential attitudes about working with diverse group members in its "Principles for Diversity-Competent Group Workers." This document contains important statements regarding the attitudes leaders should maintain as they develop an understanding of their beliefs, values, and biases relative to serving diverse group members most effectively. These attitudes include the belief that leaders should become increasingly aware and sensitive to "their own race, ethnic and cultural heritage, gender, socioeconomic status (SES), sexual orientation, abilities, and religion and spiritual beliefs, and to valuing and respecting differences" (ASGW, 2000b). Leaders should also be aware "of how their own race, ethnicity, culture, gender, SES, sexual orientation, abilities, and religion and spiritual beliefs are impacted by their own experiences and histories, which in turn influence group process and dynamics" (ASGW, 2000b). Perhaps most important, group leaders should be aware of and avoid stereotypes and focus on developing an understanding of each individual in the context of group interaction (McRae, 1994).

Lazerson and Zilbach (1993) make critical points about the need to develop awareness of culturally supported stereotypes relative to gender. They emphasize that group leaders can inadvertently intervene in a way that supports stereotypes or intentionally intervene in a way that challenges stereotypes. Group leaders who are aware of the gender stereotypes that operate in their groups can have an impact on members' interpersonal issues and social and political awareness. Group leaders who confront cultural gender stereotypes confront issues that greatly influence members' relationship attitudes and self-esteem concerns. Unfortunately, many group leaders remain oblivious to their gender biases and do not understand how their perceptions and interventions may inadvertently support stereotypes that limit or damage group members.

Being an Anarchist and Orchestrator

As groups evolve, leaders should encourage members to take risks in their relationships in group and ultimately in their relationships outside group. Leaders, too, will find that interventions are needed to help members "stretch" their ordinary boundaries of safety. The leader-anarchist intervenes to challenge customary boundaries, disrupting comfortable interaction patterns, saying what members will not say, and confronting issues that members collude to avoid. Being a leader-anarchist requires courage and a commitment that prioritizes helping members change over the leader's own comfort.

At other times, leaders will also find that group interaction engages members in productive interaction without the need for leader participation. Some leaders struggle with this, feeling that members require or need their input and direction. At these times, leaders need only orchestrate interaction to ensure that members have equal opportunities to participate. The role of leader-orchestrator will not satisfy an ego that demands being the center of attention. Rather, filling this role means that the leader values the importance of members making meaningful emotional connections and learning from one another. Filling this role signifies that members have learned how to become self-reliant interpersonal learners. Witnessing this is especially satisfying.

CONCLUSION

Both neophytes and experienced leaders benefit from developing an ongoing development plan. This plan should incorporate experiences that broaden leaders' understanding of group members' characteristics and issues and include gaining information that deepens understanding of theory and interventions. This plan should also incorporate time devoted to personal growth.

The time when leaders need to cease learning more about working with groups coincides with their retirement to life as a hermit in the wilderness. Reading and attending conferences and workshops throughout their careers allows leaders to broaden and deepen their understanding of how to lead groups in a way that can influence the lives of their groups' members. Whether this means learning more about theory or different ways to intervene, leaders should regard their ongoing learning as an important way to maintain their interest and enthusiasm. Ongoing development requires continuous change and professional growth. Leaders who choose to discontinue their development and stop challenging themselves to grow and develop become stagnant and boring, both as professionals and as persons.

Leaders should also stay keenly aware that they are parts of a broader social context. Because leaders understand how groups work, they also understand how society and its various subgroups function, occasionally to the detriment of people's welfare. Group leaders should carefully consider how to use their knowledge to confront social issues, certainly in their groups and professional organizations and, it is hoped, in society. Although leaders may debate their obligation to become social activists, they must understand that they are responsible to confront the social issues that oppress their groups' members.

Developing and growing as a group leader is both an intellectual and a personal process. Leaders should attend to their personal and spiritual growth and to their physical well-being. Ongoing personal growth should incorporate experiences that challenge comfortable personal boundaries. These experiences can include joining a therapy or a peer supervision group, attending personal growth workshops, or traveling in countries with diverse cultures. Leaders should also consider their own spiritual development, which is a matter of personal preference and can include participation in religious organizations, learning to meditate, spending time alone in the wilderness, and devoting time for quiet reflection. Finally, it is critically essential that leaders attend to their physical well-being. This is necessary if group leaders are to deal effectively with the stress of leading groups and maintain the emotional balance necessary to operate at their highest level of awareness and energy.

Appendix 1: ACA Code of Ethics and Standards of Practice*

ACA CODE OF ETHICS PREAMBLE

The American Counseling Association is an educational, scientific, and professional organization whose members are dedicated to the enhancement of human development throughout the life-span. Association members recognize diversity in our society and embrace a cross-cultural approach in support of the worth, dignity, potential, and uniqueness of each individual.

The specification of a code of ethics enables the association to clarify to current and future members, and to those served by members, the nature of the ethical responsibilities held in common by its members. As the code of ethics of the association, this document establishes principles that define the ethical behavior of association members. All members of the American Counseling Association are required to adhere to the Code of Ethics and the Standards of Practice. The Code of Ethics will serve as the basis for processing ethical complaints initiated against members of the association.

ACA Code of Ethics

Section A: The Counseling Relationship

Section B: Confidentiality

Section C: Professional Responsibility

Section D: Relationships With Other Professionals

Section E: Evaluation, Assessment, and Interpretation

Section F: Teaching, Training, and Supervision

Section G: Research and Publication

Section H: Resolving Ethical Issues

Section A: The Counseling Relationship

A.1. Client Welfare

a. *Primary Responsibility.* The primary responsibility of counselors is to respect the dignity and to promote the welfare of clients.
b. *Positive Growth and Development.* Counselors encourage client growth and development in ways that foster the clients' interest and welfare; counselors avoid fostering dependent counseling relationships.
c. *Counseling Plans.* Counselors and their clients work jointly in devising integrated, individual counseling plans that offer reasonable promise of success and are consistent with abilities and circumstances of clients. Counselors and clients regularly review counseling plans to ensure their continued viability and effectiveness, respecting clients' freedom of choice. (See A.3.b.)
d. *Family Involvement.* Counselors recognize that families are usually important in clients' lives and strive to enlist family understanding and involvement as a positive resource, when appropriate.

*Reprinted from the American Counseling Association Web Site. http://www.counseling.org/resources/codeofethics.htm. © ACA. Reprinted with permission. No further reproduction authorized without written permission of the American Counseling Association.

e. *Career and Employment Needs.* Counselors work with their clients in considering employment in jobs and circumstances that are consistent with the clients' overall abilities, vocational limitations, physical restrictions, general temperament, interest and aptitude patterns, social skills, education, general qualifications, and other relevant characteristics and needs. Counselors neither place nor participate in placing clients in positions that will result in damaging the interest and the welfare of clients, employers, or the public.

A.2. Respecting Diversity

a. *Nondiscrimination.* Counselors do not condone or engage in discrimination based on age, color, culture, disability, ethnic group, gender, race, religion, sexual orientation, marital status, or socioeconomic status. (See C.5.a., C.5.b., and D.1.i.)

b. *Respecting Differences.* Counselors will actively attempt to understand the diverse cultural backgrounds of the clients with whom they work. This includes, but is not limited to, learning how the counselor's own cultural/ethnic/racial identity impacts her or his values and beliefs about the counseling process. (See E.8. and F.2.i.)

A.3. Client Rights

a. *Disclosure to Clients.* When counseling is initiated, and throughout the counseling process as necessary, counselors inform clients of the purposes, goals, techniques, procedures, limitations, potential risks, and benefits of services to be performed, and other pertinent information. Counselors take steps to ensure that clients understand the implications of diagnosis, the intended use of tests and reports, fees, and billing arrangements. Clients have the right to expect confidentiality and to be provided with an explanation of its limitations, including supervision and/or treatment team professionals; to obtain clear information about their case records; to participate in the ongoing counseling plans; and to refuse any recommended services and be advised of the consequences of such refusal. (See E.5.a. and G.2.)

b. *Freedom of Choice.* Counselors offer clients the freedom to choose whether to enter into a counseling relationship and to determine which professional(s) will provide counseling. Restrictions that limit choices of clients are fully explained. (See A.1.c.)

c. *Inability to Give Consent.* When counseling minors or persons unable to give voluntary informed consent, counselors act in these clients' best interests. (See B.3.)

A.4. Clients Served by Others

If a client is receiving services from another mental health professional, counselors, with client consent, inform the professional persons already involved and develop clear agreements to avoid confusion and conflict for the client. (See C.6.c.)

A.5. Personal Needs and Values

a. *Personal Needs.* In the counseling relationship, counselors are aware of the intimacy and responsibilities inherent in the counseling relationship, maintain respect for clients, and avoid actions that seek to meet their personal needs at the expense of clients.

b. *Personal Values.* Counselors are aware of their own values, attitudes, beliefs, and behaviors and how these apply in a diverse society, and avoid imposing their values on clients. (See C.5.a.)

A.6. Dual Relationships

a. *Avoid When Possible.* Counselors are aware of their influential positions with respect to clients, and they avoid exploiting the trust and dependency of clients. Counselors make every effort to avoid dual relationships with clients that could impair professional judgment or increase the risk of harm to clients. (Examples of such relationships include, but are not limited to, familial, social, financial, business, or close personal relationships with clients.) When a dual relationship cannot be avoided, counselors take appropriate professional precautions such as informed consent, consultation, supervision, and documentation to ensure that judgment is not impaired and no exploitation occurs. (See F.1.b.)

b. *Superior/Subordinate Relationships.* Counselors do not accept as clients superiors or subordinates with whom they have administrative, supervisory, or evaluative relationships.

A.7. Sexual Intimacies with Clients

a. *Current Clients.* Counselors do not have any type of sexual intimacies with clients and do not counsel persons with whom they have had a sexual relationship.

b. *Former Clients.* Counselors do not engage in sexual intimacies with former clients within a minimum of 2 years after terminating the counseling relationship. Counselors who engage in such relationship after 2 years following termination have the responsibility to examine and document thoroughly that such relations did not have an exploitative nature, based on factors such as duration of counseling, amount of time since counseling, termination circumstances, client's personal history and mental status, adverse impact on the client, and actions by the counselor suggesting a plan to initiate a sexual relationship with the client after termination.

A.8. Multiple Clients

When counselors agree to provide counseling services to two or more persons who have a relationship (such as husband and wife, or parents and children), counselors clarify at the outset which person or persons are clients and the nature of the relationships they will have with each involved person. If it becomes apparent that counselors may be called upon to perform potentially conflicting roles, they clarify, adjust, or withdraw from roles appropriately. (See B.2. and B.4.d.)

A.9. Group Work

a. *Screening.* Counselors screen prospective group counseling/ therapy participants. To the extent possible, counselors select members whose needs and goals are compatible with goals of the group, who will not impede the group process, and whose well-being will not be jeopardized by the group experience.

b. *Protecting Clients.* In a group setting, counselors take reasonable precautions to protect clients from physical or psychological trauma.

A.10. Fees and Bartering (See D.3.a. and D.3.b.)

a. *Advance Understanding.* Counselors clearly explain to clients, prior to entering the counseling relationship, all financial arrangements related to professional services including the use of collection agencies or legal measures for nonpayment. (A.11.c.)

b. *Establishing Fees.* In establishing fees for professional counseling services, counselors consider the financial status of clients and locality. In the event that the established fee structure is inappropriate for a client, assistance is provided in attempting to find comparable services of acceptable cost. (See A.10.d., D.3.a., and D.3.b.)

c. *Bartering Discouraged.* Counselors ordinarily refrain from accepting goods or services from clients in return for counseling services because such arrangements create inherent potential for conflicts, exploitation, and distortion of the professional relationship. Counselors may participate in bartering only if the relationship is not exploitative, if the client requests it, if a clear written contract is established, and if such arrangements are an accepted practice among professionals in the community. (See A.6.a.)

d. *Pro Bono Service.* Counselors contribute to society by devoting a portion of their professional activity to services for which there is little or no financial return (pro bono).

A.11. Termination and Referral

a. *Abandonment Prohibited.* Counselors do not abandon or neglect clients in counseling. Counselors assist in making appropriate arrangements for the continuation of treatment, when necessary, during interruptions such as vacations, and following termination.

b. *Inability to Assist Clients.* If counselors determine an inability to be of professional assistance to clients, they avoid entering or immediately terminate a counseling relationship. Counselors are knowledgeable about referral resources and suggest appropriate alternatives. If clients decline the suggested referral, counselors should discontinue the relationship.

c. *Appropriate Termination.* Counselors terminate a counseling relationship, securing client agreement when possible, when it is reasonably clear that the client is no longer benefiting, when services are no longer required, when counseling no longer serves the client's needs or interests, when clients do not pay fees charged, or when agency or institution limits do not allow provision of further counseling services. (See A.10.b. and C.2.g.)

A.12. Computer Technology

a. *Use of Computers.* When computer applications are used in counseling services, counselors ensure that (1) the client is intellectually, emotionally, and physically capable of using the computer application; (2) the computer application is appropriate for the needs of the client; (3) the client understands the purpose and operation of the computer applications; and (4) a follow-up of client use of a computer application is provided to correct possible misconceptions, discover inappropriate use, and assess subsequent needs.

b. *Explanation of Limitations.* Counselors ensure that clients are provided information as a part of the counseling relationship that adequately explains the limitations of computer technology.

c. *Access to Computer Applications.* Counselors provide for equal access to computer applications in counseling services. (See A.2.a.)

Section B: Confidentiality

B.1. Right to Privacy

a. *Respect for Privacy.* Counselors respect their clients' right to privacy and avoid illegal and unwarranted disclosures of confidential information. (See A.3.a. and B.6.a.)

b. *Client Waiver.* The right to privacy may be waived by the client or his or her legally recognized representative.

c. *Exceptions.* The general requirement that counselors keep information confidential does not apply when disclosure is required to prevent clear and imminent danger to the client or others or when legal requirements demand that confidential information be revealed. Counselors consult with other professionals when in doubt as to the validity of an exception.

d. *Contagious, Fatal Diseases.* A counselor who receives information confirming that a client has a disease commonly known to be both communicable and fatal is justified in disclosing information to an identifiable third party, who by his or her relationship with the client is at a high risk of contracting the disease. Prior to making a disclosure the counselor should ascertain that the client has not already informed the third party about his or her disease and that the client is not intending to inform the third party in the immediate future. (See B.1.c. and B.1.f.)

e. *Court-Ordered Disclosure.* When court ordered to release confidential information without a client's permission, counselors request to the court that the disclosure not be required due to potential harm to the client or counseling relationship. (See B.1.c.)

f. *Minimal Disclosure.* When circumstances require the disclosure of confidential information, only essential information is revealed. To the extent possible, clients are informed before confidential information is disclosed.

g. *Explanation of Limitations.* When counseling is initiated and throughout the counseling process as necessary, counselors inform clients of the limitations of confidentiality and identify foreseeable situations in which confidentiality must be breached. (See G.2.a.)

h. *Subordinates.* Counselors make every effort to ensure that privacy and confidentiality of clients are maintained by subordinates including employees, supervisees, clerical assistants, and volunteers. (See B.1.a.)

i. *Treatment Teams.* If client treatment will involve a continued review by a treatment team, the client will be informed of the team's existence and composition.

B.2. Groups and Families

a. *Group Work.* In group work, counselors clearly define confidentiality and the parameters for the specific group being entered, explain its importance, and discuss the difficulties related to confidentiality involved in group work. The fact that confidentiality cannot be guaranteed is clearly communicated to group members.

b. *Family Counseling.* In family counseling, information about one family member cannot be disclosed to another member without permission. Counselors protect the privacy rights of each family member. (See A.8., B.3., and B.4.d.)

B.3. Minor or Incompetent Clients

When counseling clients who are minors or individuals who are unable to give voluntary, informed consent, parents or guardians may be included in the counseling process as appropriate. Counselors act in the best interests of clients and take measures to safeguard confidentiality. (See A.3.c.)

B.4. Records

a. *Requirement of Records.* Counselors maintain records necessary for rendering professional services to their clients and as required by laws, regulations, or agency or institution procedures.

b. *Confidentiality of Records.* Counselors are responsible for securing the safety and confidentiality of any counseling records they create, maintain, transfer, or destroy whether the records are written, taped, computerized, or stored in any other medium. (See B.1.a.)

c. *Permission to Record or Observe.* Counselors obtain permission from clients prior to electronically recording or observing sessions. (See A.3.a.)

d. *Client Access.* Counselors recognize that counseling records are kept for the benefit of clients, and therefore provide access to records and copies of records when requested by competent clients, unless the records contain information that may be misleading and detrimental to the client. In situations involving multiple clients, access to records is limited to those parts of records that do not include confidential information related to another client. (See A.8., B.1.a., and B.2.b.)

e. *Disclosure or Transfer.* Counselors obtain written permission from clients to disclose or transfer records to legitimate third parties unless exceptions to confidentiality exist as listed in Section B.1. Steps are taken to ensure that receivers of counseling records are sensitive to their confidential nature.

B.5. Research and Training

a. *Data Disguise Required.* Use of data derived from counseling relationships for purposes of training, research, or publication is confined to content that is disguised to ensure the anonymity of the individuals involved. (See B.1.g. and G.3.d.)

b. *Agreement for Identification.* Identification of a client in a presentation or publication is permissible only when the client has reviewed the material and has agreed to its presentation or publication. (See G.3.d.)

B.6. Consultation

a. *Respect for Privacy.* Information obtained in a consulting relationship is discussed for professional purposes only with persons clearly concerned with the case. Written and oral reports present data germane to the purposes of the consultation, and every effort is made to protect client identity and avoid undue invasion of privacy.

b. *Cooperating Agencies.* Before sharing information, counselors make efforts to ensure that there are defined policies in other agencies serving the counselor's clients that effectively protect the confidentiality of information.

Section C: Professional Responsibility

C.1. Standards Knowledge

Counselors have a responsibility to read, understand, and follow the Code of Ethics and the Standards of Practice.

C.2. Professional Competence

a. *Boundaries of Competence.* Counselors practice only within the boundaries of their competence, based on their education, training, supervised experience, state and national professional credentials, and appropriate professional experience. Counselors will demonstrate a commitment to gain knowledge, personal awareness, sensitivity, and skills pertinent to working with a diverse client population.

b. *New Specialty Areas of Practice.* Counselors practice in specialty areas new to them only after appropriate education, training, and supervised experience. While developing skills in new specialty areas, counselors take steps to ensure the competence of their work and to protect others from possible harm.

c. *Qualified for Employment.* Counselors accept employment only for positions for which they are qualified by education, training, supervised experience, state and national professional credentials, and appropriate professional experience. Counselors hire for professional counseling positions only individuals who are qualified and competent.

d. *Monitor Effectiveness.* Counselors continually monitor their effectiveness as professionals and take steps to improve when necessary. Counselors in private practice take reasonable steps to seek out peer supervision to evaluate their efficacy as counselors.

e. *Ethical Issues Consultation.* Counselors take reasonable steps to consult with other counselors or related professionals when they have questions regarding their ethical obligations or professional practice. (See H.1.)

f. *Continuing Education.* Counselors recognize the need for continuing education to maintain a reasonable level of awareness of current scientific and professional information in their fields of activity. They take steps to maintain competence in the skills they use, are open to new procedures, and keep current with the diverse and/or special populations with whom they work.

g. *Impairment.* Counselors refrain from offering or accepting professional services when their physical, mental, or emotional problems are likely to harm a client or others. They are alert to the signs of impairment, seek assistance for problems, and, if necessary, limit, suspend, or terminate their professional responsibilities. (See A.11.c.)

C.3. Advertising and Soliciting Clients

a. *Accurate Advertising.* There are no restrictions on advertising by counselors except those that can be specifically justified to protect the public from deceptive practices. Counselors advertise or represent their services to the public by identifying their credentials in an accurate manner that is not false, misleading, deceptive, or fraudulent. Counselors may only advertise the highest degree earned which is in counseling or a closely related field from a college or university that was accredited when the degree was awarded by one of the regional accrediting bodies recognized by the Council on Postsecondary Accreditation.

b. *Testimonials.* Counselors who use testimonials do not solicit them from clients or other persons who, because of their particular circumstances, may be vulnerable to undue influence.

c. *Statements by Others.* Counselors make reasonable efforts to ensure that statements made by others about them or the profession of counseling are accurate.

d. *Recruiting Through Employment.* Counselors do not use their places of employment or institutional affiliation to recruit or gain clients, supervisees, or consultees for their private practices. (See C.5.e.)

e. *Products and Training Advertisements.* Counselors who develop products related to their profession or conduct workshops or training events ensure that the advertisements concerning these products or events are accurate and disclose adequate information for consumers to make informed choices.

f. *Promoting to Those Served.* Counselors do not use counseling, teaching, training, or supervisory relationships to promote their products or training events in a manner that is deceptive or would exert undue influence on individuals who may be vulnerable. Counselors may adopt textbooks they have authored for instruction purposes.

g. *Professional Association Involvement.* Counselors actively participate in local, state, and national associations that foster the development and improvement of counseling.

C.4. Credentials

a. *Credentials Claimed.* Counselors claim or imply only professional credentials possessed and are responsible for correcting any known misrepresentations of their credentials by others. Professional credentials include graduate degrees in counseling or closely related mental health fields, accreditation of graduate programs, national voluntary certifications, government-issued certifications or licenses, ACA professional membership, or any other credential that might indicate to the public specialized knowledge or expertise in counseling.

b. *ACA Professional Membership.* ACA professional members may announce to the public their membership status. Regular members may not announce their ACA membership in a manner that might imply they are credentialed counselors.

c. *Credential Guidelines.* Counselors follow the guidelines for use of credentials that have been established by the entities that issue the credentials.

d. *Misrepresentation of Credentials.* Counselors do not attribute more to their credentials than the credentials represent, and do not imply that other counselors are not qualified because they do not possess certain credentials.

e. *Doctoral Degrees From Other Fields.* Counselors who hold a master's degree in counseling or a closely related mental health field, but hold a doctoral degree from other than counseling or a closely related field, do not use the title "Dr." in their practices and do not announce to the public in relation to their practice or status as a counselor that they hold a doctorate.

C.5. Public Responsibility

a. *Nondiscrimination.* Counselors do not discriminate against clients, students, or supervisees in a manner that has a negative impact based on their age, color, culture, disability, ethnic group, gender, race, religion, sexual orientation, or socioeconomic status, or for any other reason. (See A.2.a.)

b. *Sexual Harassment.* Counselors do not engage in sexual harassment. Sexual harassment is defined as sexual solicitation, physical advances, or verbal or nonverbal conduct that is sexual in nature, that occurs in connection with professional activities or roles, and that either (1) is unwelcome, is offensive, or creates a hostile workplace environment, and counselors know or are told this; or (2) is sufficiently severe or intense to be perceived as harassment to a reasonable person in the context. Sexual harassment can consist of a single intense or severe act or multiple persistent or pervasive acts.

c. *Reports to Third Parties.* Counselors are accurate, honest, and unbiased in reporting their professional activities and judgments to appropriate third parties including courts, health insurance companies, those who are the recipients of evaluation reports, and others. (See B.1.g.)

d. *Media Presentations.* When counselors provide advice or comment by means of public lectures, demonstrations, radio or television programs, prerecorded tapes, printed articles, mailed material, or other media, they take reasonable precautions to ensure that (1) the statements are based on appropriate professional counseling literature and practice; (2) the statements are otherwise consistent with the Code of Ethics and the Standards of Practice; and (3) the recipients of the information are not encouraged to infer that a professional counseling relationship has been established. (See C.6.b.)

e. *Unjustified Gains.* Counselors do not use their professional positions to seek or receive unjustified personal gains, sexual favors, unfair advantage, or unearned goods or services. (See C.3.d.)

C.6. Responsibility to Other Professionals

a. *Different Approaches.* Counselors are respectful of approaches to professional counseling that differ from their own. Counselors know and take into account the traditions and practices of other professional groups with which they work.

b. *Personal Public Statements.* When making personal statements in a public context, counselors clarify that they are speaking from their personal perspectives and that they are not speaking on behalf of all counselors or the profession. (See C.5.d.)

c. *Clients Served by Others.* When counselors learn that their clients are in a professional relationship with another mental health professional, they request release from clients to inform the other professionals and strive to establish positive and collaborative professional relationships. (See A.4.)

Section D: Relationships with Other Professionals

D.1. Relationships with Employers and Employees

a. *Role Definition.* Counselors define and describe for their employers and employees the parameters and levels of their professional roles.

b. *Agreements.* Counselors establish working agreements with supervisors, colleagues, and subordinates regarding counseling or clinical relationships, confidentiality, adherence to professional standards, distinction between public and private material, maintenance and dissemination of recorded information, work load, and accountability. Working agreements in each instance are specified and made known to those concerned.

c. *Negative Conditions.* Counselors alert their employers to conditions that may be potentially disruptive or damaging to the counselor's professional responsibilities or that may limit their effectiveness.

d. *Evaluation.* Counselors submit regularly to professional review and evaluation by their supervisor or the appropriate representative of the employer.

e. *In-Service.* Counselors are responsible for in-service development of self and staff.

f. *Goals.* Counselors inform their staff of goals and programs.

g. *Practices.* Counselors provide personnel and agency practices that respect and enhance the rights and welfare of each employee and recipient of agency services. Counselors strive to maintain the highest levels of professional services.

h. *Personnel Selection and Assignment.* Counselors select competent staff and assign responsibilities compatible with their skills and experiences.

i. *Discrimination.* Counselors, as either employers or employees, do not engage in or condone practices that are inhumane, illegal, or unjustifiable (such as considerations based on age, color, culture, disability, ethnic group, gender, race, religion, sexual orientation, or socioeconomic status) in hiring, promotion, or training. (See A.2.a. and C.5.b.)

j. *Professional Conduct.* Counselors have a responsibility both to clients and to the agency or institution within which services are performed to maintain high standards of professional conduct.

k. *Exploitative Relationships.* Counselors do not engage in exploitative relationships with individuals over whom they have supervisory, evaluative, or instructional control or authority.

l. *Employer Policies.* The acceptance of employment in an agency or institution implies that counselors are in agreement with its general policies and principles. Counselors strive to reach agreement with employers as to acceptable standards of conduct that allow for changes in institutional policy conducive to the growth and development of clients.

D.2. Consultation (See B.6.)

a. *Consultation as an Option.* Counselors may choose to consult with any other professionally competent persons about their clients. In choosing consultants, counselors avoid placing the consultant in a conflict of interest situation that would preclude the consultant being a proper party to the counselor's efforts to help the client. Should counselors be engaged in a work setting that compromises this consultation standard, they consult with other professionals whenever possible to consider justifiable alternatives.

b. *Consultant Competency.* Counselors are reasonably certain that they have or the organization represented has the necessary competencies and resources for giving the kind of consulting services needed and that appropriate referral resources are available.

c. *Understanding With Clients.* When providing consultation, counselors attempt to develop with their clients a clear understanding of problem definition, goals for change, and predicted consequences of interventions selected.

d. *Consultant Goals.* The consulting relationship is one in which client adaptability and growth toward self-direction are consistently encouraged and cultivated. (See A.1.b.)

D.3. Fees for Referral

a. *Accepting Fees From Agency Clients.* Counselors refuse a private fee or other remuneration for rendering services to persons who are entitled to such services through the counselor's employing agency or institution. The policies of a particular agency may make explicit provisions for agency clients to receive counseling services from members of its staff in private practice. In such instances, the clients must be informed of other options open to them should they seek private counseling services. (See A.10.a., A.11.b., and C.3.d.)

b. *Referral Fees.* Counselors do not accept a referral fee from other professionals.

D.4. Subcontractor Arrangements

When counselors work as subcontractors for counseling services for a third party, they have a duty to inform clients of the limitations of confidentiality that the organization may place on counselors in providing counseling services to clients. The limits of such confidentiality ordinarily are discussed as part of the intake session. (See B.1.e. and B.1.f.)

Section E: Evaluation, Assessment, and Interpretation

E.1. General

a. *Appraisal Techniques.* The primary purpose of educational and psychological assessment is to provide measures that are objective and interpretable in either comparative or absolute terms. Counselors recognize the need to interpret the statements in this section as applying to the whole range of appraisal techniques, including test and nontest data.

b. *Client Welfare.* Counselors promote the welfare and best interests of the client in the development, publication, and utilization of educational and psychological assessment techniques. They do not misuse assessment results and interpretations and take reasonable steps to prevent others from misusing the information these techniques provide. They respect the client's right to know the results, the interpretations made, and the bases for their conclusions and recommendations.

E.2. Competence to Use and Interpret Tests

a. *Limits of Competence.* Counselors recognize the limits of their competence and perform only those testing and assessment services for which they have been trained. They are familiar with reliability, validity, related standardization, error of measurement, and proper application of any technique utilized. Counselors using computer-based test interpretations are trained in the construct being measured and the specific instrument being used prior to using this type of computer application. Counselors take reasonable measures to ensure the proper use of psychological assessment techniques by persons under their supervision.

b. *Appropriate Use.* Counselors are responsible for the appropriate application, scoring, interpretation, and use of assessment instruments, whether they score and interpret such tests themselves or use computerized or other services.

c. *Decisions Based on Results.* Counselors responsible for decisions involving individuals or policies that are based on assessment results have a thorough understanding of educational and psychological measurement, including validation criteria, test research, and guidelines for test development and use.

d. *Accurate Information.* Counselors provide accurate information and avoid false claims or misconceptions when making statements about assessment instruments or techniques. Special efforts are made to avoid unwarranted connotations of such terms as IQ and grade equivalent scores. (See C.5.c.)

E.3. Informed Consent

a. *Explanation to Clients.* Prior to assessment, counselors explain the nature and purposes of assessment and the specific use of results in language the client (or other legally authorized person on behalf of the client) can understand, unless an explicit exception to this right has been agreed upon in advance. Regardless of whether scoring and interpretation are completed by counselors, by assistants, or by computer or other outside services, counselors take reasonable steps to ensure that appropriate explanations are given to the client.

b. *Recipients of Results.* The examinee's welfare, explicit understanding, and prior agreement determine the recipients of test results. Counselors include accurate and appropriate interpretations with any release of individual or group test results. (See B.1.a. and C.5.c.)

E.4. Release of Information to Competent Professionals

a. *a. Misuse of Results.* Counselors do not misuse assessment results, including test results, and interpretations, and take reasonable steps to prevent the misuse of such by others. (See C.5.c.)

b. *b. Release of Raw Data.* Counselors ordinarily release data (e.g., protocols, counseling or interview notes, or questionnaires) in which the client is identified only with the consent of the client or the client's legal representative. Such data are usually released only to persons recognized by counselors as competent to interpret the data. (See B.1.a.)

E.5. Proper Diagnosis of Mental Disorders

a. *Proper Diagnosis.* Counselors take special care to provide proper diagnosis of mental disorders. Assessment techniques (including personal interview) used to determine client care (e.g., locus of treatment, type of treatment, or recommended follow-up) are carefully selected and appropriately used. (See A.3.a. and C.5.c.)

b. *Cultural Sensitivity.* Counselors recognize that culture affects the manner in which clients' problems are defined. Clients' socioeconomic and cultural experience are considered when diagnosing mental disorders.

E.6. Test Selection

a. *Appropriateness of Instruments.* Counselors carefully consider the validity, reliability, psychometric limitations, and appropriateness of instruments when selecting tests for use in a given situation or with a particular client.

b. *Culturally Diverse Populations.* Counselors are cautious when selecting tests for culturally diverse populations to avoid inappropriateness of testing that may be outside of socialized behavioral or cognitive patterns.

E.7. Conditions of Test Administration

a. *Administration Conditions.* Counselors administer tests under the same conditions that were established in their standardization. When tests are not administered under standard conditions or when unusual behavior or irregularities occur during the testing session, those conditions are noted in interpretation, and the results may be designated as invalid or of questionable validity.

b. *Computer Administration.* Counselors are responsible for ensuring that administration programs function properly to provide clients with accurate results when a computer or other electronic methods are used for test administration. (See A.12.b.)

c. *Unsupervised Test Taking.* Counselors do not permit unsupervised or inadequately supervised use of tests or assessments unless the tests or assessments are designed, intended, and validated for self-administration and/or scoring.

   d. *Disclosure of Favorable Conditions.* Prior to test administration, conditions that produce most favorable test results are made known to the examinee.

E.8. Diversity in Testing

Counselors are cautious in using assessment techniques, making evaluations, and interpreting the performance of populations not represented in the norm group on which an instrument was standardized. They recognize the effects of age, color, culture, disability, ethnic group, gender, race, religion, sexual orientation, and socioeconomic status on test administration and interpretation and place test results in proper perspective with other relevant factors. (See A.2.a.)

E.9. Test Scoring and Interpretation

   a. *Reporting Reservations.* In reporting assessment results, counselors indicate any reservations that exist regarding validity or reliability because of the circumstances of the assessment or the inappropriateness of the norms for the person tested.
   b. *Research Instruments.* Counselors exercise caution when interpreting the results of research instruments possessing insufficient technical data to support respondent results. The specific purposes for the use of such instruments are stated explicitly to the examinee.
   c. *Testing Services.* Counselors who provide test scoring and test interpretation services to support the assessment process confirm the validity of such interpretations. They accurately describe the purpose, norms, validity, reliability, and applications of the procedures and any special qualifications applicable to their use. The public offering of an automated test interpretations service is considered a professional-to-professional consultation. The formal responsibility of the consultant is to the consultee, but the ultimate and overriding responsibility is to the client.

E.10. Test Security

Counselors maintain the integrity and security of tests and other assessment techniques consistent with legal and contractual obligations. Counselors do not appropriate, reproduce, or modify published tests or parts thereof without acknowledgment and permission from the publisher.

E.11. Obsolete Tests and Outdated Test Results

Counselors do not use data or test results that are obsolete or outdated for the current purpose. Counselors make every effort to prevent the misuse of obsolete measures and test data by others.

E.12. Test Construction

Counselors use established scientific procedures, relevant standards, and current professional knowledge for test design in the development, publication, and utilization of educational and psychological assessment techniques.

Section F: Teaching, Training, and Supervision

F.1. Counselor Educators and Trainers

   a. *Educators as Teachers and Practitioners.* Counselors who are responsible for developing, implementing, and supervising educational programs are skilled as teachers and practitioners. They are knowledgeable regarding the ethical, legal, and regulatory aspects of the profession, are skilled in applying that knowledge, and make students and supervisees aware of their responsibilities. Counselors conduct counselor education and training programs in an ethical manner and serve as role models for professional behavior. Counselor educators should make an effort to infuse material related to human diversity into all courses and/or workshops that are designed to promote the development of professional counselors.

b. *Relationship Boundaries With Students and Supervisees.* Counselors clearly define and maintain ethical, professional, and social relationship boundaries with their students and supervisees. They are aware of the differential in power that exists and the student's or supervisee's possible incomprehension of that power differential. Counselors explain to students and supervisees the potential for the relationship to become exploitive.

c. *Sexual Relationships.* Counselors do not engage in sexual relationships with students or supervisees and do not subject them to sexual harassment. (See A.6. and C.5.b.)

d. *Contributions to Research.* Counselors give credit to students or supervisees for their contributions to research and scholarly projects. Credit is given through coauthorship, acknowledgment, footnote statement, or other appropriate means, in accordance with such contributions. (See G.4.b. and G.4.c.)

e. *Close Relatives.* Counselors do not accept close relatives as students or supervisees.

f. *Supervision Preparation.* Counselors who offer clinical supervision services are adequately prepared in supervision methods and techniques. Counselors who are doctoral students serving as practicum or internship supervisors to master's level students are adequately prepared and supervised by the training program.

g. *Responsibility for Services to Clients.* Counselors who supervise the counseling services of others take reasonable measures to ensure that counseling services provided to clients are professional.

h. *Endorsement.* Counselors do not endorse students or supervisees for certification, licensure, employment, or completion of an academic or training program if they believe students or supervisees are not qualified for the endorsement. Counselors take reasonable steps to assist students or supervisees who are not qualified for endorsement to become qualified.

F.2. Counselor Education and Training Programs

a. *Orientation.* Prior to admission, counselors orient prospective students to the counselor education or training program's expectations, including but not limited to the following: (1) the type and level of skill acquisition required for successful completion of the training, (2) subject matter to be covered, (3) basis for evaluation, (4) training components that encourage self-growth or self-disclosure as part of the training process, (5) the type of supervision settings and requirements of the sites for required clinical field experiences, (6) student and supervisee evaluation and dismissal policies and procedures, and (7) up-to-date employment prospects for graduates.

b. *Integration of Study and Practice.* Counselors establish counselor education and training programs that integrate academic study and supervised practice.

c. *Evaluation.* Counselors clearly state to students and supervisees, in advance of training, the levels of competency expected, appraisal methods, and timing of evaluations for both didactic and experiential components. Counselors provide students and supervisees with periodic performance appraisal and evaluation feedback throughout the training program.

d. *Teaching Ethics.* Counselors make students and supervisees aware of the ethical responsibilities and standards of the profession and the students' and supervisees' ethical responsibilities to the profession. (See C.1. and F.3.e.)

e. *Peer Relationships.* When students or supervisees are assigned to lead counseling groups or provide clinical supervision for their peers, counselors take steps to ensure that students and supervisees placed in these roles do not have personal or adverse relationships with peers and that they understand they have the same ethical obligations as counselor educators, trainers, and supervisors. Counselors make every effort to ensure that the rights of peers are not compromised when students or supervisees are assigned to lead counseling groups or provide clinical supervision.

f. *Varied Theoretical Positions.* Counselors present varied theoretical positions so that students and supervisees may make comparisons and have opportunities to develop their own positions. Counselors provide information concerning the scientific bases of professional practice. (See C.6.a.)

g. *Field Placements.* Counselors develop clear policies within their training program regarding field placement and other clinical experiences. Counselors provide clearly stated roles and responsibilities for the student or supervisee, the site supervisor, and the program supervisor. They confirm that site supervisors are qualified to provide supervision and are informed of their professional and ethical responsibilities in this role.

h. *Dual Relationships as Supervisors.* Counselors avoid dual relationships such as performing the role of site supervisor and training program supervisor in the student's or supervisee's training program. Counselors do not accept any form of professional services, fees, commissions, reimbursement, or remuneration from a site for student or supervisee placement.

i. *Diversity in Programs.* Counselors are responsive to their institution's and program's recruitment and retention needs for training program administrators, faculty, and students with diverse backgrounds and special needs. (See A.2.a.)

F.3. Students and Supervisees

a. *Limitations.* Counselors, through ongoing evaluation and appraisal, are aware of the academic and personal limitations of students and supervisees that might impede performance. Counselors assist students and supervisees in securing remedial assistance when needed, and dismiss from the training program supervisees who are unable to provide competent service due to academic or personal limitations. Counselors seek professional consultation and document their decision to dismiss or refer students or supervisees for assistance. Counselors ensure that students and supervisees have recourse to address decisions made to require them to seek assistance or to dismiss them.

b. *Self-Growth Experiences.* Counselors use professional judgment when designing training experiences conducted by the counselors themselves that require student and supervisee self-growth or self-disclosure. Safeguards are provided so that students and supervisees are aware of the ramifications their self-disclosure may have on counselors whose primary role as teacher, trainer, or supervisor requires acting on ethical obligations to the profession. Evaluative components of experiential training experiences explicitly delineate predetermined academic standards that are separate and do not depend on the student's level of self-disclosure. (See A.6.)

c. *Counseling for Students and Supervisees.* If students or supervisees request counseling, supervisors or counselor educators provide them with acceptable referrals. Supervisors or counselor educators do not serve as counselor to students or supervisees over whom they hold administrative, teaching, or evaluative roles unless this is a brief role associated with a training experience. (See A.6.b.)

d. *Clients of Students and Supervisees.* Counselors make every effort to ensure that the clients at field placements are aware of the services rendered and the qualifications of the students and supervisees rendering those services. Clients receive professional disclosure information and are informed of the limits of confidentiality. Client permission is obtained in order for the students and supervisees to use any information concerning the counseling relationship in the training process. (See B.1.e.)

e. *Standards for Students and Supervisees.* Students and supervisees preparing to become counselors adhere to the Code of Ethics and the Standards of Practice. Students and supervisees have the same obligations to clients as those required of counselors. (See H.1.)

Section G: Research and Publication

G.1. Research Responsibilities

a. *Use of Human Subjects.* Counselors plan, design, conduct, and report research in a manner consistent with pertinent ethical principles, federal and state laws, host institutional regulations, and scientific standards governing research with human subjects. Counselors design and conduct research that reflects cultural sensitivity appropriateness.

b. *Deviation From Standard Practices.* Counselors seek consultation and observe stringent safeguards to protect the rights of research participants when a research problem suggests a deviation from standard acceptable practices. (See B.6.)

c. *Precautions to Avoid Injury.* Counselors who conduct research with human subjects are responsible for the subjects' welfare throughout the experiment and take reasonable precautions to avoid causing injurious psychological, physical, or social effects to their subjects.

d. *Principal Researcher Responsibility.* The ultimate responsibility for ethical research practice lies with the principal researcher. All others involved in the research activities share ethical obligations and full responsibility for their own actions.

e. *Minimal Interference.* Counselors take reasonable precautions to avoid causing disruptions in subjects' lives due to participation in research.

f. *Diversity.* Counselors are sensitive to diversity and research issues with special populations. They seek consultation when appropriate. (See A.2.a. and B.6.)

G.2. *Informed Consent*

a. *Topics Disclosed.* In obtaining informed consent for research, counselors use language that is understandable to research participants and that (1) accurately explains the purpose and procedures to be followed; (2) identifies any procedures that are experimental or relatively untried; (3) describes the attendant discomforts and risks; (4) describes the benefits or changes in individuals or organizations that might be reasonably expected; (5) discloses appropriate alternative procedures that would be advantageous for subjects; (6) offers to answer any inquiries concerning the procedures; (7) describes any limitations on confidentiality; and (8) instructs that subjects are free to withdraw their consent and to discontinue participation in the project at any time. (See B.1.f.)

b. *Deception.* Counselors do not conduct research involving deception unless alternative procedures are not feasible and the prospective value of the research justifies the deception. When the methodological requirements of a study necessitate concealment or deception, the investigator is required to explain clearly the reasons for this action as soon as possible.

c. *Voluntary Participation.* Participation in research is typically voluntary and without any penalty for refusal to participate. Involuntary participation is appropriate only when it can be demonstrated that participation will have no harmful effects on subjects and is essential to the investigation.

d. *Confidentiality of Information.* Information obtained about research participants during the course of an investigation is confidential. When the possibility exists that others may obtain access to such information, ethical research practice requires that the possibility, together with the plans for protecting confidentiality, be explained to participants as a part of the procedure for obtaining informed consent. (See B.1.e.)

e. *Persons Incapable of Giving Informed Consent.* When a person is incapable of giving informed consent, counselors provide an appropriate explanation, obtain agreement for participation, and obtain appropriate consent from a legally authorized person.

f. *Commitments to Participants.* Counselors take reasonable measures to honor all commitments to research participants.

g. *Explanations After Data Collection.* After data are collected, counselors provide participants with full clarification of the nature of the study to remove any misconceptions. Where scientific or human values justify delaying or withholding information, counselors take reasonable measures to avoid causing harm.

h. *Agreements to Cooperate.* Counselors who agree to cooperate with another individual in research or publication incur an obligation to cooperate as promised in terms of punctuality of performance and with regard to the completeness and accuracy of the information required.

i. *Informed Consent for Sponsors.* In the pursuit of research, counselors give sponsors, institutions, and publication channels the same respect and opportunity for giving informed consent that they accord to individual research participants. Counselors are aware of their obligation to future research workers and ensure that host institutions are given feedback information and proper acknowledgment.

G.3. *Reporting Results*

a. *Information Affecting Outcome.* When reporting research results, counselors explicitly mention all variables and conditions known to the investigator that may have affected the outcome of a study or the interpretation of data.

b. *Accurate Results.* Counselors plan, conduct, and report research accurately and in a manner that minimizes the possibility that results will be misleading. They provide thorough discussions of the limitations of their data and alternative hypotheses. Counselors do not engage in fraudulent research, distort data, misrepresent data, or deliberately bias their results.

  c. *Obligation to Report Unfavorable Results.* Counselors communicate to other counselors the results of any research judged to be of professional value. Results that reflect unfavorably on institutions, programs, services, prevailing opinions, or vested interests are not withheld.

  d. *Identity of Subjects.* Counselors who supply data, aid in the research of another person, report research results, or make original data available take due care to disguise the identity of respective subjects in the absence of specific authorization from the subjects to do otherwise. (See B.1.g. and B.5.a.)

  e. *Replication Studies.* Counselors are obligated to make available sufficient original research data to qualified professionals who may wish to replicate the study.

G.4. Publication

  a. *Recognition of Others.* When conducting and reporting research, counselors are familiar with and give recognition to previous work on the topic, observe copyright laws, and give full credit to those to whom credit is due. (See F.1.d. and G.4.c.)

  b. *Contributors.* Counselors give credit through joint authorship, acknowledgment, footnote statements, or other appropriate means to those who have contributed significantly to research or concept development in accordance with such contributions. The principal contributor is listed first and minor technical or professional contributions are acknowledged in notes or introductory statements.

  c. *Student Research.* For an article that is substantially based on a student's dissertation or thesis, the student is listed as the principal author. (See F.1.d. and G.4.a.)

  d. *Duplicate Submission.* Counselors submit manuscripts for consideration to only one journal at a time. Manuscripts that are published in whole or in substantial part in another journal or published work are not submitted for publication without acknowledgment and permission from the previous publication.

  e. *Professional Review.* Counselors who review material submitted for publication, research, or other scholarly purposes respect the confidentiality and proprietary rights of those who submitted it.

Section H: Resolving Ethical Issues

H.1. Knowledge of Standards

Counselors are familiar with the Code of Ethics and the Standards of Practice and other applicable ethics codes from other professional organizations of which they are members, or from certification and licensure bodies. Lack of knowledge or misunderstanding of an ethical responsibility is not a defense against a charge of unethical conduct. (See F.3.e.)

H.2. Suspected Violations

  a. *Ethical Behavior Expected.* Counselors expect professional associates to adhere to the Code of Ethics. When counselors possess reasonable cause that raises doubts as to whether a counselor is acting in an ethical manner, they take appropriate action. (See H.2.d. and H.2.e.)

  b. *Consultation.* When uncertain as to whether a particular situation or course of action may be in violation of the Code of Ethics, counselors consult with other counselors who are knowledgeable about ethics, with colleagues, or with appropriate authorities.

  c. *Organization Conflicts.* If the demands of an organization with which counselors are affiliated pose a conflict with the Code of Ethics, counselors specify the nature of such conflicts and express to their supervisors or other responsible officials their commitment to the Code of Ethics. When possible, counselors work toward change within the organization to allow full adherence to the Code of Ethics.

  d. *Informal Resolution.* When counselors have reasonable cause to believe that another counselor is violating an ethical standard, they attempt to first resolve the issue informally with the other counselor if feasible, providing that such action does not violate confidentiality rights that may be involved.

e. *Reporting Suspected Violations.* When an informal resolution is not appropriate or feasible, counselors, upon reasonable cause, take action such as reporting the suspected ethical violation to state or national ethics committees, unless this action conflicts with confidentiality rights that cannot be resolved.

f. *Unwarranted Complaints.* Counselors do not initiate, participate in, or encourage the filing of ethics complaints that are unwarranted or intend to harm a counselor rather than to protect clients or the public.

H.3. Cooperation with Ethics Committees

Counselors assist in the process of enforcing the Code of Ethics. Counselors cooperate with investigations, proceedings, and requirements of the ACA Ethics Committee or ethics committees of other duly constituted associations or boards having jurisdiction over those charged with a violation. Counselors are familiar with the ACA Policies and Procedures and use it as a reference in assisting the enforcement of the Code of Ethics.

ACA STANDARDS OF PRACTICE

All members of the American Counseling Association (ACA) are required to adhere to the Standards of Practice and the Code of Ethics. The Standards of Practice represent minimal behavioral statements of the Code of Ethics. Members should refer to the applicable section of the Code of Ethics for further interpretation and amplification of the applicable Standard of Practice.

Section A: The Counseling Relationship

Section B: Confidentiality

Section C: Professional Responsibility

Section D: Relationship With Other Professionals

Section E: Evaluation, Assessment and Interpretation

Section F: Teaching, Training, and Supervision

Section G: Research and Publication

Section H: Resolving Ethical Issues

Section A: The Counseling Relationship

Standard of Practice One (SP-1): Nondiscrimination.   Counselors respect diversity and must not discriminate against clients because of age, color, culture, disability, ethnic group, gender, race, religion, sexual orientation, marital status, or socioeconomic status. (see A.2.a.)

Standard of Practice Two (SP-2): Disclosure to Clients.   Counselors must adequately inform clients, preferably in writing, regarding the counseling process and counseling relationship at or before the time it begins and throughout the relationship. (See A.3.a.)

Standard of Practice Three (SP-3): Dual Relationships.   Counselors must make every effort to avoid dual relationships with clients that could impair their professional judgment or increase the risk of harm to clients. When a dual relationship cannot be avoided, counselors must take appropriate steps to ensure that judgment is not impaired and that no exploitation occurs. (See A.6.a. and A.6.b.)

Standard of Practice Four (SP-4): Sexual Intimacies with Clients.   Counselors must not engage in any type of sexual intimacies with current clients and must not engage in sexual intimacies with former clients within a minimum of 2 years after terminating the counseling relationship. Counselors who engage in such relationship after 2 years following termination have the responsibility to examine and document thoroughly that such relations did not have an exploitative nature.

Standard of Practice Five (SP-5): Protecting Clients During Group Work.   Counselors must take steps to protect clients from physical or psychological trauma resulting from interactions during group work. (See A.9.b.)

Standard of Practice Six (SP-6):Advance Understanding of Fees.   Counselors must explain to clients, prior to their entering the counseling relationship, financial arrangements related to professional services. (See A.10.a–d. and A.11.c.)

Standard of Practice Seven (SP-7):Termination.   Counselors must assist in making appropriate arrangements for the continuation of treatment of clients, when necessary, following termination of counseling relationships. (See A.11.a.)

Standard of Practice Eight (SP-8): Inability to Assist Clients.   Counselors must avoid entering or immediately terminate a counseling relationship if it is determined that they are unable to be of professional assistance to a client. The counselor may assist in making an appropriate referral for the client. (See A.11.b.)

Section B: Confidentiality

Standard of Practice Nine (SP-9):Confidentiality Requirement.   Counselors must keep information related to counseling services confidential unless disclosure is in the best interest of clients, is required for the welfare of others, or is required by law. When disclosure is required, only information that is essential is revealed and the client is informed of such disclosure. (See B.1.a. & f.)

Standard of Practice Ten (SP-10): Confidentiality Requirements for Subordinates.   Counselors must take measures to ensure that privacy and confidentiality of clients are maintained by subordinates. (See B.1.h.)

Standard of Practice Eleven (SP-11): Confidentiality in Group Work.   Counselors must clearly communicate to group members that confidentiality cannot be guaranteed in group work. (See B.2.a.)

Standard of Practice Twelve (SP-12):Confidentiality in Family Counseling.   Counselors must not disclose information about one family member in counseling to another family member without prior consent. (See B.2.b.)

Standard of Practice Thirteen (SP-13): Confidentiality of Records.   Counselors must maintain appropriate confidentiality in creating, storing, accessing, transferring, and disposing of counseling records. (See B.4.b.)

Standard of Practice Fourteen (SP-14): Permission to Record or Observe.   Counselors must obtain prior consent from clients in order to record electronically or observe sessions. (See B.4.c.)

Standard of Practice Fifteen (SP-15):Disclosure or Transfer of Records.   Counselors must obtain client consent to disclose or transfer records to third parties, unless exceptions listed in SP-9 exist. (See B.4.e.)

Standard of Practice Sixteen (SP-16):Data Disguise Required.   Counselors must disguise the identity of the client when using data for training, research, or publication. (See B.5.a.)

Section C: Professional Responsibility

Standard of Practice Seventeen (SP-17):Boundaries of Competence.   Counselors must practice only within the boundaries of their competence.(See C.2.a.)

Standard of Practice Eighteen (SP-18): Continuing Education.   Counselors must engage in continuing education to maintain their professional competence. (See C.2.f.)

Standard of Practice Nineteen (SP-19): Impairment of Professionals. Counselors must refrain from offering professional services when their personal problems or conflicts may cause harm to a client or others. (See C.2.g.)

Standard of Practice Twenty (SP-20): Accurate Advertising. Counselors must accurately represent their credentials and services when advertising. (See C.3.a.)

Standard of Practice Twenty-One (SP-21): Recruiting Through Employment. Counselors must not use their place of employment or institutional affiliation to recruit clients for their private practices. (See C.3.d.)

Standard of Practice Twenty-Two (SP-22): Credentials Claimed. Counselors must claim or imply only professional credentials possessed and must correct any known misrepresentations of their credentials by others. (See C.4.a.)

Standard of Practice Twenty-Three (SP-23): Sexual Harassment. Counselors must not engage in sexual harassment. (See C.5.b.)

Standard of Practice Twenty-Four (SP-24): Unjustified Gains. Counselors must not use their professional positions to seek or receive unjustified personal gains, sexual favors, unfair advantage, or unearned goods or services. (See C.5.e.)

Standard of Practice Twenty-Five (SP-25): Clients Served by Others. With the consent of the client, counselors must inform other mental health professionals serving the same client that a counseling relationship between the counselor and client exists. (See C.6.c.)

Standard of Practice Twenty-Six (SP-26): Negative Employment Conditions. Counselors must alert their employers to institutional policy or conditions that may be potentially disruptive or damaging to the counselor's professional responsibilities, or that may limit their effectiveness or deny clients' rights. (See D.1.c.)

Standard of Practice Twenty-Seven (SP-27): Personnel Selection and Assignment. Counselors must select competent staff and must assign responsibilities compatible with staff skills and experiences. (See D.1.h.)

Standard of Practice Twenty-Eight (SP-28): Exploitative Relationships With Subordinates. Counselors must not engage in exploitative relationships with individuals over whom they have supervisory, evaluative, or instructional control or authority. (See D.1.k.)

Section D: Relationship with Other Professionals

Standard of Practice Twenty-Nine (SP-29): Accepting Fees From Agency Clients. Counselors must not accept fees or other remuneration for consultation with persons entitled to such services through the counselor's employing agency or institution. (See D.3.a.)

Standard of Practice Thirty (SP-30): Referral Fees. Counselors must not accept referral fees. (See D.3.b.)

Section E: Evaluation, Assessment and Interpretation

Standard of Practice Thirty-One (SP-31): Limits of Competence. Counselors must perform only testing and assessment services for which they are competent. Counselors must not allow the use of psychological assessment techniques by unqualified persons under their supervision. (See E.2.a.)

Standard of Practice Thirty-Two (SP-32): Appropriate Use of Assessment Instruments. Counselors must use assessment instruments in the manner for which they were intended. (See E.2.b.)

Standard of Practice Thirty-Three (SP-33): Assessment Explanations to Clients. Counselors must provide explanations to clients prior to assessment about the nature and purposes of assessment and the specific uses of results. (See E.3.a.)

Standard of Practice Thirty-Four (SP-34): Recipients of Test Results.   Counselors must ensure that accurate and appropriate interpretations accompany any release of testing and assessment information. (See E.3.b.)

Standard of Practice Thirty-Five (SP-35): Obsolete Tests and Outdated Test Results.   Counselors must not base their assessment or intervention decisions or recommendations on data or test results that are obsolete or outdated for the current purpose. (See E.11.)

Section F: Teaching, Training, and Supervision

Standard of Practice Thirty-Six (SP-36): Sexual Relationships with Students or Supervisees.   Counselors must not engage in sexual relationships with their students and supervisees. (See F.1.c.)

Standard of Practice Thirty-Seven (SP-37): Credit for Contributions to Research.   Counselors must give credit to students or supervisees for their contributions to research and scholarly projects. (See F.1.d.)

Standard of Practice Thirty-Eight (SP-38): Supervision Preparation.   Counselors who offer clinical supervision services must be trained and prepared in supervision methods and techniques. (See F.1.f.)

Standard of Practice Thirty-Nine (SP-39): Evaluation Information.   Counselors must clearly state to students and supervisees in advance of training the levels of competency expected, appraisal methods, and timing of evaluations. Counselors must provide students and supervisees with periodic performance appraisal and evaluation feedback throughout the training program. (See F.2.c.)

Standard of Practice Forty (SP-40): Peer Relationships in Training.   Counselors must make every effort to ensure that the rights of peers are not violated when students and supervisees are assigned to lead counseling groups or provide clinical supervision. (See F.2.e.)

Standard of Practice Forty-One (SP-41): Limitations of Students and Supervisees.   Counselors must assist students and supervisees in securing remedial assistance, when needed, and must dismiss from the training program students and supervisees who are unable to provide competent service due to academic or personal limitations. (See F.3.a.)

Standard of Practice Forty-Two (SP-42): Self-Growth Experiences.   Counselors who conduct experiences for students or supervisees that include self-growth or self-disclosure must inform participants of counselors' ethical obligations to the profession and must not grade participants based on their nonacademic performance. (See F.3.b.)

Standard of Practice Forty-Three (SP-43): Standards for Students and Supervisees.   Students and supervisees preparing to become counselors must adhere to the Code of Ethics and the Standards of Practice of counselors. (See F.3.e.)

Section G: Research and Publication

Standard of Practice Forty-Four (SP-44): Precautions to Avoid Injury in Research.   Counselors must avoid causing physical, social, or psychological harm or injury to subjects in research. (See G.1.c.)

Standard of Practice Forty-Five (SP-45): Confidentiality of Research Information.   Counselors must keep confidential information obtained about research participants. (See G.2.d.)

Standard of Practice Forty-Six (SP-46): Information Affecting Research Outcome.   Counselors must report all variables and conditions known to the investigator that may have affected research data or outcomes. (See G.3.a.)

Standard of Practice Forty-Seven (SP-47): Accurate Research Results.   Counselors must not distort or misrepresent research data, nor fabricate or intentionally bias research results. (See G.3.b.)

Standard of Practice Forty-Eight (SP-48): Publication Contributors.   Counselors must give appropriate credit to those who have contributed to research. (See G.4.a. and G.4.b.)

Section H: Resolving Ethical Issues

Standard of Practice Forty-Nine (SP-49): Ethical Behavior Expected.   Counselors must take appropriate action when they possess reasonable cause that raises doubts as to whether counselors or other mental health professionals are acting in an ethical manner. (See H.2.a.)

Standard of Practice Fifty (SP-50): Unwarranted Complaints.   Counselors must not initiate, participate in, or encourage the filing of ethics complaints that are unwarranted or intended to harm a mental health professional rather than to protect clients or the public. (See H.2.f.)

Standard of Practice Fifty-One (SP-51): Cooperation With Ethics Committees.   Counselors must cooperate with investigations, proceedings, and requirements of the ACA Ethics Committee or ethics committees of other duly constituted associations or boards having jurisdiction over those charged with a violation. (See H.3.)

REFERENCES

The following documents are available to counselors as resources to guide them in their practices. These resources are not a part of the Code of Ethics and the Standards of Practice.

American Association for Counseling and Development/Association for Measurement and Evaluation in Counseling and Development. (1989). *The responsibilities of users of standardized tests* (rev.). Washington, DC: Author.

American Counseling Association. (1988) (Note: This is ACA's previous edition of its ethics code). *Ethical standards.* Alexandria, VA: Author.

American Psychological Association. (1985). *Standards for educational and psychological testing* (rev.). Washington, DC: Author.

Joint Committee on Testing Practices. (1988). *Code of fair testing practices in education.* Washington, DC: Author.

National Board for Certified Counselors. (1989). *National Board for Certified Counselors code of ethics.* Alexandria, VA: Author.

Prediger, D. J. (Ed.). (1993, March). *Multicultural assessment standards.* Alexandria, VA: Association for Assessment in Counseling.

Appendix 2: Association for Specialists in Group Work Best Practice Guidelines*

Approved by the ASGW Executive Board, March 29, 1998

The Association for Specialists in Group Work (ASGW) is a division of the American Counseling Association whose members are interested in and specialize in group work. We value the creation of community; service to our members, clients, and the profession; and value leadership as a process to facilitate the growth and development of individuals and groups. The Association for Specialists in Group Work recognizes the commitment of its members to the Code of Ethics and Standards of Practice (as revised in 1995) of its parent organization, the American Counseling Association, and nothing in this document shall be construed to supplant that code. These Best Practice Guidelines are intended to clarify the application of the ACA Code of Ethics and Standards of Practice to the field of group work by defining Group Workers' responsibility and scope of practice involving those activities, strategies and interventions that are consistent and current with effective and appropriate professional ethical and community standards. ASGW views ethical process as being integral to group work and views Group Workers as ethical agents. Group Workers, by their very nature in being responsible and responsive to their group members, necessarily embrace a certain potential for ethical vulnerability. It is incumbent upon Group Workers to give considerable attention to the intent and context of their actions because the attempts of Group Workers to influence human behavior through group work always have ethical implications. These Best Practice Guidelines address Group Workers' responsibilities in planning, performing and processing groups.

Section A: Best Practice in Planning

A.1. Professional Context and Regulatory Requirements

Group Workers actively know, understand and apply the ACA Code of Ethics and Standards of Best Practice, the ASGW Professional Standards for the Training of Group Workers, these ASGW Best Practice Guidelines, the ASGW diversity competencies, the ACA Multicultural Guidelines, relevant state laws, accreditation requirements, relevant National Board for Certified Counselors Codes and Standards, their organization's standards, and insurance requirements impacting the practice of group work.

A.2. Scope of Practice and Conceptual Framework

Group Workers define the scope of practice related to the core and specialization competencies defined in the ASGW Training Standards. Group Workers are aware of personal strengths and weaknesses in leading groups. Group Workers develop and are able to articulate a general conceptual framework to guide practice and a rationale for use of techniques that are to be used. Group Workers limit their practice to those areas for which they meet the training criteria established by the ASGW Training Standards.

A.3. Assessment

a. *Assessment of self.* Group Workers actively assess their knowledge and skills related to the specific group(s) offered. Group Workers assess their values, beliefs and theoretical orientation and how these impact upon the group, particularly when working with a diverse and multicultural population.

b. *Ecological assessment.* Group Workers assess community needs, agency or organization resources, sponsoring organization mission, staff competency, attitudes regarding group work, professional training levels of potential group leaders regarding group work; client attitudes regarding group work, and multicultural and diversity considerations. Group Workers use this information as the basis for making decisions related to their group practice, or to the implementation of groups for which they have supervisory, evaluation, or oversight responsibilities.

A.4. Program Development and Evaluation

a. Group Workers identify the type(s) of group(s) to be offered and how they relate to community needs.
b. Group Workers concisely state in writing the purpose and goals of the group. Group Workers also identify the role of the group members in influencing or determining the group goals.
c. Group Workers set fees consistent with the organization's fee schedule, taking into consideration the financial status and locality of prospective group members.
d. Group Workers choose techniques and a leadership style appropriate to the type(s) of group(s) being offered.
e. Group Workers have an evaluation plan consistent with regulatory, organization and insurance requirements, where appropriate.
f. Group Workers take into consideration current professional guidelines when using technology, including but not limited to Internet communication.

A.5. Resources

Group Workers coordinate resources related to the kind of group(s) and group activities to be provided, such as: adequate funding; the appropriateness and availability of a trained co-leader; space and privacy requirements for the type(s) of group(s) being offered; marketing and recruiting; and appropriate collaboration with other community agencies and organizations.

A.6. Professional Disclosure Statement

Group Workers have a professional disclosure statement which includes information on confidentiality and exceptions to confidentiality, theoretical orientation, information on the nature, purpose(s) and goals of the group, the group services that can be provided, the role and responsibility of group members and leaders, Group Workers; qualifications to conduct the specific group(s), specific licenses, certifications and professional affiliations, and address of licensing/credentialing body.

A.7. Group and Member Preparation

a. Group Workers screen prospective group members if appropriate to the type of group being offered. When selection of group members is appropriate, Group Workers identify group members whose needs and goals are compatible with the goals of the group.
b. Group Workers facilitate informed consent. Group Workers provide in oral and written form to prospective members (when appropriate to group type): the professional disclosure statement; group purpose and goals; group participation expectations including voluntary and involuntary membership; role expectations of members and leader(s); policies related to entering and exiting the group; policies governing substance use; policies and procedures governing mandated groups (where relevant); documentation requirements; disclosure of information to others; implications of out-of-group contact or involvement among members; procedures for consultation between group leader(s) and group member(s); fees and time parameters; and potential impacts of group participation.
c. Group Workers obtain the appropriate consent forms for work with minors and other dependent group members.
d. Group Workers define confidentiality and its limits (for example, legal and ethical exceptions and expectations; waivers implicit with treatment plans, documentation and insurance usage). Group Workers have the responsibility to inform all group participants of the need for confidentiality, potential consequences of breaching confidentiality and that legal privilege does not apply to group discussions (unless provided by state statute).

A.8. Professional Development

Group Workers recognize that professional growth is a continuous, ongoing, developmental process throughout their career.

   a. Group Workers remain current and increase knowledge and skill competencies through activities such as continuing education, professional supervision, and participation in personal and professional development activities.
   b. Group Workers seek consultation and/or supervision regarding ethical concerns that interfere with effective functioning as a group leader. Supervisors have the responsibility to keep abreast of consultation, group theory, process, and adhere to related ethical guidelines.
   c. Group Workers seek appropriate professional assistance for their own personal problems or conflicts that are likely to impair their professional judgement or work performance.
   d. Group Workers seek consultation and supervision to ensure appropriate practice whenever working with a group for which all knowledge and skill competencies have not been achieved.
   e. Group Workers keep abreast of group research and development.

A.9. Trends and Technological Changes

Group Workers are aware of and responsive to technological changes as they affect society and the profession. These include but are not limited to changes in mental health delivery systems; legislative and insurance industry reforms; shifting population demographics and client needs; and technological advances in Internet and other communication and delivery systems. Group Workers adhere to ethical guidelines related to the use of developing technologies.

Section B: Best Practice in Performing

B.1. Self Knowledge

Group Workers are aware of and monitor their strengths and weaknesses and the effects these have on group members.

B.2. Group Competencies

Group Workers have a basic knowledge of groups and the principles of group dynamics, and are able to perform the core group competencies, as described in the ASGW Professional Standards for the Training of Group Workers. Additionally, Group Workers have adequate understanding and skill in any group specialty area chosen for practice (psychotherapy, counseling, task, psychoeducation, as described in the ASGW Training Standards).

B.3. Group Plan Adaptation

   a. Group Workers apply and modify knowledge, skills and techniques appropriate to group type and stage, and to the unique needs of various cultural and ethnic groups.
   b. Group Workers monitor the group's progress toward the group goals and plan.
   c. Group Workers clearly define and maintain ethical, professional, and social relationship boundaries with group members as appropriate to their role in the organization and the type of group being offered.

B.4. Therapeutic Conditions and Dynamics

Group Workers understand and are able to implement appropriate models of group development, process observation and therapeutic conditions.

B.5. Meaning

Group Workers assist members in generating meaning from the group experience.

B.6. Collaboration

Group Workers assist members in developing individual goals and respect group members as co-equal partners in the group experience.

B.7. Evaluation

Group Workers include evaluation (both formal and informal) between sessions and at the conclusion of the group.

B.8. Diversity

Group Workers practice with broad sensitivity to client differences including but not limited to ethnic, gender, religious, sexual, psychological maturity, economic class, family history, physical characteristics or limitations, and geographic location. Group Workers continuously seek information regarding the cultural issues of the diverse population with whom they are working both by interaction with participants and from using outside resources.

B.9. Ethical Surveillance

Group Workers employ an appropriate ethical decision making model in responding to ethical challenges and issues and in determining courses of action and behavior for self and group members. In addition, Group Workers employ applicable standards as promulgated by ACA, ASGW, or other appropriate professional organizations.

Section C: Best Practice in Group Processing

C.1. Processing Schedule

Group Workers process the workings of the group with themselves, group members, supervisors or other colleagues, as appropriate. This may include assessing progress on group and member goals, leader behaviors and techniques, group dynamics and interventions; developing understanding and acceptance of meaning. Processing may occur both within sessions and before and after each session, at time of termination, and later follow up, as appropriate.

C.2. Reflective Practice

Group Workers attend to opportunities to synthesize theory and practice and to incorporate learning outcomes into ongoing groups. Group Workers attend to session dynamics of members and their interactions and also attend to the relationship between session dynamics and leader values, cognition and affect.

C.3. Evaluation and Follow-Up

a. Group Workers evaluate process and outcomes. Results are used for ongoing program planning, improvement and revisions of current group and/or to contribute to professional research literature. Group Workers follow all applicable policies and standards in using group material for research and reports.
b. Group Workers conduct follow-up contact with group members, as appropriate, to assess outcomes or when requested by a group member(s).

C.4. Consultation and Training with Other Organizations

Group Workers provide consultation and training to organizations in and out of their setting, when appropriate. Group Workers seek out consultation as needed with competent professional persons knowledgeable about group work.

Appendix 3: Association for Specialists in Group Work Principles for Diversity-Competent Group Workers*

Approved by the Executive Board, August 1, 1998

PREAMBLE

The Association for Specialists in Group Work (ASGW) is committed to understanding how issues of diversity affect all aspects of group work. This includes but is not limited to: training diversity-competent group workers; conducting research that will add to the literature on group work with diverse populations; understanding how diversity affects group process and dynamics; and assisting group facilitators in various settings to increase their awareness, knowledge, and skills as they relate to facilitating groups with diverse memberships.

As an organization, ASGW has endorsed this document with the recognition that issues of diversity affect group process and dynamics, group facilitation, training, and research. As an organization, we recognize that racism, classism, sexism, heterosexism, ableism, and so forth, affect everyone. As individual members of this organization, it is our personal responsibility to address these issues through awareness, knowledge, and skills.

As members of ASGW, we need to increase our awareness of our own biases, values, and beliefs and how they impact the groups we run. We need to increase our awareness of our group members' biases, values, and beliefs and how they also impact and influence group process and dynamics. Finally, we need to increase our knowledge in facilitating, with confidence, competence, and integrity, groups that are diverse on many dimensions.

Definitions

For the purposes of this document, it is important that the language used is understood. Terms such as "dominant," "nondominant," and "target" persons and/or populations are used to define a person or groups of persons who historically, in the United States, do not have equal access to power, money, certain privileges (such as access to mental health services because of financial constraints, or the legal right to marry, in the case of a gay or lesbian couple), and/or the ability to influence or initiate social policy because of unequal representation in government and politics. These terms are not used to denote a lack of numbers in terms of representation in the overall U.S. population. Nor are these terms used to continue to perpetuate the very biases and forms of oppression, both overt and covert, that this document attempts to address.

For the purposes of this document, the term "disabilities" refers to differences in physical, mental, emotional, and learning abilities and styles among people. It is not meant as a term to define a person, such as a learning disabled person, but rather in the context of a person with a learning disability.

*Reprinted from the Association for Specialists in Group Work Web Site. http://asgw.educ.kent.edu/diversity.htm. © ACA. Reprinted with permission. No further reproduction authorized without written permission of the American Counseling Association.

Given the history and current cultural, social, and political context in which this document is written, the authors of this document are limited to the language of this era. With this in mind, we have attempted to construct a "living document" that can and will change as the sociopolitical and cultural context changes.

THE PRINCIPLES

I. Awareness of Self

A. Attitudes and Beliefs

Diversity-competent group workers demonstrate movement from being unaware to being increasingly aware and sensitive to their own race, ethnic and cultural heritage, gender, socioeconomic status (SES), sexual orientation, abilities, and religion and spiritual beliefs, and to valuing and respecting differences.

Diversity-competent group workers demonstrate increased awareness of how their own race, ethnicity, culture, gender, SES, sexual orientation, abilities, and religion and spiritual beliefs are impacted by their own experiences and histories, which in turn influence group process and dynamics.

Diversity-competent group workers can recognize the limits of their competencies and expertise with regard to working with group members who are different from them in terms of race, ethnicity, culture (including language), SES, gender, sexual orientation, abilities, religion, and spirituality and their beliefs, values, and biases. (For further clarification on limitations, expertise, and type of group work, refer to the training standards and best practice guidelines, Association for Specialists in Group Work, 1998; and the ethical guidelines, American Counseling Association, 1995.)

Diversity-competent group workers demonstrate comfort, tolerance, and sensitivity with differences that exist between themselves and group members in terms of race, ethnicity, culture, SES, gender, sexual orientation, abilities, religion, and spirituality and their beliefs, values, and biases.

B. Knowledge

Diversity-competent group workers can identify specific knowledge about their own race, ethnicity, SES, gender, sexual orientation, abilities, religion, and spirituality, and how they personally and professionally affect their definitions of "normality" and the group process.

Diversity-skilled group workers demonstrate knowledge and understanding regarding how oppression in any form—such as, racism, classism, sexism, heterosexism, ableism, discrimination, and stereotyping—affects them personally and professionally.

Diversity-skilled group workers demonstrate knowledge about their social impact on others. They are knowledgeable about communication style differences, how their style may inhibit or foster the group process with members who are different from themselves along the different dimensions of diversity, and how to anticipate the impact they may have on others.

C. Skills

Diversity-competent group workers seek out educational, consultative, and training experiences to improve their understanding and effectiveness in working with group members who self-identify as Indigenous Peoples, African Americans, Asian Americans, Hispanics, Latinos/Latinas, gays, lesbians, bisexuals, or transgendered persons and persons with physical, mental/emotional, and/or learning disabilities, particularly with regard to race and ethnicity. Within this context, group workers are able to recognize the limits of their competencies and: (a) seek consultation, (b) seek further training or education, (c) refer members to more qualified group workers, or (d) engage in a combination of these.

Group workers who exhibit diversity competence are constantly seeking to understand themselves within their multiple identities (apparent and unapparent differences), for example, gay, Latina, Christian, working-class and female, and are constantly and actively striving to unlearn the various behaviors and processes they covertly and overtly communicate that perpetuate oppression, particularly racism.

II. Group Worker's Awareness of Group Member's Worldview
   A. Attitudes and Beliefs

   Diversity-skilled group workers exhibit awareness of any possible negative emotional reactions toward Indigenous Peoples, African Americans, Asian Americans, Hispanics, Latinos/Latinas, gays, lesbians, bisexuals, or transgendered persons and persons with physical, mental/emotional, and/or learning disabilities that they may hold. They are willing to contrast in a nonjudgmental manner their own beliefs and attitudes with those of Indigenous Peoples, African Americans, Asian Americans, Hispanics, Latinos/Latinas, gays, lesbians, bisexuals, or transgendered persons and persons with physical, mental/emotional, and/or learning disabilities who are group members.

   Diversity-competent group workers demonstrate awareness of their stereotypes and preconceived notions that they may hold toward Indigenous Peoples, African Americans, Asian Americans, Hispanics, Latinos/Latinas, gays, lesbians, bisexuals, or transgendered persons and persons with physical, mental/emotional, and/or learning disabilities.

   B. Knowledge

   Diversity-skilled group workers possess specific knowledge and information about Indigenous Peoples, African Americans, Asian Americans, Hispanics, Latinos/Latinas, gays, lesbians, bisexuals, and transgendered people and group members who have mental/emotional, physical, and/or learning disabilities with whom they are working. They are aware of the life experiences, cultural heritage, and sociopolitical background of Indigenous Peoples, African Americans, Asian Americans, Hispanics, Latinos/Latinas, gays, lesbians, bisexuals, or transgendered persons and group members with physical, mental/emotional, and/or learning disabilities. This particular knowledge-based competency is strongly linked to the various racial/minority and sexual identity development models available in the literature (Atkinson, Morten, & Sue, 1993; Cass, 1979; Cross, 1995; D'Augelli & Patterson, 1995; Helms, 1992).

   Diversity-competent group workers exhibit an understanding of how race, ethnicity, culture, gender, sexual identity, different abilities, SES, and other immutable personal characteristics may affect personality formation, vocational choices, manifestation of psychological disorders, physical "dis-ease" or somatic symptoms, help-seeking behavior(s), and the appropriateness or inappropriateness of the various types of and theoretical approaches to group work.

   Group workers who demonstrate competency in diversity in groups understand and have the knowledge about sociopolitical influences that impinge upon the lives of Indigenous Peoples, African Americans, Asian Americans, Hispanics, Latinos/Latinas, gays, lesbians, bisexuals, or transgendered persons and persons with physical, mental/emotional, and/or learning disabilities. Immigration issues, poverty, racism, oppression, stereotyping, and/or powerlessness adversely impacts many of these individuals and therefore impacts group process or dynamics.

   C. Skills

   Diversity-skilled group workers familiarize themselves with relevant research and the latest findings regarding mental health issues of Indigenous Peoples, African Americans, Asian Americans, Hispanics, Latinos/Latinas, gays, lesbians, bisexuals, or transgendered persons and persons with physical, mental/emotional, and/or learning disabilities. They actively seek out educational experiences that foster their knowledge and understanding of skills for facilitating groups across differences.

   Diversity-competent group workers become actively involved with Indigenous Peoples, African Americans, Asian Americans, Hispanics, Latinos/Latinas, gays, lesbians, bisexuals, or transgendered persons and persons with physical, mental/emotional, and/or learning disabilities outside of their group work/counseling setting (community events, social and political functions, celebrations, friendships, neighborhood groups, etc.) so that their perspective of minorities is more than academic or experienced through a third party.

III. Diversity-Appropriate Intervention Strategies
   A. Attitudes and Beliefs

   Diversity-competent group workers respect clients' religious and/or spiritual beliefs and values, because they affect worldview, psychosocial functioning, and expressions of distress.

Diversity-competent group workers respect indigenous helping practices and respect Indigenous Peoples, African Americans, Asian Americans, Hispanics, Latinos/Latinas, gays, lesbians, bisexuals, or transgendered persons and persons with physical, mental/emotional, and/or learning disabilities and can identify and utilize community intrinsic help-giving networks.

Diversity-competent group workers value bilingualism and sign language and do not view another language as an impediment to group work.

B. Knowledge
Diversity-competent group workers demonstrate a clear and explicit knowledge and understanding of generic characteristics of group work and theory and how they may clash with the beliefs, values, and traditions of Indigenous Peoples, African Americans, Asian Americans, Hispanics, Latinos/Latinas, gays, lesbians, bisexuals, or transgendered persons and persons with physical, mental/emotional, and/or learning disabilities.

Diversity-competent group workers exhibit an awareness of institutional barriers that prevent Indigenous Peoples, African Americans, Asian Americans, Hispanics, Latinos/Latinas, gays, lesbians, bisexuals, or transgendered members and members with physical, mental/emotional, and/or learning disabilities from actively participating in or using various types of groups, that is, task groups, psychoeducational groups, counseling groups, and psychotherapy groups or the settings in which the services are offered.

Diversity-competent group workers demonstrate knowledge of the potential bias in assessment instruments and use procedures and interpret findings, or actively participate in various types of evaluations of group outcome or success, keeping in mind the linguistic, cultural, and other self-identified characteristics of the group member.

Diversity-competent group workers exhibit knowledge of the family structures, hierarchies, values, and beliefs of Indigenous Peoples, African Americans, Asian Americans, Hispanics, Latinos/Latinas, gays, lesbians, bisexuals, or transgendered persons and persons with physical, mental/emotional, and/or learning disabilities. They are knowledgeable about the community characteristics and the resources in the community as well as about the family.

Diversity-competent group workers demonstrate an awareness of relevant discriminatory practices at the social and community level that may be affecting the psychological welfare of persons and access to services of the population being served.

C. Skills
Diversity-competent group workers are able to engage in a variety of verbal and nonverbal group-facilitating functions, dependent upon the type of group (task, counseling, psychoeducational, psychotherapy), and the multiple, self-identified status of various group members (such as Indigenous Peoples, African Americans, Asian Americans, Hispanics, Latinos/Latinas, gays, lesbians, bisexuals, or transgendered persons and persons with physical, mental/emotional, and/or learning disabilities). They demonstrate the ability to send and receive both verbal and nonverbal messages accurately, appropriately, and across/between the differences represented in the group. They are not tied down to one method or approach to group facilitation and recognize that helping styles and approaches may be culture-bound. When they sense that their group facilitation style is limited and potentially inappropriate, they can anticipate and ameliorate its negative impact by drawing upon other culturally relevant skill sets.

Diversity-competent group workers have the ability to exercise institutional intervention skills on behalf of their group members. They can help a member determine whether a "problem" with the institution stems from the oppression of Indigenous Peoples, African Americans, Asian Americans, Hispanics, Latinos/Latinas, gays, lesbians, bisexuals, or transgendered persons and persons with physical, mental/emotional, and/or learning disabilities, such as in the case of developing or having a "healthy" paranoia, so that group members do not inappropriately personalize problems.

Diversity-competent group workers do not exhibit a reluctance to seek consultation with traditional healers and religious and spiritual healers and practitioners in the treatment of members who are self-identified Indigenous Peoples, African Americans, Asian Americans, Hispanics, Latinos/Latinas, gays, lesbians, bisexuals, and transgendered persons and/or group members with mental/emotional, physical, and/or learning disabilities when appropriate.

Diversity-competent group workers take responsibility for interacting in the language requested by the group member(s) and, if not feasible, make an appropriate referral. A serious problem arises when the linguistic skills of a group worker and a group member or members, including sign language, do not match. The same problem occurs when the linguistic skills of one member or several members do not match. This being the case, the group worker, should (a) seek a translator with cultural knowledge and appropriate professional background, and (b) refer to a knowledgeable, competent bilingual group worker or a group worker competent or certified in sign language. In some cases, it may be necessary to have a group for group members of similar languages or to refer the group member for individual counseling.

Diversity-competent group workers are trained and have expertise in the use of traditional assessment and testing instruments related to group work, such as in screening potential members, and they also are aware of the cultural bias/limitations of these tools and processes. This allows them to use the tools for the welfare of diverse group members following culturally appropriate procedures.

Diversity-competent group workers attend to as well as work to eliminate biases, prejudices, oppression, and discriminatory practices. They are cognizant of how sociopolitical contexts may affect evaluation and provision of group work and should develop sensitivity to issues of oppression, racism, sexism, heterosexism, classism, and so forth.

Diversity-competent group workers take responsibility in educating their group members to the processes of group work, such as goals, expectations, legal rights, sound ethical practice, and the group worker's theoretical orientation with regard to facilitating groups with diverse membership.

CONCLUSION

This document is the "starting point" for group workers as we become increasingly aware, knowledgeable, and skillful in facilitating groups whose memberships represent the diversity of our society. It is not intended to be a "how to" document. It is written as a call to action and/or a guideline and represents ASGW's commitment to moving forward with an agenda for addressing and understanding the needs of the populations we serve. As a "living document," the Association for Specialists in Group Work acknowledges the changing world in which we live and work and therefore recognizes that this is the first step in working with diverse group members with competence, compassion, respect, and integrity. As our awareness, knowledge, and skills develop, so too will this document evolve. As our knowledge as a profession grows in this area and as the sociopolitical context in which this document was written, changes, new editions of these Principles for Diversity-Competent Group Workers will arise. The operationalization of this document (article in process) will begin to define appropriate group leadership skills and interventions as well as make recommendations for research in understanding how diversity in group membership affects group process and dynamics.

REFERENCES

American Counseling Association. (1995). *Code of ethics and standards.* Alexandria, VA: Author.

Association for Multicultural Counseling and Development. (1996). *Multicultural competencies.* Alexandria, VA: American Counseling Association.

Association for Specialists in Group Work. (1991). Professional standards for training of group workers. *Together,* 20, 9–14.

Association for Specialists in Group Work. (1998). Best practice guidelines. *Journal for Specialists in Group Work,* 23, 237–244.

Atkinson, D. R., Morten, G., & Sue, D. W. (Eds.). (1993). *Counseling American minorities* (4th ed.). Madison, WI: Brown & Benchmark.

Cass, V. C. (1979). Homosexual identity formation: A theoretical model. *Journal of Homosexuality*, 4, 219–236.

Cross, W. E. (1995). The psychology of Nigrescence: Revising the cross model. In J. G. Ponterotto, J. M. Casas, L. A. Suzuki, & C. M. Alexander (Eds.), *Handbook of multicultural counseling* (pp. 93–122). Thousand Oaks, CA: Sage.

D'Augelli, A. R., & Patterson, C. J. (Eds.). (1995). *Lesbian, gay and bisexual identities over the lifespan.* New York: Oxford University Press.

Helms, J. E. (1992). *A race is a nice thing to have.* Topeka, KS: Context Communications.

References

Agazarian, Y. M. (1997). *Systems-centered therapy for groups*. New York: Guilford Press.

American Counseling Association. (1995). *Code of ethics and standards of practice*. Alexandria, VA: Author.

Association for Specialists in Group Work. (2000a). Best practices guidelines. *The Group Worker, 29, 3* (Supplement, 1–5).

Association for Specialists in Group Work. (2000b). Principles for diversity-competent group workers. *The Group Worker, 29, 3* (Supplement, 1–2).

Barker, P. (1992). *Basic family therapy*. New York: Oxford University Press.

Bascue, L. O. (1978). Conceptual model for group therapy training. *International Journal of Group Psychotherapy, 28,* 445–452.

Bates, M., Johnson, C. D., & Blaker, K. E. (1982). *Group leadership: A manual for group counseling leaders* (2nd ed). Denver: Love Publishing Company.

Becvar, D. S., & Becvar, R. J. (1996). *Family therapy: A systemic integration* (3rd ed.). Needham Heights, MA: Allyn and Bacon.

Becvar, R. J., Canfield, B. S., & Becvar, D. S. (1997). *Group work: Cybernetic, constructivist, and social constructionist perspectives*. Denver: Love Publishing Company.

Benne, K. D. & Sheats, P. (1948). Functional roles of group members. *Journal of Social Issues, 2,* 42–47.

Bennis, W. G., & Shepard, H. A. (1956). A theory of group development. *Human Relations, 9,* 415–437.

Bernard, H. S., & MacKenzie, K. R. (Eds.). (1994). *Basics of group psychotherapy*. New York: Guilford Press.

Bion, W. R. (1961). *Experiences in groups*. New York: Basic Books.

Bloch, S. & Crouch, E. (1985). *Therapeutic factors in group psychotherapy*. Oxford: Oxford University Press.

Bowen, M. (1966). The use of family theory in clinical practice. *Comprehensive Psychiatry, 7,* 345–374.

Bugenthal, J. F. T. (1965). *The search for authenticity*. New York: Holt, Rinehart and Winston.

Burrow, T. (1928). The basis of group-analysis, or the analysis of the reactions of normal and neurotic individuals. *British Journal of Medical Psychology, 8,* 198–206.

Capuzzi, D., & Gross, D. R. (Eds.) (1992). *Introduction to group counseling*. Denver: Love.

Carroll, M., Bates, M., & Johnson, C. (1997). *Group leadership: Strategies for group counseling leaders* (3rd ed.). Denver: Love.

Conyne, R. K., Wilson, F. R., & Ward, D. E. (1997). *Comprehensive group work: What it means and how to teach it*. Alexandria, VA: American Counseling Association.

Corey, G. (2000). *Theory and practice of group counseling* (5th ed.). Belmont, CA: Brooks/Cole.

Corey, M. S., & Corey, G. (1997). *Groups: Process and practice* (5th ed.). Pacific Grove, CA: Brooks/Cole.

Corsini, R., & Rosenburg, B. (1955). Mechanisms of group psychotherapy processes and dynamics. *Journal of Abnormal and Social Psychology, 51,* 406–411.

Couch, R. D. (1995). Four steps for conducting a pre-group screening interview. *Journal for Specialists in Group Work, 20,* 18–25.

Council for Accreditation of Counseling and Related Educational Programs. (2000). *CACREP accreditation manual*. Alexandria, VA: Author.

Culbert, S. A. (1973). The interpersonal process of self-disclosure: It takes two to see one. In Golembiewski, R. T. & Blumberg, A. (Eds.). *Sensitivity training and the laboratory approach: Readings about concepts and applications* (2nd ed.). Itasca IL: Peacock.

D'Andrea, M., & Daniels, J. (1997). Multicultural group counseling. In S. T. Gladding (Ed.), *New developments in group counseling*. Greensboro, NC: ERIC Clearinghouse on Counseling and Student Services.

Davis, M. H., & Franzoi, S. L. (1987). Private self-consciousness and self-disclosure. In V. J. Derlega & J. H. Berg (Eds.), *Self-disclosure: Theory, research, and therapy.* New York: Plenum.

Day, M. (1993). Training and supervision in group psychotherapy. In H. I. Kaplan & B. J. Saddock (Eds.), *Comprehensive group psychotherapy* (3rd ed.). Baltimore: Williams & Wilkins.

Dies, R. R. (1993). Research on group psychotherapy: Overview and clinical applications. In A. Alonso & H. I. Swiller (Eds.), *Group therapy in clinical practice.* Washington, DC: American Psychiatric Press.

Dies, R. R. (1994). The therapist's role in group treatments. In H. S. Bernard & K. R. MacKenzie (Eds.), *Basics of group psychotherapy.* New York: Guilford Press.

Donigian, J., & Hulse-Killacky, D. (1999). *Critical incidents in group therapy* (2nd ed.). Belmont, CA: Brooks/Cole.

Donigian, J., & Malnati, R. (1997). *Systemic group therapy: A triadic model.* Pacific Grove, CA: Brooks/Cole.

Durkin, H. E. (1981). Group therapies and general systems theory as an integrative structure. In J. E. Durkin (Ed.), *Living groups: Group psychotherapy and general systems theory* (pp. 5–23). New York: Brunner/Mazel.

Durkin, J. E. (Ed.). (1981). *Living groups: Group psychotherapy and general systems theory.* New York: Brunner/Mazel.

Forsyth, D. R. (1990). *Group dynamics* (2nd ed.). Pacific Grove, CA: Brooks/Cole.

Forsyth, D. R. (1999). *Group dynamics* (3rd ed.). Belmont, CA: Brooks/Cole-Wadsworth.

Freud, S. (1922). *Group psychology and the analysis of the ego.* London: Hogarth.

Gibb, J. R. (1961). Defensive communication. *Journal of Communication, 11,* 141–148.

Gibbard, G. S., Hartman, J. J., & Mann, R. D. (Eds.). (1974). *Analysis of groups.* San Francisco: Jossey-Bass.

Gladding, S. T. (1995). *Group work: A counseling specialty* (2nd ed.). Columbus, OH: Merrill.

Gladding, S. T. (1999). *Group work: A counseling specialty* (3rd ed.). Columbus, OH: Merrill.

Goldenberg, I., & Goldenberg, H. (1991). *Family therapy: An overview* (3rd ed.). Pacific Grove, CA: Brooks/Cole.

Golembiewski, R. T., & Blumberg, A. (1970). *Sensitivity training and the laboratory approach.* Itasca, IL: Peacock.

Gray, W. (1981). The evolution of emotional-cognitive and system precursor theory. In J. E. Durkin (Ed.), *Living groups: Group psychotherapy and general systems theory* (pp. 5–23). New York: Brunner/Mazel.

Hall, C. S. & Lindzey, G. (1978). *Theories of personality* (3rd ed.). New York: John Wiley & Sons.

Hansen, J. C., Warner, R. W., & Smith, E. J. (1980). *Group counseling: Theory and process* (2nd ed.). Chicago: Rand McNally.

Horwitz, L. (2000). Narcissistic leadership in psychotherapy groups. *International Journal of Group Psychotherapy, 50,* 219–235.

Ivey, A. E. (1994). *Intentional interviewing and counseling: Facilitating client development in a multicultural society* (3rd ed.). Pacific Grove, CA: Brooks/Cole.

Ivey, A. E., Ivey, M. B., & Simek-Morgan, L. (1993). *Counseling and psychotherapy: A multicultural perspective* (3rd ed.). Boston: Allyn and Bacon.

Jacobs, E. E., Harvill, R. L., & Masson, R. L. (1994). *Group counseling: Strategies and skills* (2nd ed.). Pacific Grove, CA: Brooks/Cole.

Johnson, D. W., & Johnson, F. P. (2000). *Joining together: Group theory and group skills* (7th ed.). Boston: Allyn and Bacon.

Jourard, S. M. (1964). *The transparent self.* New York: Van Nostrand.

Jourard, S. M. (1971). *Self-disclosure: An experimental analysis of the transparent self.* New York: Wiley.

Kernberg, O. (1976). *Object relations theory and clinical psychoanalysis.* New York: Aronson.

Kerr, M. E. (1981). Family systems theory and therapy. In A. S. Gurman & D. P. Kniskern (Eds.), *Handbook of family therapy* (pp. 226–266). New York: Brunner/Mazel.

Klein, R. H. (1996). Introduction to special section on termination and group therapy. *International Journal of Group Psychotherapy, 46,* 1–4.

Kline, W. B. (1986). Working through the risks: A structured experience to facilitate self-disclosure. *Journal for Specialists in Group Work, 15,* 195–200.

Kline, W. B. (1990). Responding to problem members. *Journal for Specialists in Group Work, 15,* 195–200.

Kline, W. B. (1997). Group as a whole dynamics and the problem member: Conceptualization and intervention. In S. T. Gladding (Ed.), *New developments in group counseling*. Greensboro, NC: ERIC.

Kottler, J. A. (1994). Working with difficult group members. *Journal for Specialists in Group Work, 19*, 3–10.

Lazerson, J. S., & Zilbach, J. J. (1993). Gender issues in group psychotherapy. In H. I. Kaplan & B. J. Saddock (Eds.), *Comprehensive group psychotherapy* (3rd ed.). Baltimore: Williams & Wilkins.

Lee, C. C. (1991). New approaches to diversity: Implications for multicultural counselor training and research. In C. C. Lee & B. L. Richardson (Eds.), *Multicultural issues in counseling: New approaches to diversity*. Alexandria, VA: American Association for Counseling and Development.

Lee, R. M., & Robbins, S. B. (2000). Understanding social connectedness in college women and men. *Journal of Counseling and Development, 78*, 484–495.

Leszcz, M. (1992). The interpersonal approach to group psychotherapy. *International Journal of Group Psychotherapy, 42*, 37–62.

Levine, B. (1991). *Group psychotherapy: Practice and development*. Prospect Heights, IL: Waveland Press.

Lewin, K. (1944). The dynamics of group action. *Educational Leadership, 1*, 195–200.

Lieberman, M., Yalom, I., & Miles, M. (1973). *Encounter groups: First facts*. New York: Basic Books.

Lonergan, E. C. (1994). Using theories of group therapy. In H. S. Bernard & K. R. MacKenzie (Eds.), *Basics of group psychotherapy* (pp. 189–216). New York: Guilford Press.

MacKenzie, K. R. (1990). *Introduction to time limited group psychotherapy*. Washington, DC: American Psychiatric Press.

MacKenzie, K. R. (1992). *Classics in group psychotherapy*. New York: Guilford Press.

MacKenzie, K. R. (1994). The developing structure of the therapy group system. In H. S. Bernard & K. R. MacKenzie (Eds.), *Basics of group psychotherapy*. New York: Guilford Press.

Maslow, A. H. (1970). *Motivation and personality* (2nd ed.). New York: Harper & Row.

McRae, M. B. (1994). Interracial group dynamics: A new perspective. *Journal for Specialists in Group Work, 19*, 168–174.

Mead, W. R. (1977). Feedback: A "how to" primer for t-group participants. In R. T. Golembiewski & A. Blumberg (Eds.), *Sensitivity training and the laboratory approach: Readings about concepts and applications* (3rd ed.). Itasca, IL: Peacock.

Minuchin, S. (1974). *Families and family therapy*. Cambridge, MA: Harvard University Press.

Nicholas, M. W. (1984). *Change in the context of group therapy*. New York: Brunner/Mazel.

Nichols, M. P., & Schwartz, R. C. (1995). *Family therapy: Concepts and methods* (3rd ed.). Needham Heights, MA: Allyn and Bacon.

Ormont, L. (1990). The craft of bridging. *International Journal of Group Psychotherapy, 40*(1), 3–17.

Pearce, W. B., & Sharp, S. M. (1973). Self-disclosing communication. *Journal of Communication, 23*, 409–425.

Piper, W. E. (1993). Group psychotherapy research. In H. I. Kaplan & B. J. Saddock (Eds.), *Comprehensive group psychotherapy* (3rd ed.). Baltimore: Williams & Wilkins.

Piper, W. E., & McCallum, M. (1994). Selection of patients for group interventions. In H. S. Bernard & K. R. MacKenzie (Eds.), *Basics of group psychotherapy*. New York: Guilford Press.

Porter, L. M., & Mohr, B. (1982). Conditions for laboratory learning. In Porter, L. M. & Mohr, B. (Eds.). *Readings book for human relations training* (7th ed.). Arlington, VA: National Training Laboratory Institute.

Pratt, J. H. (1907). The class method of treating consumption in the homes of the poor. *Journal of the American Medical Association, 49*, 755–759.

Rice, C. A. (1996). Premature termination of group therapy: A clinical perspective. *International Journal of Group Psychotherapy, 46*, 5–23.

Rioch, M. J. (1975). The work of Wilfred Bion on groups. In A. D. Colman & W. H. Bexton (Eds.), *Group relations reader* (pp. 21–23). Sausalito, CA: GREX.

Rogers, C. R. (1961). *On becoming a person*. Boston: Houghton Mifflin.

Rogers, C. R. (1970). *Carl Rogers on encounter groups*. New York: Harper & Row.

Roller, B., & Nelson, V. (1993). Cotherapy. In H. I. Kaplan & B. J. Saddock (Eds.), *Comprehensive group psychotherapy* (3rd ed.). Baltimore: Williams & Wilkins.

Rosenberg, P. P. (1993). Qualities of the group psychotherapist. In H. I. Kaplan & B. J. Saddock

(Eds.), *Comprehensive group psychotherapy* (3rd ed.). Baltimore: Williams & Wilkins.

Rutan, J. S. (1993). Preface. In A. Alonso & H. I. Swiller (Eds.), *Group therapy in clinical practice.* Washington, DC: American Psychiatric Press.

Salvendy, J. T. (1993). Selection and preparation of patients and organization of the group. In H. I. Kaplan & B. J. Saddock (Eds.), *Comprehensive group psychotherapy* (3rd ed.). Baltimore: Williams & Wilkins.

Scheidlinger, S. (1993). History of group psychotherapy. In H. I. Saddock & B. J. Kaplan (Eds.), *Comprehensive group psychotherapy* (3rd ed.). Baltimore: Williams & Wilkins.

Schutz, W. C. (1966). *The interpersonal underworld.* Palo Alto, CA: Science and Behavior Books.

Schutz, W. C. (1973). *Elements of encounter.* Big Sur, CA: Joy Press.

Shapiro, J. L., Peltz, L. S., & Bernadette-Shapiro, S. B. (1998). *Brief group treatment: Practical training for therapists and counselors.* Pacific Grove, CA: Brooks/Cole.

Sharf, R. S. (1996). *Theories of psychotherapy and counseling: Concepts and cases.* Pacific Grove, CA: Brooks/Cole.

Sherif, M. (1936). *The psychology of social norms.* New York: Harper & Row.

Sklare, G., Keener, R., & Mas, C. (1990). Preparing members for "here-and-now" group counseling. *Journal for Specialists in Group Work, 15,* 141–148.

Stock, D., & Lieberman, M. A. (1962). Methodological issues in the assessment of total-group phenomena in group therapy. *International Journal of Group Psychotherapy, 12,* 312–325.

Stock, D., Whitman, R. M., & Lieberman, M. A. (1958). The deviant member in therapy groups. *Human Relations, 11,* 341–372.

Sullivan, H. S. (1953). *The collected works of Harry Stack Sullivan, M. D.* (Vol. 1). New York: Norton.

Sullivan, H. S. (1953). *The interpersonal theory of psychiatry.* New York: Norton.

Sullivan, H. S. (1955). *Conceptions of modern psychiatry.* London: Tavistock.

Tubbs, S. L. (1992). *A systems approach to small group interaction* (4th ed.). New York: McGraw-Hill.

Tuckman, B. W. (1965). Developmental sequences in small groups. *Psychological Bulletin, 63,* 384–399.

Tuckman, B. W., & Jensen, M. A. C. (1977). Stages of small group development revisited. *Group and Organizational Studies, 2,* 272–284.

Vander Kolk, C. J. (1985). *Introduction to group counseling and psychotherapy.* Columbus, OH: Merrill.

Von Bertalanffy, L. (1968). *General systems theory: Foundations, development, applications.* New York: Braziller.

Watzlawick, P., Weakland, J., & Fisch, R. (1974). *Change: Principles of problem formation and problem resolution.* New York: Norton.

Weiner, M. F. (1993). Role of the leader in group psychotherapy. In H. I. Kaplan & B. J. Saddock (Eds.), *Comprehensive group psychotherapy* (3rd ed.). Baltimore: Williams & Wilkins.

Wender, L. (1936). The dynamics of group psychotherapy and its application. *Journal of Nervous and Mental Disease, 84,* 54-60.

Wheelan, S. A. (1994). *Group processes: A developmental approach.* Boston: Allyn and Bacon.

Whitaker, D. S. (1985). *Using groups to help people.* London: Routledge.

Whitaker, D. S. (1989). Group focal conflict theory: Description, illustration and evaluation. *Group, 13,* 225–251.

Whitaker, D. S., & Lieberman, M. A. (1964). *Psychotherapy through the group process.* New York: Atherton Press.

Wright, F. (2000). The use of self in group leadership: A relational perspective. *International Journal of Group Psychotherapy, 50,* 181–198.

Yalom, I. D. (1970). *The theory and practice of group psychotherapy.* New York: Basic Books.

Yalom, I. D. (1975). *The theory and practice of group psychotherapy* (2nd ed.). New York: Basic Books.

Yalom, I. D. (1995). *The theory and practice of group psychotherapy* (4th ed.). New York: Basic Books.

Yalom, V. J., & Vinogradov, S. (1993). Interpersonal group psychotherapy. In H. I. Kaplan & B. J. Saddock (Eds.), *Comprehensive group psychotherapy* (3rd ed.) (pp. 185–195). Baltimore: Williams & Wilkins.

Young, M. E. (1992). *Counseling methods and techniques: An eclectic approach.* New York: Merrill.

Yu, A., & Gregg, C. H. (1993). Asians in groups: More than a matter of cultural awareness. *Journal for Specialists in Group Work, 18,* 86–93.

Name Index

Agazarian, Y. M., 94

Barker, P., 88
Bascue, L. O., 280
Bates, M., 154, 194
Becvar, D. S., 87, 88, 89, 162
Becvar, R. J., 87, 88, 89, 162
Benne, K. D., 24
Bennis, W. G., 35, 37, 39, 40, 41, 50, 51, 52, 54, 55, 56, 123, 166, 168
Bernadette-Shapiro, S. B., 142, 278, 279, 280, 281, 283
Bernard, H. S., 11
Bion, W. R., 34, 35, 36, 50, 51, 55, 56
Blaker, K. E., 154
Bloch, S., 4, 150, 151, 152
Blumberg, A., 37
Bowen, M., 3, 89
Bugenthal, J. F. T., 2
Burrow, T., 8, 9

Canfield, B. S., 162
Cappuzzi, D., 70
Carroll, M., 194
Conyne, R. K., 70, 71
Corey, G., 35, 70
Corey, M. S., 35
Corsini, R., 150
Couch, R. D., 121, 123
Crouch, E., 4, 150, 151, 152
Culbert, S. A., 218

D'Andrea, M., 286
Daniels, J., 286
Davis, M. H., 2
Day, M., 281, 283
Dies, R. R., 10, 11, 119, 120, 123, 129, 130, 132
Donigian, J., 70, 94, 103, 194

Durkin, H., 85, 86, 92, 93, 105, 106
Durkin, J., 90

Fisch, R., 239
Forsyth, D. R., 17, 19, 28, 33, 35
Franzoi, S. L., 2
Freud, S., 2

Gibb, J. R., 216
Gibbard, G. S., 34
Gladding, S. T., 10, 28, 35, 70, 116, 117, 140, 142, 153, 164
Goldenberg, H., 88
Goldenberg, I., 88
Golembiewski, R. T., 37
Gray, W., 93
Gregg, C. H., 286
Gross, D. R., 70

Hall, C. S., 96
Hansen, J. C., 70, 165, 166, 167, 168, 169
Hartman, J. J., 34
Harvill, R. L., 138, 142
Horwitz, L., 279, 283
Hulse-Killacky, D., 70, 103

Ivey, A. E., 186, 210, 213, 214, 215
Ivey, M. B., 210

Jacobs, E. E., 138, 142
Jensen, M. A. C., 35, 47, 56
Johnson, C. D., 154, 194
Johnson, D. W., 211, 212, 216
Johnson, F. P., 211, 212, 216
Jourard, S. M., 2, 218

Keener, R., 123
Kernberg, O., 3

Kerr, M. E., 89
Klein, R. H., 141
Kline, W. B., 146, 218, 265, 266, 270
Kottler, J. A., 265

Lazerson, J. S., 286
Lee, C. C., 286
Lee, R. M., 2
Leszcz, M., 95, 96, 98
Levine, B., 123, 124, 276, 278, 283
Lewin, K., 165
Lieberman, M., 10, 71, 76, 77, 78, 80, 108, 123, 153, 160, 161, 162, 186, 244, 245, 251, 253
Lindzey, G., 96
Lonergan, E. C., 70, 98

MacKenzie, K. R., 8, 11, 24, 25, 27, 29, 35, 36, 86, 87, 91, 93, 116, 117, 120, 122, 123, 124, 128, 129, 130, 131, 139, 140, 142, 177
Malnati, R., 70, 94, 194
Mann, R. D., 34
Mas, C., 123
Maslow, A. H., 2
Masson, R. L., 138, 142
McCallum, M., 164
McRae, M. B., 286
Mead, W. R., 223, 226
Miles, M., 153, 160, 161, 162
Minuchin, S., 88, 89
Mohr, B., 218

Nelson, V., 129, 130, 131, 132
Nicholas, M. W., 195, 196
Nichols, M. P., 88

Ormont, L., 191, 193

Pearce, W. B., 218
Peltz, L. S., 142, 278, 279, 280, 281, 283
Piper, W. E., 11, 123, 164
Porter, L. M., 218
Pratt, J. H., 8, 9

Rice, C. A., 139, 140
Rioch, M. J., 35, 36
Robbins, S. B., 2
Rogers, C. R., 2, 10, 160
Roller, B., 129, 130, 131, 132
Rosenberg, P. P., 279, 283, 285
Rosenburg, B., 150
Rutan, J. S., 9

Salvendy, J. T., 120, 122
Scheidlinger, S., 9, 10, 11
Schutz, W. C., 2, 10, 35, 41, 42, 43, 44, 45, 46, 47, 50, 51, 52, 54, 55, 56, 123
Schwartz, R. C., 88
Shapiro, J. L., 142, 278, 279, 280, 281, 283
Sharf, R. S., 2
Sharp, S. M., 218

Sheats, P., 24
Shepard, H. A., 35, 37, 39, 40, 41, 50, 51, 52, 54, 55, 56, 123, 166, 168
Sherif, M., 19
Simek-Morgan, L., 210
Sklare, G., 123
Smith, E. J., 70, 165, 166, 167, 168, 169
Stock, D., 80, 253
Sullivan, H. S., 3, 71, 96, 97

Tubbs, S. L., 210, 216, 217
Tuckman, B. W., 35, 47, 48, 49, 50, 51, 52, 54, 55, 56

Vander Kolk, C. J., 16
Vinogradov, S., 97, 98, 99, 100, 101, 102, 103, 104
Von Bertalanffy, L., 71

Ward, D. E., 70, 71
Warner, R. W., 70, 165, 166, 167, 168, 169
Watzlawick, P., 239
Weakland, J., 239

Weiner, M. F., 277, 283
Wender, L., 8, 9
Wheelan, S. A., 16, 23, 24
Whitaker, D. S., 10, 71, 76, 77, 78, 105, 106, 108, 123, 186, 244, 245, 246, 251, 284, 285
Whitman, R. M., 80
Wilson, F. R., 70, 71
Wright, F., 278, 285

Yalom, I. D., 4, 11, 17, 35, 95, 97, 98, 99, 100, 101, 102, 103, 104, 105, 106, 107, 108, 115, 116, 117, 120, 122, 123, 129, 130, 131, 137, 141, 142, 150, 152, 153, 160, 161, 162, 164, 177, 178, 179, 181, 218, 237, 266, 281, 283
Yalom, V. J., 97, 98, 99, 100, 101, 102, 103, 104
Young, M. E., 186, 193
Yu, A., 286

Zilbach, J. J., 286

Subject Index

Abdicrats, 42–43, 45, 46
Acceptance as leadership function, 160
Active participation by leaders, 169–170
Adjourning stage of group development, 49
Administration function of leaders, 164
Affection,
  need for, 41
  needs and personalities, 43–44
Affective intervention, 184
Affective objectives of group, 177
American Group Psychotherapy Association (AGPA), 10, 85, 280
Anarchist, leader as, 286–287
Anger in group interaction, 51
Anxiety,
  group, 150
  processing and, 239
  raising members, 182
  restrictive solutions for, 186
Anxiety in focal conflict, member's, 79
Anxiety in group interaction, 51, 54, 55, 58, 59, 60, 62, 78, 79
Association for Specialists in Group Work (ASGW), 10, 286
Attitudes,
  of leaders, 32
  of members, 30–32
Authoritarian leaders, 166–167
Authority continuum, 166–167
Authority issues, 55, 60–61
Authority of leaders, 284–285
Autocrats, 42, 43, 45, 46, 47

Autonomous group members, 90
Autonomy, 90–91
Avoidant role performance, 26, 27

Balance of interventions, 184–185
Basic assumption group, 35, 36
Basic facilitation sequence, 189–191
Basic interventions, 176
Basic skills, 176
Behavioral interventions, 184
Behavioral objectives of group, 179–180
Bennis and Shepard's theory of group development, 37–41, 52
Bigotry, 6
Bion's theory of group interaction, 35–36
Boundaries, 87, 146–147
  diffuse, 88–89
  impermeable, 88
  permeable, 88
Boundaries of leaders, 284–287
Boundary-closing interventions, 204
Boundary functioning, 87–91, 92
  autonomous, 93
Boundary incompatibility, 245
Boundary interventions, interpersonal, 263–264
Boundary issues, 45
Boundary management by leaders, 156–157
Boundary-opening interventions, 202–203
Boundary problems, 246, 249–250
  external, 250
Boundary setting, 202–204

Boundarying in general systems theory, 88, 92
  effective, 89–90
Bridging, 191
  about interaction, 192–193
Brief groups, 116
  size of, 117
Burrow, Trigant,
  early group work by, 8
Bypassing, 217

Caring as leadership function, 153
Cautionary roles, 24, 25
Certified Group Psychotherapists (CGP), 10, 281
Challenges, 197–199
Change, process of, 180
Clinical Registry of Certified Group Psychotherapists (CGP), 10, 281
Coercion, 248, 249
Cognitive intervention, 184
Cognitive objectives of group, 178–179
Cohesiveness in group therapy, 100, 101
Coleaders,
  competition between, 130
  conflicts between, 131
  group issues and, 131–132
  planning by, 132–133
  postgroup processing by, 132
  relationship issues of, 135–136
  relationships of, 131–132
  supervision of, 133–135
  tape review by, 134–135
Coleadership, 129–136
  benefits of, 129–130
  issues in, 130–131
Come here, go away interaction pattern, 195, 196

Communication, guidelines for effective, 211–213
Communication clarification, 199–200
Communication problems, 216–218
Communication skills, teaching, 213–216
  timing of, 215–216
Compromise solutions in focal conflict, 79
Confidentiality, 124, 125–126
  breaches in, 250
  policy, 126
Conflict in group interaction, 51
Confrontation, 193–197
  for member-to-member interaction, 194–195
Connected relationships, 2
Consensual validation in interpersonal approach, 97, 98, 99
Consensual validation subphase of development, 40–41
Contracting, 200–202
Contracts, interpersonal, 264–265
Control,
  need for, 41
  needs and personalities, 42–43
Control phase of group integration, 45–46
Core interpersonal concerns, 54–56
Core interpersonal issues,
  emergence of, 50–51
  success in resolving, 52
Corrective emotional experience, 99–100
Counseling groups, size of, 116
Counterdependence-fight subphase of development, 38–39
Counterdependent personality, 37, 38
Counterpersonal personality, 37
Covert negotiation, 242
Cultural issues of leaders, 285–286
Culture, group, 76–77

Defensive self-disclosure, 220–221
Democratic leaders, 167–168
Democrats, 42, 43
Dependence-flight subphase of development, 38
Dependence phase of development, 38–39
Dependence phase of group development, 37
Dependency, 37
Dependency assumption group, 36
Dependency issues, 54, 59–60
Dependent personality, 37
Deviant-enabling members, 265, 268
  supporting, 269
Deviant members and focal conflict, 79–81
Deviant-restrictive members, 265, 267
  intervening with, 267–268
Diffuse boundaries, 88–89, 93
Direct negotiations, 16, 17
Directed bridge, 191–192
Directive skills, 187
Disclosure-feedback-experimentation cycle, 230, 231
Disenchantment-fight subphase of development, 40
Distancing self-disclosures, 220
Disturbing motives in focal conflict, 71–72
Divergent roles, 24–25
Diversity in group members, 7–8
Diversity issues, 271
  confronting in group context, 272–273

Educational input in group, 178–179
Emotional stimulation as leadership function, 153
Empathy, 160
Enabling solutions,
  in focal conflict, 72
  supporting, 241–242

Enchantment-flight subphase of development, 39–40
Equilibrium in focal conflict, 73–75
Escape hatch, 245, 246
Executive function as leadership function, 153
Experimental behavior, 233, 260–261
Experimentation in feedback exchange, 229–233
External boundary problems, 250
External group boundaries, 156

Facilitative norm, 259
Facilitative role performance, 25
Family-of-origin experiences, 3, 105–106
Feedback, 221–224
  and interactive group environment, 224
  during final session, 143
  effective, 223
  exchange by coleaders, 134
  ineffective, 223–224
  teaching to receive, 226–227
Feedback exchange, 99,
  experimentation as objective of, 229–233
  involving group in, 227–229
  teaching, 224–226
Feedback overload, 228
Fight/flight assumption group, 36
Focal conflict perspective, 247
  obstructing norms and, 256
Focal conflicts, monitoring group interaction for, 253
Focal conflict theory, 71–83, 251
Form of intervention, 184
Forming stage of group development, 48
Frequency of intervention, 184
Funnel pattern of norm development, 19

Gender issues of leaders, 285–286
General systems theory,
  application to group counseling, 93

boundarying in, 87–91, 92
  essential concepts of, 86–98
Genuineness, 160
Ground rules,
  establishing, 242
  implementing new, 256–257
Group-as-a-system skills and in-
    terventions, 181
Group boundaries, 146–147
Group boundary problems, 246,
    249–250
Group composition, 119,
    122–123
  and solutions in focal conflict,
    75
Group counseling and therapy,
  as social systems, 50
  efficacy of, 8–12
  essential values for, 5–6
  evolution of, 9–11
  multicultural, 7–8
  research on efficacy of, 11
Group counseling and therapy
    theory,
  essential themes in, 105–109
  focal conflict, general systems,
    and interpersonal ap-
    proach compared,
    105–109
Group culture in focal conflict,
    76–77
Group development theories,
  classic, 34–49
  essential concepts, 50–52
  interactive, 56–66
  models of, 34
Group Dynamics, 10
Group dynamics, 4, 16
  essential, 16–29
Group environment, participation
    in, 30–31
Group experiences in focal con-
    flict, unsuccessful, 82
Group focal conflict, 71–72
  deviant members and, 79–81
Group guidelines, essential,
    125–127
Group interaction, 4, 16
  anger in, 51

anxiety in, 51
change in, 5
conflict in, 51
productive, 30
relevance of to real life, 5
social/cultural context of, 6
Group-level interventions,
    181
Group members,
  assessment tasks for, 120
  common fears of, 124
  recruiting, 117–118
  selection criteria, 119–120
  termination of, 141
Group process, 16
  negotiations, 16–17
Groups for children, 117
Group sessions,
  ending, 138–139
  length of, 117
  starting, 137–138
Group size, 116–117
Group structure, 17, 47, 48, 49
Group systems, 252
Group themes,
  in focal conflict, 75–76
  monitoring group interaction
    for, 253
Group therapeutic factors, 9
Guidelines for groups, essential
    operating, 125–127

Habitual personal solutions in
    focal conflict, 77
Habitual solutions, 251–253
Harm, protecting members from,
    246–250
Heterogeneous membership
    groups, 115
Hierarchy in general systems the-
    ory, 91, 93
Hindering role performance,
    25–26, 27
Homeostasis, 86
Homogeneous membership
    groups, 115

Impermeable boundaries, 88,
    93–94

Inclusion,
  need for, 41
  needs and personalities, 41–42
Inclusion phase of group devel-
    opment, 45
Independent personality, 37
Indirect negotiations, 16, 17
Individual-level skills and inter-
    ventions, 180–181
Individual subsytems of general
    systems theory, 86
Individuation issues, 55–56,
    62–63
Inference making, 217
Input, leaders requesting, 204–205
Instruction as leadership function,
    158–159
Intensity of intervention, 185–186
Interactional variety, 122
Interactive activity style by lead-
    ers, 170
Interactive authority style of lead-
    ers, 169–173
Interactive group development
    theory, 56–66
Interactive leadership functions,
    154
Interactive leadership role,
    172–173
Interactive skills, developing ef-
    fective, 147–148
Interdependence, 37
Interdependence phase of group
    development, 37, 39–41
International Journal of Group
    Psychotherapy, 10
Interpersonal affective objectives,
    177
Interpersonal approach to group
    counseling, 95–104
  essential concepts of, 98–101
  theoretical foundations for,
    96–97
  therapeutic factors in, 98
  therapeutic process in, 101–102
Interpersonal behavioral objec-
    tives, 179
Interpersonal boundaries, 146,
    245

Interpersonal boundary interventions, 263–264

Interpersonal cognitive objectives, 178

Interpersonal communication, effective, 210–229

Interpersonal communication boundaries, 87

Interpersonal confrontation, 195, 197

Interpersonal contracts, 264–265

Interpersonal interaction, structuring, 206

Interpersonal issues, 262–265

Interpersonal learning, 4, 30, 98, 101
    commitment to others', 32

Interpersonal needs of leaders, 149

Interpersonal objectives of group counseling, 108

Interpersonal relationships, 3–4

Interpersonal skills and interventions, 181

Interrole conflicts, 28

Intervention focus of group counseling, 107–108

Intervention levels, 180–181

Interventions,
    balance of, 184–185
    choosing not to use, 207
    group-as-a-system, 181
    group level, 181
    individual-level, 180–181
    intensity of, 185–186
    interpersonal, 181
    structuring, 205–206
    subgroup, 181
    timing of, 182–184
    unsuccessful, 206–207

Intimacy issues, 56, 63–65

Intrarole conflict, 28

Involvement issues, 54, 58–69

Isolation, members in, 246, 248–249

Isolation of leaders, 282

Isomorphism in general systems theory, 92, 93

Isomorphy, 50, 86

Journal for Specialists in Group Work, 10

Laissez-faire leaders, 168–169

Languaging, 179, 237
    as leadership function, 161–163
    member process, 162

Leader, role of in interpersonal approach, 102–104
    conceptualizing members' concerns, 104
    process, 104

Leader-anarchist, 287

Leader languaging, 162

Leader-orchestrator, 287

Leaders,
    active participation by, 169–170
    anarchist, 286–287
    authoritarian, 166–167, 169
    authority of, 284–285
    biases of, 286
    boundaries for relationships with members, 127
    cultural issues of, 285–286
    democratic, 167–168
    emotional reactions by, 276–278
    establishing therapeutic factors by, 150–152
    experience as group members, 280–282
    gender issues of, 285–286
    individual sessions with, 127
    intellectual demands of, 279–280
    interaction by, 149
    interactive, 172–173
    interactive activity style by, 170
    interpersonal needs of, 149
    isolation of, 282
    knowledge needed by, 280–281
    laissez-faire, 168–169
    orchestrator, 286–287
    passive, 170
    peer supervision and therapy groups for, 283
    personal boundaries of, 283–287
    personal development by, 282–283

personal involvement by, 170–171

personal issues of, 278–280

personal style of, 283

planning decisions by, 114–117

power of, 284–285

racial issues of, 285–286

religious issues of, 285–286

responsibility of, 284–285

technical skills of, 170–171

Leaders, solo, 136–137
    supervision of, 136–137
    support for, 137

Leadership functions, 153–164
    administration as, 164
    boundary management as, 156–157
    instruction as, 158–159
    interactive, 154
    languaging as, 161–163
    leader beliefs concerning, 164
    norm setting as, 154–156
    regard as, 160–161
    structuring as, 137

Leadership role, 148–152
    emotional challenges in, 276–278
    factors influencing, 148–150

Leadership style, 165–173

Level of intervention, 184

Life-cycle model of group development, 34

Linear-progressive group development model, Tuckman's, 47

Linear-progressive model of group development, 34

Listening skills, 186

Long-term groups, 122

Long-term time-limited groups, 115
    size of, 117

Loss and loneliness issues, 56, 65–66

Manipulation, 195

Meaning-attribution as leadership function, 153

Member languaging, 162

Member preparation, 123–125

Member roles, problematic, 265–270
Member selection, 119
  assessment tasks for, 120
  screening interviews, 120–122
Membership attitudes, 30–32
Messages,
  receiving, 212–213
  sending, 211–212
Monopolizing self-disclosures, 220
Multicultural,
  group counseling and therapy, 7–8
  perspective, 7

Negative feedback loops, 87
Negotiations, 16–17
  direct, 16, 17
  indirect, 16, 17
Noah's Ark Principle, 122
Norming stage of group development, 48–49
Norms, 17–23
  formation of, 18–20
  helping, 21–22
  obstructing, 20–21
Norm setting by leaders, 154–156
Norms experimentation, 259–261
Norms interventions, 256–262
Norm violations, reactions to, 18

Objective of intervention, 184
Observation skills, 188–189
Obstructing norms, 242, 256–262
  confronting, 261–262
  directing members to discuss, 258
  intervening with new ground rules, 256–257
  observing as intervention for, 257–258
Ongoing groups, 115
Open bridge, 191
Open-ended groups, 115
Open groups,
  development issues in, 128
  managing, 128–129
  realistic goals for, 128

Orchestrator, leader as, 286–287
Orientation, pregroup, 164
Overpersonal personality, 37
Overpersonals, 43, 44
Oversocials, 41, 42, 45

Pairing assumption group, 36
Paraphrasing, 214
Parataxic distortion, 97
Participation in group environment, 30–31
  importance of, 31
Passive leaders, 170
Peer supervision groups, 283
Peer therapy groups, 283
Performing stage of group development, 49
Permeable boundaries, 88
Personal boundaries of leaders, 284–287
Personal development by leaders, 282–283
Personal involvement by leaders, 170–171
Personal leadership style, 283
Personal responsibility of group members, 31
Personals, 43, 44
Physical assault, 249
Physical harm, prohibition of, 125
Planning by coleaders, 132–133
Planning decisions by leader, 114–117
Polarizing, 217
Positive feedback loops, 87
Postgroup processing by coleaders, 132
Power of leaders, 284–285
  boundaries of, 284
Pratt, Joseph, treatment of tuberculosis patients by, 8
Pregroup orientation, 164
Pregroup preparation, 123–125
Pregroup screening, 164
Premature termination, 139–140
  preventing, 140
Pressuring other members, members, 246, 247
Principle of group integration, Schutz's, 44

Principle of group resolution, Schutz's, 45
Problematic roles of members, 265–270
  conceptualizing, 266–267
  intervening with, 267–270
  leader precautions in intervening, 270
  removing from group, 270
Processing, 179, 237–241
  conceptualizing members concerns through, 239
  defining change through, 240
  developing members' insight through, 240
  engaging members in, 239
  skills, 237–241
Psychological harm, prohibition of, 125

Questioning, 214–215

Racial issues of leaders, 285–286
Reactive motives in focal conflict, 72
Receiving messages, 212–213
Recruiting group members, 117–118
Recurring-cycle model of group development, 34
  Bion's, 35
Reflecting feelings, 213
Regard as leadership function, 160–161
Relationship issues, 252–265
Religious issues of leaders, 285–286
Resistant members, 265
Resolution-catharsis subphase of development, 39
Resonance in focal conflict, 77–78
Responsibility of leaders, 284–285
Restrictive solution in focal conflict, 72, 76
Restrictive solutions, identifying and frustrating, 242–244
Risk taking by group members, 31
Risk-taking challenges, 198

Role,
  ambiguity, 28
  conflict, 28
  confusion, 28
  development, 23–24
  incompatibility, 28
  performance, 25–27
  problems, 27–28
  stress, 28
  types, 24–25
Role performance,
  avoidant, 26, 27
  facilitative, 25
  hindering, 25–26, 27
Roles, 17, 23–29
  cautionary, 24, 25
  divergent, 24–25
  negotiation of, 24
  sociable, 24
  structural, 24

Sadomasochistic setups, 195, 196
Safety, perception of, 244–246
  steps in developing, 245
Scapegoats, 247, 248
  in focal conflict, 81
Schutz's group development the-
    ory, 44–47, 52
Schutz's principle of group inte-
    gration, 44
Schutz's principle of group reso-
    lution, 45
Schutz's theory of group develop-
    ment and interpersonal
    behaviors, 41–47
Screening, pregroup, 164
Screening interviews, 120–122,
    250
Selection criteria for members,
    119–120
  assessment tasks for, 120
  screening interviews, 120–122
Self-disclosure, 2, 103, 218–221
  and interactive group environ-
      ment, 221
  coerced, 249
  defensive, 220–221
  distancing, 220
  effective, 219

  encouraging effective, 221
  monopolizing during, 221
  shocking, 220
  vulnerability in, 221
Self-esteem, 96
Self-monitoring norms, 103
Self-reflective loop, 101, 102, 237
  process and, 103–104
Sending messages, 211–212
Shocking self-disclosures, 220
Short-term groups, 115
Signal reactions, 217
Skills,
  directive, 187
  group-as-a-system, 181
  individual-level, 180–181
  interpersonal, 181
  listening, 186
  observation, 188–189
  subgroup, 181
Sociable roles, 24
Social connectedness, 2
Social/cultural context of group
    interaction, 6
Social issues,
  confronting, 271–273
  confronting in groups, 6–7
  in group context, 271
Socializing, out-of-group, 126
Social microcosm, group therapy
    as, 100, 101
Social responsibility in groups,
    6–7
Socials, 41, 42
Social systems, counseling and
    therapy groups as, 50
Solo leaders, 136–137
Solutional conflict in focal con-
    flict, 73
Solution negotiation in focal con-
    flict, 79
  member's influence on, 79
Solutions in focal conflict, 72
Stage transitions, 57
Stereotypes, 6
Stereotyping, limitations from, 6
Storming stage of group develop-
    ment, 48
Structural roles, 24

Structured groups, 115,
  starting group sessions in,
      137–138
Structuring function of leaders,
    137
Structuring interpersonal interac-
    tion, 206
Structuring interventions, 205–206
Subgroups, 87
Subgroup skills and interventions,
    181
Subsystems of general systems
    theory, 86, 87
Successful group experiences,
    250
Supervision,
  of coleaders, 133–135
  of solo leaders, 136–137
Suprasystems of general systems
    theory, 86

Tape review by coleaders,
    134–135
Task behaviors, 47, 48, 49
Technical skills of leaders,
    170–171
Termination,
  issues, avoidance of, 142
  of group, 139–143
  of group member, 141
  of time-limited group, 141–142
  premature, 139–140
  sessions, 142–143
Themes in group interaction in
    focal conflict, 75–76
Therapeutic environment, 82
Therapeutic experience, group
    member's, 77–81
Therapeutic factors,
  definitions of, 151
  establishment by leader,
      150–152
  interactive, 152
Therapeutic group environment
    of group counseling, 108
Therapeutic process,
  in focal conflict, 81–83
  in general systems theory,
      92–94

in interpersonal approach,
    101–102
of group counseling, 108–109
Therapy groups, size of, 116
Time limited groups, 114–115,
    122
    ending, 141–142
Timing of intervention, 182–184
Trust, 146–147
Trust-building process, 219
Tuckman's group development
    model, 47–49

Underpersonals, 43–44
Undersocials, 41–42, 45
Unstructured group, starting
    group sessions in, 137–138

Verbal abuse, 249
Verbal assault, 249
Viability in focal conflict, 77–78
Vulnerability in self-disclosures,
    220

Wender, Lewis, group therapeutic
    factors of, 9
Wholing, 90
Work group, 35–36
Workshops, 128